AF791198

Privatization and Economic Performance in Central and Eastern Europe

To my wife Bea, daughter
Anna, and son Máté

Research for this book was undertaken with support from the European Commission's Phare A.C.E. Programme.

Privatization and Economic Performance in Central and Eastern Europe

Lessons to be Learnt from Western Europe

Edited by

Iván Major

Senior Fellow and Head of the Center for Institutional Studies, Institute of Economics, Hungarian Academy of Sciences, Hungary

EUROPEAN ASSOCIATION FOR COMPARATIVE ECONOMIC STUDIES

Edward Elgar
Cheltenham, UK • Northampton, MA, USA

Published by
Edward Elgar Publishing Limited
Glensanda House
Montpellier Parade
Cheltenham
Glos GL50 1UA
UK

Edward Elgar Publishing, Inc.
136 West Street
Suite 202
Northampton
Massachusetts 01060
USA

A catalogue record for this book
is available from the British Library

Library of Congress Cataloguing in Publication Data

Privatization and economic performance in Central and Eastern Europe :
lessons to be learnt from Western Europe / edited by Iván Major.
European Association for Comparative Economic Studies
Includes bibliographical references.
1. Privatization—Europe, Central. 2. Privatization—Europe, Eastern. 3. Europe, Central—Economic policy. 4. Europe, Eastern—Economic policy. I. Major, Iván. II. European Association for Comparative Economic Studies.
HD4140.7.P747 1999
338.947—dc21 99–14859
CIP

ISBN 1 84064 119 3

Printed and bound in Great Britain by Biddles Ltd, Guildford and King's Lynn

Contents

List of Figures

List of Tables

Contributors

Barbara Blaszczyk, C.A.S.E., Poland

Bruno Dallago, University of Trento, Italy

Grazyna Gierszewska, C.A.S.E., Poland

Michal Górzyñski, C.A.S.E., Poland

Todor Gradev, 'Club Ekonomika 2000', Bulgaria

Tytus Kamiñski, C.A.S.E., Poland

Spartak Keremidchiev, 'Club Ekonomika 2000', Bulgaria

Iván Major, Institute of Economics, Hungary

Wojciech Maliszewski, C.A.S.E., Poland

Alari Purju, Technical University of Tallinn, Estonia

Andrea Szalavetz, Institute of World Economy, Hungary

Juhan Teder, Technical University of Tallinn, Estonia

Cristiano Vezzoni, University of Trento, Italy

Richard Woodward, C.A.S.E., Poland

Aleksander Zolnierski, C.A.S.E., Poland

Introduction: Aims and Structure of the Book

Privatization of the state-owned property of the Central and East European (CEE) countries attracted tremendous attention among Western and CEE analysts. And rightly so, for the CEE countries had to navigate the process of mass privatization on uncharted territories. After eight years of the transition most CEE countries can claim that private ownership has become dominant in their economies. Now it is time to address the issue: 'What comes after privatization?' How has privatization in particular, and the expansion of the private sector in general, affected the economic performance of the companies in the CEE countries?

The research that our team* had started two years ago addressed the above issues in the case of Bulgaria, Estonia, Hungary and Poland. We pursue a three pillar approach in analyzing the privatization and the after-privatization history of the CEE countries. First, we describe the main principles, techniques and results of privatization in the individual countries. Next, we conduct a statistical and econometric analysis of the company level data in countries where such data were accessible in order to find out what were the main factors of change in the companies' economic performance. Finally, each country team conducted interviews and case studies of a pre-selected group of companies to show the qualitative aspects of company restructuring and to analyse the impact of corporate governance on the companies' performance.

* The team consisted of six principal investigators: Barbara Blaszczyk from Poland, Johan Myhrman from Sweden, Bruno Dallago from Italy, Alari Purju from Estonia, Spartak Keremidchiev from Bulgaria and Iván Major from Hungary. It was a very sad and painful event during our research work that Professor Johan Myhrman passed away. The team was enhanced by several other team members of the participating countries whose names will be listed in the separate chapters that were prepared by the country teams. Ms. Krisztina Bedõ served as the administrative coordinator of the project.

In addition to the country studies, an introductory theoretical chapter was written by Bruno Dallago and another one by Iván Major to set the framework of the analysis. These chapters outline the main features of Western privatization and the specific aspects of East European privatization. The last chapter of the report is a summary of lessons and conclusions based on the country studies and on the additional comments of the research partners.

The structure of the book is as follows:

The first chapter is an analysis of the principles and practices of Western privatization. The second chapter discusses the different theories of privatization and the specific features of East European privatization. Chapters 3 through 6 are the country studies, starting with Bulgaria (Chapter 3). Then the chapters on Estonia (Chapter 4), Hungary (Chapter 5) and Poland (Chapter 6) will follow. Chapter 7 sums up the main lessons and conclusions of our two years research.

We organized two workshops in order to change views and experience among the research partners and to get comments from other experts. We are grateful for the valuable comments of the participants of the workshops. In addition, wc should like to thank the contribution of several analysts and company managers who helped us to do the statistical and econometric analysis and the company interviews and case studies.

1. Privatization: The Teaching of Western Experiences

Bruno Dallago

1.1 INTRODUCTION

It is generally proclaimed that privatization is implemented in order to improve the performance – usually in terms of improved efficiency – of previously publicly (for example, state-) owned firms and consequently the working of the entire economy. Various strains of economic theory have attempted to prove the intrinsic superiority of private ownership over public ownership. Among these theories, the theory of property rights, the theory of corporate control, the theory of organizations and the public choice school have outstanding importance. However, all these theories stress the superiority of already existing private firms over existing state-owned companies. They do not necessarily explain the processes that take place during privatization that are characterized by uncertainty, adaptation, learning, the striving for survival, attempts to keep established rights and control patterns and which open unique opportunities for rent seeking. Some eclectic authors have explained 'non-market failures' and worked out the fundamental privatization theorem.[1] However, there is no clear and incontrovertible evidence that privatization leads to an improvement in any case and under any circumstances.[2]

In this chapter I shall try to present a general framework for understanding the Western experiences with privatization. It is my intent to show that privatization is a complex policy and set of actions that need clarification when, under which circumstances, where and how privatization can produce socially superior results in terms of efficiency or other economically important variables.

I start the analysis of privatization by considering the subjects and some basic features of privatization (section 2) and by reviewing privatization goals and the costs it encounters (section 3). The following section (section 4) considers the organizational and environmental context, that is, those factors that are necessary for privatization to reach a socially desirable outcome. This is followed by a survey of the results obtained through quantitative measurement of the outcomes of privatization (section 5). Then I present a disaggregated systemic approach to privatization. This approach includes an examination of the limits that the features of industries and firms (section 6) and social and technical factors (section 7) impose upon privatization and of the role of the specific features of the economic system and path dependence (section 8). Conclusions of the preceding analysis are exposed in the three final sections. Here I present a simple scheme for detecting the conditions for privatization to take place (section 9), summarize the main results of this chapter (section 10) and discuss the main teaching of the Western experience for countries in transition (section 11).

My analysis is based on the following hypotheses:

1. The economic system constrains the choice and outcome of privatization policies. Beyond these, privatization has other limits and is a costly undertaking.

2. Privatization is an important, but it is an insufficient measure for improving the performance of the economy and must be supplemented by other factors.

3. Privatization policies produce spillovers that influence the economic system, the performance of the economy, other industries and firms, the firm stakeholders.

1.2 PRIVATIZATION, INSTITUTIONS, COORDINATION, AND ACTORS

The state and the firm are the subjects of privatization. They share an important feature: the exchange of goods and services internal to them does not involve direct and formal interaction mediated by the price system. In this sense, neither one is a market institution: both are indeed hierarchies. However, both may be fundamental market agents, although this is not necessarily so, and certainly not in the case of state administration and vertically integrated firms. In fact, this may depend on the features of the economic system or the specific organization of the market.

An economic system is the coordinated set of economically relevant institutions and structures that mould, constraint, address, and organise the activity of economic actors. The coordination of institutions and structures takes place via different 'coordinating mechanisms', that are the core of the system; the most important of which are markets and hierarchies. The most important economic agents are the state and the firm. Therefore, by structuring the coordination among economic actors the economic system defines economic decision making and the direction of development, promotes specific forms of relationship among actors, opens up opportunities and constrains the choices and behavior of actors, organizes the production of knowledge and the exchange of information, activates feedback mechanisms and defines institutional learning.

Privatization offers important possibilities to intervene in the balance and relation between the state and firms and their respective internal structures. In such a way, privatization is an important instrument to alter the role and relative weight of markets and hierarchies, thus changing the economic system. Unfortunately, the term 'privatization' has many and very different meanings in the literature. They range between two extremes, one narrower and one more general: (a) The sale of at least the majority of an enterprise (in general, half its shares plus one) to one or more private owners.[3] I shall denote this type as denationalization. (b) The different and separate means used to change the relationship between the state and the private business sector in favor of the latter, and to increase the role of the market and of competition.[4]

In this chapter I will use the term privatization in the latter meaning. In fact, my goal is to understand how privatization can be used to improve the functioning of the economic system by strengthening the role of the market over hierarchies and by fostering competition. To this end, it is not enough to place the accent only on formal ownership. I need also to assess how the economy actually works and who actually controls economic activity.

Markets and hierarchies coexist in market economies, as the state and firms do. The mix between market and hierarchical coordination, then, is a very delicate one and is not entirely open to free choice. Consequently, the same holds for the relation between the state and firms. The problems different economies have to face because of this uneasy relation and the opinions of scholars and action of policy makers have varied on a regular basis over the proper mix of these factors. Consequently, we have witnessed waves of nationalization followed by waves of privatization as a way to increase the role of hierarchical coordination or that of market coordination. This was done in both cases in order to improve the working of the economic system and hence the performance of the economy.

However, the situation is much more complex than that. Privatization is always based (at least, in a modern economy operating within an acceptably democratic political system) on an initial delimitation of legal rights (usually included in a privatization law). On this basis privatization changes the allocation of specific property rights (residual rights) possibly in exchange for lump sums of money or flows of payment, and consequently determines the allocation of resources, incentives and efficiency. This – given positive transaction costs and privatization costs as a special category of transaction costs – determines the overall value of production that is obtained by the privatized assets and the allocation of returns therefrom.[5]

In the present chapter, I shall not be able to deal properly with the many complex problems of legal preparation and regulation of privatization policies and actions. Besides its effects on overall production, privatization also determines the allocation of the costs deriving directly or indirectly from privatization and consequently of the returns obtained therefrom. Therefore, privatization also has consequences for equity. This – together with different goals pursued by different actors – makes the calculation of outcomes difficult and uncertain and opens privatization to the influence of political factors and rent-seeking activity. I shall consider this aspect when I discuss the costs of privatization. Because privatization is a multi-faceted policy, my goal here is to try to make economic sense of privatization. Standard approaches for privatization are based on property rights, public choice and efficiency arguments, to a complete disregard of systemic variables.[6] The only, important, exception is a part of the literature on transition countries. However, this does not concern well-established market economies. Because this raises an important question of asymmetry of analysis, I will try to bridge this gap in the case of Western market economies.

1.3 THE GOALS AND COSTS OF PRIVATIZATION

There are different types and methods of privatization.[7] The choice of a particular method depends on the goals pursued by the government, the costs that each method causes and various other factors and constraints. Each individual method, moreover, has different consequences on the life and performance of the enterprise concerned. However, not all methods can be used in every country because of the specific features of the economic system or because certain preconditions may be lacking. From this perspective, the role of the state and the existing institutions are of crucial relevance. I will briefly consider these factors in this and in the following section.

There are four main groups of goals that have been pursued through privatization:[8] (a) social, political and ideological goals. These include the reduction of political interference, weakening the role of trade-unions, increasing the number of shareholders, and attracting foreign support and capital; (b) financing the state budget; (c) short-run micro (efficiency) and macroeconomic goals (equity and macroeconomic stabilization); (d) long-run economic goals, including changing the economic system and its functioning and targets for economic development. These goals received different importance in different countries as a consequence of diverging policies, but also of the different economic systems.

Empirical analysis of different experiences show that privatization is usually fostered by a complex set of motivations, both economic and non economic in nature. An empirical analysis of privatization experiences in 49 developed and developing capitalist economies in the period 1977–96 has shown that the decision to privatize is influenced by the political majority and public sector budget constraints. However, the success of privatization processes requires, most of all, appropriate legal institutions and developed capital markets (Bortolotti et al., 1998).

The question of the costs of privatization, including limits and other obstacles, although often disregarded is particularly important. In fact, these determine the effects of privatization policies and actions on overall production, but also have distributive and equity consequences. Costs consist of direct costs which must be borne when a firm is privatized, limits deriving from the nature of industries and firms and the features of the economic system, and obstacles of various kinds that may frustrate privatization policies.

Some of these factors are of a strictly economic nature and imply the direct disbursement of resources or consist of forgone proceeds at both micro- and macroeconomic level. The prevailing features of industries and firms and the type of economic system impose limits to privatization and regulation means and techniques that can be utilized and to the goals that can be pursued. The social component of privatization may also hamper its implementation or success and add further costs. Finally, others have a technical nature: the microeconomic situation of the economy may be unfavorable for privatization implementation and privatization implies a great reorganization of the economy and this is a costly undertaking.

In this section I shall briefly review the most important costs. The analysis of the consequences of the nature of industries and firms is afforded in section 6. Section 7 deals briefly with factors of various kinds that may condition and even frustrate privatization policies. The discussion of the influence of the features of the economic system is the topic of section 8. Table 1.1 summarizes the above mentioned factors that influence, limit and provide obstacles to, privatization.

In dealing with the costs of privatization, it is important to clarify what kind of consequences may derive therefrom. Two major types of possible consequences can be distinguished: consequences on the overall production and consequences on distribution of wealth and income. Let us briefly review both these possible consequences. I shall limit the discussion to some brief general notes, because a precise answer is only possible based on a precise analysis of individual cases. I also shall greatly simplify the discussion by leaving aside such important problems as monopoly power and collusion as consequences of the implementation of privatization policies.

Table 1.1. Costs, limits and obstacles to privatization

Economic costs	Microeconomic costs	Direct disbursement of the state	Administrative costs
			Financial restructuring Physical rehabilitation Settlement of employees' claims
		Costs for the consumer	Monopoly
		Forgone proceeds	Price lower than market price
		Corruption and collusion	
	Macroeconomic costs	Direct	Privatization programs, agencies, offices
		Indirect	Unemployment, lower demand, lost budget revenues
		Lower effectiveness of state policy	Organization and regulation
Limits	Due to market features		
	Due to the economic system		
Social obstacles	Collective action	Actors, coalitions, free-riding	
Technical and macro-economic obstacles	Lack of technical a framework	Legal framework, capital, experience and expertise	
	Economic obstacles	Public debt, macro-economic instability, insufficient macro-economic demand	
	Uncertainty over property rights		

The first problem is to understand how do the actual or the opportunity costs of privatization affect the overall production that the economy reaches, all other conditions remaining unchanged. This is certainly a difficult exercise, because privatization policy does not only change property rights, but inevitably has influence on many other factors. These concern both operational conditions of privatized firms (and may include such variables as incentives, taxation, financial conditions of the activity of privatized enterprises, and the like), those of other firms, and the conditions among which policy instruments are used.[9] Supporters of privatization take for granted its positive effects on the efficiency of individual enterprises. Even if we admit that this is generally true for individual enterprises (a supposition which is not always confirmed by facts), this is not necessarily true for the entire economy – except in a world of zero transaction costs (there comprising privatization costs). In particular, supporters of the general superiority of privatization seem to forget about macroeconomic costs of privatization – a large part of which may be directly charged to the expense of the state budget.

Reviews performed on the macroeconomic consequences of privatization as presented in section 5 offer no sufficiently strong evidence of the positive consequences of privatization on the economy's growth rate. One has also to consider that privatized enterprises often change productive profile and markets, thus making comparison with the pre-privatization situation untenable. Because privatization policies have always formed a complex set of different instruments and actions – some of which have logically nothing to do with privatization proper[10] – one is clearly unable to draw a satisfactory conclusion based on case studies. It is clear, however, that some of the costs diminish aggregate demand for certain inputs, while others increase it. A precise calculation of the effects of privatization on the economy requires specific knowledge of the nature and size of the costs. Their timing (pre- or post-privatization) determines the allocation of the costs to a specific agent (respectively the public seller or the private buyer).

A second question concerns the consequences of privatization on distribution of wealth and income. Because the latter has effects on the use and expenditure of wealth and income, consequences on demand and consequently on the allocation of resources must be considered. Even in this case a precise answer requires a reliable knowledge of specific privatization processes, because – given positive privatization costs – the consequences depend on the legal and administrative context of privatization. It is these legal and administrative conditions that determine the most convenient behavior of the agents of privatization (sellers and buyers), incentives and the production and flow of information.[11] Legal and administrative conditions (there comprising the contractual agreement of sale) determine how much a buyer has to pay (relative to the competitive market price), what kind of liability he is obliged to assume (for example, for past debts or environmental damage), what kind of price policy he can follow, who enjoys the proceeds from sale, who has to pay for administrative costs of privatization, who restructures the firm, what happens with old managers and employees, whether and at what conditions marginal customers will be served, and the like. Therefore, given positive privatization costs, it is the legal and administrative context of privatization that determines distributive consequences. However, the precise nature and content of these consequences and their effect on demand and allocation of resources can only be determined case by case (firm by firm or country by country).

Therefore, the question of the costs of privatization is a crucial one and privatization involves various and major costs (World Bank, 1988). These may be substantial, especially in the case of denationalization, but they should be (in part) considered as an investment in the production of a more productive economic system. They can be divided between microeconomic and macroeconomic costs.

1.3.1 Microeconomic Costs

Microeconomic costs include all the costs that must be met in order to privatize a firm, both in the form of direct outlay of financial resources by the state and as foregone proceeds of a proportion of the potential income obtainable from the privatization. The state must meet *direct costs* of various type:

- in preparing a firm for sale. These include the costs sustained in reorganizing it internally, administrative costs (such as consultation, subscription and arbitrage fees in public auctions, arbitrage fees in private sales, marketing expenses such as advertising for the privatization operation);

- financial costs of restructuring. These comprise the acquired loans and the settling of debts, the recapitalization of the state-owned firm before it is sold, the cost of transforming the state-owned firms into joint-stock companies owned by the Treasury, the resolution of the state-owned firms' indebtedness to the state, to banks and to other state-owned firms;

- costs of physical rehabilitation. These are costs to restructure the firm, perhaps in order to break up monopolies, to renew its physical capital prior to privatization, to run the firm until the moment of its sale, to clean the environment of the pollution caused by the firm;

- costs for settlement of employees' claims. These are costs involved in order to refinance the pension fund, retrain the workforce and transfer redundant workers to other activities.

Other costs are directly paid by consumers. This is particularly the case of privatized firms that preserve their monopoly control over the market. In this case, negative consequences for consumers can be expected in terms of higher prices and lower or missing supply of non-economic services to marginal consumers. This may require compensation by the government.

Two other microeconomic costs for the state have an indirect character:

- loss of potential earnings. This happens in case of underpricing and the utilization of different incentives and devices to stimulate demand and when some social group receive ownership at conditions more favorable than those indicated by the market.[12]

- costs of corruption and collusion between private investors and public agents. This is the case of distributive coalitions which seek to exploit the privatization in order to redistribute income and wealth to their own advantage.[13]

1.3.2 Macroeconomic Costs

Macroeconomic costs comprise costs that derive to the economy as a consequence of privatization. They include:

- *direct costs* to devise and implement an overall program of privatization. In fact, privatization requires the creation and financing of special agencies and government offices.

- *indirect costs* caused by the possible consequences of privatization in terms of unemployment, lower demand, lost budget revenues.

- Costs for *reorganizing and possibly lower effectiveness of state policy*. With privatization, the state losses some of its traditional means of direct intervention in the economy. As a consequence, the state is obliged to resort to other means, such as fiscal and anti-monopoly policies, in order to achieve such social and economic goals as efficiency, equity and competition. This type of intervention imposes costs and constraints on the state and the firms and possibly diminishes the effectiveness of the economic policy measure.

1.4 THE ORGANIZATIONAL AND ENVIRONMENTAL CONTEXT

The examination of privatization experiences and the theoretical analysis clearly show that privatization as a set of measures meant to change the ownership structure and organization of individual firms is insufficient to precisely determine the outcome. In fact, the performance of a firm is determined by a complex set of factors of which the ownership structure of its assets is but one, although very important.

This is even more so when we are interested in determining the outcome of a policy of privatization on the economic system and the entire economy. The final outcome of privatization measures strongly depend on the specific features of these factors.

As I will show in section 9, the choice of privatization should be based on the consideration of both the level and the allocation of the expected benefits and the costs of intervention, and this condition holds for both the government and the prospective buyer. Both benefits and costs are expected because the conditions of privatization may rapidly change. In this section I limit myself to examine those factors that are most important in the case of the privatization of an individual firm.

There are two groups of such factors: (a) factors that belong to the organizational aspects of the firm, and (b) factors that pertain to the economic environment where the firm operates. In general, all these factors are rather strongly connected with each other. However, the situation may vary depending on the specific features of the firm, the industry where it operates, and the economic system. I will discuss these latter factors in section 6.

1.4.1 Factors Belonging to the Organizational Aspects of the Firm

These factors concern principally the complexity of the task performed by the firm, its capability to adapt to unforeseen contingencies and rapidly changing conditions and environment, the completeness and feasibility of contracts, the features of information, the firm's governance, competition in the privatization process.

a. Complexity and adaptation. The complexity of the task performed by the firm considered for privatization requires specialized knowledge and precise information to control and regulate its activity, increases the probability that intervention will occur, and renders the outcome of such actions more uncertain. As a consequence, the cost of control and regulation by the government is increased. Complexity also increases the need for rapid adaptation to unforeseen contingencies. When a task is novel and complex the formation of routines is more difficult and the appearance of unforeseen contingencies that may require rapid adaptation becomes more likely. In these cases complex and costly government action may be required to redirect activities and to limit the duration of renegotiation with the firm to pursue the social goal.[14] Such circumstances may happen, for example, in the national defense industry.

b. Completeness and feasibility of contracts. The completeness and feasibility of contracts between the firm and any level of government (which is a component of the firm in this sense) and incomplete or asymmetric information are crucial factors in determining the social outcome of privatization. Contracts cannot be completely specified because of the complexities of the relation between the firm and the government and because of the variety and variability of the economic environment, which causes lack of necessary knowledge and information. This incompleteness produces residual returns that accrue to the owner of the firm and are a powerful incentive to privatization on the demand side and to the efficient use of the acquired resources by the new owner (Alchian and Demsetz, 1972). However, contracts also cannot be complete because this is a necessary condition to confer to the owner the necessary freedom to react to changes in market conditions. From this incompleteness residual rights of control follow, which are a fundamental incentive to production and its efficiency. [15] When the firm is privatized, residual rights of control are transferred to the buyer. However, if the firm has an important social function – in particular if it produces for any level of government – the specific extent of these rights must be controlled and there is also need for regulation.[16]

However, contracts must also be feasible in the sense that they must include conditions and objectives that can actually and profitably be pursued by the firm. This is particularly important in regulated industries and in particularly complex activities involving the use of specialized assets. In such cases, contracts may comprise special requirements (for example, to serve also customers that are unprofitable for the firm) in exchange for particular advantages (for example, subsidies or a price higher than the competitive one in a protected market) or even include a stipulation on a 'fair rate of return' on invested capital or similar conditions to insure the firm against unfavorable outcomes independent from its own shortcomings.

c. Incomplete and asymmetric information. Incomplete and asymmetric information results in delegation of authority that may be socially inefficient (Sappington and Stiglitz, 1987). Often, such features of information on the situation of the firm under privatization favor its managers, who can extract a rent from their informational advantage or use it to reach socially harmful goals (for example avoid competition from other perspective buyers in the bidding process). In such circumstances, the role of the regulator of privatized firms is more difficult and less effective, thus increasing transaction costs of regulation.

d. Governance. Different undesirable governance outcomes can result from the privatization of a firm. The firm can turn out to have a weak governance structure because of the lack of clear owners or because the residual rights of control are blurred. This may be the case of a state-owned company that is turned into a public company in which different groups of owners fight for the control of the firm. In other cases the new owner may prove to be actually uninterested in the firm's activities and that the purchase was actually motivated by his desire to use the firm's physical assets (for example its real estate) in ways contrary to the intention or interest of the other social components (stakeholders) of the firm (managers, employees, customers, and suppliers). Another unfavorable case happens when the buyer is able to establish monopoly control over the market.

e. Competition in the privatization process. A competitive bidding has the effect of choosing the buyer who appears to be the most efficient producer. Insufficient competition at the bidding stage (for example obtained via a closed bidding process or in cases of asymmetric information to potential bidders) may produce rents that accrue to the selected buyer. However, this result may become useful to the government when it pursues the maximization of its privatization revenue or intends to impose inefficient production upon the firm; production that is in the interest of the government or the society (for example, serve unprofitable customers, develop particularly risky production, invest in highly specialized assets). In this sense, (part of) the rent is returned to the state or redistributed to consumers or invested in progress and development.[17] However, this solution easily leads to lack of competition also after privatization.

1.4.2 Factors Pertaining to the Economic and Social Environment

The economic environment where the privatized firm operates has a crucial importance in determining the social outcome of privatization. Such characteristics of the environment are particularly important as competition, regulation, social and legal feasibility and enforceability of contracts.

a. Competition in the market. The existence of competition in the market where the privatized firm operates is a crucial condition for a favorable social outcome of privatization. As I stress in various parts of this paper, it is competition that – given the proper organizational factors described above – can actually induce the privatized firm to pursue efficiency. In fact, one can also conclude that it is more the lack of competition than any factor intrinsic in the nature of ownership that is at the basis of the alleged lower efficiency of public firms compared to private firms. This is so not only because the competitive environment compels the firm to use its resources in the best possible way, but also because competition leads it to give up non economic goals (for example social or political goals) and to externalize all the costs that are unnecessary to the strict productive activity of the firm. As I have already observed, this charges the state with transaction costs (such as those of regulation) that the public firm is compelled to internalize

b. Regulation. Regulation is an act of centralization of government policy towards privatized enterprises that is needed to counterbalance the decentralization introduced in the economy by privatization (see Dallago and Mittone, 1996). This often leads to a greater role for hierarchies within the government as a way to foster the role of markets in the economy.[18] Regulation has at least two functions in a privatized industry (see Sappington and Stiglitz, 1987, pp. 579–80). First, regulated industries are usually characterized by economies of scale and competition is often absent. In this case, the regulator has the role of providing ongoing monitoring of the firm's performance and preventing socially harmful developments (for example by anti-monopoly regulation or via proper deregulation such as the elimination of import restrictions).[19] A further likely feature of regulated firms is complicated production technologies. Under these circumstances it is difficult to distinguish between the capabilities of the producer and the risk inherent in production. The regulator's activity involves gathering specialized knowledge and information that forms the basis of policy decisions and may limit rents that privatized firms can capture in complex and non-competitive situations. Such knowledge and information can be considered a positive spillover of regulation and lowers transaction costs of government policies compared to the case of unregulated private ownership. A further role of regulation appears when regulated industries employ specialized assets. These are costly and have limited alternative uses. Consequently, potential investors may not invest if they are not properly insured against expropriation or exploitation by a credible commitment of the government. Regulation, often involving such provisions as a 'fair rate of return' on invested capital in order to insure the firm against unfavorable outcomes independent from its own shortcomings, may supply such commitment and increase transaction costs of expropriation, thus making it less likely.

c. Social and legal feasibility and enforceability of contracts. There may exist conditions in the society, the government, the privatized firms or the law that may prevent, render difficult or ease designing or implementing contracts. Sometimes issues concerning the legality of switching a service from government to private delivery can inhibit or prevent contracting. On various occasions employees' pressure, opposition by politicians, lack or ineffectiveness of regulative means, inability to establish control or regulative bodies, concerns over the chance of service disruption or the quality of the service contracted to a private firm have prevented the approval of privatization actions. On other occasions social or ideological pressure for privatization have induced the government to give up proper carefulness in stipulating and enacting contracts.

1.5 THE OUTCOME OF PRIVATIZATION THROUGH THE EVALUATION OF EXPERIENCES

Numerous studies have been promoted and implemented to analyse and measure the consequences of privatization. An important number among these have consisted in attempts to arrive at some conclusions on the outcome of privatization based on the analysis of quantitative data. All existing studies greatly simplified the problem in order to elaborate the data and manage to reach some conclusion. Moreover, the quality of the data, their consistency and completeness, and their comparability through time, sectors, and countries – in particular for those studies that consider more than one sector or country – is often doubtful.

A further problem with quantitative analyses is that they must rely on factors that are more easily measurable and quantifiable. Such factors are usually different types of efficiency, most often microeconomic static efficiency. By doing so, these studies disregard other important aspects of privatization policies, such as their direct consequences and spillovers on the economic system, equity, incentives. Also, such studies must oversimplify what privatization is about by putting together different institutional solutions and disregarding important policy, institutional and systemic factors. Among the latter of particular importance is that countries not only differ in the weight that the public sector has, but also because of the role of the public hand in the economy (for example through regulation). The great importance of these factors – that I discussed in section 4 – throws uncertainty on the real value and meaning of the results of quantitative analysis. The latter also disregard that different governments may pursue different goals through the use of public firms and that in any case the latter purses goals that are different from those of the private firms. Often, public firms exist in sectors different from those where private firms operate: usually the former operates in non-competitive or only partially competitive sectors. Microeconomic comparisons also suffer from disregarding costs that are often internalized in public firms but not in private ones: for example costs of regulation and enforcement, and costs of unemployment. Usually, they do not control what happens in the public sector after privatization. If privatization is not followed by restructuring of public sector, privatization may simply add new costs to (social) production (that is the costs of resources utilized by private production in addition to resources previously employed within the public sector).

In spite of all these flaws, it seems useful to start from a survey of the main results reached through some of the existing quantitative analysis. In fact, these studies offer the only attempts to reach some type of measurable conclusions on the effects of privatization. This, if properly interpreted, helps to explain other factors and can aid to specify the trade-offs that may exist between different variables involved. However, this can only be a starting point, for the reasons just mentioned and for the incompleteness of the present survey. I will consider some of the studies that compare the outcome of privatization in various countries and divide these studies according to the methodology utilized. Two main approaches can consequently be distinguished: (a) evaluation of the microeconomic efficiency of privatization, and (b) evaluation of its outcome in terms of macroeconomic efficiency.

1.5.1 Microeconomic Comparisons

These comparisons are usually static and consider one or more sectors in one or more countries. An article by Borcherding, Pommerehne and Schneider (1982) reviews the results obtained by fifty studies concerning the consequences of privatization on productive microeconomic efficiency in the United States, the Federal Republic of Germany, Australia, Canada and Switzerland. The five countries considered are federal states and the studies reviewed focus on the comparison of public output of goods and services at different levels of government (federal, state, and local) and private output in nineteen different sectors.

The results obtained by these authors are complex and critical. Apparently, public firms are microeconomically less efficient than their private counterparts and various scholars have revealed the waste implied by public production in terms of excess costs over private production. However, this is probably the result of lack of competition more than of transferability of ownership.

In reality, some of the excess costs of public firms could be considered as the price for delivering desirable outputs whose characteristics would be provided in different amounts and ratios by private supply and not necessarily as transfers in the form of higher wages, reduced effort, corruption, and some other deliberate form of redistribution. In sum, the authors conclude that:

> Government 'waste' is after all a sick consideration neglecting those sizeable costs of contracting, monitoring ad controlling which may arise when private production is preferred over the public one. Also some part of the 'waste' is the result of the political process of redistribution, where public production is used as an effi-

> cient means for selecting and discriminating. Thus we expect that the claim for 'more market and less government' has no real addressee and that the chance of most proposals of how to decrease public production or to increase its efficiency is rather modest. (Borcherding, Pommerehne and Schneider, 1982, pp. 146–7)

Another article by Boardman and Vining reviews 55 quantitative studies, which partially overlap with those analysed in the preceding review. The findings apparently show an 'edge' for the private sector. However, the results vary considerably across industries depending on the conditions of competition. Superior public efficiency is registered in those industries (electricity and water) where there is limited competition or the private firms are highly regulated. Greater efficiency of private companies is in the delivery of services (for example refuse collection, fire protection, and non-rail transit) where subcontracting to private producers and monitoring costs are relatively low.

The same article also attempts to overcome a gap in the literature that does not deal with comparisons of private–public performance in the competitive sector. This is done with an original comparison of the performance of the 500 largest manufacturing and mining corporations in the world outside the United States as compiled by *Fortune* magazine in 1983. Among these, 409 are private firms, 23 are mixed firms and 57 are state-owed firms. There is a different sectoral and country concentration of each type of ownership.

The model utilized intends to test the property rights hypothesis and includes (a) four different measures of profitability and two measures that relate to aspects of X-efficiency; (b) four different dummy variables for state-owned and mixed firm, thereby making private firms the benchmark; and (c) concentration and dummy variables for each of the fifteen industrial sectors and each of the six countries (Canada, France, Germany, Great Britain, Italy, Japan) considered, in order to reflect the nature of the regulatory/competitive environments.

The result of the estimate exercise is that:

> While each dependent variable has some weakness as a performance measure, the consistent direction and magnitude of the estimates across all equations provides robust evidence that state enterprises and mixed enterprises are less profitable and less efficient than private corporations. With respect to profitability, mixed enterprises perform about the same or worse than SOEs, while in terms of efficiency, mixed enterprises perform about the same or slightly better than SOEs. (Boardman and Vining, 1989, p. 17)

A study undertaken as a doctoral dissertation at the RAND Graduate School by Randy Ross reaches some mixed results.[20] The study compares performance in the public and private sectors in electric power (public sector more efficient), production and insurance in mental health (private sector more efficient), and school bus transportation (private sector more efficient). The study shows that relative performance varies not only through ownership sectors, but also according to specific solutions that are utilized in production. For instance, institutional arrangements involving a combination of public and private sector operations in school bus transportation performs nearly as well as private operations alone.

Other studies that were implemented in the United States reach results that are more in favor of the private sector (see Wolf, 1994, p. 140). Three studies were performed in the first half of the 1980s. The first was performed by the Chief Administrative Officer of Los Angeles County and concerned the outcome of the Los Angeles privatization program. It covers health services, facilities management, data processing, parks and recreation, public social services, and other functions. The outcome is higher efficiency of the privatized sector. A study completed in 1984 for the Department of Housing and Urban Development covers street construction, street cleaning, janitorial services, traffic-signal maintenance, tree pruning. In each case results show greater efficiency of private supply, after controlling for differences in the quality of service. The Office of Management and Budget analysed 235 contracts awarded by the Department of Defense in fiscal years 1981 and 1982 and found that contractor operation was substantially less costly than in-house operation.

In a review of private approaches for delivery of public services, Harry P. Hatry examined a number of eleven options that local governments can utilize to increase use of the private sector (Hatry, 198X). These options include contracting out, franchising, grants and subsidies, use of vouchers, use of volunteers, encouraging self-help, altering regulation or tax policy, encouraging private agencies to take over an activity, demarket or reduce the demand, obtain temporary help from private firms, use fees and charges to adjust demand. His review showed that different solutions have different impact on the costs of government and on other variables (the effect on the cost paid by clients, on increasing the client choice, on improving or maintaining service quality, on distributional effects, on likelihood of disruption of service, on difficulty of implementation). Costs of government are reduced most by franchising and by encouraging private takeover. Contracting out and self-help also have fair impact. However, in particular franchising and private takeover by nonprofit organizations have considerable difficulty of implementation that – if some crucial conditions are not respected, like a strong level of competition or control – may revert the outcome in terms of cost efficiency. The reduced costs often appear to consist essentially in shifting costs directly to customers.

Table 1.2. A summary of the results of some quantitative microeconomic comparisons

Greater efficiency	Private goods	Services	Utilities	Provision of public services	Competitive sectors
Private sector	**1.** Forestry (2), Housing (3), Ocean tanker repair and maintenance (1), Slaughterhouses (1) **4.** Data processing, Street construction	**1.** Airlines (1), Banks (1), Bus service (1), Debt collection (1), Insurance claims processing (1), Insurance sales and servicing (1), Savings and loans (1) **2.** Nonrail transit (4) **4.** School bus transportationFacilities management-Janitorial services, Traffic-signal maintenanceDefense services	**1.** Electric utilities (2), Water utilities (3) **2.** Electric utilities (5), Water utilities (2)	**1.** Cleaning services (2), Fire protection (1), Hospitals (3), Refuse collection (6), Weather forecasting (1) **2.** Health-related services (7), Refuse collection (2), Fire services (1), **4.** Production ad insurance of mental health, Health services, Public social services, Street cleaning, Parks and recreation, Tree pruning **5.** Local contracting out of public services (60)	**2.** 15 industrial sectors **3.** Jute (1)
Public sector			**1.** Electric utilities (1) **2.** Electric utilities (2), Water utilities (2) **4.** Electric power distribution	**1.** Hospitals (1), Refuse collection (1) **5.** Local contracting out of public services (15)	
The same or result is ambiguous		**1.** Insurance sales and servicing (1), Railroads (1) **2.** Airlines (3), Railroads (1), Financial institutions (1)	**1.** Electric utilities (1) **2.** Electric utilities (4), Water utilities (1)	**1.** Refuse collection (4) **2.** Health-related services (1), Refuse collection (1)	

Source: **1.** Borcherding, Pommerehne, Schneider (1982); **2.** Boardman and Vining (1989) (excluding 19 studies included in Borcherding et al.'s study); **3.** Bhaskar, Khan (1995); **4.** Wolf (1994); **5.** Hatry (198X).

Note: Number in parenthesis indicate the number of cases considered. Public sector includes different levels of government and nonprofit sector.

Another article estimates the consequences of privatization on employment and output in the jute industry in Bangladesh (Bashkar and Khan, 1995). Therefore, its approach is different from the preceding ones both because it only considers one sector in one country and because comparison takes place through time. Privatization of the jute industry involved 31 mills out of the 62 in the sector, which accounted for 38 per cent of capacity of the sector and was implemented in 1984. It was accompanied by extensive regulation concerning wage rates. The results of the estimate show that 'privatization has reduced employment significantly, while the reduction in output is not statistically significant ... The reduction in employment was primarily directed toward clerical and managerial employees ... and to lesser extent toward permanent manual workers' (op. cit., p. 267). Privatization had a negative effect on aggregate output, but this effect is not statistically significant. However, by disaggregating the data at the product-group level, a statistically significant change in output composition between privatized and public sector mills is disclosed. In fact, privatized mills shifted toward more profitable production (sacking) away from a relatively less profitable one. Therefore and although the outcome seems to be overall advantageous to privatization in terms of microeconomic (allocative and probably also X–) efficiency, there is a clear trade–off with quantity and quality of employment. Also the shift in the product–group production softens the meaning of the results obtained and raises the questions of spillovers of privatization.[21]

1.5.2 Macroeconomic Comparisons

Macroeconomic comparisons try to establish the relation between the relative size of the public sector and the growth rates of the economy (as a proxy for dynamic efficiency) of different countries. This kind of comparison meets with a set of at least four important difficulties and flaws. One first such difficulty is given by the choice of an appropriate scale for measuring the relative size of the private and public sectors. This is usually either tax revenue or government spending. Both present problems and are only very imperfect proxies of government size and role in the economy. In fact, and apart from possibly different relative prices in different countries, considering that public sectors are usually non-competitive the latter also depends on differences in regulation, policies, legislation, administrative intervention, morale standards, and so on.

A second problem derives from the quality of existing data that vary through countries and may also vary through time. This problem may be substantial when comparisons include countries at different level of development and with important differences in systemic features, from which usually follow great differences in national accounting systems. For instance, figures for government spending may include varying proportions of transfer payments, and a large part of the private economy may be unregistered, especially in countries at a low level of development. A third problem concerns the comparability of data, and derives from the necessity of converting all data into a common numerator (usually US or international dollars). A fourth problem arises from variability in the economic system and from differences in the level of development, culture and history. Under different circumstances, the same figure may have quite a different meaning.

In spite of all these difficulties, macroeconomic dynamic comparisons provide important insights if they are correctly and carefully interpreted. A study by Keith Mardsen is based on a sample of ten paired countries at different levels of development and covers the period 1970–79 (Marsden, 1983). Each pair includes countries characterized by approximately the same level of development, but sharply different ratios between tax revenues and GDP. The author regresses the real average annual growth of each country rate in the 1970s on its corresponding ratio of tax revenues to GDP. The main result of the regression is a statistically significant negative relationship between the two variables. Moreover, the variation in the ratio of tax revenues to GDP explains nearly 45 per cent of the variation in average annual growth rates across the sample. A further finding is that the positive result of the low taxation/high growth countries is not at the expense of other important variables (equity of income distribution, consumption growth, improvement in government services, changes in infant mortality and life expectancy). One wonders whether these findings reflect more the underdevelopment trap rather than strictly the disadvantages of a large government sector.

Another empirical study was implemented by Charles Wolf Jr. and Randy Ross at RAND and covered the period 1972–82. Later it was updated to cover the period 1983–87 (quoted in Wolf, 1994, pp. 145–51). The methodology utilized is rather similar to that used by the World Bank study and is based on annual growth rates of real GDP. However, the RAND study also uses total government spending – in addition to tax revenues – related to GDP as independent variables in the regression analysis. Another difference is that the RAND sample is somewhat larger (27 countries) than the one utilized in the World Bank study.

In addition the finding of the RAND study points to a negative relation between the size of the government sector and the rate of growth of the economy. However, there are some substantial differences with the World Bank study that highlight the necessity to be very careful in interpreting and utilizing the outcome of these exercises. The results of the RAND regression show a much weaker relation between the variables considered than the World Bank study. The difference is great in the case of both low-income and middle- and high-income countries. A further difference concerns the coefficient of determination R^2: in the RAND study tax revenues (government spending) explain 25 per cent (32 per cent) of the intercountry variation in growth rates in the years 1972–82 and the explanatory proportion is further reduced to a bare 19 per cent (10 per cent) in the following period. In the World Bank study the coefficient resulted to be 0.45.

Another study by Daniel Landau also finds a clear negative relationship between government consumption expenditures and per capita economic growth for the 1961–76 period (Landau, 1983). However, other studies do not find any clear relationship in this sense. Frederic Pryor, who compares the growth rates in the OECD and CMEA countries, finds no difference between growth rates in the two groups of countries in the 1950–80 period, after allowing for other explanatory factors besides the systemic difference in the role of government (Pryor, 1985). Nor does Mancur Olson find any reliable relation between the size of government and growth rates in his study of long-term secular growth, except possibly since the 1970s (Olson, 1982).

To summarize, microeconomic quantitative studies of efficiency do not reach an incontrovertible conclusion on the unchallenged superiority of private ownership over public one. This is so because of many and various factors: the uncertainty of quantitative data; the actual impossibility of basing estimates on a *ceteris paribus* condition, because of the many factors involved and the likely change in policy priorities during privatization programs; the usual disregard of the general costs of privatization (that are allocated to the government) and of other kinds of positive and negative spillovers.

As to macroeconomic dynamic efficiency as explained in the studies reviewed in the previous section, its results are even more uncertain. Although a negative relationship appears to exist between the economic role of the government and growth, this relationship explains a relatively minor part of the variation of growth rates across countries at different level of development. But even more important is the fact that we do not receive an answer as to what are the *original* factors that determined the growth of governments. One is left with the suspicion that governments grew more in some countries that in others to respond to the incapability of the private sector to solve serious economic difficulties. This is a well-known trap in development economics.

However, other factors are also important that are not directly reflected in the microeconomic and macroeconomic efficiency considered above, although the effect of these factors may be only indirectly measured. The most important such factors are included in the concept of institutional efficiency, that comprises X-efficiency and capabilities. The former denotes that individual firms may be internally inefficient (in the sense that they operate below the production possibility frontier) even when allocative efficiency holds

(Leibenstein, 1966). This type of inefficiency derives from organizational problems and from the incentive system that does not promote organizational efforts.

The second component of institutional efficiency includes the endogenously determined capability of the firm to originate motivation to use existing resources and economic opportunities as effectively as they might be used, to promote adaptation to a changing environment, and to avoid processes that hinder and distort technical and institutional learning and discovery, the diffusion of knowledge and information, that cause systematic organizational errors, preclude or discourage the generation of trials and the coordination of decision-making processes.

Privatization, by diminishing bureaucratic red tape and opening the way to the action of competition, may play an important role also in this sense. However, even in this case other elements – particularly the structure of payoffs and clearness and enforcement of property rights – appear more important, although privatization can do a lot to bring them in line with the requirements of institutional efficiency. However, one cannot reject the possibility that the structure of payoffs and of property rights promoted by privatization encourage rent-seeking behavior and activity more than productive ones.[22]

1.6 THE FEATURES OF INDUSTRIES AND FIRMS

The features of industries where the firm to be privatized operates and those of the firm itself impose limits to privatization and regulation means and techniques and to the goals that can actually be pursued and influence the outcome of privatization. The explanatory variables considered here are supply conditions and the prospects of demand:[23] these explain why investors should be interested in buying a firm to be privatized and what should be the organization of the industry once enterprises are privatized. On this basis, privatization (understood principally as denationalization) may yield results of varying desirability for the goals pursued by the government.

Clearly, the easiest and more favorable cases are those when demand prospects are good. However, here we can have different situations on the side of supply conditions. When state-owned firms operate in industries potentially characterized by competitive conditions on the supply side, privatization may produce considerable gains in efficiency (in any sense) by actually introducing competition. Typical cases are those of large-sized industries such as air transport, telecommunications on a national or international scale, electricity and gas production. Privatization of these industries should be given priority if the intention is to increase consumer welfare and hence create a climate of public opinion in favor of privatization.

When demand prospects are unfavorable – such as in the case of the steel industry, the production of transport means, shipbuilding – there is no serious probability that private monopolies will form and international competition is usually strong. Consequently, consumers will not gain significant advantages from privatization; these will accrue to taxpayers insofar as privatization will eliminate the contributions and subsidies that the state pays to these industries when they are publicly-owned.

Privatization of monopolies with good demand perspectives, such as local electricity and gas distribution networks and telephone networks, may be more risky than beneficial for consumers, because conditions on the supply side are not favorable to competition. It would therefore seem useful to increase competition among public firms by removing barriers to entry and by restructuring the industries. If privatization is chosen for some reason, regulation of privatized firms should receive priority. The danger that private monopolies will be born when privatizing public monopolies with bad demand perspectives – such as the railway and the postal service – is not significant, because these are industries in decline and there exist alternative services which consumers find preferable. In this case, privatization leads to diminish supply; and it will therefore be used if the intention is to reduce the use of resources in these sectors and perhaps to increase their efficiency.

Services for national defense, public hospitals, and prisons are examples of industries producing goods that are sold only to the state. These captive industries are characterized by non-competitive conditions on the side of supply. Here there is great deal of room for privatization through denationalization and contracting out, although straightforward deregulation may also lead to substantial improvements by increasing competition. Rather similar is the situation of those firms that operate in industries such as gasoline, tollways, television networks, transportation, some basic goods, where conditions may be closely regulated. Because these industries are usually competitive, deregulation can often substantially improve efficiency – although maybe at the expense of the social goals pursued previously.

Vertically integrated firms are often found in public utilities, in particular telecommunications, transportation and electricity. This form of organization may be useful at a certain stage of development when the lack of private capital is a major obstacle to development and when the technological prerequisites of economies of scale favor it. However, when these prerequisites disappear, these cases became identical with that of monopoly discussed above. Other organizations implement transfers to specific groups of population (such as the poor, the unemployed, large families, the homeless), geographical areas (underdeveloped regions), industries (infant or obsolete ones), and produce public goods (such as defense, law and order, justice). Although there is no or very little room for denationalization and even contracting out in these cases, deregulation may help to improve efficiency of supply.

1.7 SOCIAL, TECHNICAL AND MACROECONOMIC FACTORS

Privatization is a complex social undertaking that may produce socially desirable results, but also has socially undesirable outcomes for some actors and in any case subverts routines and established interests. Therefore, the social component of privatization may also influence its implementation or success and add further costs. Finally, other factors inhibiting or promoting privatization have a general technical, legal and macroeconomic nature: the macroeconomic situation of the economy may be unfavorable for privatization implementation and privatization implies great reorganization of the economy which is a costly undertaking.

Social obstacles. Privatization involves changes of a social nature. Consequently, it raises a major problem of collective action. For the privatization to be successful, cooperation is necessary between the actors who promote and implement it (the government and interested buyers) and between these and the other stakeholders in the firm (managers, employees, suppliers, customers). The conflict with the actors who may lose from privatization (old managers of state-owned enterprises and possibly employees, but also consumers and suppliers) should not be allowed to block the process if the latter is justified by its social desirability. The attempt to reach a compromise among all the actors concerned may give rise to the so-called 'paradox of privatization'.

When an institutional change threatens some actors with the loss of important privileges – as happens with managers and possibly employees of state-owned enterprises to be privatized – rational actors may prefer to invest substantial resources in the defense of their privileges and consequently in stopping or conditioning changes that are considered unfavorable.

The literature on privatization has stressed how the paradox of privatization raises doubts over the use of privatization in order to increase productive efficiency (Kay and Thompson, 1986, p. 18). The conviction that private firms are more efficient than public ones is based on the fact that private managers are subject to economically more rigorous discipline and incentives than their public counterparts. If this is true, one might expect managers of public companies to be opposed to privatization, and the same would apply to the workers. This they can do, for example, by decapitalizing the firms or accumulating inter–enterprise arrears or by using their connections and strength to obtain concessions by the government and the new owners in order to avoid the more rigorous discipline and incentives than privatization promises to introduce in the firms.

Yet without the consensus and participation, or at least the acquiescence of managers, privatization would be difficult to accomplish. In actual fact, concessions are usually made to managers in order to gain their assent to privatization, thus creating or strengthening path dependence of privatization. The most important of these concessions is the maintenance of the firm's dominant position in the market in which it operates, that is, the exclusion of competition. If this goal is achieved,[24] then the government fails in its objective of increased efficiency. And this concession also rules out the possibility of introducing competition in the future: because this would worsen the prospects of profit for the privatized monopoly and reduce the market value of its shares, it would be vigorously opposed.

Technical obstacles. These include the difficult valuation of the goods to privatize, lack of capital, and the inadequate experience and expertise of the individuals and organizations delegated to implement privatization. In particular, the nature and development of capital markets is fundamental in determining the feasibility of privatization, the privatization methods that can be used, and the outcome (Bortolotti et al., 1998).

Macroeconomic obstacles. These comprise public debt, macroeconomic instability, and insufficient macroeconomic demand. In fact, privatization is usually placed on the agenda when the economy is in difficulty and the government pursues the increase of its revenue or decrease of its costs directly by privatizing public assets and indirectly via increased fiscal revenue or decreased disbursement for subsidies following improved efficiency of privatized enterprises. This situation incites the government to privatize and may diminish social obstacles to it, but may render potential purchasers less willing to buy.

Legal obstacles. These consist of the absence of the necessary legislative structure and uncertainty over property rights. Sometimes property rights are unclear or their registration is lost. This problem arises in particular when the government wishes to return totally or partially expropriated goods to their former owners. However, cases of conflict – in particular over rights on the proceeds of privatization – between the government and the management of the organ (such as state holdings) in control of the enterprise to be privatized are rather frequent. Other conflicts may take place within the government concerning the use of the revenue from privatization.

1.8 VARIETIES OF CAPITALISM, CORPORATE GOVERNANCE AND PATH DEPENDENCE

The type and features of the economic system existing in a country have a great influence on privatization. This influence concerns the implementability of privatization *via* specific means (such as through the stock exchange), the willingness and actual possibility of the government to divest itself of property rights and specific functions, the social acceptability of a privatization program, and the economic and social outcomes of privatization policy. Different types of capitalism are distinguished by technical features, by the working of the economy, by ownership structures, and by types of corporate governance.[25] This causes path dependence that produces different problems, preferences and choices, limits and solutions for privatization. I distinguish three fundamental types of capitalism in economically developed economies. They are as follows:

1. *Competitive managerial capitalism.* Its prototype is Anglo-Saxon capitalism. This type of capitalism is characterized by two elements: a high number of enterprises in a competitive environment and a developed financial market that is important for corporate governance. Both elements are based on rather dispersed private ownership that gives managers a very important or even dominant role in the control of enterprises. In the countries of Anglo-Saxon capitalism (Great Britain and the United States in particular) the state has a relatively minor role in the ownership structure and in managing firms, and the market for corporate control is quite active. As a consequence, privatization can easily be implemented through the financial market (stock exchange, in particular), can result in a relatively dispersed ownership, and can promote competition more easily than in other cases.
2. *Concentrated (bank-centric) capitalism.* This can also be termed as German-type capitalism. It is characterized by a limited number of organizations (mostly non-financial companies) that own and control a large part of the economy. Banks have a fundamental role in corporate governance, but this role is more indirect than in Japan and is largely exercised via delegated rights deriving from the management of shares owned by other investors. The industrial structure is dominated by the presence of large companies, that also have an important role in corporate governance via widespread cross-ownership. The role of the state in the economy is consequently secondary and generally indirect and devoted to establish and enforce clear rules and rights and coordinate and control the few large controlling organizations. Privatization in these circumstances is likely to be controlled by large banks and by the large groups of non-financial institutions that already control the economy. Privatized enterprises easily become directly or indirectly part of

those same groups. As a consequence, privatization is likely to strengthen the degree of concentration of corporate control and also of ownership.
3. *Family (bargaining) capitalism.* This is close to the traditional Italian-type capitalism and is characterized by an extremely high concentration of ownership and control of individual firms in the hands of capitalist families and groups, the great role of the state as an owner and a manager, and the modest role of financial institutions and capital markets in corporate control. In Italy, separation between ownership and control is guaranteed by a mix of state ownership, pyramidal groups and implicit rules, namely family relations and coalitions among owners sharing common interests or values, while control-oriented financial institutions, takeover and fiduciary duties are lacking. Dominant features are consequently limited degree of separation, high stability of control – which spurs entrepreneurs' commitment and investments – and obstacles to mobility and control – which hamper growth and restructuring and limit people's opportunities. In this type of capitalism, privatized enterprises are often included in the few existing family empires or groups, that are often the only strong buyers. A further danger exists: the government and the agents of politics (such as political parties) and the representatives of social groups (such as trade unions) may be strongly involved in business life and business relations and disputes. As a consequence, the chances are that privatization can also be used to reward political supporters – individuals, enterprises or social groups. Thus it can easily fail to pursue competition and to strengthen capital markets and to introduce an impersonal system of corporate control.

One can draw an important conclusion from these few notes, a conclusion that concerns the relation between the economic system and privatization: the dominant features of the economic system affect the implementation of privatization, restrict choices of techniques utilized and goals pursued, and influence the outcome. This is certainly not a deterministic process: in any economy and any system privatization offers great chances to modify or even change the economic system. However, the system creates conditions and factors that may easily produce path dependence in privatization.

Path dependence is the consequence of the stickiness of institutions, but it is also a rational outcome of agents who try to reduce transaction, adaptation and information costs that are necessary to adapt to the new situation, overcome uncertainty and take advantage of opportunities offered by privatization. Those agents who have an important role in the system and possess highly valuable and possibly specialized assets, thus being favored by asymmetric information and bargaining power – such as policy makers, owners or entrepreneurs of large private businesses, managers of large state-owned companies – may prefer to buy and restructure already existing former state-owned companies than setting up and developing entirely new enterprises. By buying an existing firm, they also buy its intangible assets (such as knowledge, know-how, business connections, reputation) and may also enjoy rents. Therefore, the allocation of capital, corporate control and entrepreneurship after privatization is determined by the allocation of capital, corporate control and entrepreneurship before privatization. Path dependence renders privatization a weaker instrument for changing the working of the system than hoped by its supporters. It follows that the role of privatization in the economy reflects the features of the economic system and in order to contribute to change the latter privatization must be strongly supported by political will to reform the system. In this sense, privatization is a political process.

However, path dependence does not necessarily play a negative role. In fact, it may have a productive outcome, because the still valuable assets of the old state-owned enterprises have a technical value that may be of help in the new situation. This decreases transaction costs of privatization, because the new structure of payoffs can reinforce tendencies already existing, thus reducing institutional resistance to changes and increasing the effect of institutional externalities. This effect is likely to be more important in certain types of capitalism (competitive managerial capitalism, and possibly also concentrated capitalism).

1.9 THE RATIONALE FOR PRIVATIZATION

The results of the studies reviewed in section 5 and the factors considered in the other sections present us with a rather complex and contradictory picture of the nature and consequences of privatization. In general, it turns out that privatization may have useful and important outcomes in terms of different types of efficiency. However, the outcome crucially depends on a set of other factors, first among which is the existence of a competitive environment. In this section I shall work out a simple scheme for detecting the conditions for privatization to take place as a socially feasible and advantageous undertaking. In order to simplify the analysis, I shall consider that privatization is initiated by the government as a rational decision based on the advantages for society. Therefore, I shall consider government as a benevolent agent that pursues the well-being of society.[26] I shall also disregard the role of those social and economic agents other than the seller and the buyer who can have a stake in privatization (for example managers and employees, consumers and suppliers). In a first approximation, private agents, who are the demand side of the privatization process, are interested in privatization when the return they can obtain by using those assets to produce goods or services covers at least the costs they have to incur to buy or obtain a privatized firm.

However, I shall also consider that private agents may be interested in pursuing a purely redistributive outcome, that is, the net transfer of government income or wealth through privatization.

Within this simple framework, the government will privatize when the advantages for society are greater than costs. In balancing these factors, the government usually considers long-term dynamic effects and the various positive and negative spillovers of privatization. In fact, any change of routines and existing organizational structures of the economy implies advantages that go beyond the specific action undertaken. However, such change also involves costs for those who promote them (organizations and possibly individuals within the government) and for the society at large, costs that are more general because they may not be limited to the subject of privatization (the specific privatized firm). For instance, there may be costs for the state budget. Consequently, the net outcome of privatization for promoters must be positive in order to cover those more general costs; that is, it must be greater than implementation costs of specific privatization cases. I shall call the former type macroeconomic costs of privatization because they accrue directly or indirectly to the society at large. I shall call the latter type of costs microeconomic costs of privatization, because they accrue directly to the individual acts of privatization, although they are not necessarily paid directly by the buyer.

The government has responsibility for privatization in two different ways. First, the government may decide to establish a wide-ranging privatization program, including the privatization of many and different assets. This is usually done in the framework of a reform policy for improving the working of the economic system. In this context, systemic and dynamic outcomes are important. I shall call this type of privatization macroeconomic privatization. It involves many different costs of privatization, comprising establishing privatization structures, and various types of positive and negative spillovers that concern a large part of the economy. Here one should notice that macroeconomic costs of privatization are not limited to macroeconomic privatization, although they are mostly the consequence of the latter. However, some of these costs may also be the consequence of privatization of specific assets, for instance, the social costs for financing unemployment deriving from the privatization of individual firms.

The government decides to start a privatization program when:

$$R + D + S \geq C_M + C_m \qquad (1.1)$$

Where:

R is the revenue that society obtains from privatization. It includes the value of the privatization program (the aggregate sale price of privatized assets), the taxes that the government raises from firms after their privatization (net of lost taxes that were paid by the same firms before privatization), the value of unnecessary investment of privatized firms (net of crowding out of other investments caused by privatization and net of subsidies paid to the privatized firms over those enjoyed before privatization).

D indicates dynamic outcomes of privatization. These include the net gain to consumers from lower prices charged by privatized firms compared to the situation before privatization and from net improvement of quality/choice of goods and services supplied by privatized firms, and net effects on the economy growth rate, technical progress and institutional reform.

S includes the value of net spillovers of privatization on the rest of the economy (for example in terms of increased creditworthiness of the state, greater efficiency via increased competition or net increase of demand by privatized firms).

C_M denotes macroeconomic costs. These consist of the direct costs of privatization (to prepare and implement privatization programs, and establish privatization structures), of indirect costs (from net increase of unemployment, decreased aggregate demand, loss to the budget of the revenues of firms before privatization), and of policy costs (costs of alternative policy instruments and actions necessary after privatization both to regulate privatized firms and to compensate negative outcomes of privatization in terms of equity or else net of the costs for running state-owed companies previously met).

C_m marks microeconomic costs. These include the aggregate net value of administrative costs, the costs of financial restructuring and physical rehabilitation of firms before privatization, the settlement of employees' claims, the losses deriving to the firm from uncertainty before privatization, the value of underpricing in the sale of firms, the cost of corruption and collusion that may accompany the sale.

Privatization as a general policy is successful when the above condition holds and, after discounting all values to the time of sale, there is presently no alternative action that is more convenient. Second, the government may decide to sell individual assets, be it in the framework of a general program of privatization or simply on an *ad hoc* basis. In the former case the government can also afford microeconomic losses, in the sense that it can accept a net revenue from privatization lower than the market value of the firm privatized. Usually the government also gives up the share of macroeconomic costs of privatization that pertain to the individual firm. In this case the gain for society can derive from dynamic effects and spillovers.[27] Therefore, the minimum condition for privatization of individual assets and firms to take place is:

$$r_g + d_g + s_g \geq c_{mg} \tag{1.2}$$

Where:

r_g is the revenue that society obtains from privatization of an individual firm or asset (the aggregated price of sale of the privatized firm or asset, plus net taxes, plus the net value of unnecessary investment). As said above, this net revenue may even be lower than the firm or asset market value, thus implying a loss over potential revenue.
d_g indicates dynamic outcomes of the individual privatization action. These also include the outcome of the individual privatization action on the success of the privatization program (for example sale of one firm via underpricing may increase the chances of success in later sales).
s_g includes the value of net spillovers of individual privatization actions on the rest of the economy (in general, in the specific market where the firm operates).
c_{mg} marks microeconomic costs relative to the specific firms that is privatized.

Similarly, buyers have to pay a price for getting the privatized firm or for obtaining a contract, but they also have to afford different transaction costs. These derive from the need to acquire information on the privatization program and the privatized firm, work out a development strategy and reach a decision, and sign a contract balancing this with other investment opportunities. I shall call these costs for the buyer purchase costs of privatization. One can easily suppose that purchase costs for the individual buyer cannot be higher than the value of the revenue expected from the privatized firms discounted to the time of privatization. This can possibly be augmented by spillovers that the purchase can have on other activities of the buyer (for example via decreased transaction costs or by permitting diversification and vertical integration) and by dynamic effects (for example the establishment of monopoly power or economies of scale). The condition for purchase to take place is:

$$r_p + d_p + s_p \geq c_{mp} \tag{1.3}$$

Where:

r_p is the discounted flow of profits that the buyer expects to obtain from the individual firm or asset (net of taxes).
d_p indicates dynamic effects of the individual privatization action for the buyer.
s_p includes the value of net spillovers of the individual privatization action on the other activities of the buyer.
c_{mp} marks microeconomic costs relative to the purchase of the specific firm that is privatized. These costs are possibly decreased by the effect of underpricing and by other facilities offered by the government (for example credit for financing the purchase, technical assistance during the process of privatization). However, microeconomic costs are increased by the necessity to restructure the firm.

Individual actions of privatization are successful when the following minimum condition holds:

$$r_g + d_g + s_g - c_{mg} \geq r_p + d_p + s_p - c_{mp} \tag{1.4}$$

No similar condition is necessary for macroeconomic privatization. Indeed, this can be considered as a unilateral decision of the government to invest resources in order to improve the efficiency of the economy and consequently increase overall production.

1.10 SUMMARY AND CONCLUSIONS

The analysis of the preceding sections brings some interesting conclusions on the features, importance, circumstances, and consequences of privatization in market economies. I summarize the main conclusions in this section. I will extend those conclusions to countries in transition in the next section.

Being largely an economic undertaking, given the goals pursued, privatization policy is particularly sensitive to the question of its costs. I divided those costs into two groups: microeconomic costs that are easily ascribable to individual acts of privatization, and macroeconomic costs that are not accounted to individual actions but are directly paid by society via public budgets. This divergence between individual and general costs blurs the possibility of establishing the actual social profitability of individual privatization actions. The goals pursued and the costs are crucial factors in the choice of privatization methods. The outcome of privatization not only depends on the content of direct privatization policies and actions, goals pursued, techniques utilized, sequencing, speed. In fact, there exists a set of important factors that belong to the organizational aspects of the firm and another group of factors that jointly form the environment of privatization and whose activity strongly influences the course of privatization and its outcome. The examination of these factors is the topic of section 4. In doing this, I have particularly addressed the question of which environmental conditions are necessary to reach a socially desirable outcome. I concluded that various factors are important, among which competition and regulation stand out.

Section 5 presents a survey of the results obtained by quantitative analyses of the microeconomic and macroeconomic consequences of privatization. Such analyses are rather unilateral, because they usually consider only one of the aspects of privatization, although important, namely efficiency. The main conclusion has been that although there is some evidence that private companies obtain results that are superior to comparable state-owned companies, this result is likely to be the consequence more of competition than of any intrinsic feature of ownership. A further interesting result is that results of privatization vary in different sectors and contexts. It is concluded that also institutional efficiency should be considered in order to have a full picture of the consequences of privatization.

In the sections presented so far, I have supposed that there are no constraints on privatization, except those that derive from the content of privatization policy and actions. However, this is not so and the next sections of the chapter are devoted to presenting a more disaggregated systemic approach to privatization. Section 6 examines the constraints that the features of industries and firms impose upon privatization. The independent variables considered for industries are supply conditions and the prospects of demand. Independent variables for firms are different degrees of competition or monopoly. Together, these explain why investors should be interested in buying a firm to be privatized and what should be the organization of the industry once enterprises are privatized. On this basis, privatization may yield results of varying desirability for the goals pursued by the government.

The discussion of social and technical factors that impose constraints upon privatization is presented in section 7. These factors extend from the existence of groups and coalitions that determine collective action to the lack of legal framework, insufficient resources and expertise, through macroeconomic problems. These may be important factors that must be carefully considered in designing proper privatization policy and implementing it.

Section 8 discusses the role of the specific features of the economic system and path dependence. It is shown that there are different types of economic system and each one presents different problems, advantages and disadvantages for privatization. Consequently, privatization policies should be system-tailored, at least because the features of the system are in any case able to impose their influence upon the implementation process and its outcome through path dependence.

Because privatization not only has consequences on revenues and costs, but also has dynamic outcomes and different spillovers, I concluded that all these effects must be considered to reach a complex and reliable picture of the advantages and disadvantages of privatization.

A set of conclusions arise from the above analysis:

1. The problem setting varies according to the specific features of the economic system. Different types of capitalism have fundamental consequences for corporate governance. Consequently, the institutional framework that makes up the economic system, together with the features of economic actors, render privatization policies path dependent. However, a well-designed policy of privatization may support the transformation of the economic system in the desired direction, thus helping the success of privatization. In fact, one has to consider that the evolution or change of the type of capitalism have important implications for the economic organization and may require a different mix between market and hierarchy.

2. There is no completely free choice concerning the actual content of privatization policies. This is so because privatization has institutional and technical limits, meets obstacles and implies costs.

3. Privatization is not enough to improve the performance of the economy. In fact, its social consequences crucially depend upon concomitant factors, in particular competition and regulation.

4. Policies of reform are subject to the pressure of interest groups, ideologies, political influence, changing preferences, foreign influence, lack of coordination, administrative rigidities, technical mistakes. These have various undesirable consequences. Among these, of particular relevance is the possibility that – because of the lack of actual consideration for the complexity of policies privatization – the policy 'pendulum' swings excessively in this direction. This may produce negative externalities or spillovers on the economy that easily lead to disappointing outcomes of such policies.

5. In a systemic perspective it is not enough to consider the outcome of privatization on individual firms and not even on individual industries. In fact, the privatization of a firm has many and varied 'hidden' consequences on the economic system, the entire economy, other industries and firms.

1.11 SOME TEACHING FOR TRANSITION ECONOMIES

The analysis of the previous sections and the findings I arrived at there refer to privatization in well-established market economies. Therefore, it is not easy to extend them to the case of transition economies in Central-Eastern Europe. In fact, privatization is in this latter case a much wider and deeper undertaking that involves the entire organization of the economy. It is not addressed at improving the working of a well-established market economy or at reforming it. On the contrary, it is implemented in order to radically change the economic system by establishing a previously non-existing private property regime.

Therefore, the goal of privatization in transition economies is firstly a general, social one: laying the organizational and systemic basis for a market economy. In this sense, it would be reductive to evaluate the outcome of privatization on a purely microeconomic basis. For instance, the improvement of productive and allocative efficiency or of the income performance of each company, or the income obtained by the state through privatization, or the establishment of clear and enforceable property rights are certainly important outcomes.

However, these are far from being sufficient to the success of transition. What matters most are the complex outcomes that derive from the interaction of all these factors and the contribution this gives to the establishment of the organizational and institutional basis on which the new system can evolve and produce in the long run results that are socially superior to the outcome produced by the old system. All this makes privatization in transition economies a more important and a much wider and deeper undertaking than in well-established market economies; an undertaking that is consequently more complex and difficult. However, for these very reasons it may be better to introduce other factors, such as competition, that can be important concomitant factors of privatization.

It is impossible, in these few conclusive notes, to treat satisfactorily such a wide and complex set of factors. I will limit myself to sketching out some suggestions for transition economies that derive from the study of Western experiences. I will assume as my privileged point of observation what I consider to be the most important one for transition economies, namely the contribution of privatization to the success of systemic change. This is mainly a general, social point of view. However, it comprises in itself the fundamental microeconomic components: only if the microeconomic factors of the companies' activity improve is the outcome of transition for the economy at large (the social outcome) positive.

A. The first, general outcome of the preceding analysis is that we should not expect too much from quantitative measurement of the progress of privatization. This is very difficult even in developed market economies, where quantitative data are usually of good quality and change processes less general, deep and fast than in transition economies. A further reason for caution should derive from the actual impossibility to correctly measure or consider all the factors involved. Privatization in the strict sense of the word is but one of these factors in determining the performance of companies, let alone the outcome of transition. Many other variables strongly influence the outcome, variables that may change through countries, time, and sectors. Measurement is quite important both for the results it can give and the rigor it may introduce in the analysis, but one should be careful in interpreting the results.

B. From the very nature of privatization in transition economies it follows that the simple scheme that I worked out in section 9 for detecting the conditions for privatization to take place should be carefully interpreted. In fact, in transition economies the dynamic outcomes and different spillovers of privatization are particularly important and the government should not be limited in its privatization action by short-term and microeconomic considerations. However important the latter are, long-term dynamic considerations should prevail in establishing a privatization policy and possibly also individual privatization decisions.

C. The choice of privatization techniques is particularly delicate and important during transition. This is so because each technique has various limits, requires proper circumstances to be successful, and effectively reaches certain goals more than others. It is also important to consider that the use of each technique may have different consequences for the social and political parties involved in privatization. Also, the use of specific techniques may be more difficult during transition, while the utilization of others may be socially and politically easier. If the final goal is to establish a modern market economy, clearly market methods should be preferred to distributive methods. This is so for the teaching, knowledge, and incentive aspects of the former, because this method requires the active and rational participation of individual actors in the privatization process. However, in certain circumstances their choice may be made too difficult and the outcome uncertain because of lack of time, political support, or private capital. In these circumstances, alternative methods may be preferable to immobilism. However, one should be careful in considering such methods as restitution. In fact, these involve a delicate problem of social justice for present and future generations that may be induced to passive or hostile attitudes by the 'return to the past'.

D. The multiplicity of goals pursued by means of privatization may be a serious disadvantage. In fact, this may be the cause of missing clear priorities in privatization action and trade-off, and may open greater opportunities to pressure groups. As stressed above, the traditional goals of privatization in market economies, namely micro-efficiency or the income produced for the state, should not shadow the fundamental goal of privatization. More important is the contribution of privatization to systemic change, in particular to the establishment of new market institutions. In this sense, privatization should play a fundamental role in producing new market knowledge and incentives. Market methods are clearly superior to others from this point of view. Also speed may be misleading or plainly negative when it is to the disadvantage of institutional restructuring and when it favors rent-seeking attitudes. In fact, it may lead companies to fight for survival by pushing them in a difficult situation due to reasons independent from their decisions and actions. This is hardly a situation in which companies can learn and adapt in the new environment. Learning, adaptation and establishing new incentives need time. Use of privatization to finance the public debt is always risky, but may be very useful to prove the determination the government has in establishing a hard budget constraint for itself, a major institutional breakthrough for transition economies.

E. Because of its novelty, extent, and lack of proper institutions and organizations, privatization in transition economies is a much more costly undertaking than in market economies. This is so for both individual companies and society. Costs depend on the specific privatization method used and the specific circumstances of individual branches. However, high costs should not be an excuse to stop privatization. This is so also because privatization may enjoy increasing returns: for example the greater is the quantitative progress in privatization, the more privatization agencies learn how to privatize and private businessmen how to run a private business. Also, it is only when privatization reaches a certain critical mass that competition starts to assert its beneficial effect. The great costs of privatization should give rise to a double consideration. First, being microeconomic costs high, the state (comprising local governments and international agencies) should carefully consider various options to support private businesses in their initial period of life and even more so to give potential entrepreneurs the opportunity to start their own business. Second, being macroeconomic costs high the (positive) social outcome of privatization should be a primary goal of any privatization policy. For this reason the social outcome should be carefully monitored. Policy measures should be implemented in order to reach such an outcome: for example by regulating (such as establishing authorities to prevent exploitation of monopoly power) or by liberalizing.

F. Various factors are important to the success of privatization which belong to the organizational aspects of the firm or in the economic environment. These factors are particularly important and delicate in transition economies, because the market environment is still undeveloped. This stresses that there is an urgent need to rebuild a market-friendly state to overcome market failures in all those circumstances when alternative methods are non-existent, undeveloped or simply less effective. These factors include, for example governance, regulation, and competition, that require careful public legal action and control. The solution of these problems should accompany privatization, not follow it, in order to address privatization towards socially productive outcomes.

G. In transition economies there is a great danger that particularly well-informed and powerful groups get a strong advantage in privatization. In this case, clear and enforceable property rights are not sufficient to originate a socially productive outcome of privatization. In fact, there may be various negative economic, social, and political consequences to this. One is certainly that such an outcome may prevent competition from displaying its beneficial role in the new market economy. To prevent this, the privatization process should be as open as possible, information should circulate widely, and capital concentration (direct and indirect, open and hidden) should be avoided in all the cases when transaction costs considerations or investment requirements do not prevail. Also this requires that the role of public organs be particularly delicate and important.

H. The experience gained in Western economies based on different industries 'desirability' of privatization may not necessarily be a guideline for transition countries. In fact, in the latter case, the primary importance of privatization is to establish market institutions. However, careful consideration of the perspectives and outcomes of privatization in different industries is certainly important for the success of privatization, namely for finding private buyers and for establishing sustainable and desirable economic conditions in the new system. An accurate choice of industry approach and priorities is also an important factor in determining the specific features of the new economic system. Although this is influenced by the past system via path dependence, privatization can do a lot to influence the final outcome. In this sense a transparent market privatization presents many advantages in the long run.

NOTES

1. Compare, respectively Wolf (1994) and Sappington and Stiglitz (1987). Sappington and Stiglitz (1987) have formulated the fundamental theorem of privatization in order to specify the conditions under which government cannot improve upon private production. However, these conditions are very restrictive. Moreover, both private and public production appear quite similar in some respects. The main difference between them concerns the transaction costs that the government faces when attempting to intervene in the delegated production activities. However, such intervention is generally less costly under public ownership than under private ownership.

2. Stiglitz (1994) observes that, even in the transition economies of Central-Eastern Europe, 'These general theoretical arguments, as well as the empirical evidence, do not make the case for privatization as compelling as some of the stronger advocates for market mechanism would suggest ... The case for privatization is a political one' (p. 173).
3. See for example, Beesley and Littlechild (1983, p. 1), Bös (1991, p. 2).
4. See for example, Domberger and Piggott (1986, pp. 145–6), Hensher (1986, p. 147), Kay (1987, p. 344), Kay and Thompson, (1986, p. 18).
5. This conclusion can easily be derived from Coase's (1960) analysis when transaction costs are positive by comparing privatization to the action of business firms that have favorable effects on others. Thus, a privatization policy is implemented because it is believed to increase the overall net value of production. Coase (1960, p. 115) states that: 'In these conditions, the initial delimitation of legal rights does have an effect on the efficiency with which the economic system operates. One arrangement of rights may bring about a greater value of production than any other. But unless this is the arrangement of rights established by the legal system, the costs of reaching the same result by altering and combining rights through the market may be so great that this optimal arrangement of rights, and the greater value of production which it would bring, may never be achieved.'
6. Borcherding, Pommerehne and Schneider (1982) offer an interesting survey of the literature by distinguishing between property rights approach and public choice approach.
7. World Bank (1988, vol. I, pp. 8–40), Yarrow (1986), Vickers and Yarrow (1988).
8. I leave out of consideration illicit, illegal or even criminal goals that usually accompany privatization, because I consider these goals as deviations from normality.
9. Coase (1960) is particularly precise and deep in dealing with the various aspects of actions having external effects. (op. cit., pp. 155–6).
10. I consider that the change in the budget constraint of enterprises or an increase in competition are changes that are logically different from privatization. These changes can also be introduced independently from privatization. However, it is true that the implementation of privatization policies also offers *de facto* an effective opportunity to introduce such changes.
11. Coase (1988) stresses that: 'Once we take transaction costs into account, the various parties have no incentive (or a reduced incentive) to disclose the information needed to formulate an optimal liability rule. Indeed, this information may not even be known to them, since those who have no incentive to disclose information have no reason for discovering what it is ... With positive transaction costs, some or all of these contractual arrangements become too costly to carry out ... What incentives will be lacking depends on what the law is, since this determines what contractual arrangements will have to be made to bring about those actions which maximize the value of production' (p. 178). As a consequence, 'in the presence of transaction costs, the liability rule cannot be optimal' (p. 178).
12. Underpricing generally accompanies privatization. Its nature is far from being clearly determined and univocal. It is usually defined as a discount of the subscription (sale) price compared to the price that is determined in the market on the first day of flotation after privatization (market price). However, even disregarding the many contingent factors that may influence the latter, the market price reflects the value of the privatized firm, while the sale price reflects the value of the public firm. If privatization promises to increase efficiency or to free the enterprise of social or political constraints, the market price must obviously be higher than the sale price, because it reflects an economically and institutionally different condition of the firm. As a consequence, underpricing is difficult to define, even when it is purposefully utilized by the seller as a sale technique.
13. Milgrom and Roberts (1990) have proposed the concept of 'influence costs' to indicate the costs connected with the centralized and discretionary power of the public and pri-

vate economic organizations whose members seek to influence, for personal gain, the decisions taken by the organization's internal authorities.

14. This point has been raised by Sappington and Stiglitz (1987, pp. 580–81).
15. Grossman and Hart (1986), and Schmidt (1996) present a model of privatization using an incomplete contracts approach, in which different allocations of ownership rights lead to different allocations of inside information about the firm, which in turn affect both allocative and productive efficiency. It is concluded that '*The evidence suggests that private ownership has efficiency advantages in competitive conditions, but does not show either public or private ownership to be generally superior when market power is present*' (p. 17, italics in the original).
16. The ownership of residual returns and residual rights of control only coincide when the firm is managed by its owner. In firms controlled by managers such coincidence is not complete. This may have important consequences for efficiency of production. See, Milgrom and Roberts (1992).
17. Honderich (1996) offers an interesting treatment of the different aspects rents may assume.
18. Wolf (1994, pp. 162–9) discusses the role of government in improving and extending markets.
19. Høj, Kato and Pilat (1995) presents a careful survey of the impact of regulation and regulatory reform in the case of the privatization in the service sector in OECD countries. Services considered are distribution, construction, road transport, telecommunications, airlines, energy, postal services, and railways. The sectoral evidence 'suggests that regulatory reform in services, if properly designed and implemented, can help to increase the degree of competition in the service sector and can contribute to improved performance' (p. 63). Ayres (1996) offers an interesting discussion of regulation and deregulation in the case of Brazilian privatization.
20. Ross (1988). Quoted in Wolf (1994, p. 141).
21. Qantitative comparisons about the results of privatization were made by Borcherding, Pommerehne, Schneider (1982), Boardman and Vining (1989), Bhaskar and Khan (1995), and Wolf (1994).
22. An important contribution to the comprehension of this danger is offered by Baumol's (1993) analysis of entrepreneurship.
23. Hensher (1986) proposes an interpretation based on the type of goods produced.
24. This goal has usually been achieved in British privatization. See, Kay and Thompson (1986, pp. 29–31).
25. The definition of different types of capitalism presented here draws on the following sources: Barca (1996), Barca et al. (1994), Chew (1997), Dietl (1998), Edwards and Fisher (1994), Ide (1998), Kester (1992).
26. This apparently naïve approach is justified by the fact that the institutional framework in a developed democratic market economy is such as to determine – via the selection of public agents and the constraints of their actions – a reasonably positive result for society, at least on average and in the long run.
27. Cantor (1996) works out a simple model of microeconomic privatization based on some simplified assumption. He concludes that 'a firm should be privatized if the weighted after-tax value of the privatized firm's investment is greater than the weighted value of the transaction costs less the net externalities associated with transferring the firm to private ownership' (p. 105).

REFERENCES

Alchian, A. A. and Demsetz, H. (1972), 'Production, Information Costs and Economic Organization', *American Economic Review*, **62**, 777–95.

Ayres, R. (1996), 'The Economics of Privatization and Regulation: The Brazilian Experience 1990–94', *Review of Political Economy*, **8** (3), 303–24.

Barca, F. (1966), 'On Corporate Governance in Italy: Issue, Facts and Agenda', *Corporate Governance and Property Rights*, Milan: Fondazione Eni Enrico Mattei.

Barca, F., Bianchi, M., Brioschi, F., Buzzacchi, L., Casavola, P., Filippa, L. and Pagnini, M. (1994), *Assetti proprietari e mercato delle imprese. Vol. II: Gruppo, proprietà e controllo nelle imprese italiane medio-grandi*, Bologna: Il Mulino.

Baumol, W.J. (1993), *Entrepreneurship, Management, and the Structure of Payoffs*, Cambridge, MA: The MIT Press.

Beesley, M. and Littlechild, S. (1983), 'Privatization: Principles, Problems and Priorities', *Lloyds Bank Review*, (July), 1–20.

Bhaskar, V. and Khan, M. (1995), 'Privatization ad Employment: A Study on the Jute Industry in Bangladesh', *The American Economic Review*, March, pp. 267–73.

Boardman, A.E. and Vining, A.R. (1989), 'Owership and Performance in Competiive Environments: A Comparison of the Performance of Private, Mixed, and State-Owned Enterprises', *Journal of Law and Economics*, (April), 1–33.

Borcherding, T.E., Pommerehne, W.W. and Schneider, F. (1982), 'Comparing the Efficiency of Private and Public Production: The Evidence from Five Countries', *Zeitschrift für Nationalökonomie*, (Suppl. 2), 127–56.

Bortolotti, B., Fantini, M., Siniscalco, D. and Vitalini, S. (1998), *Privatisations and Institutions: A Cross-Country Analysis*, Milan: Fondazione ENI Enrico Mattei.

Bös, D. (1991), *Privatization. A Theoretical Treatment*, Oxford: Clarendon Press.

Cantor P. (1996), 'To Privatize or Not to Privatize: That is the Question; What is the Answer?', *Review of Radical Political Economics*, **28** (1), 96–111.

Chew, D.H. (1997) (ed.), *Studies in International Corporate Finance and Governance Systems*, New York and Oxford: Oxford University Press.

Coase, R. (1960), 'The Problem of Social Cost', *The Journal of Law and Economics*, (3), 1–44, reprinted in R. Coase, *The Firm, the Market and the Law*, Chicago: The University of Chicago Press, 1988, pp. 95–156 (quotation in the text is from this latter source).

Coase, R.H. (1988), 'Notes on the Problem of Social Cost', in R. Coase, *The Firm, the Market and the Law*, Chicago: The University of Chicago Press, pp. 157–85.

Dallago, B. and Mittone, L. (1996) 'The State and the Firm: the Centralization and Decentralization of Economic Institutions. An Introduction', in B. Dallago and L. Mittone (eds), *Economic Institutions, Markets and Competition*, Aldershot, UK and Brookfield, US: Edward Elgar, pp. 1–30.

Dietl, H.M. (1998), *Capital Markets and Corporate Goverance in Japan Germany and the United States. Organizational response to market inefficiencies*, London: Routledge.

Domberger, S. and Piggott, J. (1986), 'Privatization Policies and Public Enterprise: A Survey', *The Economic Record*, (June), 145–62.

Edwards, J. and Fisher, K. (1994), *Banks, Finance and Investment in Germany*, Cambridge: Cambridge University Press.

Grossman, S. and Hart, O. (1986), 'The Costs and Benefits of Ownership: A Theory of Vertical and Lateral Integration', *Journal of Political Economy*, **94**, 691–719.

Hatry, H.P. (198X), A *Review of Private Approaches for Delivery of Public Services*, Washington, DC: The Urban Institute Press.

Hensher, D.A. (1986), 'Privatization: An Interpretative Essay', *Australian Economic Papers*, (December), 147–74.

Honderich, K. (1996), 'Producers and Parasites: The Uses of Rent Seeking', *Review of Radical Political Economics*, **28** (2), 54–76.

Høj, J., Kato, T. and Pilat, D. (1995), 'Deregulation and Privatization in the Service Sector', *OECD Economic Studies*, No. 25, 1995/II, 37–74.

Ide, Masasuke (1998), *Japanese Corporate Finance and International Competition. Japanese Capitalism versus American Capitalism*, Houndmills, Basingstoke: Macmillan Press.

Kay, J.A. (1987), 'Introduction: Public Ownership, Public Regulation or Public Subsidy?' *European Economic Review*, **31** (1–2), 343–5.

Kay, J.A. and Thompson, D.J. (1986), 'Privatization: A Policy in Search of a Rational', *The Economic Journal*, (March), 18–32.

Kester, C.W. (1992), 'Governance, Contracting, and Investment Horizon: A Look at Japan and Germany', *Journal of Applied and Corporate Finance*, **5** (2), 83–98.

Landau, D. (1983), 'Government Expenditure and Economic Growth: A Cross-Country Study', *Southern Economic Journal*, **49** (3), 783–92.

Leibenstein, H. (1966), 'Allocative Efficiency vs. X-Efficiency', *American Economic Review*, (3), 392–415.

Marsden, K. (1983), *Links between Taxes and Economic Growth: Some Empirical Evidence*, World Bank Staff Working Paper 605, Washington, DC.

Milgrom, P. and Roberts, J. (1990), 'Bargaining Costs, Influence Costs and the Organization of Economic Activity', in J. Alt and K. Shepsle (eds) (1990), *Perspectives in Positive Political Economy*, Cambridge: Cambridge University Press, pp. 57–89.

Milgrom, P. and Roberts, J. (1992), *Economics, Organization and Management*, New Jersey: Prentice Hall.

North D.C. (1991), *Institutions, Institutional Change and Economic Performance*, Cambridge: Cambridge University Press.

Olson, M. (1982), *The Rise and Decline of Nations*, New Haven, Conn.: Yale University Press.

Pryor, F.L. (1985), 'Growth and Fluctuations of Production in OECD and East European Countries', *World Politics*, **37** (January), 204–37.

Ross, R.L. (1988), *Government and the Private Sector: Who Should Do What?*, New York, NY: Taylor & Francis.

Sappington, D.E.M. and Stiglitz, J. (1987), 'Privatization, Information, Incentives', *Journal of Political Analysis and Management*, **6** (4), 567–82.

Schmidt, K. (1996), 'The Costs and Benefits of Privatization: An Incomplete Contracts Approach', *The Journal of Law, Economics and Organization*, **12** (1), 1–24.

Stiglitz, J.E. (1994), *Whither Socialism?*, Cambridge, MA: The MIT Press.

Vickers, J. and Yarrow, G. (1988), *Privatization: An Economic Analysis*, Cambridge, MA: The MIT Press.

Wolf, C.Jr. (1994), *Markets or Governments. Choosing between Imperfect Alternatives*, 2nd edn, Cambridge, MA: The MIT Press.

World Bank (1988), *Techniques of Privatization of State-Owned Enterprises*, 3 Vols, Washington, DC: The World Bank.

Yarrow, G. (1986), 'Privatization in Theory and Practice', *Economic Policy*, **1** (2), 324–77.

2. Theories of Privatization and The Specific Features of East European Privatization

Iván Major

2.1 INTRODUCTION: AN ANALYTICAL FRAMEWORK

At first sight, it seems convenient to consider privatization of the state-owned property as an ordinary market transaction. Notably, there is a distinguishable and valuable good that is owned by the seller, that is, by the state, and there are potential buyers who are willing to pay a price for that good. Thus, the sale's price will be set at a level where demand for, and supply of, the state-owned property are in equilibrium. However in reality, privatization has never occurred according to the handbook rules of ordinary market transactions. Not even in advanced market economies can privatization transactions be described by the Walrasian or Arrowian, or Leontiefian equilibrium models, or by the equilibrium models of the game theory, where these transactions take place in a fairly organic way – that is, those are driven by the dominance of private property rights – and in a market environment. Western privatization also have some peculiar features as compared to ordinary company takeovers, since the state as the seller may pursue non-economic goals. Privatization can even less be explained by ordinary market mechanisms in the transforming Central and East European countries where privatizing the state-owned property is taking place in a mass scale and where competitive markets and private property rights are non-existent or they are in a premature state.

It would be very appealing to explain the peculiarities of privatization by the *complexity of factors* that explain supply and demand and price formation on the privatization market. However, it would also be misleading. It is not complexity, but the *uniqueness* of the transactions that distinguishes the privatization market from other types of markets. I shall discuss the nature of this uniqueness and the mechanism of transactions in sections 2 and 3 below.

In section 2, I outline the basic difference between the 'transaction cost' approach and the 'economic constitution' approach in relation to the analysis of East European privatization. The point of departure in discussing the transaction cost approach is Coase (1937, 1960). Coase's theory also served as a basis for Alchian and Demsetz (1973) and Demsetz (1988) where they described the institutional framework of a market economy and the structure of the private firm. O.E. Williamson (1985) and Pejovich (1990) have moved away from the orthodox theory of transaction costs toward an institutional theory of private property rights, but they have not arrived at a theory that could be tested against the experience of East European privatization.

The 'economic constitution' approach can be traced back to D. North (1981, 1991), but it was most clearly presented by Brennan and Buchanan (1985). The last two authors did not have East European countries in mind when they discussed how economic constitutions can be changed and how do they really change. Nevertheless, they provided us with a very useful way of looking at the privatization experience of Central and East Europe.

In section 3, I describe the main factors of supply, demand and price formation on the privatization market and I shall discuss their dynamics. The empirical and analytical works of many authors served as a good basis for the analysis of the privatization market.[1]

I also started analysing the factors of supply and demand on the privatization market in Major (1994a). In doing so I was inspired by Mihály Laki, who suggested that I should try to describe the peculiar 'clockwork' of the privatization market. This article would not have been born without his critical and helpful comments.[2]

2.2 IS IT POSSIBLE TO CONSTRUCT A FEASIBLE THEORY OF PRIVATIZATION?

When mass privatization started in Central and Eastern Europe, these countries could not rely on a vast literature on how to turn the state-owned property into private hands since such an extensive literature did not exist. Nor could they adopt the privatization methods of the advanced market economies for at least two reasons. First, although a massive wave of privatization and deregulation started in the West in the 1970s, actual privatization transactions occurred as individual cases rather than an all-embracing process that would have altered the basic rules and institutions of the Western market economies. Contrary to Western privatization, privatization has been the core of the economic transformation in Eastern Europe. And economic transformation aimed at the shifting of the socialist economic system as a whole into a radically different system, notably into a market economy. Thus, Western privatization seemed to be simple market transactions compared to the immense task of the Central and East European countries that had to turn their whole economic system around.

Western privatization focused mostly on public utilities. Privatizing public utilities, many of which used to be natural monopolies, is a very special exercise. Some of its lessons can be applied to any kind of privatization but others can not. Consequently, privatization of the electricity or gas works or telecommunications in the West could not serve as a model for East European countries (Valentiny, 1991, Valentiny, Buck and Wright, 1992 and Major, 1991).

Second, there was not a clear theoretical answer to the question even in the West whether privatization was only or mostly an issue of everyday politics or it could and should be directly related to the basic institutions and rules of the economic system. The 'classical' work on Western privatization was published by Vickers and Yarrow (1988). The authors described privatization as an almost ordinary market transaction that has, at the same time, several special features. Vickers and Yarrow considered privatization as an issue for economic analysis, but they also admitted – and they showed in several case studies in their book – that turning the state-owned property into private hands has political implications, too, beside the economic considerations. The deregulation and privatization literature of the 1970s and 1980s in the USA and in Western Europe also pointed out that privatization is directly intertwined with politics but it did not provide us with a comprehensive theory. Consequently, the question remained still unanswered if an economic theory of privatization is feasible at all?

2.2.1 Transaction Cost Theory and the Evolution of Economic Institutions

An obvious point of departure to construct an economic theory of privatization is the institutionalist theory of the firm (Coase, 1937; Demsetz, 1988), the theory of transaction costs or social costs (Coase, 1960) and the theory of property rights (Alchian and Demsetz, 1973; Pejovich, 1990). These theories properly describe the necessary and sufficient conditions for the viability of an economic system where the individuals and the firms act as autonomous economic agents. That is to say, the theories mentioned above show under what conditions private ownership can prevail. Moreover, these theories also outline the patterns of the actual transactions among the economic agents by which private property rights can be and they are being exercised. Thus, the theories of an 'organic' evolution of private ownership provide us with a comprehensive picture of what *mass privatization* should accomplish at the end. But they say little about the way privatization can move an economic system to that final stage.

Transaction cost theory and the theory of the firm as well as the theory of property rights have individual transactions and owners or firms in mind. When these theories show how individual owners and firms can minimize the cost of transaction of a certain property both for the individuals themselves and for the society as a whole, they implicitly assume that those transactions occur on a 'regular' market, that is, on a market where sellers and buyers are equally autonomous and they both follow the rules of maximizing economic benefits. Economic benefits are defined as utilities that can have a definitive equilibrium price and these benefits result from transactions that can be repeated under the same market conditions. Consequently, an evolutionary theory of privatization that is based on the above theories must assume that privatization itself is a series of ordinary market transactions.

However, it is not, because it cannot be the case. First, the seller(s) and the buyer(s) are not in an equal position on this market because they do not equally perceive their property rights. The buyer – a private investor – considers his investment as a business decision. After having paid the price for the property, he wants to have exclusive rights in utilizing the acquired asset. The state as a seller, on the other hand, pursues non-economic goals – beside economic considerations – when it offers its assets for sale and it aims to have some control over the sold property even after the transaction had been concluded. Hence, the state is reluctant to accept the clear and impermeable boundaries between the owner and the non-owners of a property. Were the sellers of the property the managers of the state-owned enterprises themselves, inequality among sellers and buyers would be much smaller, but it would still be present. Managers of the state-owned companies would still be the *representatives* of the owner – that is, the state or the people – while buyers are *per definitionem* private owners. Consequently, an unambiguous equilibrium price cannot be defined since sellers' supply is determined by other, often non-economic, factors than buyers' demand. Thus, the factors determining sellers' supply belong to another space than the factors that set buyers' demand.

Second, privatization transactions cannot be repeated. Each transaction is unique, for privatizing a company can only occur once.[3] And the individual transaction is very much affected by the specifics of the property for sale. Consequently, experience from other privatization transactions can only be used to a limited extent. It is so even if several similar or even identical components can be shown in different privatization transactions.

If there is no definitive equilibrium price and there is no possibility of repeating the market transactions, we cannot speak of an 'ordinary' market. Thus, the construction of a theory of privatization that aims to be an *eco-*

nomic theory and to be a theory that is compatible with the microeconomics of the market economy is *not* feasible. For the above reasons and for the reasons mentioned in the previous section, Central and East European mass privatization cannot be based on, nor can they be modeled by, the neo-classical theory and by the theory of transaction cost, or by the theories of the private firm and private property rights.

2.2.2 Institution Building and Changing the Economic Constitution

The emergence of the decisive institutions of an economic system that set the framework for, and the 'rules of the game', that is, the mechanics of, the actual economic transactions, is not fully determined by – hence, it cannot be deducted exclusively from – economic factors. Historical and cultural traditions, moreover, sociological and social psychological trends as well as geographical factors also heavily influence the evolution of economic institutions. The recognition of the important role of the above non-economic factors had been so obvious for the classical political economy, first of all for Adam Smith, that the prominent thinkers had not felt the need to discuss those factors extensively and separately from economic theory. In addition, historical time was much 'slower' in the age of late feudalism and early capitalism. Thus, the emergence of the institutions of capitalism could be considered as an organic process, although it was not.

From the neo-classical perspective the non-economic factors could not be reconciled with the economic ones in describing the formation of an economic system. It was the chief invention of institutional economics and the new political economy that the birth of the economic institutions cannot be explained only by economic factors. North (1981, 1991) was among the first authors who outlined a multi-disciplinary evolutionary theory of the economic institutions of capitalism. Williamson (1985) tried to bridge the gap between a pure economic theory of capitalism and the non-endogenous theory of capitalist institutions by flexibly applying the theory of the firm and the transaction cost theory. But he only achieved a limited success for he also assumed that the new economic organizations emerge in an economic and social environment where the basic institutions of the regular market transactions are in place and those institutions largely determine the behavior of the economic agents. Since neither Williamson – nor any other author of the evolutionary school – solved the problem how a non-evolutionary theory could be formulated in order to explain the 'jump' from socialism to capitalism, we cannot deduct a comprehensive theory of *mass* privatization either from North's evolutionary theory or Williamson's institutional theory of the capitalist firm.

The proper clue to the theory of privatization was provided by the new political economy and by the theory of collective choice. More concretely, it was the theory of the theory of 'public choice' (Buchanan, 1978), and the theory of 'economic constitutions' (Brennan and Buchanan, 1985), (Buchanan and Tullock, 1989), moreover the theory of 'collective action' (Olson, 1982) that made it feasible to place the main issues of privatization on a firm theoretical basis. While the evolutionary theories of capitalism showed us why private firms and private property rights result in a higher level of productive and allocative efficiency of the companies and the economies as a whole, than a collectivist and centralized economic system, and those theories also outlined why the individual and social costs of transactions are lower under private property rights than in an economic system of public or 'state' property rights, Buchanan, Brennan and Olson provided economics with directions on how to get from one economic system to another.[4] The institutionalist theory of the firm and transactions can show how markets function and evolve when they already exist, while the theories of economic constitution and collective action explain how an economy can be transferred from a system of non-market coordination to the system of market coordination.[5]

The constitution theory and the theory of collective action proved that moving from one economic system to another, such as, for example, from the collectivist socialist economic system to a market economy with dominant private ownership, cannot be accomplished by merely changing the economic institutions however deep those institutional changes are. New institutions will only become viable if the all-embracing economic constitution of the system is changed. Thus, privatization is not only about selling or giving away the state's right of control of individual companies to private owners. Privatization is itself the process of redefining the economic constitution of the system. Without incorporating the change of constitution into the process of privatization, turning the state-owned property into private hands cannot be successful because the private companies will not be viable. And those private companies cannot be viable because they must operate and survive under the rule of an economic constitution that is incompatible with private property rights. This incompatibility between the economic constitution on the one hand and the institutions on the other, has resulted in a very limited success of privatization in terms of economic restructuring and improving the productive efficiency of the private companies in Eastern Europe so far.

The theories of economic constitution and collective action do not provide us with a blueprint of mass privatization, nor do these theories offer specific techniques as to how property rights of a state-owned company could and should be changed. But these theories describe how 'the rules of the game', that is, the economic institutions themselves and the relations among those institutions, can be altered in a consistent manner that is compatible with economic rationality. Some cornerstones of these rules are:

(1) It is the obligation and the privilege of the state, that is, the parliament and the government, to formulate the legal framework of the transition. This legal framework determines what can*not* be done by the economic actors when state ownership is being transferred into private ownership.

(2) As a rule, the government administration should not act as a seller or a buyer on the privatization market since government agencies and other state authorities are driven by other interests than the economic actors whose benefit from the market transactions can be defined in economic terms. Should the government be involved in individual privatization transactions – such as, for example, privatization of nation-wide public utilities, where the issues of national security, market regulation and international coordination may be relevant beside the economic considerations – these transactions must be clearly separated from 'ordinary' transactions that occur in a mass scale on the privatization market.

(3) Since the central state and the local governments are the legal owners of the non-private property, these institutions can and should authorize the private agents or managers of the state-owned enterprises to conclude the individual privatization transactions. By doing so, the state refrains from interfering in economic transactions with non-economic interests. It is a common wisdom that – because of the information asymmetry – the managers of the state-owned enterprises will use privatization for their own benefit. But this kind of asymmetry will be present even if the state agencies try to administer every single privatization transaction for those agencies need to rely on the information of the company managers. And under such conditions the managers will not have any incentive to strive for a successful privatization. Thus, the state will be better off if it lets economic agents conclude individual privatization on the privatization market, although under unique market conditions. The delegation of the state's as an owner's authority to economic agents is the only way to put privatization under the control of economic rationality. But privatization will only be guided by economic rationality if the rules of the delegation of the ownership rights and the actual procedures of the individual transactions are transparent, predictable and competitive rather than discretionary. Even if the above conditions are met, privatization still remains a unique transaction on a peculiar market.

2.3 COMMODITY MARKETS, CAPITAL MARKET AND THE MARKET FOR COMPANIES TO BE PRIVATIZED

In this section we compare the main features of different markets in order to show that the 'privatization market' cannot be described solely with the notions and mechanisms of an 'ordinary market'.

2.3.1 Factors of Demand and Supply and Price Formation on 'Ordinary' Markets

The functioning of ordinary markets is not homogenous as regards the regularities of the generation of demand and supply and the regularities of price formation. Ordinary markets differ depending on the rules of entry and exit and on the fact of whether a market is competitive or non-competitive. A market can be non-competitive for several reasons. One of the reasons is that the nature of the goods traded on that market exclude competition. In such cases market transactions are guided by the rules of a 'natural monopoly' and the goods that are traded are called 'non-tradable' goods. Markets can be monopolistic or oligopolistic for reasons others than the presence of a natural monopoly. For instance, monopolies emerge because of historical, cultural traditions.

Notwithstanding the fact of whether a market is competitive or non-competitive, 'ordinary' commodity markets and capital markets – including money markets – are considered as ordinary because the goods traded on such markets are reproducible and, first of all, the *transactions* themselves are reproducible. The factors that determine the magnitude of demand for and supply of such goods, as well as the rules of price formation, can be described as a repetitive game between buyers and sellers. Reproducibility and repetitiveness of the market transactions do not mean static stability. Neither the factors of demand and supply, nor the prices themselves are stable, but the rules of the transactions on such markets are. It is so even if the actors on such markets are not equal, that is, the state as a buyer or seller cannot act on ordinary markets as a not ordinary agent.

The factors and mechanisms that determine or influence the magnitude of demand and supply and the mechanics of price formation are well described and well known from the economic literature. Hence, there is no need for a detailed discussion of the nature of market transactions on ordinary markets. There is one market where the state as an agent has a privileged position: the privatization market. On this market the state as a seller strives to fully exploit its exclusive and unilateral rights to initiate and administer privatization transactions. The state is a dominating actor on the privatization market even if it is under pressure to sell its property.

2.3.2 Supply, Demand and Prices on the Privatization Market

It is the unilateral right of the state to initiate the sale or give-away of a state-owned property. This right of the state is not different from the right of private owners who can deliberately sell their properties. But there is still a substantial difference between private sales and the sale of the state-owned assets. Notably, privately owned assets have a market value and a market price that are determined by regular transactions and by standardized methods of evaluation. As regards the joint stock companies, the price of their shares, that is, their unit value, is perpetually set by ordinary market transactions. Consequently, there is always a *potential demand* for a privately-owned asset. Thus, a potential buyer may become an actual buyer by initiating a market transaction. The magnitude of demand and the demand price offer are guided by the regular rules of market transactions.

Privatization as a market transaction usually aims at the sale of an existing company or business unit that is still in function. This fact is also true for privately-owned companies that are sold on the capital market. But the state as a seller selects the buyer of its assets by taking into account numerous considerations. Apart from the potential buyers' price offer and beside the technological level and market force of the potential buyers the state usually strives for specific *commitments* from the selected buyer. These commitments may include a predetermined level of employment in the acquired company, a certain amount of investment into the company, the transfer of know-how and marketing and management methods, the reorganization and restructuring of the company, access to international markets, and several other requests of the state as seller, all provided by the buyer.

The commitments requested by the seller, and in optimal cases accepted by the buyer, are the buyer's *promises* for the future – promises the fulfillment of which very much depend on the buyer's own business strategy, and on his or her perception of the macro and micro-level conditions of the company's operation he or she acquired. The more 'marketized' a transforming economy is, the higher is the probability that the private owner will fulfill her/his promises. Notably, as soon as the state transferred its property rights to the private owner, it has very feeble tools, and mostly non-economic tools, to enforce the fulfillment of the new owner's former promises. Only transparent and stable property rights, the well-rooted and solid institutions and the well-established markets can generate enough pressure that will prevent the private owners from circumventing the rules of the 'economic constitution' in a country.

It is obvious from what was outlined above, that supply of, and demand for, the state-owned property are generated in a completely different way from supply and demand on an ordinary market. While each transaction is guided by similar economic considerations on both sides, that is, on the seller's side and on the buyer's side, as regards the ordinary market transactions, a privatization transaction, on the other hand, is a unique event. It is unique because the seller strives for goals others than just to achieve the best price for its property. These goals are partly non-economic ones and in part they often contradict to each other. For instance, the state wants its company to be restructured by the private owner, but the state also wants to preserve a pre-specified number of jobs. It may aim at the safeguarding of industrial cultures in the country, but it also would like to see high technology industries emerge. Moreover, the procedure of evaluation of the property for sale is a complex bargaining process between the seller and the buyer that will not result, because it cannot result, in a 'regular' price. The price will not be regular because it will be set for only one occasion: for that specific deal that will be concluded on a certain date and between a certain buyer and the seller. Should the deal fail, the seller and the new potential buyers will start the bargaining process all over again.

Bargaining may change the price of a commodity in a regular market transaction, too. But the new price cannot be set in an arbitrary way. It will be constrained by the price of the substitute and by the complementary products. Meanwhile, in a privatization transaction, there are no comparable prices for the price of the other, comparable companies is also undetermined. In addition, 'the product' itself is not well defined since it is not a set of equipment that is for sale, but a complex organization, with special skills and with a certain amount of accumulated knowledge. Finally, the seller (the state) may further confuse the bargaining process with pursuing too many goals.

We can also formulate the above statement in a more formalized way. The supply function and the demand function of the privatization transactions are not continuous, consequently they are not differentiable. Thus, the price of a state-owned property cannot be determined as a unique function of supply and demand, for two reasons. First, the supply and demand functions are undetermined themselves, consequently the price is not an unambiguous function of supply and demand. Second, the privatization price is influenced by several factors others than supply of, and demand for, the state-owned property. These 'exogenous' factors are usually more important in setting the price requirement of the seller (the state) than the regular and endogenous factors of supply and demand.

It seems possible to define the price function in the framework of the game theory. But this would be unfeasible because the non-economic factors that affect price formation on the privatization market play a very important role in the 'privatization game'. And the relationship between these non-economic factors and the privatization price cannot be described with the tools of the game theory.

Another and frequently quoted approach to the determination of the 'objective' or 'realistic' price of the assets to be privatized finds its roots in Tobin's *q*-theory (Tobin, 1971, 1978). According to this approach, the 'realistic' price of a state-owned asset is the discounted value of the sum of future profits that can and will be generated by that asset. But the above definition of the asset's price assumes that a state-owned asset already has a market value and it also implies that privatization will not radically change the profitability of a state-owned enterprise.

None of the assumptions outlined above hold. First, the state-owned asset cannot have a market price because there is no capital market that could objectively evaluate that asset. A robust capital market can only emerge *after* mass privatization, that is, after private property rights had already become dominant in an economy. Second, it is the essence and *raison d'être* of privatization that it will induce a massive restructuring of the formerly state-owned companies. The privatized companies will usually operate on other markets and under very different market conditions and with another level of economic efficiency than the state-owned enterprises did before privatization. Thus, it is almost impossible to determine the expected profitability of a state-owned enterprise that will be privatized and radically restructured. Consequently, Tobin's theory of the capital evaluation could only be applied if privatization would be an *evolutionary* process that would not substantially alter the marginal productivity of the companies' assets. But this assumption is unrealistic in the case of the Central and East European countries. One can observe that we ended up with the same problem as we did when we tried to construct a theory of privatization from the evolutionary theories of the firm and private property rights.

It is reasonable to argue that there are other goods, beside the state-owned assets for privatization, the purchase and sale of which occur only infrequently. Such goods are, for instance, valuable works of art or real estates and agricultural land. Still, the transaction of these goods more or less follow the principles of regular market transactions. Why would the privatization transaction be so much different from the transactions mentioned above that it needs a distinct analysis? As long as the seller and the buyer of the state-owned property act in a similar way as those of a unique picture or a real estate, privatization can be regarded as one of the cases of the auction type markets. However, it cannot be assumed that the state administration as the seller of the state-owned assets does not have other types of considerations than the seller of a private albeit unique property. The basic difference between privatization on the one hand and the transaction of precious goods on the other is not related to the characteristics of the goods but to the different endeavors of the actors of the transactions.

Ultimately, we can conclude: if demand for, and supply of, the state-owned property, as well as price formation on the privatization market are not guided dominantly by the rules of ordinary market transactions or by other economic principles, then a pure economic theory of privatization is not feasible. Privatization is a political rather than an economic process during systemic transformation that can nevertheless be subordinated to the principles of economic rationality. If the organizations of the state – more concretely the parliament, the government and the municipalities – are capable of constraining themselves to the *political task* of setting the legal and regulatory framework for private property rights and for the transfer of the state-owned property into private hands, then the danger of political and bureaucratic interference in individual property transactions will be smaller. Moreover, should the individual privatization transactions be left to the economic agents, the distance between the privatization market and the 'ordinary markets' will be decisively smaller.

2.4 CONCLUSIONS

I showed in this chapter that privatization in Central and East Europe cannot be compared to the individual privatization cases that have occurred in advanced market economies or to the privatization in less mature but still existing market economies, such as, for example, the South European or South American market economies. Although privatization is a unique transaction in these countries, too, it does not have the function to substantially change the whole institutional system in that country, while in Central and East Europe privatization is the essence of the economic transformation because this is the way to radically change the *economic constitution* in these countries.

We saw from the experience of Hungarian privatization – and it can also be seen from the privatization process in other Central and East European countries – that privatization transactions are not guided by the rules and mechanics of an ordinary market (see, for example, Earle et al, 1994, Kornai, 1991, Mihályi, 1998, Móra, 1990, and Voszka, 1995). Privatization in Eastern Europe is a series of unique transactions whereby the state as the seller strives for several goals that are out of the terrain of the economic principles and considerations. Consequently, the 'privatization market' is a peculiar market the functioning of which cannot be described by any economic theory of the market. I also tried to deduct a feasible economic theory of privatization from the institutionalist theories of the firm and private property rights. We saw that these evolutionary theories can explain the structure and functioning of a market economy with dominant private ownership. But they are unable to provide us with a comprehensive set of economic principles that could outline how will an economic system with state ownership and political, bureaucratic regulation be transformed into an economy with private ownership and market coordination.

The clue to a feasible theory of privatization and economic transformation was provided by the theory of economic constitution and by the theory of collective action, that is, by the new political economy. Notably, it can be deducted from these theories that privatization of a whole economy is not a homogenous economic process that could be explained by a pure economic theory. The theoretical background of East European privatization and economic transformation can only be created from *economic* and *political* principles jointly. Thus, privatization, that is, changing the constitution of an economic system is *per se* the subject of the *political economy*. But we could also observe that the political economy cannot offer specific tools and methods either that could be directly implemented in the Central and East European countries in transition. The actual privatization transactions can and they should be guided by rational economic principles. But the rule of economic principles can only prevail if the state as a genuinely non-economic agent is constrained in its rights of interference in the privatization transactions. The collective action of private agents is a more efficient way of fostering sensible privatization than the omnipotent action of the state administration. The state has the right and obligation to create the legal and regulatory framework for the implementation and sustainable functioning of private property rights. Otherwise the state's active participation in privatization cannot be reconciled with the rational economic principles. This does not mean that the state must fully be excluded from the individual privatization transactions. But the state's activities in privatization have to be fully transparent and it must also be subordinated to the same economic principles as the privatization transactions of the other economic agents. This is the only way that the gap between mass privatization as the totality of unique transactions on a peculiar market on the one hand, and ordinary market transactions on the other, can be narrowed and ultimately bridged over.

NOTES

1. The long list of studies are given in Major (1993). Moreover, I heavily relied on the valuable works of Aslund (1991, 1995), Blanchard et al. (1991), Frydman, Rapaczynski and Earle (1993a, 1993b), and Earle, Frydman, Rapaczynski and Turkewitz (1994), Frydman and Rapaczynski (1994), Kornai (1990, 1991), Laki (1993), Lipton and Sachs (1990),

(1990), Filatotchev, Buck and Wright (1992), Mihályi (1998), Roland and Verdier (1991), Voszka (1995).

2. Laki also discussed some of the issues regarding the state's role in privatization (Laki, 1993). His analysis of the state's as seller's behavior in the 'privatization game' also emphasizes the multitude of contradicting goals that the state wants to meet. In this regard, Laki's study goes along similar lines as the following article. But he uses the analogy of a 'final clearance sale' to describe the state's attitudes in the privatization transactions, which seems to me too far fetched and it is not supported by facts.
3. In principle, and strangely enough, in Eastern Europe in practice, a state-owned enterprise can be privatized more than once. It can happen if the new private owner of the company goes bankrupt and she or he returns the company to the state. However, even in this case the second privatization of the company cannot be considered as a repetition of the same privatization transaction.
4. The evolutionary theories of capitalism and the theories of economic constitution and collective action have, of course, their antecedents. The former theories can directly be related to von Hayek's (1944) and von Mises's (1935) critique of the collectivist economic system. The new political economy can be traced back to the classical political economy of Adam Smith (1937). Schumpeter (1962, 1987) can be considered as a bridge over the two, not very distant, schools of thought.
5. Dahrendorf expressed similar ideas in his interview to *La Repubblica*, November 17–18, 1991. He said: 'I therefore believe it is important to establish the inviolable principles of what I would call an *economic constitution*'. The economic constitution approach was applied to describe the Polish economic transition by Federowicz (1994).

REFERENCES

Alchian, Armen A. and Demsetz, Harold (1973), 'The Property Rights Paradigm', *Journal of Economic History,* **33** (17), 16–27.

Aslund, Anders (1991), 'Principles of Privatization', in László Csaba (ed.), *Systemic Change and Stabilization in Eastern Europe*, Aldershot: Dartmouth.

Aslund, Anders (1995), *How Russia Became a Market Economy?* Washington, DC: The Brookings Institution.

Blanchard, Olivier, Dornbusch, Rudiger, Krugman, Paul, Layard, Richard and Summers, Lawrence (1991), *Reform in Eastern Europe,* Cambridge, MA: MIT Press.

Brennan, Geoffrey and Buchanan, James M. (1985), *The Reason of Rules: Constitutional Political Economy,* Cambridge: Cambridge University Press.

Buchanan, James M. (1978), *Cost and Choice: An Inquiry in Economic Theory,* Chicago: The University of Chicago Press.

Buchanan, James and Tullock, Gordon (1989), *The Calculus of Consent: Logical Foundations of Constitutional Democracy,* Ann Arbor: The University of Michigan Press.

Coase, Ronald H. (1937), 'The Nature of the Firm', *Economica,* (4), 386–405.

Coase, Ronald H. (1960), 'The problem of social cost', *Journal of Law and Economics,* (3), 1–44.

Demsetz, Harold (1988), *Ownership, Control, and the Firm,* Oxford: Basil Blackwell.

Earle, John S., Frydman, Roman, Rapaczynski, Andrzej and Turkewitz, Joel (1994), *Small Privatization,* CEU Privatization Reports, Vol. 3, London and Budapest: Central European University Press.

Federowicz, M. (1994), *Poland's Economic Order: Persistence and Transformation,* Warsaw: Friedrich Ebert Foundation.

Filatotchev, I., Buck, T. and Wright, M. (1992), 'Privatization and Entrepreneurship in the Break-Up of the USSR', *World Economy,* **15** (4), 505–24.

Frydman, Roman, Rapaczynski, Andrej and Earle, John S. (1993a), *The Privatization Process in Central Europe,* CEU Privatization Reports, Vol. 1, London: Central European University Press.

Frydman, Roman, Rapaczynski, Andrej and Earle, John S. (1993b), *The Privatization Process in the Republics of the Former Soviet Union,* CEU Privatization Reports, Vol. 2, London: Central European University Press.

Frydman, Roman and Rapaczynski, Andzej (1994), *Privatization in Eastern Europe: Is the State Withering Away?* London: Central European University Press.

Hayek, Friedrich von (1944), *The Road to Serfdom,* Chicago, IL: University of Chicago Press.

Kornai, János (1990), *The Road to a Free Economy. Shifting from a System: The Example of Hungary,* New York, NY: Norton.

Kornai, János (1991), 'A privatizáció elvei Kelet-Európában' (The Principles of Privatization in Eastern Europe), *Közgazdasági Szemle,* **XXXVIII** (11), 1021–40.

Kornai, János (1993), 'Transzformációs visszaesés' (Transformation Recession), *Közgazdasági Szemle*, **XL** (7–8), 569–99.

Laki, Mihály (1993), 'The Post-Socialist State as a Seller of Enterprises and other State-Owned Assets', Working paper #2, July 1993, Central European University, Budapest.

Lipton, David and Sachs, Jeffrey (1990), 'Privatization in Eastern Europe: the Case of Poland', *Brookings Papers on Economic Activity,* no. 2, Washington, DC.

Major, Iván (1993), *Privatization in Eastern Europe: A Critical Approach,* Aldershot, UK and Brookfield, US: Edward Elgar.
Major, Iván (1994), 'The Constraints On Privatization in Hungary: Insufficient Demand or Inelastic Supply?', *Most,* **4** (Special Issue), 107–45.
Mihályi, Péter (1998), *A magyar privatizáció krónikája, 1989–1996.* (The Chronicle of Hungarian Privatization, 1989–1996), Budapest: Közgazdasági és Jogi Ltd.
Mises, Ludwig von (1935), 'Economic Calculation in the Socialist Common-wealth', in Friedrich von Hayek (ed.) *Collectivist Economic Planning,* London: Routledge & Kegan Paul, pp. 87–130.
Móra, Mária (1990), 'Changes in the Structure and Ownership Form of State Enterprises (1987–1990)', *Economic Papers,* Budapest: Economic Research Institute.
North, Douglass C. (1981), *Structure and Change in Economic History.* New York and London: Norton.
North, Douglass C. (1991), *Institutions, Institutional Change and Economic Performance,* Cambridge: Cambridge University Press.
Olson, Mancur (1982), *The Rise and Decline of Nations: Economic Growth, Stagflation and Social Rigidities,* New Haven, London: Yale University Press.
Pejovich, Svetosar (1990), *The Economics of Property Rights: Towards a Theory of Comparative Systems,* Dordrecht: Kluwer.
Roland, Gerard and Verdier, Thierry (1991), 'Privatization in Eastern Europe: Irreversibility and Critical Mass Effects' Discussion Paper No. 9105 (June), Centre d'Economie Mathematique et d'Econometrie.
Schumpeter, Joseph A. (1962), *Theorie der wirtscahftlichen Entwicklung,* München-Leipzig: Duncker-Humboldt.
Schumpeter, Joseph A. (1987), *Capitalism, Socialism and Democracy,* London: Allen & Unwin.
Smith, Adam (1937), *The Wealth of Nations,* New York, NY: Random House.
Tobin, James (1971), 'A General Equilibrium Approach to Monetary Theory' in *Essays in Economics, Vol. 1: Macroeconomics,* Amsterdam: North Holland, pp. 322–38.
Tobin, James (1978), 'Monetary Policies and the Economy: The Transmission Mechanism', *Southern Economic Journal,* (January) pp. 421–31.
Valentiny, Pál (1991), 'Hungarian Privatization in International Perspective', *Public Enterprise,* **11** (2–3), 141–50.
Valentiny, Pál, Bruck, T. and Wright, M. (1992), 'The Pricing and Valuation of Public Assets: Experiences in the UK and Hungary' *Annals of Public and Cooperative Economics,* **63** (4), 601–20.
Vickers, John and Yarrow, George (1988), *Privatization: An Economic Analysis,* Cambridge, MA: MIT Press.
Voszka, Éva (1995), *Az agyaglábakon álló óriás,* (The Gholem), Budapest: Pénzügykutató Rt.
Williamson, Oliver E. (1985), *The Economic Institutions of Capitalism: Firms, Markets, Relational Contracting,* London: Macmillan.

3. Company Restructuring in the Bulgarian Transition

Spartak Keremidchiev and Todor Gradev

3.1 INTRODUCTION

Toward the end of the first decade of its peaceful transition to democracy, the Bulgarian society has little grounds to be proud of its new place in the world economic order. Marginalized on the periphery of Europe, the Bulgarian economy and industry need to struggle both with geography and history. Geographically, the distance to the increasingly exclusive European high-technology core renders many Bulgarian industries as second-tier subcontractors, allowed to enter only the markets for conventional, or less sophisticated commodities with little scientific ingredients. In the context of history, the Bulgarian economy suffered more severely that any other country in the European East from the landslide disintegration of the Council of Mutual Economic Assistance (CMEA), and faced the highest hurdles in its efforts to realign its productive capacities for exports from East to West. Moreover, history has placed Bulgaria in a troubled region prone to conflicts, too fragmented and too risky to be properly credited by the international flow of investments.

Yet changes do take place, even though not always in the most desirable direction. In this chapter, we address the transitional changes that have occurred in the Bulgarian industry since 1989 as a result of corporate restructuring and privatization. Empirically, our study is based on a sample of ten newly privatized companies in three Bulgarian industries: mechanical engineering, textiles and clothing, and food. Although these companies have been in private ownership for about two years on average, we trace their development from the beginning of the transition, and in some cases back from the immediate pre-transitional period of the late 1980s.

Industrial restructuring can be depicted as a movement of the firm from one equilibrium position to another in pursuit of momentous optimality. Together, all these equilibrium points form the equilibrium development path of the restructuring process. Under pressure, firms can shed labor and discard machinery, reshuffle personnel, fuse or split departments, realign production processes, reorganize work and overhaul finances – in short, firms can adjust and readjust. Firms which ignore market signals and fail to adjust go bust, sooner or later.

The restructuring moves of the firm toward a new equilibrium position are within a feasible set of actions. There are only a certain number of alternatives for which the company managers can opt under the pressure to restructure. While each particular managerial choice of action is endogenous for the firm, the feasible set – the range of actions from which company managers can choose – has its exogenous limitations. It is the macroeconomic environment, the governmental policies, the international trade agreements of the country, and so on, that sets the bounds of the feasible set of actions allowable to company managers.

A central notion underlying our discussion in this chapter is the belief that structural changes in the economy and industry are path dependent: instantaneous actions and motivations of firms, industries, and national economies are embedded in their legacies and their allowable development paths. We also try to make the distinction, where applicable, between instantaneous movements to a new equilibrium position under market pressures to readjust, and a shift, or a redirection of the entire equilibrium development path. The latter reflects the quality of the restructuring process, measurable for example by the level of science-based commodities in the product range of the firm.

For, whatever the external influences, the moves in a democratic society are determined endogenously, and they always reflect the 'enlightened self-interest' of its citizens who coordinate on an equilibrium agreement by mutual consent. Since there are always multiple equilibria of acceptable social contracts, the society moves are of necessity incremental, from one social contract to the nearest higher adjacent. To stay on its equilibrium path, the society must stay within its feasible set of action. The bounds of the set of an entire society are determined first and foremost endogenously – they are delineated by the 'common knowledge'[1] of history and culture available within this same society (Binmore, 1994). Sadly, it is in this respect that the experience of the Bulgarian transition so far can count as a warning, mostly to actors outside rather than inside the countries of Central and Eastern Europe. In this chapter, we consider the impact of these processes on the industrial restructuring underway in the Bulgarian economy primarily at a company level. We analyse the internal and external factors at play that have a bearing on the restructuring process in the Bulgarian industrial enterprises. Although the main target of analysis is the recently privatized companies, their behavior, motivations, aspirations, financial and economic viability are evaluated in the wider context of their respective markets, industries, local and regional economies and broader economic environment.

The first part of the chapter reflects on the determinants of firm behavior in the Bulgarian transition. A brief account is given in section 2 of the pre-transitional developments that have led to the shocks of the transition that in their turn shape the current macroeconomic environment of the Bulgarian economy, in which the companies operate. Section 3 reports on the corporate and financial governance aspects of the transition. The second part of the study focuses on the empirical results from the interviews with the designated privatized companies. After a brief description of the sample of companies and the methods of their privatization as the background of the privatization process in Bulgaria, their emerging corporate structures are put in the context of their conduct and performance. The next section considers the product differentiation strategies of the companies in the sample in their search for new market niches. The effects of restructuring of the product range are analysed from two perspectives: changes due to the former specificity of company assets and changes necessitated or influenced by the respective market structure. Lastly, adjustments in the cost structure and company finances, and improvements in the work organization after privatization complete the restructuring stories of the selected companies. We sum up the data in tables at the end of each section.

3.2 EXTERNAL DETERMINANTS OF FIRM BEHAVIOR

In the late 1980s, Bulgaria was a middle income country in South Eastern Europe with population of a little over 9 million people living on a territory of 110,994 square kilometers. In the entire postwar period, the country was a typical example of rigid economic control by the state over nearly all segments of economic activity. With the notable exception of privately-owned housing – unique in the entire East European block – and small subsidiary agricultural plots allocated mainly to the rural population, there was virtually no private ownership of land and other tangible assets in the country (Ehrlich, 1985).

Some tinkering with superficial cosmetic reforms has taken place in Bulgaria only since the beginning of the 1980s, carried out by ever-changing 'innovators' of the late Zhivkov governments. These reforms however, seen to be geared towards creating an imagery of ostensible change while preserving the political status quo of an aging regime, had little appeal among the population. The first real move to partial decentralization of the economic decision making was made only in January 1989 with Decree No. 56 on Economic Activity[2] issued by the State Council, a body of mixed functions of executive and legislature above the Council of Ministers, which existed in the last years of the totalitarian regime.

International trade has played a significant role in the Bulgarian economy. Total foreign trade turnover (exports and imports) have been traditionally very high, equivalent to about 80 per cent of the GDP in 1989. Throughout the years, about two-thirds of the trade has been with CMEA countries, primarily the Soviet Union. Insulated from the stormy events in the world economy by a complicated mix of subsidies and taxes, administrative setting of the exchange rate and rationing of the foreign currency, the Bulgarian economy hardly ever experienced the first and the second oil shocks. Consequently, close to nothing was done to restructure the industry in line with the challenges to the global economy, stemming from scarcity of resources and increased prices of energy in the 1970s and 1980s. This fabulous reluctance to adapt to the external environment only aggravated the severity of the multiple shocks on the economy caused by the demise of central planning and the collapse of CMEA. The over-reliance on the Soviet markets, and the absence of strong reformist wings within the communist party up until the late-1980's made the subsequent transition more painful than it had been ever expected.

Starting from the 1970s, the Bulgarian economy featured a persistently rising deficit of convertible currency. This deficit deteriorated radically in the second half of the 1980s, from $0.7 billion in 1986 to $1.3 billion in 1989. In addition, payment arrears began to accumulate on the $2 billion export credits extended by Bulgaria to some developing countries (Iraq, Libya and Syria being among the biggest debtors). The hard currency deficit of Bulgaria was financed through borrowing, primarily from private commercial banks in Western Europe (about 80 per cent of the total debt). The loans were frequently taken very irresponsibly, at high interest rates and very short maturity. The debt–service ratio of Bulgaria (export earnings to annual repayments) increased to 36 per cent of the exports in 1989, and the total external debt rose to over $9 billion in 1989 to add up to the complexities of the political and economic transformation of the Bulgarian society at the turbulent end of this relatively smooth and prosperous decade.

In 1990–91, Bulgaria entered the transition with profoundly dislocated economic resources. Unlike Poland and Hungary, Bulgaria had not been toying with reforms for one decade or more. Unlike Czechoslovakia, Bulgaria started from the bottom. Unlike Romania, Albania, and the former Soviet folks, Bulgaria had known better times in the immediate past. And to make things worse, out of the 1990–91 Iraqi embargo, Bulgaria found herself pushed by the Soviets into a triangle deal with Iraq, whereby Russian arms deliveries to Iraq were to be repaid with Iraqi oil to Bulgaria, and the oil counted for payment purposes in Bulgaria as 'imported from Russia'. With the embargo in force in 1990 and 1991 and the payment mechanism of CMEA at a broke, there was no petrol whatever for private consumption in Bulgaria during the entire 1990.

The austerity package of January 1991 was thus launched with shop shelves just emptied of goods and streets just emptied of cars; with milk and meat malnutrition and other food rationed; with loose money known to be of no value tomorrow; with huge foreign debt that had miraculously piled up since 1985. And with not so tightly held from the center, but still politically obedient, landlords in production and trade. Overnight, the state-managed foreign trade was abolished, and prices were freed to end up in a soaring 396 per cent inflation.[3] Bulgarian money was made internally convertible at a unified and market determined rate. Monetary and fiscal belts were successfully tightened to curb the sweeping inflation. Political control from the center evaporated. The industrial landlords found themselves free and became fully-fledged feudal masters. The problem is – as figures of inflation, industrial production and employment will show in the next section – that the society did undertake the jump, even though there was no consensus. Inevitably, the process went astray. The desired equilibrium was beyond the feasible set of the Bulgarian society, determined by its history and culture. The balance between macro-stabilization and micro restructuring had been ineptly planned: the macro-effort overshot to suffocate and stiffen the micro-motivations. Let us illustrate this point with a brief account of the effects of the shocks of the early transition.

The shocks experienced have been external and internal. The internal shocks stemmed primarily from plummeted consumer demand and high costs of credit. The fall in consumer demand was due to sharply decreased living standards and affected the consumer good industries, most noticeably food processing, where output dropped more than 20 per cent in 1991 and 10 per cent in 1990. The high cost of credit has led to huge depreciation in the capital-intensive industries, such as mechanical engineering, chemicals, and metallurgy.

In the absence of bankruptcy legislation and enforcement mechanisms in Bulgaria, the only feasible adjustment policy for these industries consisted of writing off equipment, shedding labor, and piling up debts. Unemployment rocketed from virtually none in 1989 to 16.8 per cent in 1993, contributing in a 'snowball' effect to the squeeze in consumer demand. Interest rates, although prohibitively high for entrepreneurs, remained negative, well below inflation. At such rates, the savings of the population in banks – short of any other investment opportunity – effectively pumped out resources from households to the government (Avramov, 1994) to subsidize various kinds of X-inefficiency, thus further aggravating the squeeze in consumer demand. The internal shocks experienced by the Bulgarian industries in 1991 and

1992 have been shocks inflicted by the crushingly quick 'introduction' of the market, which challenged the very survivability of firms, households, and the nation.

The external shocks resulted from the international environment of the early 1990s. The Gulf War embargo and the trade sanctions against Serbia, from which the country suffered severely indeed, are often blamed as major reasons for the poor trade performance in 1991–93. They were, however, mere incidents, and their occurrence simultaneously with other international events adversely affecting the Bulgarian industry may obscure more systematic failures. Among those systemic failures, the most important was the landslide disintegration of Eastern Europe after the collapse of CMEA. In spite of its clumsiness, its political, ideological and nationalistic biases, the former CMEA was a highly sophisticated system of commercial, technological, informational, infrastructural, financial, scientific and other relationships. The overnight elimination of these relationships has led to disrupted supply and production chains, prematurely terminated research, misallocated resources, and caused idle capacity in existing infrastructure and bottlenecks in other inadequately developed networks. In fact, the transaction costs of these interrupted linkages have been immeasurably higher than the immediate effects of the lost markets and the higher prices.

On the surface, however, all internationally inflicted evils upon the Bulgarian industry boiled down to increases in input prices and vanishing output markets. Since redirection of trade flows from the East to the West had to be accomplished by the Bulgarian enterprises when facing manifold increases in prices of energy and raw materials, unreliable supplies of components and overvalued domestic currency, the contraction of the industries in 1991 and 1992 could well be anticipated. At the same time, excessive import liberalization – higher than in the more prudent countries of Central Europe (see, for example, European Bank for Reconstruction and Development (EBRD) 1994, 1995) – opened the Bulgarian market completely for the invasion of (often-subsidized) foreign consumer goods. Whereas the internal shocks to the industry were evoked by the severity of the macro-stabilization adjustment, the external shocks have produced an 'adverse selection' problem. The size of plants in many industries had been originally set with a view of exploiting economies of scale on the entire CMEA market. With the evaporation of the latter, some sound companies with a bigger share of CMEA exports, or of imported inputs in their cost structure suffered more than others that were less effective, but relied on domestic supplies. Mostly hit were industries that had previously enjoyed utmost priority in the division of labor within CMEA and possessed the most advanced technology, but also the deepest product integration with enterprises in other countries.

Table 3.1. Key indicators of economic development in Bulgaria, 1989–96

Indicators	1989	1990	1991	1992	1993	1994	1995	1996
GDP (per cent)	–0.3	–9.1	–16.7	–12.4	–6.2	1.4	2.6	–9.2
Industry (per cent)	–1.4	–16.5	–22.4	–18.2	– 7.0	0.5	1.2	–10.5
Agriculture (per cent)	–0.3	–3.7	–9.8	–7.7	–2.3	0.1	0.2	–2.4
Consumer's Price Inflation (per cent)	6.4	30.0	334.0	82.0	56.0	87.1	62.7	109.0
Producer's Price In-flation (per cent)	7.1	22.8	396.4	55.9	32.2	85.0	55.8	126.0
Unemployement rate (per cent)	0.1	3.0	11.1	15.2	16.8	14.1	10.7	12.3
Retired to Employed (per cent)	44.0	48.0	66.0	80.0	86.0	84.0	88.0	85.0
Balance of Payments, ($US bn)	–0.9	–1.1	– 0.9	0.4	–0.9	–0.9	–1.0	–1.1
Budget Deficit to GDP (per cent)	0.8	3.6	3.8	5.7	10.9	5.8	5.7	10.9
Gross Foreign Debt, ($US bn)	9.8	10.6	11.3	13.8	13.9	11.4	10.2	9.6
Foreign Debt Service Ratio, (per cent)	16.5	20.4	28.7	17.0	14.6	11.5	18.7	21.9*
Reserves of National Bank, ($US bn)	2.6	1.5	0.3	0.9	0.7	0.8	1.0	0.6
Gross Investment to GDP	4.0	–0.2	–19.9	–1.5	–9.0	–7.0	–1.0	–2.0
FDI, ($US m)	10.0	30.0	40.0	65.0	127.0	220.0	105.0	202.0

* Forecast

Sources: National Statistics Institute, Avramov (1994), Institute of Economics, Bulgarian Academy of Sciences, OECD, The World Bank, EBRD, own calculations.

Table 3.2. Gross foreign debt of Bulgaria, 1991–96, (million US$)

	1991	1992	1993	1994	1995	1996
Gross Foreign Debt (A+B)	11 301.1	13 857.7	13 889.4	11 411.4	10 229.0	9 627.0
A. Long-term	2 676.0	3 167.0	3 256.6	9 267.9	8 841.3	8 253.0
I. Public Institutions	1 872.0	2 256.0	2 338.0	3 216.0	3 084.6	2 939.0
II. Private Creditors	804.0	911.0	918.6	6 051.9	5 756.7	5 323.9
B. Short-term	9 625.1	10 690.7	10 632.8	2 143.5	1 387.9	1 374.0

Source: Angelov et al, 1997.

Table 3.3. Service of the foreign debt of Bulgaria, 1995–99

	1995	1996	1997	1998	1999
Gross Foreign Debt ($US m)	10 229.0	9 627.0	9 800.0	9 500.0	8 900.0
Maturing Debt ($US m)	650.0	1 040.0	990.0	1 250.0	1 170.0
Maturing Debt to GDP (per cent)	7.7	10.7	8.4*	7.8*	5.6*
Maturing Debt to Export (per cent)	18.7	21.9	20.7*	24.6*	22.1*

* Forecast

Source: Angelov et al, 1997.

We provided some statistical evidence above to support the claims made in the previous section. We have summarized in Table 3.1 a detailed breakdown of the indicators of the Bulgarian economy between 1989 and 1996.

The biggest challenge to the economy and to industry in 1989 was the huge foreign debt, which the country, with only limited and decreasing reserves, was in no position to service. In our opinion, the foreign debt service has been one of the factors suffocating the Bulgarian economy during the transition, and perhaps the biggest contributor to the renewed loss of macroeconomic stability in 1996. Therefore, we showed additional data on the debt in Tables 3.2 and 3.3, which illustrate our reasoning.

Table 3.4. Geographical distribution of trade of five European countries of former CMEA (Share in total export/import, per cent)

Country	CMEA Area			OECD Countries		Developing Countries	
	1988	of which USSR	1994	1988	1994	1988	1994
Bulgaria							
– export	*82.59*	*62.34*	*35.70*[a]	*6.42*	*46.60*	*9.43*	*5.10*
– import	*75.32*	*53.52*	*40.30*[a]	*15.45*	*48.50*	*7.85*	*1.70*
Czechoslovakia[b]							
– export	75.14	43.06	37.30	16.28	55.40	4.70	7.30
– import	74.09	40.29	15.10	18.56	58.30	3.51	5.40
Hungary							
– export	45.48	27.61	19.00	40.54	72.00	8.88	5.00
– import	44.25	25.04	22.20	43.61	70.60	7.38	4.00
Poland							
– export	41.10	24.53	n.a.	43.53	63.90	9.94	n.a.
– import	40.90	23.30	n.a.	45.89	59.60	7.00	n.a.
Romania[c]							
– export	36.93	21.36	n.a.	33.63	56.60	24.13	n.a.
– import	44.70	22.42	n.a.	16.98	63.50	32.80	n.a.
USSR[d]							
– export	58.18	–	14.40	21.85	62.50	14.25	11.90
– import	61.24	–	8.00	25.09	67.40	8.22	14.10

Notes

[a] Including the successor-states of former Yugoslavia, of which trade with Macedonia has grown in importance, reaching 6.44 per cent of the Bulgarian export in 1994.

[b] Data for 1994 is for the Czech Republic only. Export to CMEA area in 1994 (37.30 per cent) includes 16.30 per cent export to Slovakia.

[c] The columns for 1988 contains the last available data for 1985.

[d] Data for 1994 is for Russia only.

Source: Own computations based on *Comecon Data*, 1990, and Country Reports of the Economist Intelligence Unit, various issues of 1995 and 1996.

Finally, a few words about the redirection of Bulgarian foreign trade from the East to the West. As Table 3.4 shows in a comparative perspective, given its high embeddedness into the ex-socialist trade, Bulgaria seems to have had a remarkable success between 1988 and 1994: the share of export to OECD countries has expanded from 6.4 per cent to 46.6 per cent, and the share of export to the former CMEA block has contracted from 82.6 per cent to 35.7 per cent.[4] However, the shift in the geographical distribution of exports is accompanied for Bulgaria by the strongest – among the countries in the sample – shift in the commodity composition of the exports.

3.3 THE BULGARIAN FIRM AND ITS GOVERNANCE

3.3.1 Corporate Governance

It is a well-established fact that new corporate governance structures emerge with privatization. However, a critical mass of private ownership is needed to enable explicit manifestation of the new features of the corporate relationships. In Bulgaria, such a critical mass is not yet available. As illustrated so far, privatization has not been abundant, and the few private companies still operate in a predominantly state-owned environment. In section 3.4 we discuss the new corporate structures evolving in our sample of ten recently privatized companies. Here, we stay with the corporate governance issues of the firms before their privatization. We find this approach useful, because the pre-privatization corporate structures inevitably have a repercussion on the corporate relationships after privatization.

The essence of corporate relationships has not changed much in the state sector in Bulgaria during the years of transition. Although the legal form and corporate structure of all existing state-owned enterprises has changed, the subordination, attitudes and incentives within the enterprises are basically the same. This is hardly surprising, because even revolutionary changes in the political environment and in the formal rules for doing business only marginally affect the inertia of industrial relations and shop-floor attitudes to work. At face value, the new corporate governance in the Bulgarian industry has meant 'corporatization' of all enterprises and institutionalization of a monitoring body over the executives. In reality, it has relinquished state control and boosted up the discretionary powers of the managers of state-owned enterprises.

Corporatization of enterprises is understood here as their legal transfer into one of the forms of commercial entities in accordance with the Bulgarian legislation. The initial legal framework for 'incorporating' a company in Bulgaria was given by the Decree No. 56 for Economic Activity of January 1989, which re-established the company structure that had been in existence before 1951, when the old pre-war Commercial Code was abolished (*State Gazette*, 4 January, 1989). In June 1991, a new Commercial Code superseded Decree 56, but the registration of those companies that had already 'incorporated' under Decree 56 was recognized. A short-lived Law on Incorporating

Single-Owner Firms with State Property was in force for several months in 1991. Final and comprehensive legal procedures for incorporation of state-owned enterprises were provided by the Privatization Law of February 1992[5] (*State Gazette,* 12 July, 1989).

Nowadays, all companies in Bulgaria are registered as one of the following type of company: private merchants, general partnership, limited partnership, public limited partnership, limited liability company, joint stock company. Most state-owned companies have adopted the legal form of limited liability company and joint stock company. The owner of all shares and stakes, except for the shares of some state banks, is the Bulgarian state. There is no special state organ to ensure enforceability of the ownership rights of the state: usually, state bureaucrats from the ministries sit on the supervisory boards of the enterprises. Since they are paid for this position by the enterprise, and their remuneration is usually much higher than the salaries received form the state, board members are more often seen to collude with managers rather than to than to exercise control.

The corporate governance structure evolving in Bulgaria seems to follow the patterns of 'internal' capital markets (Germany, Japan), as opposed to the 'external' example set by the UK and USA. An issue of crucial importance in this process is known to be the adequate provision for, and the enforceability of, corporate control. Whereas in Germany bank representatives on companies' boards prudently monitor how enterprises perform, ministerial bureaucrats on the boards in Bulgaria are more often seen as an extension of the political lobbying apparatus of the company, pleading for preferential treatment of the enterprises (or industry), for example, for state subsidies, for a ban on imports of similar products, for various quotas, restrictions, or their abolition. In the wake of privatization, state bureaucrats are also seen to arrange for a privatization scheme to the benefit of company managers, and for provision of credits from state banks, if within their reach and power. Not least, they are also seen to push ahead their own private interests in the future privatization of the said company. Apart from the function of control, where 'corporatization' has performed poorly so far in Bulgaria, the other important aspect of this policy is its expected effect on managerial and employees' incentives. Here too 'corporatization' without subsequent privatization seems to have underperformed.

The shocks of the Bulgarian economic transition have not only empowered managers beyond imagination, they have also heavily taxed the sustainability of decency in industrial relations. Huge lay-offs for party-political reasons have moved employees between industries, to the private sector and to the dole. In 1991, managerial decisions could only be challenged by the rising power of the unions, mainly PODKREPA, who were embroiled in the political life of the moment and could give their militancy a political and ideological clue. Later – in 1992 and afterwards – when PODKREPA withdrew from politics,[6] its influence over managers became less strenuous. Yet even now it is strong enough in politically sensitive industries like steel and mining. Nonetheless, enterprise managers in Bulgaria nowadays seem to breath more freely, and until now – and perhaps until the effects of the mass privatization take shape and reside – they are often accountable to none.

In the absence of comprehensive and transparent privatization process in Bulgaria, SOE managers have displayed two types of incentives. One is to strip the assets illegally – either to shift them to their parallel businesses, or simply in get-rich-quick moves of different shape and disguise. The other – to guard the property of the enterprise before its legal private acquisition. To be true, the second type of behavior has involved deliberate depreciation of the capital stock and undervaluation geared at a cheaper subsequent deal. Yet it has been less perilous than the other, for in this case managers would do no harm to the assets, but they would pay valuators (with enterprise money) to make valuations look less attractive to potential outsiders.

Regrettably, the indecisive policies of governments with short time horizons towards legal privatization have encouraged many managers to switch to the first type of behavior. The asymmetry of information between managers and the owner–state is huge, and opportunities for theft have abounded. Political instability and personal insecurity in the face of party-political dismissals have rarely encouraged a pursuit of legal privatization – it goes beyond the political cycle marked by the next dismissal. Consequently, little or no restructuring could happen prior to privatization, and vice versa, little privatization could happen with companies in decay and tiny prospects for survival.[7] Among other things, the sustained political disequilibrium of the Bulgarian transition has arrested the possibility for corporate restructuring before privatization.

3.3.2 Financial Governance

The early shocks of the transition have also contributed to a grave deterioration of the financial situation of the Bulgarian enterprises. In 1991–92, most of them found themselves suffering from extensive and corrosive internal debt problems. The sheer proportion of company indebtedness began to blur the distinction between good and bad management, and made even more difficult the tasks of hardening enterprise budget constraints and privatization. Inevitably, financial overhauling through debt restructuring was to become a vital ingredient of the overall enterprise restructuring. In Bulgaria – as in many other countries of CEE – enterprise debt restructuring came with a wrong sequencing, too late, and without the necessary preparations. Therefore, the desirable positive effects believed to be implanted into its design failed to materialize. Moreover, it could not cure, because the treatment was applied to the symptoms of the disease, instead of attacking its causes. And because the Bulgarian economy was already out of equilibrium, the treatment could not be innocuous – it delivered an additional disequilibrating push.

Let us juxtapose symptoms and causes first. The symptoms were easy to diagnose: the companies had debts, and for the most part these debts could not be honored. However, the causes of the existing debts had not been correctly identified: these debts were not the legacy of the old regime. The old pre-transitional company debts had been eradicated by the nearly 400 per cent inflation of 1991. In their larger part, the debts reported by state-owned enterprises in 1992 and 1993 were a result of recently and currently accrued losses due to the radically changed structure of relative prices of inputs and outputs. They were the outcome of sudden and massive deterioration of company profitability, inflicted on a grand scale by the shocks of the early transition. These losses were a consequence of the radical changes in the geographical distribution of exports, and the shifts in the commodity composition of production and exports, which we discussed earlier. In the case of Bulgaria, they also had to do with the conversion rates of 'transferable' rubles into convertible currencies and into Bulgarian levs. Moreover, the losses continued to grow and to give rise to further debts.

Thus there were the 'stock' problems of the debt – the symptoms – and the 'flow' problems of the debt – its continued growth.[8] Logically, to eliminate the problems at source, one had first to stop the accumulation of further debts. Attacking the causes of the disease would have meant creating conditions to prevent the accumulation of further losses. This should have translated into an effort to keep afloat at least those companies that were sound and would have been able – under normal circumstances – to register positive cash flows and add value to the national economy.

One suggestion for such a policy was the introduction of temporary trade protection, or a temporary reduction of the payroll taxation (Flemming, 1993). Other policies could have been devised as well, if the society was in consensus, if the government had leeway to act and could signal credibility. None of these was possible at the end of 1993, when the issue of enterprise debt restructuring was addressed for the first time in Bulgaria. Not only was the unelected government of the time – the government of Professor Berov – internally unstable, it also had to appease external creditors and sponsors.[9] Moreover, actions had to be taken fast for Bulgaria was already gaining the aura of a slow-mover. Sidestepping the 'flow' problem of the debt and ignoring its causes, the government and parliament attacked the symptoms. A law was passed – the famous ZUNK[10] law – under which enterprise debt to the banks totaling Lv. 32 billion ($640 million) was transformed into a debt of enterprises to the state budget. The law was relevant only to debts – and interests accrued on these debts – accumulated before 1990. Thus it failed to amend the negative influences on profitability due to the shocks of transition. Having attacked directly the 'stock' problem of the debt, this financial restructuring did nothing to prevent its further explosion.

And explode it did, for – as mentioned – the medicine was not innocuous: it created a 'moral hazard' problem. With such restructuring, the incentives of company managers to make profits were dulled: if losses could be 'restructured' there was no need to try to avoid them. All that mattered was to focus on political lobbyism in expectation of the next restructuring campaign. The access of loss-making companies to new cheap credits was not closed. In addition, the credibility of the government was further undermined, because the selection of companies to be restructured was inevitably arbitrary. Company managers had to discover for themselves that profitability is nothing more than a concept which – as one manager put it – matters only for books of history, not of accounting.

3.4 THE EFFECTS OF PRIVATIZATION: THE EVIDENCE

3.4.1 General Description of the Sample

The fact that few privatization transactions had been concluded in the period between 1993 and 1995 made the selection of companies in our sample difficult. At the end of 1994, there had been only a handful large privatization transactions in Bulgaria (Table 3.5), few of them accessible for our investigation. Therefore, to enable analysis of post-privatization restructuring, we looked at enterprises that had been in private ownership for at least one financial year. Thus the sample of the companies investigated in the current study constitutes of ten enterprises privatized not later than the end of 1995, so that they have operated as private companies at least throughout 1996. This criterion was one of the major factors influencing the selection of the sample. The chosen methods of investigation were face-to-face interviews with company managers, matched independently with analysis of the balance sheets, and compared with information published in the local press, wherever applicable.

The companies in our sample (Table 3.6) represent three industries: textiles and clothing, mechanical engineering (with focus on pneumatics which happen to be favored by foreign investors) and foods.

Table 3.5. The biggest privatization transactions in Bulgaria (December 1994)

	Company	Date of privatization	Branch	Share sold (per cent)	Liabilities (mln)	Future Investment (mln)	Foreign buyer
1.	Tzarevitchni Producti	May 12,1993	Food	81.0		$20.0	Belgium
2.	Republika	Nov. 15, 1993	Food	82.08		$10.0	USA
3.	Hidroprobivna Technika	Feb. 10, 1994	Machinery	98.11	BGL 6.37	$0.35	Denmark
4.	Gazobeton	Feb. 11, 1994	Construct.	100.0	BGL 5.361	DM 5.6	Germany
5.	Sh.Z.I. – Sofia	June 13, 1994	Food	75.9	$ 4.274	$7.0	Switzerland
6.	SOMAT SC	Aug. 2, 1994	Transport	55.0	$46.782	$48.0	Germany
7.	Eskos Dograma	Sept. 16, 1994	Wood proc.	80.0	BGL 96.0	DM4.0	Italy
8.	Zagorka	Oct.28, 1994	Brewery	80.0		$41.4	Greece
9.	Unit of Vamo	Nov. 3, 1994	Machinery	100.0		GBP3.5	UK
10.	Hotel Vitosha	Dec. 14, 1994	Tourism	80.0			Germany
11.	Kamenitza	Jan. 25, 1995	Brewery	70.0		DM31.87	Belgium
12.	Burgasko Pivo	Apr. 27, 1995	Brewery	67.0	BGL33.9	$19.7	Belgium
13.	Storko	Nov. 2, 1995	Food	80.0	$12.8	$ 6.5	UK
14.	Pirinska Mura	Nov.3, 1995	Wood proc.	67.0		BGL 350.0	USA-Bulg.
15.	Instrument	July 3,1996	Machine tools	78.94		DM 1.5	Austria
16.	Complast	Aug. 14, 1996	Plastics	77.0	$2.42	$1.55	Austria-Bulg.
17.	Avangard	Aug. 15, 1996	El.engineer.	67.0	$1.264	DM1.70	Switzerland
18.	Varnenchik hotel	Aug. 21, 1996	Tourism	100.0		BGL 920.0	Russia
19.	Vitamina	Aug. 30, 1996	Food	60.0	BGL 1700	BGL 160.7	USA
20.	Eltos	Sept. 5, 1996	El.engineer.	55.0	BGL 2252	DM12.0	Germany
21.	'Diana' hotel	Sept. 5, 1996	Tourism	100.0		BGL 820.0	Russia
22.	Sheraton Sofia	Sept. 23, 1996	Tourism	67.0		$5.0	South-Korea
23.	Microelektronik	Sept. 24, 1996	Machine tools	100.0			Japan

Table 3.5 continued

24.	'Vidima'	Oct. 17, 1996	Sanit. fittings	77.0		$5.0	USA
25.	Elprom Nayden Kirov	Oct. 31, 1996	El.engineer.	76.0	BGL 153. 9	$0.49	Israel
26.	Incoms El. i Mechanika	Oct. 31, 1996	El.engineer.	40.0	DEM3	BGL 35.0	Switzerland
27.	Feromagnit	Nov. 8, 1996	Engineering	75.0	BGL 294.4	$1.34	Czech Rep.
28.	'Mraz'	Dec. 20, 1996	Freezing techn.	67.0	$2	$1.0	France-Ireland-Bulg.
29.	'Milksi'	Dec. 20, 1996	Dairy	80.0	BGL 315	$0.1	Austria
30.	Ceramics W.shop	Jan. 10, 1997	Ceramics	100.0	BGL 4.4	$0.08	UK
31.	'Stind'	Jan. 13,1997	Glass ind.	70.0	BGL 386.2	$27.33	Cyprus
32.	Gipsfazer	Jan. 31, 1997	Build. materials	60.0	$1.1	$5.41	Austria
33.	Magnitni Glavi	Feb. 28,1997	Electronics	80.0		$2.33	USA
34.	Sodi-Devnya	Apr. 14,1997	Chemical ind.	60.0		$67.0	Belgium
35.	Devnya Cement	n.a.	Cement prod.	70.0		$209.45	Spain – Bulg.
36.	Bules-Bourgas	May 26,1997	Wood proc.	51.0		$7.0	Austria
37.	Kambana – Bourgas	n.a.	Food	68.0		$23.0	Holland
38.	Interpred WTC-Sofia	n.a.	Trade	70.0		$5.0	South-Korea
39.	Agromashina-Rousse	June 20,1997	Mach. Building	70.0	BGL 707.0	BGL 1500	Germany
40.	Elprom-Trapho	n.a.	El. Engineer.	70.0		$4.0	South-Korea
41.	Lesoplast-Troyan	July 28,1997	Wood proc.	24.4			Austria
42.	MDK-Pirdop	Sept.10,1997	Copper prod.	56.0		$220.0	Belgium

Source: Privatization Agency of the Republic of Bulgaria

The companies are situated in different geographical locations of the country, in towns varying in size and regional administrative importance. Most companies are a major employer in their respective region – the number of their employees varies from 166 to 1,820. Then, Table 3.7 outlines the key data of the companies in our sample. All companies have been privatized through a sale of a major stake to private investors. In seven of them the majority shareholder is a foreign company, holding a stake from 51 per cent to 81 per cent. Three of the companies have been privatized through MBO/ESOP schemes (80 per cent). In all companies except for the one that is employee-owned, minority shareholders are the managers and employees, Bulgarian banks (usually the main creditors of the firm), former owners (compensated with shares through the restitution process for their pre-World War II ownership in a different company) and privatization funds (in one case where a minor stake of the company has been subsequently offered through the mass privatization).

Table 3.6. Panel of companies and their key data

Industry	Location	Number of staff	Method of privatization	Biggest holding	Markets, per cent of output
Textile & clothing	Regional center	1550	Sales priv., MBO/ESOP	80% (manag & empl.)	Foreign 75%
Textile & clothing	Small town	1100	1. Sale, MBO/ESOP	80% (manag & empl.)	Foreign 75%
Textile & clothing	Small town	850	1. Sales priv. 2. Mass priv.	66% (manag & employ-ees)	Domestic
Mech engin. (rotat-ing heads)	Medium town	1030	Sales privatization	80% (for-eign inves-tor)	Foreign
Mech. engin. (non-standard spare parts)	Medium town	166	Sales privatization	62.2% (for-eign inves-tor)	Foreign 60%
Mech. engin (san-tech equipment)	Small town	280	Joint venture	51% (for-eign inves-tor)	Foreign 99%
Mech. engineer. (hydro-pneum. equipment)	Regional center, big city	470	Sales privatization	77% (for-eign inves-tor)	Foreign 65% Domestic 35%
Mech. engineer. (pneum. engines)	Medium town	860	Sales privatization	80% (for-eign inves-tor)	Foreign 100%
Foods (dairy factory)	Sofia	1820	Sales privatization	67% (for-eign inves-tor)	Domestic 99%
Foods (cereals, maize products)	Medium regional center	850	Sales privatization	81% (for-eign inves-tor)	Domestic 70%

Table 3.7. Data on privatization of the companies in our sample

Year	Company	Sold (per cent)	Price (millions)	Committed investment (millions)	Debts accepted by investor (millions)	Buyer
1994	Maize Products	81	$20.0	$120.0	–	AMYLUM
1993	Republica	80	$2.0	$10.0	–	Kraft Gen Foods
1994	Chocolate Produce	70	$2.1	$7.0	$4274	Nestle S.A.
1994	*Zagorka* Brewery	80	$21.7	$41.4	–	Brewinvest S.A.
1994	HydroTechnik	97	$0.35	$0.35	Lv6371	Breakers A/S Co
1994	GasBeton Construct	100	DM5.0	DM5.6	Lv5361	Ytong Ltd
1994	SO-MAT Transport	55	$55.0	$48.0	–	Willi Betz Int Sp
1994	ESKOS Fittings	80	DM0.7	DM4.0	Lv96	Gibu Ltd

In terms of distribution of their output, all companies are either predominantly export-oriented, or rely mainly on the domestic market. As it is, the mechanical engineering firms in our sample deliver the bulk of their production to the international markets. These are usually cross-border deliveries in the production chain of the acquiring Western company, and it has often been a reason for their acquisition by the foreign investor. The main markets of the textile and food companies in the sample are also abroad, utilizing old or newly established distribution channels.

Clearly, the study of just ten companies does not allow for statistically significant conclusions about the respective industries, because the firms selected are among the few available to respond to the criteria of this study, mainly the presence of sufficient post-privatization experience. Yet given their different starting points, development paths, industrial environment, international linkages and market penetration, the analysis allows for identification of major trends and the forces at play in the restructuring process taking place at company level in the Bulgarian industry.

3.5 PRIVATIZATION PROCESS AND METHODS

3.5.1 The Privatization Process

The privatization process in Bulgaria, in which the companies in our sample have changed their owners, reflects the power struggle of problematic political downturns. It has displayed elements of thinking and practices pursued elsewhere in Central Europe, yet so far with less consistency and unequivocal persuasion. The swings and sways of all transitional governments in Bulgaria have turned around the dilemma of commercial and non-commercial, or give-away privatization. Epitomized by the two extremes – Hungary for the market-driven privatization, and the Czech Republic for the give-away schemes – these two modes of privatizing have gained different prominence in the different stages of development and maturity of the Bulgarian transition.

The owners-to-be had to pay, or make a credible commitment to their belief in the market. So, privatization through sales became the new religion. Witnessing such a middle class emerging in Hungary, many Bulgarian politicians of 1991–93 failed to notice that there it was the product of two-decade market-driven developments, with considerable wealth already accumulated in private accounts. There was no such wealth in the Bulgarian private accounts. Wherever there was, it was stolen money by the former partocracy, which began rapidly to regroup through a process which in Bulgaria acquired the name of 'quiet privatization'. To counter it, the New Right lavished properties to its supporters against their restitution claims, a process seen as thoroughly unjust by the socialistic-minded Bulgarian society of 1992/93. So it went, with peaceful yet fierce clashes between Left and Right on more issues than one, with three general elections producing eight governments in seven years, none of them stable enough to pursue credible and persistent privatization.

Since the adoption of the Privatization Law in February 1992 in Bulgaria, for three years at least auctions and public tenders remained without bidders, the piecemeal sales of smaller properties by municipalities and branch ministries remained low profile and, wherever successful, tainted by allegations of corruption. Gradually, it became obvious that a more radical approach was needed to make the much needed go ahead. In 1995, all eyes of the Western hemisphere were cheeringly focused on the 'successes' of the Czech mass privatization. Prodded again by the multilaterals, the Bulgarian government of the day decided to adopt the approach and sell it to the public. Yet with respect to the companies in our sample, mass privatization did not matter much. Only in one of the firms was a minor stake of shares disbursed in the mass privatization scheme. The other privatization transactions took place through sales, and these were rare examples of good beginnings. Therefore, we outline the procedures which most of them had to undergo.[11] As a rule, privatization through sales included the following steps:

1. formal decision taken by the Privatization Agency;
2. submission of claims by former owners (if applicable);
3. legal analysis clarifying the current entitlements;
4. economic analysis and appraisal (by at least two methods, discounting of future cash flows, and net asset value) by an independent contractor;
5. choice of method and share of the assets to be privatized;
6. publication of the method of privatization;
7. pre-selection of highest bidders and/or direct negotiations on particulars of the bids (depending on the method chosen);
8. signing of contract;
9. payments;
10. transfer of property rights;
11. post-privatization control (especially in the sales of big enterprises).

Before proceeding, we need to mention in passing the Bulgarian mass privatization program. The implementation of this program is still very young, and so far nothing substantial has happened in terms of enterprise restructuring, that would need coverage in this chapter. Mass privatization in Bulgaria closely follows the Czech model, and given the current problematic developments in Prague it probably needs considerable re-thinking. One substantial advantage of the Bulgarian process over the events we witnessed in the Czech Republic is the fact that everything seems to be more carefully and prudently organized in Bulgaria, with legislation and regulation going ahead of actions. Hopefully, this will result in better transparency and less illusions. But for the time being, mass privatization bears little evidence for company restructuring. What will matter in the immediate future is the behavior of the major shareholders and market players – the privatization funds – and the ability of governmental regulation to make them play by the rules, complying to standards of transparency and disclosure. Taking stock of the present Czech misfortunes, there is at least hope that at this juncture the Bulgarian model will diverge.

3.5.2 Privatization Results

Seven of the ten companies in our sample have been privatized through a tender offer and subsequent direct negotiations for the sale of a major stake to the current majority owner. One company – VIDIMA in Sevlievo – has been established as a joint venture between a foreign investor and a divested part of a Bulgarian state-owned enterprise. Two companies have been sold to the employees through an ESOP scheme. In two of the tendered sales the tender results have been revoked due to irregularities in the legal analysis of the companies prior to the tender. Yet even in these two cases, the highest bidders of the tenders have been pre-selected by the Privatization Agency for subsequent negotiations, and eventually they turned out to be the new owners.

In all tenders, there has been some competition among the bidders: the number of bidders has been two, three, and four. The price has not been the only reason for success – other factors too have been taken into consideration, like commitments for future investments, employment and personnel development, and even industrial experience and excellence in the respective production, a concept vaguely defined and difficult to be quantified by an arbitrator. Naturally, this has left some scope for subjectivity in the decision-making, and has made the decision rule questionable. In one of the cases, the loser in a tender has challenged the decision of the Privatization Agency in court. The court challenge was not successful, but it delayed the legal transfer of the property rights for about half a year. The privatization procedures of the firms in our sample – including the preparation of the tender, the subsequent negotiations, payment and ownership transfer – have been very protracted, up to 1.5–2 years from the initial announcement of the respective decision for privatization. Actually, so far this has been the usual period for completion of a privatization procedure by sale.

In all privatization transactions in our sample, the payments have been effected in Bulgarian currency and in securities accepted as legal tenders in such transactions: all three emissions of Brady bonds, and the ZUNK bonds issued against company debt in 1993. These securities can be acquired only for a fraction of their face value, but they are accepted for payment at face value. Before 1996, up to 70 per cent of the payments could be effected in such securities, thus allowing for a discount of about 25–30 per cent on the total price. After the adoption of the 1996 privatization program, no more than 30 per cent of the payment can be made in legal tenders other than Bulgarian currency.

The MBO/ESOP schemes applied in the privatization of one of the companies in our sample is somewhat different. To begin with, the managers and employees were the only candidates to acquire the firm. Then, there was some pressure from the trade unions: the company had just recovered some markets and was on its way back to profitability, but this was insider information known only to the managers. There were no claims from previous owners. And lastly, all steps of the privatization procedure were executed swiftly and efficiently. The ESOP scheme allows for payments in installment for up to 10 years. On purchase, only 10 per cent of the negotiated price has to be paid. Due to the highly volatile macro-environment, annual installments are being fixed separately each year, with interest equal to 50 per cent of the mean of the interest rate fixings for the preceding year.

The hyperinflation of 1996 made all prices fixed in Bulgaria earlier – and especially before 1995 – ridiculously low. Therefore, all companies under a MBO/ESOP scheme in Bulgaria hastened to pay their dues entirely, benefiting from the grossly devalued Bulgarian currency and the negative interest rate. For the same reason, all companies in our sample fulfilled their obligations for subsequent investment, also fixed in the privatization agreements in the devalued Bulgarian currency. In one of the companies in our sample, the methods of sales privatization were mixed with partial divestiture through the mass privatization program.

3.6 THE NEW CORPORATE STRUCTURES

After privatization, all companies in our sample but one (except for the ESOP privatizations) adopted a two-level governance structure, whereby the shareholders elect a Supervisory Board, which in turn nominates the Board of Directors. The company privatized through the ESOP scheme retained its previous one-board structure. The company managers interviewed – most of them members of the Board of Directors in a two-tier structure – pointed out the following reasons in favor of the two-board scheme:

1. A two-tier governance structure ostensibly makes the accountability issue more transparent. In the eyes of all stakeholders of the firm – owners, workers, local government and community, and so on – there is someone who is monitoring the directors on a regular basis, and can share the responsibility if things go wrong.
2. A Supervisory Board allows for better representation and alignment of the interests of all those concerned with the firm, and at least formally, all

interests and concerns can be listened to. All companies in our sample have reserved on their Supervisory Boards seats for the minority shareholders and the workers' representatives (but not for the unions!). In three companies there are seats for members of the local government, and in two companies (without even a minority participation of the state) – for representatives of the respective ministry.

3. If properly constituted, the Supervisory Board can be of assistance in the day-to-day running of the company. Members of the Supervisory Board can help not only with their experience, but also with lobbyism, influence, and technical expertise, where applicable. In one of the companies, a professor from the Sofia Technical University is a member of the Board, taking a seat nominated for the Ministry of Industry.
4. Members of the Supervisory Board can take up a sizable fraction of the 'community burden' of the company management – attending public meetings, communicating results, even occupying the attention of the media.
5. The sympathy and understanding of the banks which service the accounts and secure loans can be secured through nominations of seats for them on the Supervisory Board.
6. There has been no industrial conflict so far in any of the companies in our sample, but the managers think that even if it were to come, a two-tier governance structure would handle it in an easier way.

The role of the Supervisory Board should not be exaggerated: the general impression is that its constitution is well managed and under the control of the Central Executive Officer – whose title in most Bulgarian companies is Executive Director – with the tacit approval of the majority shareholder. In the companies interviewed, there seems to be no clear demarcation between the decisions put for discussion on either of the boards, and the contacts between internal and external directors also seem to be very operational. By constitution, the Supervisory Board should do little more than annual approval of the balance and nomination of the directors. In reality, it is formally convened every quarter to hear a broad range of problems currently facing the executive management. In between these quarterly meetings, members of the Supervisory Board are asked to intervene on many occasions. Perhaps because all companies in the sample have a clear majority owner to take the important decisions, the functions of the two boards are somewhat diluted.

Yet decision making is definitely done in the executive boardroom. In the companies where the majority shareholder is a foreign firm, there are two Executive Managers, where one of them is a representative of the foreign investor, with whom most of the day-to-day running of the company has to be consulted on and coordinated. The two companies that have retained their previous one-tier board structure have introduced some additional elected organs to assist and control various aspects of the managerial process. For example, one company under the MBO/ESOP scheme has established a unit to monitor and report the implementation of the decisions taken by the board and the general assembly of the shareholders. Similar units – to monitor various aspects of the performance, such as innovativeness, adaptation of the personnel to a new technology, and so on – are created in some of the production departments of the firm. So far, there are little tangible results of these activities, and for the most part they are performed on a voluntary basis.

If any fruit is to be easily recognized out of the post-privatization corporate restructuring, it is the fact that contracts begin to matter. This is true not so much of the external contracts of the firm, as it is for the internal contractual relationships between department, sub-divisions and even individuals, even the implicit ones. In the words of one of the directors, it is as if responsibilities automatically became better defined, and now workers need less prodding. Directors are also under scrutiny: in one case the general assembly refused to determine the Supervisory Board member's remuneration, effectively leaving them without payment for more than six months. In only one company an executive manager complained of loosened coordination and diluted responsibilities as a result of excessive interventions of the Supervisory Board. In another company, the Supervisory Board had failed to finalize the contracts with the Executive Board members for no obvious reason at all, except for poor coordination, leaving them without salaries for about four months.

As an example of a new corporate structure, Vidima Plc adopted a two-tier governance structure. The management of the company is responsible to the general assembly of the shareholders via the intermediation of a Supervisory Board. The control package of the shares – 51 per cent – is owned by American Standard Inc., USA. The remaining shares are owned by the United Bulgarian Bank (18 per cent), the employees (10 per cent), and the Bulgarian state. In addition, seats in the Supervisory Board are reserved for the local government and one local bank. The governance structure of Vidima Ideal consists of a Supervisory Board, Managerial Board, functional departments and production departments (production lines). The Managerial Board includes the general manager and the respective managers for production, finance, sales and marketing. The company has functional departments dealing with legal aspects, administrative issues, environmental protection, technical control, sales and marketing, material inputs and quality control, engineering and innovation.

3.7 THE CONQUEST OF NEW MARKETS AND MARKET SHARES

3.7.1 Product Differentiation I: The Lessons of Asset Specificity

Forced into the red with the initial 'stabilization' and 'opening-up' shocks of the 1991 'austerity' package, all companies in our sample have had hard times staying afloat until the beginning of 1994, when a modest revival began to pick up momentum in the Bulgarian economy. Between 1989 and 1991/92, they had lost most of their traditional markets, which had resulted in low capacity utilization, redundancies (30–40 per cent of the workforce on average), arrears in the payment of wages and salaries, forced unpaid leave of the remaining personnel for 3 to 6 months, indebtedness to banks and to the budget. In short, they all had suffered from the common decease of the Bulgarian economy in the early 1990s: industrial slump and stagflation. Yet these companies were among the few to be privatized relatively early in the otherwise delayed privatization process of Bulgaria, and this must have been for a reason: obviously they had been 'discovered' as potential above-the-average profit earners by their current owners.

Before 1989, all companies in our sample had been relative success stories, with well-established and secure markets for the range of products that they had been producing. The textile companies were selling their fiber mainly to the Bulgarian sewing factories, which in turn exported ready-made clothes both to the East and West, but mainly to the Soviet Union. The five mechanical engineering companies had been constituent parts of larger Bulgarian conglomerates, and one of them (producing numerically programmed rotating heads) was part of a joint Bulgarian–Soviet enterprise. In the 1980s, all five mechanical engineering firms in the sample had been tuning their product range according to their CMEA specialization and priorities; they had enjoyed subsidies and beneficial investment credits for import of state-of-the-art machinery and equipment. The two companies in the food sector had been local monopolies (in the supply of maize and dairy products) in their respective regions; while the company for maize products had had some exports to Western Europe, the dairy firm in Sofia was the sole supplier of milk and yogurts to the capital city and the adjacent small towns and villages. It was also producing various white and yellow cheeses for distribution throughout the country, and insignificant quantities of white (fetta) cheese for export to the Soviet Union.

Product differentiation was pursued in the companies of our sample according to the particularities of their exposure to external shocks, and their opportunities to find a new market niche. As these vary, in what follows we shall discuss them separately for each of the represented industry. Most of them feature one common characteristic discussed earlier: a shift from vertical to horizontal integration in their co-operative linkages and supply-chain relationships. As we shall see, the benefits of this shift have not always been unequivocal. The search for new markets in all companies has been contingent on the degree of specificity of their fixed assets. It is well known that under market conditions, high degree of asset specificity leads to a 'hold-up' problem and underinvestment. This is due to the precautions partners take to safeguard their investment: they are afraid that part of their *ex-ante* relationship-specific investment can be expropriated *ex-post* by the partner under a threat to renege the contract, which would render such relationship-specific investment useless, or at least less productive (if the asset is adaptable for alternative use). So, investing heavily into an asset specifically designed and purpose-built to serve a customer, a firm makes itself vulnerable to the discretionary whims of that particular customer in any *ex-post* bargaining process. The specificity of the *ex-ante* investment may not be necessarily technical or technological: it can be locational (situating the asset close to customers and/or suppliers), or logistical (investments into the particular requirements, for example, packaging, of a distribution network). Therefore, in a market economy a company would typically underinvest into the asset-specific relationship, thereby retaining some flexibility for readjustment if things go contractually wrong.[12]

This had not been the case when investment decisions were made back in the 1980s in the mechanical engineering companies in our sample. Not only was the possibility of 1989 non-existent in the eyes of the Bulgarian investment planners of earlier years; even as late as 1987/88 they were still emphasizing the necessity to foster CMEA cross-border 'specialization and cooperation' – popular ideological fad of the time, urging companies to develop 'direct links' with foreign (socialist) partners, and to disassemble production lines – across borders, if necessary – in search of specialization advantages.

Even though the ideology behind the fad did not work, cooperation agreements did go ahead at company level, and in the case of Bulgaria they were particularly well pronounced with ex-Soviet enterprises and conglomerates. In present-day terminology, these days probably saw the beginnings of some sort of 'strategic alliances', whereby 'tacit knowledge' and organizational learning were being transferred between companies located in different countries without much regard to the underlying commercial principles and objectives (Senker and Faulkner, 1996). Gradually, production processes were becoming more and more complimentary across the borders. Moreover, in the case of three of the mechanical engineering companies in our sample, future complementarity in technology and production was a precondition to obtain CMEA investment credits and state subsidies. And anyway, their Soviet market looked boundless and eternal.

These companies had been amongst the CMEA flagships in their respective subsectors, and within their respective administrative conglomerates. Most of them had expanded, or were substantially modernized in the second half of the 1980s under the auspices of the 1985 CMEA 'Program for Scientific and Technical Progress', one of the priority of which was the development of flexible engineering in robotics.

Except for the joint venture in Sevlievo – formed with a privatized splinter firm from a larger Bulgarian state-owned enterprise – while in public ownership, all mechanical engineering companies in our sample had been separate legal entities. Yet their original technical design, and for most their technological processes had imposed such a degree of vertical integration that in some aspects it was unimaginable for them to produce their primary products independently, outside their respective branch/foreign trade conglomerate. For one thing, the managers of these companies had been well trained technically, but they had little, if any, experience with foreign trade and international markets. For another, to compete in Western markets they had limited administrative experience and managerial skills needed to organize production processes efficiently, along the new globalization currents of the 1990s. New learning from the West was not at all encouraged by the new financial difficulties in which the companies had found themselves, and even less so by the new prohibitive visa restriction imposed by Western Europe, which since 1990 made every trip abroad an ordeal. Stuck amongst their otherwise not bad, but dismembered and hence purposeless machinery, facing insurmountable evils and blames, they could not understand – in the words of one manager – why the rest of the world had suddenly turned so nasty, and why had it started treating them as if they had contracted leprosy.

Albeit not in the most efficient and profitable way, the mechanical engineering companies in our sample could readjust under the pressures of the new markets. As it is, the ability to switch to products salable in the West has been a major factor for their privatization: now they all export predominantly to the Western markets. Their acquisition by a foreign investor who would secure a market outlet was perceived as their ultimate salvation – both by the Bulgarian authorities and by their employees. Indeed, privatization has saved these companies from certain extinction, and has enabled them – also financially – to realign their production lines. But what matters for our study are the details of this realignment.

To be sure, managerial and mainly marketing know-how and experience have been, and are being transferred after privatization. Since all investigated companies in this sector have a foreign firm as a majority shareholder, the Bulgarian managers would usually work with an interchangeable foreign partner–director who would provide the liaison with the mother company abroad, and especially with the respective unit (or separate company) in charge of sales and marketing. At the same time, most of the organizational changes after privatization have been undertaken under the initiative of the indigenous Bulgarian managers, and the foreign directors are typically seen as doing 'monitoring' and 'advising' work. And of course, what matters for the product differentiation, the foreign directors are the conduits for any decisions of the mother company for changes and modifications of the product range.

In all companies, production lines have been reconfigured to meet the demand of the new market niches: old products have been modified, and – though mostly for the domestic rather than for the foreign markets – new products and services have been developed. Thus to respond to the new demand in the newly discovered market niches, one of the companies in our sample has to maintain a product range of about 2,500 components, details, and spare parts, that are sold to some 500 customers. Yet since the domestic sales of these companies are very limited in terms of their turnover, so are the genuinely new products and services developed. What did take place in the re-adjustment process following privatization was mostly the switch to products that these companies had been capable of producing before, but their assets – mainly machinery and equipment – had not been originally designed to turn our such products. Of course, this was made possible through the import of technological know-how after privatization, but without any significant investment on the part of the new owner.

In terms of asset specificity, this entailed a loss in technological efficiency: the companies were switching to conventional, or in any case to less sophisticated, commodities than their assets would otherwise allow them to produce. In a normal economic and financial environment, this would entail pure economic loss. As a pursuit-for-survival strategy in the catastrophic industrial and economic environment of Bulgaria, this simply was the only strategy that worked. And then, there was the hope that this is only the beginning of these companies' new family lives, and the future might be (technologically) brighter. This technological downgrading of the companies occurred concomitantly with their switch from vertical to horizontal integration and supply-chain relationships. In their 'ex-socialist life', most of the companies have been specializing on purpose-built specific details and components which would enter a subsequent production line – in Bulgaria or abroad – with increasing sophistication. With the evaporation of the latter, the company-supplier had to switch to 'horizontal' relationships with other clients, who would mostly require details and components for conventional, or more general use. It had also to broaden the range of products manufactured in order to meet the existing demand, whatever the technical complexity of the components required. For example, a basic set of 40–50 components would satisfy the needs for a whole spectrum of 2,500 final products based on those components. Thus the *ex-ante* relationship-specific investment for state-of-the-art equipment – although not expropriated by anyone, as the 'holding-up' literature would suggest – remained unutilized. Moreover, with this patterns of development, further technology-driven investment would be discouraged even if it were financially plausible.

A distinct example for such technological downgrading is the company for rotating heads in Stara Zagora, formerly part of a Bulgarian–Soviet joint venture. Clearly, this is a technology where massive R&D is needed to keep track of new developments and new competition. Set up in the early 1980s with CMEA blessing, this company was supposed to enter the new world of computer-controlled robotics. Among other things, it developed the production of a rotating and sliding head holding a knife (for cutting metals) capable of performing 48 numerically programmed operations. To be sure, as experimental production this was far from perfect: the programs would occasionally fail on the more difficult bendings, the sequencing of the operations and the transmission mechanisms would also give some faults. But back in the mid-1980s, 48 operations were more than a typical production line – even in the West – would normally require from a cutting knife: the computer-controlled flexibility of the 1990s had yet to come. What was needed in the 1980s, were basic 7–8 rotating and sliding operations which would enable metals to be cut with high precision, and therefore had to be numerically programmable. In these operations, the Bulgarian machine was pretty reliable. Its major market was the metal-processing factories of the ex-Soviet Union, and it was even able to make some inroads into the highly demanding market of Northern Italy. As we explained, a small firm in Italy – subcontracted by a major high-tech manufacturer to deliver a certain component – would buy the Bulgarian machine and let it do only three or four operations, but it would be working around the clock, without any interruption for 3–4 months, thus completing a full amortization cycle.

Yet this company could not enter the mass computerization of the 1990s, when computers are being linked to robots to set up the new standards of flexible specialization: it suffered from the disintegration shocks exactly at the time when massive further investment was needed to make the next technological jump. In the 1980s, it had been an experimental base of the Institute of Robotics and the Institute of Computing and Informatics at the Bulgarian Academy of Sciences. After 1991, the company was left all to itself, and all it could do was to consolidate on what it could produce well, and look for clients of the products developed in the mid-1980s. For example, after privatization, the rotating head was simplified to make four basic operations, and currently this sells well on the conventional 'general use' markets for this product. As another example, the a.m. company now produces mostly standardized spare parts – some of them import-substituting – instead of serving its primary purpose: to focus on the development of non-standard purpose-designed components of experimental machine tools. So in this company too, many of the specialized machines and instruments available are not fully utilized.

3.7.2 Product Differentiation II: Competition versus Concentration

Product differentiation in the textile and clothing and food companies in our sample display a different pattern of development. The degree of asset specificity in these companies was relatively low: it had to do with the established contractual relationships and locational advantages, both of which disappeared in 1990. Yet the costs to re-establish new distribution channels – although inflated by the speedy import liberalization of 1991/92, hugely out of proportion with the access granted to Bulgarian products abroad, as well as by the chaotic economic and political environment at home – have not been insurmountable for these companies. As it happened, the textile-clothing companies are mainly domestically-owned, whereas the majority owners of the two food companies are foreign multinationals. Both the textile and the food companies sell their produce mainly on the domestic market, while the clothing companies sell predominantly abroad. It seems that this is the line of development to be followed by their new owners. Thus having different types of owners and clearly distinguishable markets in this part of our sample, it is interesting to compare the different approaches pursued by the companies when developing the marketing and product strategies for their respective market segments.

The post-privatization behavior of these companies is best made explicit when their responses to competitive pressures are matched with the respective market structures, or the level of concentration of their main markets. The structure of the market on which private firms operate is a major determinant of their behavior. Assuming that private agents are rational and consistent, their behavior in pursuit of benefits – profits, rents, subsidies, and so on – is contingent on two factors: first, on their strategic interdependencies with other agents on the same market; and second, on the size of this market.

The strategic interdependencies of rationally motivated private agents on a well-regulated market is determined, among other things, by their sheer number. Thus, for example, a market with only a few firms infers oligopolistic pricing with tacit collusion and subnormal profits; a market with many suppliers is indicative of marginal cost pricing and competitive behavior of the agents. As far as market size is concerned, a larger market is seldom more concentrated than a smaller one. In our cases, the sizes of the respective market segments are difficult to quantify exactly, but the approximate number of the players and their interrelationships are clearly discernible. Therefore, the following argument is based on intuitive understanding of the evidence presenting itself from the company data and the interviews, and on independent observations of the respective markets. The strategies of product differentiation are being pursued differently in the textile and clothing, and in the food companies in our sample, depending on the characteristics of their markets and the types of their owners. As a result, different market structures emerge to spell out different product diversity, product quality and organizational efficiency. While the textile and clothing companies have undoubtedly adopted the approach of horizontal product differentiation, the conduct of the food companies features distinct symptoms of vertical product differentiation, typical for the behavior of multinational firms.

In the context of the industrial organization literature, *horizontal product differentiation* is defined as one in which either all consumers have different tastes and the product is the same (Hotelling, 1929), or all consumers have the same tastes, but the products differ (Dixit and Stiglitz, 1977). In the most popular model, the 'umbrella' of Hotelling, where the differences in consumers' preferences are depicted as different distances to the vendor, there is always a possibility to install a new vendor between any existing two, and the new entrant may be able to capture bits of the market shares of his neighbors, thereby making the market more fragmented and less concentrated. Thus horizontal product differentiation makes the market more competitive, pushes prices down, and adds to the product diversity on offer. Usually in these cases, the sunk costs of entry are exogenously fixed, hence they are equal for all potential entrants. Therefore, with horizontal product differentiation a new product may or may not be identified by the customers as superior to the other products on offer: what matters is the balance between pricing and quality, and these are obvious to all customers.[13]

The textile and clothing companies in our sample have inserted themselves into their current market segments in a fashion similar to the vendors in the Hotelling umbrella. The fibers and clothes they have been producing – although different in substance, pattern, color, texture, thickness, and so on – are replaceable and not difficult to emulate by their competitors. In any case, there are clear-cut criteria for the relationship between price and quality of this product. In 1996, there have been 38 registered textile-producing firms in Bulgaria based on wool and cotton, and many more firms importing such materials (what actually makes the market size immeasurable). In the production of clothes, the number of sizable manufacturers goes well into the hundreds. Therefore, it is safe to assume that this market is very fragmented and competitive in Bulgaria.

To conquer new market segments, the textile companies in the sample had to move along with the changing requirements of the Bulgarian market for clothes. For the most part, their previous distribution channels had disappeared, at least for the materials they had been producing: either the sewing companies contracted, or – after their revival – they requested different textiles for the different clothes they began to produce. The managers of the textile companies had to promote their products – and glean ideas how to readjust – not only on textile fairs and exhibitions, but also in fashion saloons and shows, and by cruising the newly emerging private sewing workshops. One company transformed a company bus into a 'road-show', driving their promotions and samples into small towns and villages in search of new customers.

Initially, the textile and clothing sector had suffered from two types of shocks originating from, first, the heavily suppressed consumer demand for domestically-produced clothes, and second, from the 'de-collectivization' turmoil in the Bulgarian agriculture, their major supplier of cotton and wool. (Previously, cotton had also been imported from Uzbekistan, but these deliveries were terminated with the collapse of the Soviet Union.) Yet at the end, these companies were able to readjust and find new clients: their main customers, the Bulgarian sewing factories, were amongst the first to revive and redirect their production from East to West, and many new private sewing shops emerged in Bulgaria after 1992/93. With little organizational improvements, mainly in the packaging and sorting, the textile companies in our sample were also able to secure some exports: now the share of their export is between 25 per cent and 35 per cent of their total output. One clothing company in our sample is working almost entirely for export.

The redirection of the Bulgarian sewing firms from Soviet to Western markets entailed increased requirements to the quality of the clothes and the materials that went into them. It required a wider variety of models and fibers produced in smaller batches, better stickiness of the painting inks, increased responsiveness to fashion, more frequent changes of colors, patterns, and so on, in short more efforts and hence higher costs. While the huge depreciation of the Bulgarian currency – conducive to exports for most of the time – could offset some of the cost increases, what mattered most to make firms rationalize costs in pursuit of profits was the vivid competition. The ubiquity of domestic producers and importers – especially from other low wage countries in Asia and Africa – kept the pressure to optimize and diversify constant. Nowadays, the textile and clothing companies investigated have a track record of 1–2 post-privatization years of decent profitability, and orders secured for 6 to 8 months ahead. Yet their managers do not feel confident in the future of their market shares, and seem to be always on the alert. In general, horizontal product differentiation after privatization has resulted in a brand-, color, quality, and price proliferation in the Bulgarian market for clothes and textiles.

Not so in the investigated companies of the foods sector: there – as will be shown below – privatized local and regional monopolies differentiated vertically and sunk costs endogenously to keep, at least so far, the market concentrated and undersupplied. Before privatization, the food companies in our sample had faced problems different from those of the textile companies discussed above. Being local monopolies in their respective regions and for their product range, the maize company in Razgrad and the dairy company in Sofia were still able to sell their products; yet they suffered from the disruptions in the supplies of their inputs: maize and milk respectively. They also suffered from the low, and even negative profitability imposed upon them by the price regulator in the absence of any further subsidies.

The disruptions in the supplies of milk and grain were also in this case partially due to the organizational mismanagement of the 'de-collectivization' process in the Bulgarian agriculture. However, the primary source of this disruption was the inconsistent pricing policy of the ever-changing governments after 1991. Until recently, milk and grain had been among the products with regulated prices at which the products were purchased from the producers, and the regulatory mechanism usually failed to match inflation and volatile exchange and interest rates: the prices were either too high, or too low, or too late to adjust – at any rate, they were piling up to the insecurity that precluded any sensible business and investment planning. Little wonder that few private initiatives for milk and grain production could ever be brought to fruition in Bulgaria, and the market still remains thin and shallow.

Bowing to populist demands, up until mid-1997 all weakling-governments of the Bulgarian transition have kept under price caps in absolute figures the prices of bread, animal feed, cereals and dairy products, that is, the commodities turned our by the privatized firms in our sample. The effects of the price caps on these companies have been twofold. First, they have stimulated collusive, and perhaps – not to be entirely dismissed – corruptive practices in the distribution of raw milk and flour, hitting back the supply chains for inputs. More importantly, the price caps kept the profitability of these companies very low, at times negative, effectively depriving them of even amortization payments to offset the depreciation of the capital stock.

Let us be clear at this junction: the above argument is no sentiment against a prudent and consistent market regulation – including price regulation – in pursuit of a well-defined public policy. What has been taking place in Bulgaria, however, – as far as regulation of prices is concerned, – are stop-and-go populist practices in the absence of any coherent policy. Keeping the poor out of starvation with low prices of milk and bread had needed custom protection and no custom protection, high taxes and low taxes, subsidized credits to producers and no subsidized credits, and many other contradictory and mutually conflicting policy measures. Rushing from one extreme to the other, the authorities often created havoc and panic. Yet the successive Bulgarian governments of different colors are hardly to blame: poverty and malnutrition have descended upon the Bulgarian society at a scale unknown since after the First World War. More than in any other domain, the pricing policies with respect to the 'first necessity commodities' – including milk and bread – have displayed the swings and sways of a society in disequilibrium, pushed out of its equilibrium path by the initial shocks of transition.

The sweeping reduction of living standards after 1990 – urging the necessity to keep the prices of milk, bread and dairy products artificially low – resulted in general, as was mentioned above, in very low profitability of the companies in these sectors. This has kept the markets highly concentrated, and has impeded the advance of competitive, market-driven behavior of new private agents. As it looks now, the purchase of the dairy and grain companies in our sample by foreign multinationals was a purchase into their monopoly position in their respective regional markets – with all the textbook implications of mark-up pricing and lower quantity of the output – and there is little evidence that these newly privatized companies are willing to abandon their monopoly privileges. Entering – through their respective privatization – a highly concentrated market, the two food multinationals are seen to differentiate their product range vertically, which can contribute little, if at all, to product diversity, higher quality and lower prices.

To elucidate the idea and the observed practices of vertical product differentiation, we shall make a reference to the notion of endogenous sunk costs, developed by Sutton (Sutton, 1992). *Endogenous sunk costs* are the costs that the firm can set endogenously at will, with a view to future profits, aspired market shares and growth. Endogenous sunk costs usually include the outlays for advertising and research into market penetration. Vivid manifestation of endogenizing the sunk costs of entry is the advent of the advertising-intensive industries, in which the most successful advertising-intensive companies are the multinational enterprises; the Bulgarian companies in the food sector in our sample seem to be no exception.

We mentioned above that the set-up costs of entry in the textile and clothing industry are exogenous – determined by the roughly similar technical level of all textile factories in Bulgaria – and the competing firms have no leverage to influence them: these costs are equal for all new entrants into the market. This has resulted in a competitive and highly diverse market for textiles in Bulgaria. However, if – as was the case with the two multinationals entering a mass commodity market – the firm itself can choose the level of the set-up costs before entering a market, that is, if it is able to determine *endogenously* the level and amount of costs to sink in order to achieve its ends once inside, the outcomes for the degree of future competition on that market, and its interplay with industrial concentration become profoundly different.

Inherent to the aggressive high intensity advertising is the vertical product differentiation. In contrast to horizontal product differentiation, *vertical product differentiation* (Shaked and Sutton, 1982, 1987; Sutton, 1989) is understood here as the pursuit of a marketing and product strategy to convince *all* consumers that the *perceived* quality of the new product is unambiguously higher. On the contrary, vertical product differentiation can not only keep the market oligopolistic; it can even make it more concentrated and less competitive. The profits of the incumbent – once established in the new market – will need to recover the initially sunk outlays, hence it becomes imperative for him that all potential new entrants are kept out, at a respectable distance away from his market segment. This is achieved by shifting upwards the endogenously set threshold for entry, for example, the costs of advertising needed for an entry into that industry's market to be successful. Thus to shunt competitors away, a vertically differentiating firm would escalate advertising costs and eventually push prices up, at the same time leaving the market less diversified.

Let us take the example of the dairy company. Having acquired a fraction of a former SOE – dairy factory in Sofia – the purchasing multinational has also acquired an almost monopolistic market for dairy products in Sofia and around. To be true, in recent years this market gradually turned into oligopolistic, and the SOE remained the market leader with about 70–80 per cent of the market share. Inroads into the market of the capital city are made not by new private entrants, but by the milk- and yogurt state-owned factories in other big cities – as far away as Stara Zagora (350 km) and Burgas (420 km) – which happen to have spare production capacity and better access to dairy farms. The milk market in Sofia is also occasionally invaded by another multinational's acquisition in Montana, about 150 km to the north-west of the capital city. For these companies, to deliver their produce to Sofia is costly, and one would expect higher prices. Instead, their prices are usually lower than those of the SOE's products, which implies even lower profitability. They also enter only the market for lower-quality milk and yogurt, whereas the newly-privatized SOE put stringent requirements on the quality of the raw milk supplied by the farmers. Yet being outsiders, their access to the distribution network of Sofia is more difficult: their deliveries go only to a certain number of shops, not at the best locations.

What changed in the eyes of the consumer after the privatization of the big SOE, was its public image. It began to show up on TV commercials, adds in the papers, and mainly on posters throughout the city. The packaging of the yogurts were slightly improved; in fact, managers refer to the new multicolored labeling as the only reason for the price increases. In terms of diversity, little has changed, except for a few new fruit mixtures of the Bulgarian yogurt.

In sectors that are less advertising-intensive – as in the case of the maize products company in our sample – the sunk cost endogeneity of the new post-privatization entrant may have different implications. The inability to influence directly the tastes of the consumers may infer the necessity to struggle for market shares by means of product proliferation and other price and cost advantages. The foreign investor may even decide to endogenously sink the subsidy for the first several years of operation, if this subsidy is justified by higher returns in future out of improved market position, reskilled personnel, better work organization, or upgraded technology. This must be the case in the company in our sample, where a substantial expansion of the production capacity was undertaken immediately after privatization.

To sum up, new and more sophisticated products have seldom been a post-privatization occurrence in Bulgaria. Typically, the foreign investment would introduce know-how to utilize existing technologies, and produce for whatever market niches can be found.

3.8 MANAGING COSTS AND FINANCES

Some of the most clearly distinguishable restructuring changes occurred in the financial management of the investigated companies. These changes concern the adjustment of the companies in accord with their new cost structures, emerging under the pressures of the macroeconomic environment. In view of the severity of the shocks that these firms had to undergo, it is difficult to estimate how much of the restructuring process was forced upon them, and how much restructuring was added at their own initiative (what usually company managers would claim for themselves). The comparison of cost structures was made on the basis of company balance sheets between 1989/90 (the pre-shock period) and 1996/97, when all firms in the sample have already been in private ownership (for 1997 we have only rough estimates based on the first and second quarter results).

The strongest shocks pressing for cost restructuring have been, and still are, the steep rises of the prices of most inputs. These have imposed a shift in the balance between internal inputs – like labor – and external inputs, usually beyond the grasp and influence of the respective company. On balance, almost everywhere the new cost structure has evolved toward reducing the share of labor costs, and reducing – or wiping out entirely – the share of the retained profit to be allocated for re-investment.

Among the external inputs, the highest increases have been in the prices of electricity, water, fuels, and communications (faxes, telephones, and so on). These prices are still determined in a centralized fashion in Bulgaria, either directly by the government, or by a designated governmental agency. Since the beginning of 1996, the electricity prices for industrial consumers have been increased 3–4 fold, and the postal and telecommunication services 2–3 fold. While communication services could be administratively curtailed, the consumption of electricity is technologically determined, and not easily reducible – at least not in the short run, and not without further investment. Its share is highest in the textile companies in our sample.

Throughout 1996, utility prices have risen unexpectedly, without much prior warning (usually 2–3 weeks). Since the beginning of 1997, prices of electricity and water are officially linked to the exchange rate of the Bulgarian lev. This makes them publicly known, and they should not be so unpredictable as managers claim, because in US dollar terms they are among the requirements of the conditional policy lending institutions – IMF and the World Bank. What makes them unpredictable, especially in hyperinflationary 1997, is the volatility of the exchange rate of the Bulgarian currency. The bulk of the contracts of the companies in our sample are being concluded for one year ahead, the prices are fixed in Bulgarian currency, and there is no practice in Bulgaria to include clauses for effective currency hedging. The volatile exchange rate and the constant depreciation of the Bulgarian currency have been harmful in more than one aspect for the companies in our sample. Some of them, mainly in mechanical engineering, are importing material inputs. Others, for example, the maize company, have to repay credits in convertible currency. And all of them have to obey the Bulgarian law, which makes illegal any transactions conducted in Bulgaria in a currency other than the Bulgarian lev.

The escape from the lev took various forms in 1996 and 1997. The companies would usually keep most of their finances in foreign exchange accounts in Bulgarian banks. (Given the precarious conditions of the banks, they would also 'freeze' considerable amounts of cash in safe deposit boxes, and would try to obfuscate this fact in the company accounts.) They would usually sign an unofficial 'amendment' to the legally binding contract, stipulating a price in hard currency for the commodity contracted. (Such 'amendment' is not enforceable in court, hence very much in the business relations depends on loyalty, ethics, and trust.) Then, on the day of the transaction, the currency would be exchanged and payment would be effected in Bulgarian levs.

The additional administrative costs of these operations are the minor evil: the biggest problem is the financial rigidity, which prevents cost-effective financial management. It also makes the transactions more expensive: payments usually have to be effected in cash, in advance, or in installments with large deposits. Commercial credit is something which has practically ceased to exist in Bulgaria since 1996 – when BNB set the base interest rate at 25 per cent per month – and even though the new government went to the other extreme reducing it to 5.5 per cent in July 1997, it will take some time until the credibility of the banking system is restored. Fortunately for most of our companies, their older credits to suppliers have been paid by their new owners as one of the conditions of the privatization transactions. None of them seems to have any old dues to the state budget – they have been either paid up, or annulled by the government as a sweetener for their privatization.

Where financial restructuring did take place at company management level and initiative, is the realignment and reorganization of the internal inputs: labor and capital stock. After privatization, all companies have remained unionized. A 'collective labor contract' is signed annually between union and the company management, stipulating basic conditions of work and the rate of increase of the wages and salaries. The collective bargaining process in Bulgaria is a mixture between the German (industry level) and British (company level) models. Usually, ministers and branch union leaders negotiate ceilings and floors, and issue a recommended wage level pegged to inflation (actually, much of the bargaining is over the true level of the inflation). Then, each company signs a separate wage contract, more or less sticking to the industry level.

In all companies investigated, a steep reduction of the labor cost was observed in the overall cost structure. The decrease of the wages and salaries in real terms is usually attributed to exchange rate deprecations, rather than to internal company reasons. Nowadays, workers' representatives (but not the unions) would usually sit on the Supervisory Board, but their voices would not be heard to make much noise. Collective bargaining is not a problematic process in these privatized companies, because on average workers seem to be better paid than their colleagues in the state-owned enterprises. Problems arise when not enough orders can be secured, and personnel has to be laid off. Even in such cases, no grave deterioration of the industrial relations has been recorded in the investigated companies.

As a part of the restructuring process, in some of the companies depreciated capital stock has been sold to the personnel after privatization at reduced prices. According to the Bulgarian Privatization Law, capital stock (for example, machinery) worth up to 10 million levs can be purchased by the company employees with repayment in installments within six years, if they continue to use it for its designated purposes. In some of the textile and mechanical engineering companies, separate production lines – mainly on grounds of their different location from the main company – have been divested and established as independent legal entities and subcontractors, whereby the mother company would still be an important, though not necessarily a majority shareholder.

3.9 OUTLOOK: THE ULTIMATE ARRIVAL?

The findings of this chapter show that the story of enterprise restructuring in the Bulgarian transition is far from unambiguous. While changes have taken place, they have been in response to shocks rather than to pressures. For the companies, these changes have resulted in positive and negative consequences. On the positive side, companies are now more responsive to signals of the market. They are more flexible, more adaptive, more persistent and consistent in their policies and strategies. The direct exposure to the international markets has made company managers more open-minded and outward-looking.

Table 3.8. A summary of company restructuring

Problem	Resolved	Close to resolved	Close to unresolved	Unresolved
Ownership	X			
Markets		X		
Product range		X		
Pricing		X		
Financial restructuring	X			
Investments		X		
Personnel		X		
Access to retailing outlets on the domestic market			X	
Cost restructuring			X	
Governance		X		
Horizontal and vertical integration				X
Diversification of investments				X

On the negative side, in several aspects the restructuring process in the Bulgarian industry seems to have a bias toward practices that have given capitalism a bad name in the past, and pays little attention to the realities of the coming twenty-first century. This concerns technology, industrial relations and work organization. In technology, most industrial enterprises are slipping down the road of cheap conventional mass-consumption commodities, and pay little respect to innovativeness, information technology and quality upgrading. In industrial relations, the prevailing consensus is vulnerable. In work organization there is little, or no, evidence of involvement-fostering participatory practices. Table 3.8 above sums up the restructuring process in the investigated Bulgarian companies of our sample.

Yet if anything must have become unambiguously clear by now, it is the fact that efforts toward industrial restructuring are futile as long as ownership is diffused. While privatization in our sample of companies happened after restructuring had begun, the transfer of ownership has given the strongest impulses that made changes irreversible. The speed of restructuring is highest in the companies that have been acquired by foreign firms and work for foreign markets. Least changes – also due to the little time elapsed – have occurred in the companies privatized in the mass privatization program, or those producing mainly for the domestic market. All companies investigated in our sample have been a relative success story of industrial restructuring. This is possibly due to the fact that in the Bulgarian privatization, the first firms to be privatized were also the best. However, on many occasions the awareness convincingly emerges that privatization itself is not the ultimate arrival.

NOTES

1. In a game-theoretical framework of reasoning, a group has *common knowledge*, if all participants of the group share the same information, and everybody knows this, and everybody knows that everybody knows this, and so on *ad infinitum*. For formal definition of common knowledge, see Aumann, 1976.
2. *State Gazette*, 4 January 1989. This Decree was superseded by the subsequent legislation, mainly by the *Commercial Code* (*State Gazette* of 18 June 1991) and the *Privatization Law* (*State Gazette* of 8 May 1992), but some of its provision, especially with respect to the activity of the state-owned enterprises, are still in force.
3. This is the average figure for 1991. The immediate price upsurge in February compared with January 1991 was about 1600 per cent.
4. The reduction of Bulgarian trade with the countries of Central Europe was also due to the 'cumulation of local content' clause of those countries' Association Agreements with the European Union, which separated the trade within the Visegrad group (Czech Republic, Hungary, Poland, and Slovakia) from their trade with Bulgaria and Romania. According to this clause, intermediate imports of semi-finished goods could count as 'local content' for the purposes of value added – and hence make the final product qualify for access to the market of EU – *only within* each of the two groups of countries, but not between them (EBRD 1993, 1994). This has obviously discouraged the Visegrad contries from industrial cooperation with Bulgaria and Romania.
5. For a comprehensive coverage of the Privatization Law, and the Bulgarian privatization process and legislation up to the point when the mass privatization idea gained ground, see, for example, Frydman et al., 1993. Very little has happened thereafter in terms of privatization (sales) transactions.
6. Although a founding member of the UDF, PODKREPA withdrew from it when the UDF won the 1991 election. The reason announced publicly was that PODKREPA wished to 'preserve its nature of a trade union' and as such it could not participate in any government.
7. Hence the small number of privatized state-owned companies in Bulgaria as late as 1994–95 from which the sample – to be discussed in the next section – could be drawn.
8. The distinction between the 'stock' and the 'flow' problems of enterprise debt, and the misplaced sequencing of its restructuring, were drawn to our attention by John Flemming.

9. At the time, Bulgaria still had to sign the re-shedding agreement on its external debt with the London Club – represented by Deutsche Bank – and still had to secure new IMF stand-by credit to make these repayments possible.
10. This is an acronym of the Bulgarian transliteration of the name of the law.
11. For a good coverage of the basic privatization legislation in Bulgaria before the advent of the mass privatization see *inter alia* Frydman et al., 1993.
12. Actually, a good part of the economic theory today is preoccupied with the question how to overcome this 'hold-up' problem leading to underinvestment, and to induce firms to invest optimally (for a summary see Hart, 1995).
13. For an extensive analysis of differentiated markets, and a survey of the literature on product differentiation see for example, Hay and Morris, 1991.

REFERENCES

Agency for Economic Development and Forecasting (1992–96), *Annual Report on the Bulgarian Economy,* various issues, Sofia.

Angelov, I., Dimitrov, A., Dulev, S., Hubenova-Delislavkova, T. and Konsulov, V. (1994), *'Ikonomikata na Bulgaria do 1999 godina'* (The Bulgarian Economy until 1999), Institute of Economics, Bulgarian Academy of Sciences, Sofia.

Aumann, R. (1976), 'Agreeing to Disagree,' *Annals of Statistics*, (4), 1236–9.

Avramov, R. (1994), *Prehodat* (The Transition), Agency for Economic Coordination and Development, Sofia (in Bulgarian).

Binmore K. (1994), *Playing Fair. Game Theory and the Social Contract,* Volume 1, Cambridge, Mass.: The MIT Press.

Bulgarian National Bank (1988–96), *Annual Report,* various issues, Sofia.

Bulgarian National Bank (1988–96), *Monthly Bulletin*, various issues, Sofia.

Comecon Data (1990), Edited by the Vienna Institute for Comparative Economic Studies, London: Macmillan.

Dixit, A.K. and Stiglitz, J.E. (1977), 'Monopolistic Competition and Optimum Product Diversity', *American Economic Review,* **67**, 297–308.

Economist Intelligence Unit (1995/96), *The Economist,* various issues of country reports for Bulgaria, the Czech Republic, Hungary, Poland, Romania and Russia, London.

Ehrlich, Éva (1985), 'The Size Structure of Manufacturing Establishments and Enterprises: An International Comparison', *Journal of Comparative Economics*, (9), 267–95.

European Bank for Reconstruction and Development (1993), *Current Economic Issues,* July 1993, London.

European Bank for Reconstruction and Development (1994), *Transition Report. Economic Transition in Eastern Europe and the Former Soviet Union*, London.

European Bank for Reconstruction and Development (1995), *Transition Report Update. Economic Transition in Eastern Europe and the Former Soviet Union*, London.

Flemming, John (1993), *Speech at the IX International Summer Seminar of Club 'Economika 2000'*, Albena, September 1993, Discussion Paper of Club 'Economika 2000', Sofia, 1993.

Frydman, R., Rapaczynski, A., Earle, J., et al. (1993), *The Privatization Process in Central Europe: Bulgaria, Czechoslovakia, Hungary, Poland, Romania,* CEU Privatization Reports, Vol. 1, Budapest, London and New York: CEU Press.

Hart, O. (1995), *Firms, Contracts, and Financial Structure*, Oxford: Clarendon Press.

Hay, D.A. and Morris, D.J. (1991), *Industrial Economics and Organization. Theory and Evidence*, Oxford: Oxford University Press.

Hotelling, H. (1929), 'Stability in Competition,' *Economic Journal*, **39**, 41–57.

International Bank for Reconstruction and Development (1993), *Trends in Developing Economies. Extracts,* Washington, DC: The World Bank.

National Statistical Institute (1996), *Statistical Notebook: Bulgaria,* Sofia.

Senker, J. and Faulkner, W. (1996), 'Networks, Tacit Knowledge and Innovation', in Coombs, R., Saviotti, A. and Walsh V. (eds), *Technological Collaboration: Dynamics of Cooperation in Industrial Innovation,* Aldershot, UK and Brookfield, US: Edward Elgar, pp. 76–97.

Shaked, A. and Sutton, J. (1982), 'Relaxing Price Competition through Product Differentiation', *Review of Economic Studies,* **49**, 3–13.

Shaked, A. and Sutton, J. (1987), 'Product Differentiation and Industrial Structure', *Journal of Industrial Economics,* **36**, 131–46.
State Gazette of the Republic of Bulgaria, 1990–1997, various issues.
Statistical Yearbook of the (People's) Republic of Bulgaria, 1988–1996, various issues.
Sutton, J. (1989), 'Endogenous Sunk Costs and Market Structure,' in Bonanno, G. and Brandolini, D. (eds), *Market Structure and the New Industrial Economics*, Oxford: Oxford University Press.
Sutton, J. (1992), *Sunk Costs and Market Structure. Price Competition, Advertising, and the Evolution of Concentration,* Cambridge, Mass.: The MIT Press.

4. Company Restructuring in Estonia between 1992 and 1995

Alari Purju and Juhan Teder

4.1 INTRODUCTION

Estonian economic reform has been in several respects very similar to developments in the other East and Central European countries (see, Frydman, Rapaczynski and Earle, 1993). At the same time some important specific features occurred in Estonia which determined the outcomes of the reform. Estonia was one of the constituent republics of the former Soviet Union and therefore it did not have several attributes of an independent state (own currency, foreign embassies, central bank, foreign trade organizations, and so on). Although formally the Republic of Estonia was restored from the state that had existed between the two World Wars, in several aspects we can speak about the introduction of completely new institutions and regulations after Estonia regained independence in August 1991. This had a strong impact on the transition from the planned to a market economy and on the creation of social and political structures of a democratic state.

Such a situation had its positive and negative sides. It was relatively easy to introduce a very hard and restrictive monetary policy which was, at least in its first stage, the most important factor determining the structural changes in the economy, and it created a relatively sound basis for future development. Also, social expenditures were relatively low and the tax burden of enterprises and individuals was lower than in most other East European countries. This means that there were more resources for investment and a relatively fast accumulation of capital occurred. One special factor in Estonia's move toward a market economy has been its linguistic and cultural closeness to Finland. A very large number of Estonian business contacts with the Western world started from that neighboring country.

On the other hand, this specific situation also had its drawbacks. The institutional development of Estonia was relatively modest compared to countries which had some prehistory of reforms and closer contacts with market economies. Though Estonia created a rather sound banking sector, which is an advanced one in the Eastern European framework, the development in other sectors (especially the introduction of a sound legal regulation) has not been so successful. In the near future coordination of the interests of different social groups can be expected to be of great importance (Purju, 1996).

Ownership reform has a very strong impact on the transition among all these common and specific features. Due to the missing prehistory of reforms and to a somewhat simplified understanding of all nuances of a developed market economy, the need for a dominating private sector and the belief that the dominance of the private sector itself would solve most economic problems were very widely spread.[1] The result of such attitudes was that Estonia applied an approach in the privatization of enterprises that guaranteed the speed and it was dominated by economic goals.[2] The result was that by the end of 1996 practically all enterprises in the manufacturing and service sectors were privatized and the private sector was dominating in these fields.[3]

On the other hand, restitution had a rather important role in the Estonian privatization scheme. Though some attempts were made to apply methods enabling the renovation of the pre-World War II ownership relations in the privatization of enterprises, basically different methods prevailed in this field. Retaining minority shares of some enterprises by the state for selling those shares against vouchers expressed this attitude. At the same time, in the privatization of land and housing the restitution approach has been very strong.

Changes in the macroeconomic environment and a restrictive monetary policy realized in the form of a currency board with a fixed foreign exchange rate have been very important factors determining the economic performance of enterprises. This is one of the reasons why the current chapter starts, after a short introduction, with a description of the basic features of that policy. The next section of the report is dedicated to the general trends of privatization in Estonia. After that, in the fourth section, the changes in the ownership structure and trends of output, exports and employment are analysed. The fifth section is an analysis of enterprises privatized between 1992 and 1995. The output, employment and financial results of these enterprises are covered. The sixth section is based on case studies and on the answers of company managers to a respective questionnaire. The analysis ends with conclusions from the privatization process and its influence on the economic behavior of enterprises.

4.2 MACROECONOMIC AND POLITICAL FACTORS

4.2.1 The Monetary Reform

The economic reform has been going along with the restoration of political independence in Estonia. Restoration of Estonia's independence in August 1991 brought along several changes in the institutional framework of the economy but Estonia still remained in the ruble zone. The monetary reform conducted in June 1992 was a major turning point in the history of economic reforms. As the list of articles written on the details of the Estonian economic reform is rather long, only some of its more general features which determined the direction of changes of foreign trade are described here.[4] The currency board arrangement and convertibility of the Estonian kroon were introduced. The exchange rate of the kroon was fixed to the DEM (1 DEM = 8 EEK). Both private individuals and enterprises can convert the kroon in foreign currency without restrictions.

At the introduction of the exchange rate of the kroon the rate of the foreign exchange auctions was used with the result of the kroon being by some estimations even 7–8 times cheaper than the purchasing power parity (PPP) rate. The purchasing power of the domestic market suffered due to the drastic devaluation of the kroon. The combination of low wages as a cost side factor and a low purchasing power on the domestic market as a result of the undervalued currency and a low domestic demand forced the enterprises to export. However, the producers really need much imported equipment to produce exports acceptable for other markets. If they do not manage to export their products, low revenues obtained on the domestic market will not satisfy investment requirements, yet to export they will need resources for investments.

4.2.2 Changes in the Structure of Economy

It has been characteristic of the Estonian economic reform that no branch of the economy has been preferred; practically the single determining factor in the restructuring has been the ability of an enterprise to adapt itself to the economic conditions, especially the ability to orientate itself to Western markets. It has been caused by the indeterminacy of the economic situation, the sharply increasing relative prices and by the rapid contraction of the East European markets. But it has also been caused by the trust in the efficiency of the strict monetary policy used by different governments and the determining effects of the market-oriented economic environment created by it.

Table 4.1. Main economic indicators of the Estonian economy, 1992–96

	1992	1993	1994	1995	1996
GDP, in current prices, billion kroons		22.1	30.3	40.7	52.4
Real GDP change rate (per cent)	–14.2	–8.5	–2.7	4.3	4.0
Industrial output, change (per cent)	–35.6	–18.7	–3.0	1.9	2.9
Consumer price index (per cent)	952.0	35.6	41.7	28.9	23.1
Unemployment (per cent)[a]	1.9	2.6	2.2	9.7	10.0
Average monthly salary, kroons[b]	802.0	1165.0	2096.0	2375.0	2985.0
Exchange rate/DEM	8.0	8.0	8.0	8.0	8.0
Exports (bn.kr.)	5.4	10.6	16.9	21.1	25.0
Import (bn.kr.)	5.1	11.9	21.5	29.1	38.9
Foreign trade balance, (bn. kr.)	0.3	–1.3	–4.6	–8.0	–13.9
Foreign trade surplus (deficit)/GDP, (per cent)	2.0	–5.9	–15.2	–19.7	–26.5
Exports/GDP (per cent)	41.2	48.0	55.8	51.8	47.7

Notes

[a] Proportion of employment-age population receiving unemployment benefits

[b] Average wage in the fourth quarter of each year

Sources: Estonian Statistics Monthly (1997), No. 2, pp. 18–19, 29–32, 35–9; *Eesti Bank Bulletin* No. 3, 1997, pp. 21–36, and *Statistical Yearbook of Estonia* (1998), pp. 25–7, 164–5, 189–90, 197–8, 236–7, 287–8.

The most direct consequence of the changed economic environment has been the sharp decline of production in all branches of the economy. Economic changes were very much forced by the prices and foreign economic shocks. As a result, the GDP fell by 3.6 per cent in 1990, 13.6 per cent in 1991, 14.2 per cent in 1992, 8.5 per cent in 1993 and by 1.8 per cent in 1994.

Table 4.2. The structure of the Estonian GDP between 1989 and 1995, in per cent

	1989	1991	1992	1993	1994	1995
Agriculture, forestry	22.0[a]	15.0	12.3	9.4	8.5	6.7
Fishing		1.9	0.8	0.5	0.5	0.4
Mining, quarrying	1.7	1.6	2.5	1.7	1.6	1.5
Manufacturing	35.1	32.7	28.7	17.1	16.6	15.7
Electricity, gas and water	2.0	1.7	4.3	3.2	2.9	3.5
Construction	9.2	6.1	4.6	5.9	5.6	5.3
Trade	7.0[b]	7.2	13.0	15.2	13.5	14.8
Restaurants, hotels		0.8	1.5	1.2	1.0	1.0
Transport, storage and communication	6.9	6.2	12.0	11.1	10.1	9.4
Financial institutions, insurance		0.8	1.7	2.6	2.8	3.3
Real estate, business services		1.6	5.3	6.6	7.3	8.5
Public administration	16.1[c]	1.7	2.1	3.1	3.9	4.4
Education		2.4	3.5	5.1	5.0	5.4
Health and social care		1.6	0.5	2.3	3.1	3.6
Other		8.7	2.2	4.8	5.1	6.1
GDP in basic value	99.8	90.1	94.2	89.8	87.5	89.6
Net taxes	0.2	10.9	5.8	10.2	12.5	10.4
GDP, in current prices, million kroons		1 832	13 054	22 060	30 268	40 705

Notes

a Fishing is included in this figure

b Services of restaurants and hotels are included in this figure

c Services of financial institutions, insurance, business activities, education, health and social care are included in this figure.

Sources: Statistical Yearbook of Estonia (1998), pp. 23–5.

The cumulative decline of the GDP during the period of 1990–94 was 36 per cent. The decline of industrial production began in 1991 and it was 10 per cent then. A further decline of 35.6 per cent followed in 1992, a 18.7 per cent decline occurred in 1993 and 3.0 per cent in 1994. But the GDP increased by 4.3 per cent in 1995 and by 4.0 per cent in 1996. Industrial output increased respectively by 1.9 per cent and by 2.9 per cent. However, the figures published by the Statistical Office of Estonia have been strongly criticized. The Bank of Estonia estimated some economic growth in 1994. Several reasons could be presented why statistical figures underestimate real economic changes (Table 4.1).

A rapid increase in small enterprises not covered by regular statistics and attempts to diminish their turnover and incomes, a large share of the shadow economy, are some of these reasons. Growth occurred for two reasons in 1995. First, in 1995 large-scale privatization in Estonian industry was very close to its end, and the private sector attained a dominant role. This clarification of ownership relations is a very important starting point for future economic growth. And secondly, there has been a very deep decline in Estonian industry, and growth would be possible mainly on the basis of the already existing production capacities.

Foreign and domestic investments in certain branches and access to new markets are factors supporting this growth. Estonia is a very small country and one large investment by some big international corporation in the cement industry, or in the manufacturing of wood and paper, could change the growth rates and the structure of the whole economy.

Estonia is overcoming the economic crisis with a notably changed economic structure. The shares of the trade, transportation and service sector have increased rapidly. The share of manufacturing was 35.1 per cent and that of agriculture (together with hunting and forestry) 22.0 per cent in the GDP in 1989. In 1994 the shares of these branches were respectively 16.6 and 8.5 per cent and in 1995 15.2 per cent and 6.7 per cent. The structure of the Estonian GDP has become rather close to the structure of the GDP of developed countries, but these structural shifts happened during a deep decline in the economy and a foreign trade shock, which was more complicated for industrial enterprises. Some restoration of the role of these industries should be expected during the next years (Table 4.2).

4.3 PRIVATIZATION: GENERAL TRENDS

Privatization in Estonia has many similar features with the same process in other Eastern European countries. However, there are also some specific preconditions for ownership reform in Estonia: an extensive migration from other republics of the former Soviet Union; a commitment to the ruble zone (the national currency, the Estonian kroon, was only introduced in 1992), and the predominant role of state ownership in housing. There was a very strong readiness for the transition to a market economy and to the concomitant economic reforms, because the goals of these changes were identified with that of achieving the political independence of Estonia. Therefore, the population was prepared to suffer the pains created by the reform.

The following dilemmas have been mentioned in discussions over privatization as being most important: (i) should ownership reform be comprehensive and rapid or should firms be sold off gradually after the new rules of economic behavior emerge; (ii) should state property be sold or given away (also using vouchers); (iii) should restitution play a major part in ownership reform, or is it necessary to take into account other considerations restricting the scope of restitution; (iv) should the employees of privatized enterprises get a special claim, or should there be no preferences for them as state assets were created through an unfair redistribution of resources from one sector to another; (v) is it especially important to support domestic firms, or do we need to encourage foreign investors to participate in privatization? In Estonia during privatization, the second and third dilemmas were mainly discussed.

Since 1990, all the Estonian governments have declared privatization to be the central issue of the continuing reforms. Differences have occurred between the political parties about privatization methods and which interested groups should be preferred in the process. Two approaches may be distinguished: (1) the so-called restitution approach, which gave priority to restitution and also distribution by vouchers; and (2) the entrepreneurial approach, which stresses in the process of privatization the role of core investors and management. During the period 1990–96 seven governments preferring both approaches have been in office. However, though some changes of emphasis on different methods have occurred, the privatization process has continued following the same path.

4.3.1 Small-Scale Privatization

At the beginning of 1991 the total number of privatized small-scale units was estimated to be 1200 service facilities, 500 shops, 350 booths and 800 catering facilities (Klein and Tali, 1995, p. 146). Later, during the time real privatization took place, this number decreased due to liquidation of several entities, bankruptcies, and so on. The Department of State Property organized the small-scale privatization utilizing one of the following methods: (i) auctions; (ii) selling of shares; (iii) competition of business ideas (tender). However, at the request of the local government, insiders, local inhabitants or current leaseholders could be given pre-emptive rights in the auction process. One reason for awarding pre-emptive rights was the desire to avoid drastic changes in the existing structure of services (especially in small towns and villages). The pre-emptive rights were accompanied by a requirement not to change the usage of the property for at least five years.

By the end of 1992, the list of enterprises to be privatized totaled 1212 entities. Of this, 211 entities with a total purchasing price of 18.2 million rubles were sold in 1991 and 556 entities with an estimated total purchasing price of 41.9 million kroons (during the first half of 1992 enterprises were sold for rubles, during the second half of 1992 for Estonian kroons) in 1992. From this list, 767 entities with an estimated price of 43.6 million kroons were sold by the end of 1992. During the first half of 1993, 193 entities with a price of 104.2 million kroons were sold. Altogether 960 entities from the initial small privatization list were sold by June 1993. After this date, the small privatization program underwent major changes. Part of the unsold entities were transferred to municipal ownership, but several entities were sold also in 1993 and 1994.

The 'Privatization Law' adopted by the Parliament in June 1993, legally equalized small-scale and large-scale privatization. Since the middle of 1993, it has been possible to speak about small-scale privatization, in the sense that for smaller enterprises the auction method was used for ownership transformation. On the other hand, any quantitative ceiling for including enterprises into the list for privatization by this method was abolished. Besides service, trade and catering enterprises several small manufacturing and transportation enterprises were also privatized using the auction method. During the second half of 1993 additionally 50 entities were sold, taking the total number of small entities to 243 with a purchasing price of 124.7 million kroons for 1993. In 1994, 126 entities with a purchasing price of 68.2 million kroons were sold. In 1995, these numbers were respectively 121 and 79.8 million kroons, and in 1996 85 and 148.7 million kroons (*Estonian Privatization Agency*).

Small-scale privatization was relatively successful in Estonia, despite several changes in legal regulation. The private sector offered 89 per cent of real estate, renting and business services and 84 per cent of other services in 1996. The private sector of wholesaling was 98 per cent in 1996. In retail sales, the private sector share was 96 per cent in 1996. More than 90 per cent of enterprises now active in the trade and service sectors belonged to the state and municipalities in 1991. Competition has emerged and these sectors are the fastest growing area of the Estonian economy.

4.3.2 Large-Scale Privatization

The so-called pilot privatization of seven large enterprises by sale from summer 1991 until April 1992, was the prelude of large-scale privatization in Estonia. This program was based on the legal regulation of small-scale privatization and was launched to give privatizers some experience in using different forms and procedures of privatization. One of the reasons for such a limited program was the negative attitude of the public and politicians toward selling large-scale enterprises for inflating rubles.

The large-scale privatization program was introduced in August 1992, when two acts regulating the privatization of entities with a book value over 600 000 kroons were passed in the Parliament. Also, the Treuhand-type Estonian Privatization Enterprise was founded in September 1992. The Estonian Privatization Enterprise used the know-how, consultants and the financial support of the German Treuhand. The 'Law on Privatization' passed on 17 June 1993, uniformed the privatization of enterprises, specified more clearly the methods of privatization and it also introduced organizational changes. The Estonian Privatization Agency was founded on the basis of the Department of State Property and the Privatization Holding. The Privatization Agency and its Board obtained more independence in the process of managing the privatization process. The Minister for Economic Reforms filled the chairman's post on the board. The law only regulates the privatization of enterprises; agricultural reform and the privatization of dwellings are regulated by other legislation. The 'Privatization Law' envisages the following methods of privatization:

1. The sale of shares of an enterprise or its structural units by way of tenders with preliminary negotiations

This method is used in cases where the organizer of a privatization sets additional conditions alongside the price. These additional conditions cover employment guarantees, the creation of new jobs, investment guarantees, environmental issues, and other conditions regulating the activity of the enterprise or its structural units. The Privatization Agency sets no initial price for assets or shares, the bidders have to provide the enterprise they are applying to buy with three-year business plan and a bank guarantee of 5 per cent of the value of the bid.

2. The sale of property or shares of enterprises or their structural units at a public or restricted auction

For an auction, no specific conditions are set. The auction lists are only published locally. The organizer of the auction sets an initial price for the asset to be privatized. The price is based on the book value and on the experts' estimate. All participants must pay the participation fees and guarantees, usually 10 per cent of the initial price. Objects are sold to the highest bidder.

3. Public offering of shares

The minority shares of privatized enterprises are sold through a public offering of shares. On average, the sale of 25 per cent of shares of 33 companies was realized by the Privatization Agency during 1995–96. The most important characteristic of the public offering in Estonia, is that shares can be bought only for vouchers (details of this method are discussed in the paragraph on use of vouchers).

4. The sale of property or shares of enterprises or their structural units, by the method established by the organizer of privatization in cases where no purchaser was found using the other methods (sale of so-called leftovers)
In this case there is no deadline for a submission of the bid. The Board of the Privatization Agency can make a decision on selling when the first suitable bid is received. This method has been rather popular among purchasers because the price of assets or shares has been relatively low.

Altogether 410 enterprises were offered in 15 tenders and 452 purchasing contracts were made for the total sum of 3.0 billion kroons (approximately $US 250 million). However, the figures for enterprises offered and sold are not directly comparable, because in several cases units of the same enterprise were sold to different buyers and separate contracts were concluded for every unit. From the enterprises listed before 1 January, 1997 at least one contract has been made on 337. Additionally, some contracts were signed for the enterprises that were not included in the list of 15 tenders. The state mainly sold some minority part of the shares that it still held in several private enterprises. It is possible to say that approximately 80 per cent of the enterprises included in the list of tenders were sold completely. Enterprises which were not sold during the first tenders were again offered in the later tender lists (for example, Keila Terko, a grain processing company, was offered in the third and sixth tenders, but was finally sold only in the eighth tender). Starting from the sixth tender another method, the method of selling the so-called leftovers, is used after the failure of sale through tender. Such enterprises and their units are sold to the first buyer without any deadline for bidding. Approximately 16 per cent of the total purchasing price was paid by foreign buyers. Although some tenders were announced only locally, there were no restrictions for foreigners to participate.

It should be noted that the purchasing price does not equal the proceedings from privatization. As mentioned previously, the Privatization Agency subtracts from the purchasing price the costs related to the organization of the process. Another important point here is that in the majority of cases the purchaser paid only 20 per cent of the price immediately and another 80 per cent by installments up to ten years after the contract was signed. In June 1996, together with introducing by Government decree the possibility to pay 50 per cent of the purchasing price with vouchers, the share of the compulsory initial payment was increased from 20 to 50 per cent of the price.

It is interesting to note that in the last tenders the total sum of guaranteed investments was relatively large in comparison with the purchasing price. There are several interrelated reasons for this. First, the quality of enterprises sold in the last tenders was on average somewhat lower than that of the enterprises sold at the beginning. Second, government institutions seem to have overestimated the readiness of foreign investors to participate in the privatization of Estonian enterprises. Third, the financial situation of most enterprises worsened during their time on the list of privatizable enterprises. Furthermore, their managers did not invest in the enterprises' capital stock due to the uncertain situation. Now the new owner has an additional investment requirement and very often there was a trade-off situation between the higher price and the investment guarantees. Although in some earlier contracts investment guarantees were fixed, the Privatization Agency has had problems in several cases forcing a new owner to make these promised investments.

Another important factor which has influenced the purchase price has been the liabilities taken over by a new owner. All discussions about these issues have been rather complicated. One reason for this is that enterprises have quite different structures of financial obligations. Tax arrears create a rather big share of them. If the new owner agreed to take over a substantial part of the liabilities, it was possible to apply for a lower price in the bidding process. There were ten cases among 452 contracts where the purchasing price of an enterprise was 1 kroon. The new owner took over a substantial number of liabilities and gave investment guarantees. Table 4.3 describes the proportions of these indicators from the point of view of investors. The total purchasing price, liabilities and investment guarantees are compared with a share of each component.

Another important aspect is related to the role of foreign investors in the privatization process. Although the respective figures do not give a complete picture of foreign participation in the process, they make it possible to estimate some general features. Table 4.4 describes the role of foreign investments in the total purchasing price, investment guarantees and employment guarantees. It is necessary to mention here that in most cases investment and employment guarantees were compulsory for a three-year period after the privatization contract was signed. The last row sums up the respective parameters during the period 1993–96, and also average shares of purchasing price, investment and employment guarantees fixed in contracts with the foreign investor are presented.

The figures in Tables 4.3 and 4.4 confirm that investment guarantees started to be more important than the purchasing price of enterprises in the end of the period. This aspect was considered to be important especially in the case of contracts signed with foreign investors. On the other hand, employment guarantees were less important in deals with foreign participation. This phenomenon could be explained by two reasons: (1) it was rather complicated to force foreign investors to keep excess labor force in privatized enterprises; (2) very often the most important advantage of the foreign offer was the investment guarantee with transformation of know-how, and with promising future development perspectives. It was not reasonable to introduce obstacles for the foreign investor in such cases.

The figures in Table 4.4 clearly underestimate the role of foreign investors in Estonian privatization. One reason for this is that Estonian legislation provided domestic investors with one rather important preference: they only had to pay part of the purchasing price at once and they received an opportunity to pay the remaining part in installments. Several foreign participants preferred first to create a joint venture with a formally dominating ownership of Estonians registered in Estonia. Such a company then participated in the privatization as an Estonian company.

Part of the shares of several enterprises have been retained for a public sale against vouchers since the fifth tender. The shares of 33 enterprises were sold by public auctions against vouchers from December 1994 until December 1996. The shares of two of the first enterprises (49 per cent of the shares of the Tallinn Department Store in December 1994 and 20 per cent of the shares of the Saku Brewery in April and May 1995) were sold at a fixed price in voucher kroons. Although the price was in both cases substantially higher than the face value of the sold shares, the shares of both enterprises were significantly oversubscribed. Small investors were preferred and 200 shares with a face value of 10 kroons was the maximum amount for every subscriber. As the demand for shares was over four times higher than the number of shares offered, every investor got a quarter of the shares he had subscribed to in the case of Saku Brewery (more exactly, 46 shares if the investor had applied for 200 shares) for the same fixed price of 26 voucher kroons per share with the face value of ten kroons.

Table 4.3. Purchasing prices, investment guarantees and liabilities in Estonian privatization

Year	Purchasing price		Liabilities		Investment guarantees		TOTAL	
	mln.kr	per cent	mln.kr	per cent	mln.kr.	per cent	mln.kr.	per cent
1993	353.2	45.0	195.6	24.9	236.8	30.1	785.6	100.0
1994	1333.8	46.3	689.2	24.0	855.5	29.7	2878.5	100.0
1995	874.9	37.7	538.9	23.2	906.2	39.1	2320.0	100.0
1996	473.6	40.9	230.3	19.9	453.6	39.2	1157.5	100.0
Total	3035.5	42.5	1654.0	23.2	2452.1	34.3	7141.6	100.0

Source: Author's calculations

Table 4.4. The role of foreign investors in Estonian privatization

Years	Purchasing price			Investment guarantees		
	Total (mln kr.)	Foreign invest-ments (mln. kr.)	Share of foreign investors (per cent)	Total (mln kr.)	Foreign invest-ments (mln. kr.)	Share of foreign investors (per cent)
1993	353.2	91.0	25.8	236.8	87.1	36.8
1994	1 333.8	108.1	8.1	855.5	130.7	15.3
1995	874.9	76.7	8.8	906.2	193.4	21.3
1996	473.6	208.4	44.0	453.6	338.0	74.5
Total	3 035.5	484.2	16.0	2452.1	749.2	30.6

Employment			
	Total	In companies of foreign investors	Share of companies of foreign investors (per cent)
1993	9 099	1 939	21.3
1994	25 483	2 917	11.4
1995	7 950	1 460	18.4
1996	1 274	50	4.2
Total	43 776	6 370	14.6

Source: Author's calculations

On 24 June, 1995, the Privatization Agency announced the sale of minority shares of six enterprises for vouchers. In this case, and later, a different system for bidding and the determination of the price of shares was used. The public could use two methods for applying for the shares. In the case of using method I, the subscriber determines the value of vouchers he or she reserves for buying shares of some enterprise. The number of shares he or she really gets is determined by the equilibrium price and the value of reserved voucher kroons. By method II, the investor also shows the maximum price he or she is ready to pay for a share of an enterprise. If the equilibrium price is higher than accepted by the investor, the investor will get his/her voucher kroons back.

As a maximum, 49 per cent of a joint-stock company's shares was sold for vouchers (8 cases of the total of 33). Usually 20–25 per cent of the shares were sold for vouchers, but before that a majority stake was already sold to the core investor. The lowest price was fixed at the level of 3 kroons for a share with a face value of 10 kroons. Only in four cases the equilibrium price was lower than the face value of the respective share. The highest price was 235 times higher than the face value of the respective share of the well-known confectionery factory *Kalev* (*Eesti erastamisagentuuri*, 1996 *aasta tegevusaruanne*, 1997). However, it should be mentioned here that we are speaking about voucher kroons, whose market value was at that time approximately one fifth of cash kroons.

4.3.3 Privatization of Public Utilities

The step-by-step approach should prevail in the privatization of infrastructure, oil shale mines and power stations, as the Government and the Privatization Agency stated (*Erastamisprogramm valitsusse*, 1995). First, all state-owned companies in this field will be reorganized into joint-stock holding companies. Second, several parts which have mainly supportive functions for the main activity in the respective field will be privatized. Third, the privatization of the main activities may be privatized. The predominant part of shares could be sold to some core investor or to several foreign partners, with the Estonian state remaining a minority shareholder. The Estonian state could diminish its participation by selling shares for vouchers to those resident in Estonia.

The Privatization Agency formed a special working group at the end of 1995 to prepare privatization plans for public utilities. Financial support of the Phare program was used for this purpose. Initial privatization plans were presented to the Government in June 1996. Further, respective ministries, the Privatization Agency and Phare consultants had to prepare more detailed privatization schedules for *Eesti Energia* (the power engineering company) and *Eesti Põlevkivi* (the oil shale mining company) on 1 November, 1996 and for other infrastructure enterprises on 1 January, 1997. The special department was founded in the Privatization Agency to deal with the privatization of infrastructure.

In May 1996, 66 per cent of shares of Estonian Air were already sold. Also 100 per cent of the shares of the state-owned insurance company *Eesti Kindlustus* were sold. In August 1996 a two-level tender of 70 per cent of *Eesti Merelaevandus* ((the marine transportation company) was announced. This process was in its second stage in May 1997. There is in the stage of preparation of master plan the privatization of *Eesti Energia*. However, several legal and administrative problems must be solved before privatization can began in this field. For example, for privatization of power stations, the legal act regulating the supply of electricity and establishment of an institution supervising the process has been considered necessary. Also, the price of electricity is regulated by the state and relatively low. The same is true in the case of railway transportation, where the tickets for passengers are several times lower then costs. For these reasons there seems to be some socially needed time lag to prepare privatization in these fields. The project of the law regulating energy market is still discussed in respective government institutions.

4.3.4 Privatization Securities (Vouchers)

Two types of privatization securities are used in Estonia (Hänni, 1993). The National Capital Bonds (NCBs) are issued on the basis of a person's period of employment. Every employment year is considered to be worth 300 kroons. The Compensation Securities (CS) are issued to the former owners of unlawfully expropriated property and their heirs, if they do not want this property back, or if the return of this property is not possible. The value of the property in 1940 is determined first and then recalculated into 1992 EEK by multiplying by 10 (by 40 for land). In privatization the NCB and the CS are used in a similar way. A specific feature of the Estonian scheme is that vouchers can be used for buying flats, land and shares of enterprises. On the one hand, an opportunity has been created to promote privatization in different areas of the economy. On the other hand, this brings about many difficulties, as it is necessary to compare the value of very different assets.

As described above, there are two types of privatization securities. As to NCB, the sum 8.5 billion kroons is final because the issue of cards is now completed (Hänni, 1993). The total value of CS depends on the number of claims, as well as the relationship between physical return and compensation. The smaller the amount of physically returned property, the greater the value of issued CS, and vice versa. This factor has a direct effect on the vouchers side and assets side of the balance but does not influence equilibrium. In May 1997 the value of issued CSs was 5.5 billion kroons and the forecast of total amount was diminished to 8.5 billion kroons (*Erastamisväärtpaberite väljaandmine ja kasutamine,* 1997). So, the total value of vouchers could be 17 billion kroons. As people could buy their flats using a card which was issued on the basis of the length of employment (voucher kroons with a value of 2.1 billion kroons were utilized for buying flats), the expected value of vouchers would be 14.9 billion kroons. On privatization accounts were 7 billion kroons, the value of assets sold for vouchers was 6.2 billion kroons (plus dwellings with an estimated value of 2.1 billion kroons) on 10 March, 1997.

The value of privatized property can only be roughly estimated. It will also depend on political decisions concerning the amount of assets to be privatized, and the behavior of persons in the privatization process. The land, dwelling rooms, shares and other assets of enterprises are in an economic sense very different and their estimation in the framework of a single scheme is fraught with difficulty. Also, the mechanisms for evaluation and sale are very important for determining how vouchers are covered with assets. Some assets are privatized to their users for the calculated nominal value (flats, land). Another part of the property will be sold through auction-type mechanisms for cash or for vouchers. A greater share of the property sold through the auction-type mechanism should help absorb more privatization securities.

The adjustment of the demand and supply sides of the voucher scheme over a longer period is very important for creating proper expectations. The deep decline of the price of vouchers below their nominal value has caused heated political debates. At the same time, the interest of private economic agents in vouchers has rapidly increased. Although, the speed of privatization has been much slower than different political parties have claimed, especially during election campaigns, the investment funds and real estate firms realized that through this scheme a large amount of property is transformed and it is possible to make a very good business there. Large amount of shares which were bought for vouchers, but are now tradable for cash, have been introduced for trading in the tiny Estonian securities market through this scheme.

4.3.5 The Compensation Fund

The activity of the Compensation Fund is very important for balancing the whole system. The Compensation Fund was financed through the transfers of 50 per cent of the money earned from privatization for cash to it. In 1996, this share was reduced to 45 per cent when state-owned assets are sold and to 25 per cent when municipal property is sold.[5] The Compensation Fund is to buy the privatization securities for bonds and invest the money received from privatization for cash into other financial institutions, which will lend out the money. This money should be invested in Estonian enterprises, the construction of dwellings or reconstruction of infrastructure. The sum of money received by the Compensation Fund has already diminished by privatization costs. The issued bonds will be repurchased by the Compensation Fund after 1 January, 2000. The total amount of the Funds' assets was 496 million kroons on 11 September, 1995 (*Eesti Sónumid,* 1995). In the end of March, 1997, the amount of assets has been increased to 1220 million kroons (*Äripäev*, 1997b).

During 1994, 1995, and 1996 the Fund had eight series of issues of bonds worth a total value of 360 million kroons. On 7 May, 1997 the Compensation Fund announced the ninth issue of bonds. The Fund sells its bonds with a nominal value of 100 kroons for voucher kroons at a price that is equal to the price of vouchers in the open market. As the value of vouchers has been far below their nominal value (vouchers were traded at a price of 25–30 per cent of their nominal value at the end of May 1997, which means that if one working year was equalized to 300 kroons then the equivalent of it is traded for 75–90 kroons), the bonds are sold for the price that is closest to 400 voucher kroons.

The Compensation Fund also paid interests for bonds twice a year. There was a fixed 7 per cent base interest rate per annum. The extra interest rate was paid on top of the basic rate according to the financial results of the Fund. Altogether the interest rate paid by the Compensation Fund bonds was 16.85 per cent in 1994 and for the first half of 1995 15.6 per cent calculated for the whole year. For the second half of 1996 the interest rate was 12 per cent. Since 1997 was introduced a new system, according to which the interest rate is based on the interbank interest rate of the money market of Estonia (Talibor) plus 1.5 per cent (the interest rate could be approximately between 6 and 8 per cent). The maturity time of the ninth issue was shortened from six to five years. The Compensation Fund will be closed when all of its obligations are fulfilled.

4.4 CHANGES IN THE OWNERSHIP STRUCTURE AND ITS IMPACT ON NET TURNOVER, EXPORTS AND EMPLOYMENT OF THE COMPANIES

4.4.1 The Data and Problems of Adequate Interpretation

General data about the ownership structure of turnover, exports and employment in different branches has been published by the Statistical Office of the Republic of Estonia. The following forms of property are classified: (1) state property; (2) municipal property, (3) Estonian private property, (4) foreign property. The classification of enterprises by ownership is based on the dominating owner (that is, on the owner who owns the majority of shares). If the proportion of shares between the state and a private owner, or some other owner, is 50:50, then the enterprise is considered to be in state ownership. To be classified as a foreign company, the foreign owner should have at least 51 per cent of the shares of the company (*Eesti ettevõtete finantsnäitajad 1995 I*, 1996).

Another problem is related to the change of the classification in ownership forms introduced from 1 January, 1995. Firms rented from the state by the employees were considered to be private companies before that deadline and have been classified as SOEs since that date. This complicates the comparison of figures for 1993–94 and 1995. The classification covers only enterprises that are corporatized or in another legal form (general partnerships, co-operatives and so on). So, most of the public units in education, health care and public administration are not covered by this classification. Also in insurance and finances the respective institutions are not included, the list covers only enterprises offering supportive services in these fields. All the enterprises with more than 49 employees were included in the sample by the Statistical Office. To other firms simple random sampling was applied. The statistical profile of the Estonian Enterprises Register based on economically active companies was also used in the sampling process.

4.4.2 Changes in the Ownership Structure Due to Privatization

There were 940 SOEs, 688 municipal enterprises, 49 053 Estonian private firms, 5756 foreign companies and 255 other enterprises not mentioned before. Altogether, 56 692 firms were registered in the Register of Enterprises on 2 January, 1997. The largest number of enterprises, 27 834, were in the wholesale and retail trade, followed by 7858 enterprises in manufacturing, 6464 in real estate, renting and business activities, 3809 in construction, 2463 in hotels and restaurant services, 2295 in transport, storage and communications and so on (*Estonian Statistics Monthly*, No. 1, 1997).

Looking at these numbers, we can see that Estonian private enterprises and foreign enterprises are dominating. But several of the domestic private firms are not active any longer. By the estimation of the Statistical Office approximately 40 000 enterprises were active in the middle of 1996, among them 11 000 private farms. If we work on the figure of 29 000 enterprises and assume that non-active enterprises are registered as private enterprises and those whose activity was classified under 'other', then the share of state-owned enterprises is 3.5 per cent, that of municipal enterprises 2.5 per cent, foreign enterprises 20.2 per cent and of Estonian private enterprises 73.8 per cent.[6] Considering that most foreign enterprises are private enterprises, the total percentage of private enterprises in the Estonian economy is around 94. This is of course a very preliminary estimation of the share of the private sector and could be used as a starting point for our analysis of the ownership structure of the economy.

If we compare the number of Estonian private and foreign companies with the number of privatized enterprises, then we can say that privatization had a very modest role in forming the private sector. There were altogether 27 260 acting Estonian private and foreign enterprises in Estonia. The number of enterprises sold in the process of small-scale privatization (in the framework of different laws) was 1342, and the number of contracts signed in the process of large-scale privatization was 452 until the end of 1996. So, we could say that 1794 private enterprises, or 6.6 per cent of all private enterprises were created directly as a result of privatization of state-owned or municipal enterprises. That figure clearly underestimates the role of privatization in creating the private sector. A large number of private firms were created for the privatization of some state-owned company. Managers or workers created a new private firm before privatization, which formally did not have any linkage to the state-owned company. On the basis of one such company several private units emerged, which competed with each other and outsiders in the privatization process. Several private firms that were not created for privatization could later participate in the auctions of equipment or buildings of some privatized company.

Another possible way of comparing the importance of privatization in creating the private sector is to evaluate investments made into fixed assets of enterprises. As an indirect parameter we could use here the volume of investment guarantees compared to investments into the private sector. By an estimation of the Statistical Office of Estonia, the amount of investments into fixed assets was 4.4 billion kroons in 1993, 6.8 billion kroons in 1994 and 8.8 billion kroons in 1995. Of them, 52 per cent was invested into Estonian private and foreign enterprises in 1993, 53 per cent in 1994 and 61 per cent in 1995 (*Statistical Yearbook of Estonia,* 1996; *Reealinvesteeringud*, 1994, 1995, 1996). On the basis of these figures, the total investments in fixed assets of Estonian private and foreign enterprises made up 11.3 billion kroons during the period 1993–95. Investment guarantees offered by new owners to companies privatized during the same period were 2.0 billion kroons. Investment guarantees are a very approximate estimation, but if we use this figure, it is possible to say that 18 per cent of the investments into these companies are due to privatization.

The share of investments made in connection with privatization might be even higher. The audit of 342 privatized enterprises made by the Estonian Privatization Agency during 1996 showed that the real investments in these companies were 1.564 billion kroons compared to investment guarantees of 0.796 billion kroons fixed in respective contracts (*Eesti erastamisagentuuri 1996 aata tegevusaruanne*, 1997). This means that the real investments, at least in that sample of enterprises, were two times as high as the guarantees. If we widen that figure on the total number of privatized enterprises, the share of investments due to privatization increases to 36 per cent level of investments into Estonian private and foreign enterprises.

Another possibility is to compare employment guarantees in privatized enterprises with employment in Estonian private and foreign companies. In 1995, the total labor force of different types of enterprises was 442 108 persons. Of them, 76.5 per cent or 338 212 persons worked in Estonian private and foreign enterprises (Statistical Office of Estonia). Employment guarantees amounted during 1993–95 to 42 502 jobs. On the basis of these figures, the share of privatization in creating jobs in Estonian private and foreign enterprises is 13 per cent. This figure is probably at least two times lower than the real influence of privatization, because employment guarantees were not required in the process of small-scale privatization.

Different figures indicate that, in a direct sense, privatization played a minor role in creating the private sector. However, the role of privatization was much higher in other terms. Privatization confirmed the political will of different governments of Estonia to create a market economy based on the private sector and that very clear political signal promoted activities of various domestic and foreign economic agents in introducing their private businesses.

4.4.3 Share of the Companies with Different Ownership Forms in Net Turnover and Exports

As we described above, privatization and the creation of the private sector were a very rapid process in Estonia. From the total net turnover, the share of the private sector was 48.7 per cent in 1992 and it grew to 68.9 per cent in 1994 and to 66.8 per cent in 1995. The high share of the private sector in 1992 is worth special notice. There are several reasons for such a high share. To begin with, as mentioned above, privatization, which gained full speed only in 1992, played a relatively modest role in quantitative terms in creating a private sector. First, the creation of new-type co-operatives (different from the old type in agriculture, kolkhozes) had started already in 1987 and after that the private sector began to grow. A large number of private enterprises emerged, especially in trade and the service sector. Secondly, most collective farms and state farms were in the process of reorganization already in 1992, which made the share of state and municipal ownership relatively low. Thirdly, there was also a reason related to statistics. As was mentioned above, since 1995 all state-owned enterprises that rented out their assets were qualified as private. This artificially increased the number of private enterprises, especially in 1992 and 1993. In the privatization process during 1992–95 most such enterprises were privatized, but as they were already classed as private enterprises, the increase of the private sector seemed in statistical terms more moderate than it actually was.

A notable increase occurred in foreign ownership, especially in 1995. It grew to 15.7 per cent of the total net turnover. The share of enterprises with foreign ownership was the highest in manufacturing with 23.6 per cent. During the following years the share of companies with foreign ownership increased, because several big enterprises were privatized to foreign investors. It should be said here that due to the applied statistical methods the role of foreign owners is diminished, because the company is qualified as a foreign company only if the foreign owners have at least 51 per cent of the shares, as mentioned above. However, there was a minor foreign ownership in several other enterprises. In some of them the foreign owners played a leading role having the largest proportion of shares, but less than 51 per cent (Table 4.5).

Though there are several problems that diminish the credibility of data on the ownership structure, it is possible to prove that the Estonian private sector had a dominant role in several branches (agriculture, fishing, wholesale and retail trade, hotel and restaurant services, real estate, renting and business activities, construction, and manufacturing). Basically this private ownership was accompanied by foreign ownership. State-owned and municipal enterprises were of very limited importance in these fields. On the other hand, in fields qualified as infrastructure (mining; power, gas and water supply; transport; storage and communications) privatization did not start until 1995 and the share of Estonian private and foreign investors increased in the process. Such a development was desired for several reasons, because these fields need large investments and as the privatization process improved foreign investors in particular made large investments in the Estonian economy.

As to the relationship between ownership and exports of the respective groups of enterprises, more comprehensive figures are available only starting from 1995, after the new statistical form was enacted. On the other hand, 1995 is a relatively good year for making such comparisons, because the influence of privatization in the establishment of the private sector became more evident only in this year. As was described above, in 1995 the peak of privatization in different fields, except infrastructure, was over and the ownership structure in the economy was stabilizing.

In different branches the share of exports is determined by very specific reasons. So, it is risky to speak about very clear tendencies, especially in connection with the ownership structure. However, there are some features which should be underlined. The figures in Table 4.6 show that when the average level of exports was 23.0 per cent of turnover, there were certain differences in the share of exports in certain groups of enterprises with different owners. The share of exports was the highest (33.0 per cent) in the enterprises belonging to foreign owners. These were followed by enterprises with state and municipal ownership (23.0 per cent) and enterprises in Estonian private ownership (15.4 per cent). The exports/GDP ratio, that also describes the openness of economy, stood at 51.1 per cent in 1995.

The relatively high share of exports in enterprises with foreign ownership is in accordance with evidences from other researches showing that foreign investors with larger available financial resources could manage to restructure the existing enterprises faster and make them competitive in foreign markets, or they established new companies in Estonia keeping in mind future exports (Purju, 1996, 1997; Terk and Pihlak, 1996). However, especially considering privatized enterprises, the reason could be that foreign investors purchased the state-owned enterprises in a more sound financial and technological state and were thus able to export more.

Table 4.5. The share of net turnover by ownership in different fields of economic activities

Branch	Net turnover (current prices, bn kr.)				State and municipal ownership (per cent)			
	92	93	94	95	92	93	94	95
Agriculture., forestry, hunting	1.1	2.2	2.7	3.5	23.1	12.5	6.2	3.0
Fishing	0.3	0.4	0.4	0.5	0	0	0	0
Mining	0.6	0.8	1.2	1.6	92.4	91.9	91.6	87.9
Manuf.	9.3	14.5	19.9	27.4	68.1	52.8	33.8	18.4
Electr., gas, water	2.0	3.2	4.6	6.0	93.2	91.0	80.1	75.5
Construction	1.9	3.8	5.1	8.3	23.2	17.1	14.2	4.3
Wholesale and retail trade	8.7	18.1	28.0	47.9	29.0	13.0	7.5	3.2
Hotels and restaurants	0.6	1.1	1.1	1.4	20.0	17.1	7.3	15.4
Transport, storage, commun.	3.5	7.1	9.8	11.4	66.7	59.8	41.3	46.0
Real estate, renting and business act.	0.8	1.8	2.5	4.5	27.0	28.8	27.0	23.5
Other services	0.4	1.2	1.1	1.5				
TOTAL	29.2	54.2	76.4	114	50.8	36.7	25.8	17.5

Branch	Estonian private ownership				Foreign ownership			
	92	93	94	95	92	93	94	95
Agriculture, forestry, hunting	76.8	86.4	90.9	85.7	0.1	1.1	2.9	11.2
Fishing	100.0	100.0	100.0	100.0	0	0	0	0
Mining	7.6	8.1	8.4	12.1	0	0	0	0
Manufacturing	31.7	45.2	59.6	58.0	0.2	2.0	6.6	23.6
Electr., gas, water	6.8	9.0	19.9	7.0	0	0	0	17.5
Construction	76.8	82.5	83.8	89.8	0	0.4	2.0	5.9
Wholesale and retail trade	69.9	83.3	84.7	80.8	1.2	3.7	7.8	16.0
Hotels and restaurants	80.0	82.6	91.8	75.3	0	0.3	0.9	9.4
Transport, storage, commun.	33.3	40.1	56.9	45.0	0	0.1	1.8	9.0
Real estate, renting and business act.	71.6	69.3	68.9	65.4	1.4	1.9	4.1	11.1
Other services								
TOTAL	48.7	61.2	68.9	66.8	0.5	1.9	5.3	15.7

Table 4.6. The share of exports in the net turnover in 1995

Branch	**Total in the field of activities**			**State and municipal ownership**		
	Net turnover (bn. kr.)	**Exp. (bn. kr.)**	**Share of exp. (per cent)**	**Net turnover (bn. kr.)**	**Exp. (bn. kr.)**	**Share of exp. %**
Agriculture, forestry, hunt.	3.509	0.721	20.5	0.110	0.005	3.5
Fishing	0.454	0.303	66.7			
Mining	1.579	0.106	6.7	1.388	0.021	1.6
Manufact.	27.438	10.161	37.0	5.051	1.426	28.2
Electricity, gas and water	5.958	0.264	4.4	4.496	0.257	5.7
Construction	8.338	1.044	12.5	0.354	0.102	29.0
Wholesale and retail trade	47.887	6.042	12.6	1.565	0.414	26.5
Hotels and restaurants	1.446	0.053	3.7	0.222	0.011	5.0
Transport, storage, communic.	11.369	7.032	61.9	5.256	2.794	53.2
Real estate, business serv.	4.460	0.446	10.0	1.050	0.004	0.4
Other services	1.686	0.147	8.7	0.460	0.011	2.6
TOTAL	114.1	26.3	23.0	19.9	5.5	27.6
Branch	**Estonian private ownership**			**Foreign ownership**		
Agric., forestry, hunt.	3.006	0.425	14.1	0.393	0.291	73.9
Fishing	0.454	0.303	66.7			
Mining	0.191	0.085	44.5			
Manufactur.	15.900	5.455	34.3	6.487	3.280	50.6
Electricity, gas and water	0.420	0.002	0.5	1.042	0.005	0.5
Construction	7.489	0.822	11.0	0.495	0.120	24.2
Wholesale and retail trade	38.679	4.393	11.4	7.642	1.236	16.2
Hotels and restaurants	1.088	0.040	3.7	0.136	0.002	1.5
Transport, storage, communic.	5.115	3.508	68.6	0.998	0.730	73.1
Real estate, business serv.	2.915	0.314	10.8	0.495	0.128	25.8
Other services	0.978	0.060	6.1	0.248	0.074	29.8
TOTAL	76.2	15.4	20.2	17.9	5.9	33.0

Source: Statistical Office of Estonia

Another reason for a higher share of exports in enterprises with foreign ownership is that very often the foreign owners had better and more reliable relationships with foreign wholesale and retail trade companies. Also, as exports cover subcontracting and other forms of international cooperation between enterprises, the additional explanation for the higher share of exports in those firms is that the respective Estonian enterprises were included in the technological chain with foreign companies and this increased their foreign supply. The higher share of exports of state-owned and municipal enterprises compared to Estonian private enterprises has branch-related explanations. Particularly in construction a large share of exports was given by joint ventures (mainly with Finnish private firms), where the Estonian state was formally the major shareholder and which offered services in Russia. In electricity, gas and water supply the higher share of exports of state-owned and municipal companies than of private firms could be explained by the fact that public companies had been predominating in offering respective goods and services. On the other hand, the relatively low level of Estonian private firms gives a critical signal about their readiness for international competition.

A comparison of the share of exports in various fields of activities reveals differences. The highest export share is in fishing, where only private firms (66.7 per cent) are listed. Next come transportation, storage and communications with a total share of exports of 61.9 per cent (state-owned and municipal companies having a 53.2 per cent share of exports, Estonian private companies 68.6 per cent and foreign companies 73.1 per cent), followed by manufacturing with a total of 37.0 per cent (groups of companies by ownership respectively 28.2, 34.3 and 50.6 per cent).

4.4.4 Ownership and Employment

There are more complete figures about employment in enterprises with different ownership since 1995. A comparison of the structure of employment by fields of activities with the respective structure of the GDP (Table 4.2) gives some idea about the efficiency of the use of labor (see Table 4.7). Technological peculiarities related to labor or capital of certain branches have importance here (compare, for example, agriculture or trade with electricity and so on). Nevertheless, it is remarkable that in 1995 manufacturing had a two times higher share in employment (30.3 per cent) than in the GDP (14.9 per cent). There is also a relatively big difference in construction (respectively 8.4 per cent and 4.7 per cent), but there the so-called 'envelope wages' could play a more important role.[7] In other branches the differences are not so huge.

Table 4.7. Employment by field of activities in enterprises with different ownership structure in 1995

Field of activities	Total employment		State and municipal ownership		Estonian private ownership		Foreign ownership	
	Persons	per cent	Persons	per cent	Persons	per cent	Persons	per cent
Agricult., forestry, hunting	36 673	8.3	1 698	4.7	34 004	92.7	971	2.6
Fishing	4 110.0	0.9			4 110	100.0		
Mining	11 386	2.6	9 709	85.3	1 677	14.7		
Manufact.	134 111	30.3	21 341	15.9	95 474	71.2	17 296	12.9
Electricity gas, water supply	17 514	4.0	14 809	84.6	2 108	12.0	597	3.4
Construction	36 989	8.4	2 719	7.3	33 136	89.6	1 134	3.1
Wholesale and retail trade	90 878	20.6	3 754	4.1	80 606	88.7	6 518	7.2
Hotels and restaurants	12 895	2.9	1 138	8.8	10 841	84.1	916	2.9
Transport, storage, communication	50 779	11.5	32 481	64.0	16 874	33.2	1 424	2.8
Real estate, business services	30 234	6.8	10 036	33.1	18 921	62.6	1 277	4.2
Other services	16 539	3.7	6 161	37.2	9706	58.7	672	4.1
TOTAL	442 108	100	103 846	23.5	307 457	69.5	30 805	7.0

Source: Statistical Office of Estonia

If we compare the net turnover and employment in different fields of activities by ownership, there is a striking difference between enterprises with foreign ownership on the one hand and the Estonian private and state and municipal enterprises on the other. Enterprises of foreign ownership had 2.6 per cent of the labor force in agriculture, forestry and hunting and 11.2 per cent of net turnover; in manufacturing the respective figures were 12.9 and 23.6 per cent; in electricity, gas and water supply 3.4 and 17.5 per cent; in construction 3.4 and 5.9 per cent; in wholesale and retail trade 7.2 and 16.0 per cent; in hotels and restaurants 2.9 and 9.4 per cent; in transport, storage and communication 2.8 and 9.0 per cent; in real estate, renting and business services 4.2 and 11.1 per cent. In total enterprises with foreign ownership hired 7.0 per cent of the labor and produced 15.7 per cent of the total net turnover. This means that on average such an enterprise had a 2.3 times higher performance per employee than Estonian private enterprises and a 3.0 times higher performance than Estonian state-owned and municipal enterprises in 1995 (Table 4.8).

Between state and municipal enterprises on the one hand, and Estonian private enterprises on the other, differences are smaller: the average turnover of private enterprises was 1.3 times higher. There are several branches where the net turnover in state and municipal enterprises is higher than in the Estonian private sector: in manufacturing the state and municipal enterprises hired 15.9 per cent of the labor and gave 18.4 per cent of the turnover, for the Estonian private sector the respective figures were 71.2 and 58.0 per cent. The average turnover per employee is 1.4 times higher in the first group of enterprises. The situation was similar in electricity, gas and water supply, where the state and municipal enterprises had 84.6 per cent of the labor and gave 80.1 per cent of the turnover, while for the Estonian private sector the respective figures were 12.0 and 7.0. The average turnover per employee was 1.5 times higher in the first group of enterprises. In this field the economies of scale, concentrated into the public sector, determined the result.

There are several fields where the private sector is more efficient. In construction the state and municipal enterprises had 7.3 per cent of the labor and 4.3 per cent of the turnover, the Estonian private enterprises had 89.6 per cent of the labor and 89.8 per cent of the turnover (the private sector is 1.7 times more efficient); in transport, storage and communications the respective figures for the state and municipal enterprises were 64.0 and 46.0 per cent and for the Estonian private sector 33.2 and 45.0 per cent (the private sector is 1.9 times more efficient) (see Table 4.8).

There are several reasons for such tendencies. The fact that most Estonian enterprises have relatively outdated technologies and equipment could be one reason for low efficiency. It is also important how the private enterprises were created. The economic results were better when new enterprises started with the required capital for investments. On the other hand, in manufacturing the privatization process itself deteriorated the economic situation of enterprises, especially if they had to wait for a contract in the list of privatized enterprises. One conclusion that can be drawn from the figures above is that Estonian enterprises have to work hard. As long as wages are relatively low, this will not be a burden. However, with increasing wage levels excessive labor will be a very critical factor.

Table 4.8. Net turnover per employee in different fields of activities in 1995

Branch	Total in the field of activities			State and municipal ownership		
	Net turnover (bn. kr.)	No. of employed	Turnov./ employee ('000 kr)	Net turnover (bn. kr.)	No. of employed	Turnov./ employee ('000 kr.)
Agric., forestry	3.509	36 673	95.7	0.110	1 698	64.8
Fishing	0.454	4 110	110.5			
Mining	1.579	11 386	138.6	1.388	9 709	143.0
Manufacturing	27.438	134 111	204.6	5.051	21 341	236.7
Electricity, gas, water	5.958	17 514	340.2	4.496	14 809	303.6
Construct.	8.338	36 989	225.4	0.354	2 719	130.2
Trade	47.887	90 878	526.9	1.565	3 754	416.9
Tourism	1.446	12 895	112.1	0.222	1 138	195.0
Transport, storage, comunic.	11.369	50 779	223.9	5.256	32 481	161.8
Real est., business serv.	4.460	30 234	147.5	1.050	10 036	104.6
Other serv.	1.686	16 539	101.9	0.460	6 161	74.7
TOTAL	114.1	442 108	258.1	19.9	103 846	191.6

Branch	Estonian private ownership			Foreign ownership		
Agric., forestry	3.006	34 004	88.4	0.393	971	404.7
Fishing	0.454	4 110	110.5			
Mining	0.191	1677	113.9			
Manufacturing	15.900	95 474	166.5	6.487	17 296	375.1
Electricity, gas, water	0.420	2 108	199.2	1.042	597	1745.4
Construct.	7.489	33 136	226.0	0.495	1 134	436.5
Trade	38.679	80 606	479.9	7.642	6 518	1172.4
Tourism	1.088	10 841	100.4	0.136	916	148.5
Transport, storage, comm.	5.115	16 874	303.1	0.998	1 424	700.8
Real est., business services	2.915	18 921	154.1	0.495	1 277	387.6
Other serv.	0.978	9 706	100.8	0.248	672	369.0
TOTAL	76.2	307 457	247.8	17.9	30 805	581.1

4.4.5 Selected Data about Companies with Different Ownership and with More than 100 Employees

Our incomplete data set makes evaluation of changes in employment during the examined time period rather difficult. There is a sample of 462 enterprises with more than 100 employees (and at least that number of persons were employed during the whole period) with data about employment for every year of the period 1993–96 present. Also no changes occurred in their dominant ownership during that period. In 1995 a total of 136 445 persons were employed, this means that the enterprises in the sample cover approximately 30 per cent of the total employment in entrepreneurship.

Total employment decreased by 6 per cent from 1993 to 1996 in that sample of enterprises. The basic reason is general economic decline until 1994, the economy only started to grow in 1995 (Table 4.7, see also Table 4.1). Compared to the decline of output the decrease of labor is rather modest. On the other hand, when the economy started to grow the modest decrease of employment continued. The decrease in employment was relatively bigger in municipal enterprises. There are several reasons for that, basically the decline was due to activities given over to private units (in communal services, for example). Employment increased every year in the group of enterprises with foreign ownership which first is related to their output increase. Our analysis based on the ownership structure in different fields of activities showed that in enterprises with foreign ownership the net turnover per employee was much higher than in the enterprises with Estonian owners. That gives us the basis to say that probably the increase of employment was connected with the increase of output and widening activities of foreign enterprises in Estonia. So, the sector of foreign enterprises grew during the whole period. However, as it was relatively small, the positive results of that group of enterprises had a modest influence on the economy as a whole.

4.4.6 Financial Indicators

Financial indicators were applied to analyse different aspects of the economic activities of enterprises and their performance (liquidity, turnover of assets, sources of finances and return of assets). Seven basic indicators were used: (1) current ratio = current assets : current liabilities; (2) total assets turnover = sales : average total assets; (3) liabilities of long-term capital = long-term debt : (long-term debt + equity); (4) equity ratio = equity : total assets; (5) net profit margin = net profit after tax : sales; (6) return on total assets = net profit after tax : average total assets; (7) return on equity = net profit after tax : average total equity. Data are available on all enterprises for the period 1992–95, but for enterprises with different ownership more detailed data exist only for 1995, partly due to a change of methodology used by the Statistical Office for grouping enterprises by ownership.

The indicators describing liquidity and return (current ratio, net profit margin, return on total assets and return on equity) deteriorated every year. Total assets turnover deteriorated in 1993 but then started to improve. The equity-ratio and liabilities of long-term capital show that enterprises have been using more credits from year to year. The stabilized economic situation, additional resources of banks, decreasing levels of inflation and interest rates have been important for these changes (Tables 4.9–4.11).

Indicators describing returns on assets and equity, and net profit margin have been deteriorating partly because enterprises had various possibilities to diminish their profits to pay less taxes. This seems to be one reason why the total profits of Estonian enterprises and the sum of corporate income tax have been decreasing from year to year. Another reason for that tendency could be an increase of input costs (especially wages). As Estonia had a fixed foreign exchange rate of DEM 1 = EEK 8 from 1992 until summer 1997 and the CPI and other price indexes increased several times during that period, the increase of the cost of domestic inputs was also notable and decreased profitability of exports. This time series of financial indicators describes general tendencies and makes it possible to take them into account also in evaluating the financial situation of enterprises with different ownership. Data in Table 4.11 describe the financial situation of enterprises that presented their balance sheets and other reports. When evaluating these figures we should be careful, because the field of activities-related factors have been rather influential in forming several indicators. For example, manufacturing, agriculture and fishing as a branch made losses in 1995.

Financial indicators of enterprises in mining, electricity, gas and water supply were influenced by the increase in state-regulated prices of their production and so on The following tendencies deserve special emphasis: (1) Enterprises in state and municipal ownership used much less loan capital than foreign or Estonian private enterprises. (2) For Estonian private and foreign enterprises, return on equity was higher than for state and municipal enterprises. There are two possible explanations for this. First, private owners use their own money and that is the reason for the higher return. Second, the share capital of state-owned and municipal enterprises has very often been calculated on the basis of balance sheet figures, and it is not really the money the owners have put into the company. (3) Returns on total assets for all types of companies differ less, because the Estonian private and foreign enterprises use more loan capital. (4) SOEs as a whole made losses in 1995. (5) Current ratios that express liquidity of assets differ less than other indicators, being the lowest in Estonian private enterprises. (6) The turnover of total assets was the fastest in the Estonian private enterprises, however, here the fields of activities are of great importance. Since among SOEs electricity, gas and water supply, a branch with a low turnover of assets, has a rather big share, the low turnover figure for SOEs is determined by the branch structure of enterprises. On the other hand, in the wholesale and retail trade, a branch with a fast turnover of assets, private Estonian enterprises are predominating.

Table 4.9. Changes in employment (end of respective year)

Ownership group	**Number of enterprises**	**1993**	**1994**	**1995**	**1996**
State ownership	68	32 567	29 793	29 994	31 584
Municipal ownership	20	8 852	7 960	7 914	7 501
Estonian private ownership	359	100 960	99 675	95 318	94 043
Foreign ownership	15	2 729	3 164	3 219	3 227
TOTAL	462	145 108	140 592	136 445	136 355

Table 4.10. Key financial ratios for companies between 1992 and 1995

Year	**Current ratio (times)**	**Total assets turn-over (times)**	**Liabili-ties of long term capital (times)**	**Equity ratio (times)**	**Net profit margin (per cent)**	**Return on total assets (per cent)**	**Return on equity (per cent)**
1992	1.48	2.19	0.13	0.49	7.7	16.8	31.3
1993	1.33	1.42	0.14	0.59	1.7	2.4	3.9
1994	1.27	1.65	0.19	0.54	1.0	1.7	3.0
1995	1.17	1.86	0.25	0.46	0.6	1.1	2.3

Table 4.11. Key financial ratios for companies by ownership in 1995

Ownership	**Cur-rent ratio (times)**	**Total assets/ turn-over (times)**	**Liabili-ties of long term capital (times)**	**Equity ratio (times)**	**Net profit margin (per cent)**	**Return on total assets (per cent)**	**Return on equity (per cent)**
State	1.30	1.11	0.15	0.66	–0.6	–0.6	–0.9
Municipal	1.26	0.76	0.11	0.72	1.1	0.8	1.1
Estonian private ownership	1.13	2.50	0.29	0.37	0.7	1.8	4.7
Foreign ownership	1.20	1.55	0.37	0.38	1.0	1.6	4.1

Source of Tables 4.9–4.11: Statistical Office of Estonia

4.5 ANALYSIS OF THE COMPANIES PRIVATIZED BETWEEN 1993 AND 1995

4.5.1 The Data

The list of privatized enterprises was offered by the Estonian Privatization Agency. Detailed information on output, employment and financial indicators for that set of enterprises was ordered for this report from the Estonian Register of Enterprises. The sample included privatized enterprises with more than 100 employees at the end of 1996. The data were taken from the balance sheets and profit and loss statements of enterprises. The respective documents were available for 1994 and 1995, but as the balance sheet of a certain year also includes figures for the previous year, the data are for the period 1993–95.

Unfortunately, the reporting discipline is rather low among Estonian enterprises and not all privatized enterprises had presented their balance sheets for every year of the period. The list of privatized enterprises with more than 100 employees consisted of 112 units, the balance sheets of 1994 been presented to the Estonian Enterprise Register by 93 enterprises of that set, and the balance sheets of 1995 by 70 enterprises. The balance sheets for 1994 and 1995 had been presented by 62 enterprises, which make up our sample of future analysis. Here we should say that one reason for slack discipline of reporting in 1995 was a new form of balance sheet which was introduced together with the new Law on Accounting enacted from 1 January, 1995. Figures on employment were available for the period of 1993–96 and were presented for every year of the period by 83 enterprises (privatized in 1993–95 and with employees over 100).

We used the following classification of new owners in our analysis: (1) employees of the privatized enterprise (management buy-out in most of the cases), (2) other Estonian enterprise in the same field, (3) foreign enterprise in the same field, and (4) outside financial investors. The list of enterprises in every group was offered by the vice director of the Estonian Privatization Agency, Kostel Gerndorf. In several cases questions emerged about the type of owner. For example, in some cases different groups competed for the deal and very often the investors who won asked the competing group of managers of the privatized enterprise to share the ownership. In this case the distribution of shares between the new owners was the basis for classification, or in other words, the dominant owner determined the type of ownership.

4.5.2 The Composition of Ownership

As was mentioned before, there were altogether 112 enterprises with more than 100 employees privatized during the period 1993–95, and for these years financial indicators were available for 62 enterprises. Table 4.12 contains figures on the number of the new owners whose financial indicators we analysed. The figures show that nearly half of the enterprises were privatized to employees of the same enterprise. The figures for enterprises privatized to other Estonian enterprise in the same field and to outside financial investors are very close. What is remarkable is that financial investors started to participate in privatization only in 1994. This is in accordance with the development of the Estonian financial sector. Namely, 1994 is the first year when Estonian private investment companies accumulated enough resources and guarantees to be supported by banks and to be active agents in buying enterprises. A very limited number of enterprises had been bought by foreign enterprises in the same field in our sample. So, we have to be rather careful in generalizing figures on that group of enterprises.

4.5.3 Changes of Employment in Privatized Companies

Data on the changes in employment are presented in Table 4.13. As was mentioned above, the sample of enterprises on which employment figures are available is bigger than the sample of enterprises with financial reports. However, general tendencies in employment can be described on the basis of that information. The total employment decreased by 25.8 per cent in this sample of enterprises from 1993 to 1996. It is noteworthy that a rather similar decrease occurred before and after privatization (look, for example, at the figures for 1993, 1994, 1995 and 1996 for enterprises privatized in 1994 or 1995). Also interesting is that the general dynamics of economy (decrease in 1994 and growth in 1995 and 1996) did not have a considerable influence on employment in this sample of enterprises.

4.5.4 Changes of Net Turnover and Profits in Privatized Companies

Turnover figures are influenced by the general price increase: the CPI was 41.7 per cent in 1994 and 28.9 per cent in 1995, the PPI of industrial output was respectively 36.2 and 25.6 per cent (see, *Statistical Yearbook of Estonia 1996,* pp. 147, 156). Included are enterprises privatized in 1993 and 1994. The economic results were better in 1993 and deteriorated later (Table 4.14). The economic results during the whole period were better for enterprises privatized in 1993. There are several reasons for that. A specialist from the

Estonian Privatization Agency commented that as a rule enterprises privatized at the beginning of that process were in better shape.

Table 4.12. Number of enterprises by types of new owners

Year of privatization	Employees of the privatized enterprise	Other Estonian enterprise in the same field	Foreign enterprise in the same field	Outside financial investors	Other	TOTAL
1993	8	1	3	0	0	12
1994	12	10	0	7	1	30
1995	9	4	1	6	0	20
TOTAL	29	15	4	13	1	62

Source: Estonian Privatization Agency

Table 4.13. Changes of employment in companies privatized in different years

Year of privatization	Number of enterprises	Number of employees			
		1993	1994	1995	1996
1993	16	5 431	4 912	4 559	3 927
1994	33	13 980	11 490	12 373	11 700
1995	34	16 960	14 332	12 610	11 307
TOTAL	83	36 371	30 734	29 542	26 994

Source: Estonian Register of Enterprises

Table 4.14. Changes in total net turnover and profits of privatized enterprises by the year of privatization

Year of privatization	1994/1993 (times, in current prices)[a]		1995/1994 (times, in current prices)[a]	
	Net turnover	Net profit after tax	Net turnover	Net profit after tax
1993	2.02	2.23 (50)	1.26	1.20 (50)
1994	1.25	1.20 (70)	1.24	0.80 (50)
1995	1.25	1.25 (37)[b]	1.10	–1.65 (44)[c]

Notes

a In brackets the percentage of enterprises increasing the profit or decreasing the losses.

b Total sum of profits increased due to substantial decrease of losses of one big textile company. The total sum of profits of all other enterprises decreased 1.15 times.

c The net loss of 1995 was 1.65 times larger than the net profit of 1994.

If enterprises had no major economic problems, it was easier and faster to make all the necessary procedures to prepare the enterprise for the process and it was listed earlier. It was easier also to find investors interested in purchasing such enterprises. Moreover, if an enterprise remained in the list of privatized enterprises for a long time, deterioration of its economic solvency was fast. This was a rather logical development, especially if managers were interested in participating in privatization. Lower quality and bigger liabilities of the enterprise decreased its purchasing price. We may also ask whether privatization itself improved the economic results of enterprises concerned. A very preliminary answer can be given by comparing the economic results for different years and linking this analysis with the year of privatization, which was done in Table 4.15.

For enterprises privatized in 1993 the turnover and profit figures increased in 1994 and 1995, that is, after privatization. For enterprises privatized in 1994, the turnover and profit increased in the year of privatization. In 1995, that is, a year after privatization, the turnover continued increasing, but the total profit of those enterprises decreased and the number of enterprises increasing their profit (or decreasing losses) was equal to the number of enterprises whose profit decreased (or losses increased). This suggests that privatization itself did not influence the economic results. That is, turning state-owned enterprises into private ownership did not exert any short-run influence on economic results. The influence of the duration of the privatization process (that is, how long the enterprise was in the list of privatized units) and who was the new owner was much stronger. Of course, our sample is very limited and the time period is too short to draw any final conclusions.

The indicators on economic performance calculated per employee also show that the general tendency was the decline of efficiency while the influence of privatization as such is more limited. The indicators in Table 4.16 describe the relationship between the type of new owner and economic performance. The time period for comparisons is very short and only preliminary comments can be given. It is also necessary to take into account that during the period we are discussing a general diminishing of growth rates and deteriorating of profitability of enterprises occurred. The economic results were better in enterprises that had been privatized to foreign enterprises in the same field. Of course, the number of such enterprises in our sample is very limited (three), but that result is in accordance with evidences from other parts of our analysis showing that enterprises in foreign ownership had relatively good economic results. Net profits increased both in enterprises privatized to the employees of the same enterprise and to the other firms in the same field.

The share of enterprises that increased their net profit after tax was higher among enterprises of the three first types of new owners in 1994 than in

1995. There were only 36 per cent of such enterprises in 1995. The share of those increasing their profit was higher in 1995 than in 1994 only among the enterprises privatized to outside financial investors (respectively 80 and 60 per cent). On the basis of these figures it is possible to draw a conclusion that availability of financial resources has been critical for privatized enterprises (both foreign enterprises and outside financial investors were in a better situation in that sense compared to Estonian industrialists). In the case of foreign enterprises in the same field better access to export markets could be one more reason supporting better economic results.

Table 4.15. Changes in net turnover and profits per employee of privatized companies by year of privatization

Year of privatization	1994/1993 (times, in current prices)		1995/1994 (times, in current prices)	
	Net turnover	Net profit after tax	Net turnover	Net profit after tax
1993	2.40	2.53	1.25	1.31
1994	1.70	1.47	1.39	0.90
1995	1.46	1.47	1.24	–2.25

Source: Authors' calculations

Table 4.16. Changes in net turnover and profits of privatized companies by types of new owners

Type of new owner	1994/1993 (times, in current prices)*		1995/1994 (times, in current prices)*	
	Net turnover	Net profit after tax	Net turnover	Net profit after tax
Employees of privatized enterprise	1.40	0.99 (65)	1.19	0.74 (41)
Other Estonian enterprises in the same field	1.08	1.34 (66)	1.20	0.58 (36)
Foreign enterprise in the same field	2.19	3.54 (100)	1.34	1.18 (67)
Outside financial investors	1.63	1.19 (60)	1.32	1.13 (80)

Note: * In brackets the percentage of enterprises increasing the profit or decreasing the losses.

Source: Authors' calculations

4.5.5 Financial Indicators of the Privatized Companies

The same set of financial indicators was used here as in the previous section (Table 4.17). The economic results of enterprises privatized in 1993 were better than those privatized in 1994 and in 1995. If for Estonian enterprises in general the decrease of return on total assets and equity was characteristic in 1995, then the respective indicators for enterprises privatized in 1993 improved in 1995. The returns on total assets and equity of enterprises privatized in 1994 were also higher than the Estonian average in 1994 and 1995. On the other hand, the same indicators for enterprises privatized in 1995 were lower. The reason for that is the long period of waiting for privatization, when the future of the enterprise was unclear, a minimum amount of investments was made and it was very hard to get credits for such enterprises. There may be also interdependence: privatization was prolonged because the financial situation of a certain firm was already very weak before it was included in the process of privatization. In addition to the indicators of return on total assets and equity, the relatively good shape of privatized enterprises compared to the Estonian average is proved by liquidity indicators (current ratio). However, the relatively high figure for enterprises privatized in 1995 could be somewhat misleading because it is first of all related to the low level of loan capital (Table 4.17).

Table 4.17. Key financial indicators for enterprises between 1993 and 1995

Year of privatization	Current ratio		Total assets per turnover		Liabilities of long-term capital		Equity ratio	
	94	95	94	95	94	95	94	95
1993	1.73	1.59	1.69	1.86	0.36	0.29	0.46	0.47
1994	1.52	1.31	2.36	2.15	0.19	0.25	0.54	0.47
1995	1.56	1.69	1.51	1.43	0.08	0.08	0.68	0.72

Year of privatization	Net profit margin (per cent)		Return on total assets (per cent)		Return on equity (per cent)	
	94	95	94	95	94	95
1993	6.8	7.3	11.6	14.3	25.2	28.7
1994	4.1	2.7	6.6	5.8	13.6	11.4
1995	1.2	−1.8	1.8	−2.6	2.6	−3.7

The current ratio of all enterprises has declined, but the situation is relatively good in enterprises privatized to a foreign enterprise in the same field, and weaker in enterprises privatized to other Estonian units in same field. The net profit margin, return on total assets and equity indicators have all been higher in privatized to foreign enterprises cases. These figures declined generally for all types of enterprises. The exception was the return on equity in firms privatized to outside investors, which was higher in 1995 than in 1994. These indicators also support the conclusion that enterprises with foreign ownership have been relatively successful (Table 4.18).

Table 4.18. Key financial ratios for companies by ownership in 1995

Ownership	Current ratio		Total assets per turnover		Liabilities of long-term capital	
	94	95	94	95	94	95
Employees	1.75	1.53	1.11	1.87	0.34	0.31
Other Estonian firms, same field	1.26	1.03	3.18	2.47	0.34	0.24
Foreign firms, same field	2.36	1.73	2.48	1.92	0.35	0.28
Financial investors	1.65	1.33	1.88	1.42	0.07	0.18

Ownership	Equity ratio		Net profit margin		Return on total assets		Return on equity	
	94	95	94	95	94	95	94	95
Employees	0.43	0.43	4.2	2.6	7.3	4.9	14.0	11.3
Other Estonian firms, same field	0.38	0.42	2.4	1.2	4.8	2.9	11.4	3.6
Foreign firms, same field	0.55	0.55	10.5	8.8	20.5	17.0	37.4	30.7
Financial investors	0.62	0.56	6.5	5.6	8.1	7.9	11.2	13.7

Source: Authors' calculations

4.6 RESULTS OF THE CASE STUDIES

4.6.1 Data and Methodology

Representatives of a total of 18 enterprises were interviewed using a standard questionnaire worked out in the framework of the current research. The enterprises were classified into groups according to the following indicators: (1) industry (clothing, mechanical engineering and electrical machinery); (2) country of owners (foreign or domestic ownership); (3) relationships of owners with economic activities (managers, another enterprise in the same field or investment institution). Also, we included in the sample enterprises of different sizes (medium-sized, that is, with less than 500 employees, and large enterprises, with 500 and more employees) and enterprises from Tallinn and other towns of Estonia. All enterprises in the sample had been formed as a result of privatization or had some linkage with that process (for example, ELCOTEQ Tallinn is a Finnish company, which bought a unit of a privatized company). (A list of enterprises included into the sample is presented in Table 4.19.)

Table 4.19. Companies in the sample

Company	Industry	Ownership	Size	Geographical location
Elina	Clothing	Foreign enterprise in the same field	Medium	Tallinn
Klementi	Clothing	Domestic, outside investor	Large	Tallinn
Linette	Clothing	Domestic, managers	Medium	Tallinn
Marat	Clothing	Domestic, managers	Large	Tallinn
Sangar	Clothing	Domestic, managers	Large	Tartu
Sulev	Clothing	Domestic, managers	Medium	Haapsalu
Tallinna Moemaja	Clothing	Domestic, outside investor	Medium	Tallinn
Valko	Clothing	Domestic, outside investor	Medium	Valga
Virulane	Clothing	Domestic, managers	Medium	Rakvere
Eesti Talleks	Mechanical engineering	Domestic, outside investor	Large	Tallinn
ELCOTEQ Tallinn	Electronic equipment	Foreign, outside investor	Medium	Tallinn
Estel	Electrical machinery	Domestic, managers	Medium	Tallinn
Ilmarine	Mechanical engineering	Foreign, enterprise in the same field	Medium	Tallinn
Norma	Mechanical engineering	Domestic, outside investor	Large	Tallinn
Pioneer	Mechanical engineering	Domestic, managers	Medium	Tallinn
Rõngu Tehas	Electrical machinery	Domestic, managers	Medium	Rõngu
Tarkon	Electronic equipment	Foreign, enterprise in the same field	Medium	Tartu
Tondi Elektroonika	Electrical machinery	Domestic, managers	Large	Tallinn

Most Estonian enterprises were privatized before 1996. So, a very limited number of state-owned enterprises still exist. There are some large enterprises in manufacturing, which produced mainly for military purpose in Soviet time, and in power engineering and transportation that still belong to the state. Privatization projects have been prepared and are under discussion also for those enterprises. Therefore, there is no group of enterprises with state ownership that could be used for comparative analysis of different ownership types. In the framework of this research we concentrated on the analysis of the influence of different types of private owners on corporate governance of enterprises. The different topics are ordered in our analysis in accordance with the respective grouping of questions in the questionnaire.

4.6.2 General Information about the Companies in the Sample

Most of the companies (except ELCOTEQ Tallinn) were established several decades before the transition to market economy began in Estonia. Some of them had even historical predecessors in the Republic of Estonia before World War II. In the 1970s and 1980s they expanded their output. Their production was orientated basically to the other republics of the Soviet Union, which was a big market of mainly low-quality goods. However, some enterprises managed to get resources for more modern Western equipment and technologies from the state budget. As Estonia's role in the all-Union division of labor was, partly, the production of substitutes of Western consumer goods, several clothing enterprises in our sample (Klementi, Marat, Sangar and so on), had modern and new equipment by the end of the 1980s. Also several enterprises in mechanical engineering and electrical machinery had equipment bought for hard currency. Sometimes the reason was that the production of those enterprises was unique for other firms in the Soviet Union (for example, fixtures, powder metallurgy products, aluminum and plastic casting by Pioneer). Several other enterprises made products for military purposes (Tarkon, Tondi Elektroonika).

Enterprises in the sample underwent major changes in 1992–95. The majority of enterprises had several problems in the privatization process. There are cases where enterprises were privatized, went bankrupt and started afterwards with a new owner (Pioneer). There is an example where the competition between two groups from the same company competing in the privatization process had very critical results for the company and later caused deep structural changes due to lost markets (Eesti Talleks).

Approximately half of the enterprises were privatized to managers and employees of the same company. The companies that now had an investor outside Estonia took a critical path after privatization and Estonian commercial banks supporting them are now important shareholders (Klementi,

Valko, Eesti Talleks). There are a few cases where the dominant owner is a foreign company in the same field of activities. The outside investor of ELCOTEQ Tallinn the sole case in our sample. This case is in some sense unique and is used here basically for making comparisons with other ownership types in corporate governance. It could also be considered as a greenfield investment. The Finnish company ELCOTEQ purchased a department of a privatized Estonian company only in order to use its relatively new building in Tallinn. All technical equipment was brought from Finland and a completely new company was built up in Tallinn. There are 12 enterprises from Tallinn, from the area of fastest economic growth. Southern Estonia, a critical area for the economy, is represented by four enterprises (two from Tartu, one firm from Valga and another from Rõngu). Western Estonia is represented by one firm from Haapsalu and eastern Estonia by one firm from Rakvere.

4.6.3 Reorientation of Business

Most Estonian large companies have always exported the bulk of their output. Before political and economic changes very often 80–90 per cent of their production was sold in different Soviet republics. A very deep economic shock in 1991–92 with high inflation and payment crises in the Soviet Union forced a very deep change in the foreign trade pattern. A rather typical situation is that in 1992 the company exported two-thirds of the production to Russia, and though in 1994 the share of exports was the same, two-thirds of products went to the West.

The price of that significant reorientation of trade was, for most of the enterprises (in clothing, but also in mechanical engineering), a switch from final products to subcontracting. The net profit margin, return on total assets and equity depend for most enterprises on the type of market rather than on other factors. Because of more complicated access to Western markets with final products, the profitability of those markets decreased. Of course, some enterprises also managed to increase the share and total amount of final products sold in these markets (Klementi), but this increase was rather modest compared to the increase of input costs in Estonia.

The most profitable markets for several enterprises have been Russia and other CIS markets. However, Estonia has certain specific problems in trading with Russia. These are the so-called double customs tariffs. Estonian enterprises have to pay double tariffs because Estonia does not have the MFN status in trade with Russia and those countries cannot have access to that market with preferential tariffs. For some Estonian traditional export articles (food products, furniture) these tariffs are high, up to 60 per cent of the value of the product. Several Estonian enterprises are selling their products via

Finnish companies or have introduced subsidiaries or joint ventures in Russia to avoid the problem. In 1997, several enterprises are expecting that the state should solve that problem and Russia is seen as a profitable market for Estonian companies.

The share of the domestic market has also increased due to the increasing purchasing power of local people. Though the Estonian domestic market is very tiny, with 1.5 million inhabitants, clothing firms in particular were claiming that the profitability of that market was improving because they can sell final products here. At the same time they mentioned that the share of the domestic market would never be very big (for most companies, the maximum share of the domestic market could be up to 20 per cent). Big risks are connected to the Russian market. The first problem is related to payments. Customers in Russia did not pay or paid for products after a big delay. Partly the reason was that they did not have enough financial resources. There were also cases where the partner just disappeared. One enterprise in the sample (Sulev) will probably go bankrupt because it has not received payment for one big shipment of goods. There have also been problems with Russian banks and transfer of payments.[8]

In business orientation, one extreme situation (with the predominance of the Eastern markets) was substituted by another extreme situation (a very clear cut with Eastern markets and a switch toward Western markets). Now enterprises seem to examine their risks and profits offered by different markets more carefully. There are enterprises that managed to balance these risks so that they have some big clients in the West, but earn the largest share of their incomes in the East (Norma). Also the share of other Baltic states, Latvia and Lithuania, has been increasing. One reason for that was the intermediary role of some enterprises in re-exporting products to the Russian market (Latvia and Lithuania have the MFN status in trade with Russia and therefore their customs tariffs are lower).

For most enterprises profitability was determined by the proportion of subcontracting and final products (in clothing and mechanical engineering). In clothing, the share of own models (final products) varied between 10 and 30 per cent. The percentage was bigger in smaller companies, which sold more of their products in the domestic market. Since 1992 the profitability, in general, has decreased. The rapidly increasing input costs (especially wages and energy costs) were the main reason for that. Due to the fixed exchange rate, the loss of profitability was larger in Western markets, and smaller in domestic and Eastern markets. The only way to avoid the influence of deteriorating economic conditions was to increase final products.

The dominating price model for the clothing industry was cost-based pricing. Enterprises also followed the prices of their competitors and made some adjustments on that basis. There are some differences in certain enterprises in mechanical engineering, which had better opportunities for determining the prices of their products (Norma, Ilmarine). Some enterprises also used lower prices to gain a market share in a new market, but that was more often a forced solution without very clear prospects for success.

Enterprises increased the number of their customers in general, but the goal was not so much the number of customers itself in one market, but a larger number of customers in different markets and in that way cutting risks.

The capacity utilization declined very rapidly at the beginning of the 1990s (in some enterprises 20–30 per cent of capacities were utilized). On the other hand, the utilization rate itself does not tell us too much, because the main reason for changes of that indicator in most of the enterprises (especially in mechanical engineering and electrical machinery) was the low quality of output with such equipment. The enterprises had to restructure their production capacities and an increase in the capacity utilization rate was achieved in later years, partly thanks to more intensive use of equipment, partly also due to reducing the equipment by selling it off (very often as scrap metal).

4.6.4 Personnel Management and Financial Management – Changes in the Cost Structure of Enterprises

Employment decreased in most enterprises very rapidly until 1994. After that the general tendency changed and rather different strategies in employing people were adopted. There are enterprises in which the number of employees still continued to decrease (Pioneer, Estel, Tarkon). In most enterprises, the number of employees stabilized after 1994, and there were smaller fluctuations in both directions. A very different example is ELCOTEQ Tallinn, which started to operate in 1993 with 200 employees and increased employment by the end of 1994 to 400, in 1996 to 800, in the middle of 1997 to 1650.

An increase of production personnel at the expense of managers and other office staff was typical in most enterprises. The increase of wages followed the CPI in general. In 1996 the wages were 50 per cent higher than in 1994 and 2.5–3 times higher than in 1992. Enterprises with Estonian ownership financed the dominating part of the production, investments and exports from their own resources until recently. Only in 1995 and 1996 did commercial banks become more interested in crediting enterprises. A large share of enterprises faced financial problems due to these restrictions; for several enterprises the situation was somewhat critical in 1993–94.

Different ways have been used to overcome the lack of resources. Subcontracting had positive features for production and investments, because the foreign partner credited the purchase of the required materials and provided equipment, technologies or models. Several companies (especially in clothing) introduced permanent relationships with certain banks to get loans to buy materials or to credit exports. There are some cases where the price of such support was part of the shares of the respective company.

Several funds have been introduced to credit exports, to offer export guarantees and to support participation of enterprises at fairs and exhibitions (the Estonian Export Credit Fund) or to support different projects (Small Enterprises Support Fund, Rural Enterprises Support Fund). The resources of those funds have been so limited that in our sample there were only two cases mentioned where the enterprises received some support.

After economic transformation, the main ways to raise additional funding were new loans, increasing revenues from sales, rental revenues and sale of equipment not required or other assets. The shares of two companies, Norma and Klementi, have been on the list of Tallinn Stock Exchange since 1996 and 1997, respectively. Norma raised a large amount of money from the stock exchange, because its shares with a nominal value of 10 kroons were traded at around 90 kroons in July 1997. The company had introduced a joint venture in India in 1995 (50 per cent of the shares belong to Norma) and a subsidiary in Russia. The Norma Group, a financial institution and a major shareholder of Norma (formed by managers of Norma) was established in 1996. In July 1997 that institution sold 12 per cent of the shares of Norma to Western investors. This is an example of how an investment group grew up from a successful manufacturing enterprise. The group started to invest into buildings belonging to Norma and to develop that investment as a real estate project. Klementi, a clothing company, was not so successful on the stock exchange (its shares with a face value of 10 kroons were traded at the level of 19 kroons in July), but owners of that company also introduced a holding company. One Estonian commercial bank became the strategic owner of the company. Eesti Talleks is a company in our sample which raised certain financial resources from rental payments.

The rapid increase in wages and energy costs was mentioned by most enterprises. The reason for wage increases was mainly the macroeconomic environment. A minor role was played by the more intensive use of labor in the production process. In the structure of wages, the faster increase in the wages of managers and salespersons was a characteristic feature. The rapid growth in the price of electricity and heating was the main reason for the increase of energy costs. The price of these goods has been regulated by the state and, particularly for social reasons, has been kept rather low. On the other hand, the increase of costs in the energy sector and a need for investments forced high price increases.

The increase of material costs was modest and for several enterprises has been caused by the change from lower quality inputs to more expensive materials. There were some unexpected increases of purchased materials in the Eastern market. Some suppliers of these materials have announced that they have had to increase their prices due to increasing costs, although a contract for a certain period including the prices of respective materials had been signed (Sulev). At the same level was the increase in the price of various services bought from outside the enterprise. The costs related to general expenses also increased. Financial costs decreased in the sense that credits started to be cheaper due to decreasing interest rates. For several enterprises the possibility of paying half of the purchase price of privatized property in vouchers significantly decreased the outcomes related to that liability.

4.6.5 Investment Patterns and Motives

Investment patterns of enterprises depend on ownership type rather than on other characteristics of economic behavior. A typical feature for enterprises privatized to their managers was lack of financial resources. Part of that problem was created by the purchasing price they had to pay to the Estonian Privatization Agency. As was mentioned above, that burden has diminished due to the state economic policy during the last years. Another reason for the shortage of financial resources has been the limited resources of banks and their rather careful credit policy. That problem has been aggravated by the limited guarantees the enterprises could offer to banks (which was partly related to the very slow process of land privatization and the creation of real estate units eligible for mortgage and other guarantees related to property). An improvement in financial conditions began in 1995 and by 1997 the capital market had widened considerably.[9] Enterprises with foreign ownership received credits more widely and for lower interest rates from foreign banks, but also from Estonian commercial banks. One very good example is the ELCOTEQ Tallinn, widening production in Tallinn due to big investments.

The lack of financial resources has been one reason why in several privatized companies some shares were sold to foreign investors. There are also some examples where the managers who initially owned the company had to sell it to a foreign partner (very often to the partner ordering subcontracting) or to Estonian banks. As was mentioned above, for enterprises subcontracting to foreign companies, investments were very often made in kind, in the form of used machinery.

Considering the investments after economic transformation started, we have to say that their structure varied. In most companies that agreed to disclose those figures, investments into capital equipment and new technology dominated. During the first years of transformation and in enterprises of Estonian ownership, those investments practically crowded out all other vestments. Only very limited investments were made into training, marketing and quality control (altogether less than 10 per cent of the investments in most of those companies). In 1995 and 1996, the structure of investments changed. The share of investments into capital equipment and new technology decreased and investments into training and plant maintenance gained importance. The development of the Tallinn Stock Exchange introduced a new goal for investments: shares and bonds. As the price of most shares listed on the stock exchange increased very rapidly, such investments started to be popular among enterprises.

In companies with foreign ownership the structure of investments differed. Investments into capital equipment and new technology had the largest share, but training, plant maintenance and marketing were more important than for companies with Estonian ownership. So we could say that in recent years the structure of investments in companies with Estonian ownership started to be closer to the structure of companies with foreign ownership. There is one peculiarity in those comparisons: a large number of managers of even very small Estonian companies prefer expensive luxury Western cars (Mercedes-Benz, BMW and Audi have been in high demand).

The most important incentive for investments into capital equipment was that without those investments it was impossible to follow the quality requirements of more advanced markets. In clothing, but also in mechanical engineering, another reason for those investments was better utilization of materials. As labor costs have been increasing during the past years, enterprises have felt a stronger need to economize labor as one special incentive for investments. A special purpose for investments was to get certification of ISO standards. In our sample, ELCOTEQ Tallinn had ISO 9000 and Norma had ISO 9002 certificates.

The average age of capital equipment was rather high. The companies where as much as half of the capital equipment was older than 10 years have been considered as relatively modern. The age structure of capital equipment improved from 1992 to 1996. At the same time, it is rather hard to say, and our studies did not provide exact evidence, how important new investments were in that process, and what was the share of liquidated and sold assets.

4.6.6 Results and Tasks Ahead: the Role of Corporate Governance

For the majority of enterprises in our sample, the most important achievement was a switch from Eastern markets to Western markets and adjustment to those rapidly changing circumstances. In particular clothing enterprises saw the main task for the future as being an increase of their own models in their output. Marketing and design are very critical issues in the process of achieving that goal and need big investments.

Several enterprises in mechanical engineering and electrical machinery were very interested in following special quality standards and applying for respective certificates (ISO standards, but also specific standards proving that certain critical operations are at the required level). The enterprises were worried about increasing costs. That is one factor that forces several changes in the structure of production and requires additional investments. Most companies were planning substantial investments in the near future. Another strategic problem was related to future markets. We could say on the basis of our sample that there were two groups of enterprises. One group was in some sense disappointed by the results on Western markets and was following with great interest developments in Russia. They have also been interested in introducing contacts with other regions of the former Soviet Union (first of all Ukraine). The other group of enterprises planned to widen their market area in Western countries. Norma was the sole example which managed best in balancing the two types of markets producing, nevertheless, a major part of its production for the Russian market.

Leaders of most companies in our sample represent a mixture of managers and owners. In Estonian companies owned by managers, but also in companies with an outside owner, the management of the company is involved in ownership problems. Only in recent years in some enterprises with a higher organizational culture have these functions started to be separated, and people have to choose their roles in the executive or on the side of the owners. The situation was much clearer in companies with foreign ownership.

The members of the Supervisory Board represent the owners. Very often there is a representative of one commercial bank (not only in the case where the bank is a shareholder, but also when the bank is servicing that enterprise). The members of the Board are basically representatives of different management structures. The members of the Supervisory Board are elected by the general meeting of shareholders. That meeting also determines the salaries and other benefits of the members of the Supervisory Board. The Supervisory Board approves the salaries and other benefits of executives.

The law leaves two opportunities for selecting the members of the Board. They could be elected by the general meeting of shareholders or determined by the Supervisory Board. Companies have to determine in their statute which method they use for creating the Board. The strategy of enterprises was mainly worked out by the managers (board). Sometimes business-plan type documents were ordered or certain projects were analysed with representatives of commercial banks.

4.7 CONCLUSIONS

Estonian privatization had some specific preconditions in comparison with other East and Central European countries: significant migration from other regions of the Soviet Union after World War II, which affected the claims for restitution and added specific features to the privatization of the housing sector; lack of its own currency before June 1992 when the Estonian kroon was introduced, and a significant share of state ownership in the housing sector. That is why Estonian privatization had its own characteristic features: the important role of compensation and return of property in kind, that had been nationalized in the 1940s, the issue of national capital bonds and compensation securities into the scheme of privatization securities; the realization of very different property for privatization securities such as dwelling rooms, land and shares of privatized enterprises. The serious criticism of selling state-owned property for cash before the kroon was introduced was a consequence of these specific features.

Economic aspects dominated in the privatization of enterprises, the main features being: the selling of enterprises for cash (especially after 1992); no privileges for employees of privatized enterprises; limited role of privatization securities and finding a core investor for privatized enterprise before some part of the shares was sold for privatization securities (from 452 contracts made on selling enterprises in 33 cases 5–49 per cent of shares were reserved for selling for privatization securities).

An auction type mechanism dominated in small-scale privatization and the highest offered price has been the main criterion for contracts. The total purchasing price, investment and employment guarantees and environmental requirements have been the main factors in making decisions about the new owners in large-scale privatization. Very often the new owner had to also take over the liabilities of the privatized enterprise. A comparison of the privatization contracts of different years shows that the importance of the purchase price and the liabilities taken over has been diminishing and that of investment guarantees increasing in the contracts. One reason for this is that privatization started with more successful enterprises. The financial situation of enterprises staying for a longer time in the list of enterprises to be privatized deteriorated due to lack of really interested owners and this had its influence on the purchase price of the enterprise (ten enterprises have been sold for a symbolic price of one kroon). On the other hand, the future competitiveness of enterprises became more important in privatization policy.

Foreign investors had an important role in privatization. The new owners with foreign participation paid 16 per cent of the total purchasing price in 1993–96, but offered 30.6 per cent of all investment guarantees. An important advantage was given to the domestic owners during that period: they had the right to pay by installments and the period of paying was up to ten years. All other conditions have been equal for different buyers.

There were altogether 27 260 Estonian private and foreign enterprises operating in Estonia. The number of enterprises sold in the process of small-scale privatization (in the framework of different laws) was 1342, and the number of contracts signed in the process of large-scale privatization was 452 until the end of 1996. So we could say that 1794 private enterprises, or 6.6 per cent of all private enterprises, were created directly as a result of privatization of state-owned or municipal enterprises. This figure clearly underestimates the role of privatization in creating the private sector. A large number of private firms were created for the privatization of a state-owned company. Managers or workers created a new private firm before privatization, which formally did not have any linkage to the state-owned company. On the basis of one such company several private units emerged, which competed with each other and outsiders in the privatization process. Several private firms that were not created for privatization could later participate in the auctions of equipment or buildings of some privatized company.

As an indirect parameter we could use here the volume of investment guarantees compared to investments in the private sector. By an estimation of the Statistical Office of Estonia, the amount of investments into fixed assets was 4.4 billion kroons in 1993, 6.8 billion kroons in 1994 and 8.8 billion kroons in 1995. Of these, 52 per cent was invested into Estonian private and foreign enterprises in 1993, 53 per cent in 1994 and 61 per cent in 1995. On the basis of these figures, the total investments into fixed assets of Estonian private and foreign enterprises were 11.3 billion kroons during the period 1993–95. Investment guarantees offered by new owners to companies privatized during the same period were 2.0 billion kroons. Investment guarantees are a very approximate estimation, but if we use this figure it is possible to say that 18 per cent of the investments into these companies are due to privatization.

The share of investments made in connection with privatization might be even higher. The audit of 342 privatized enterprises made by the Estonian Privatization Agency during 1996 showed that the real investments in these companies were 1.564 billion kroons compared to investment guarantees of 0.796 billion kroons fixed in respective contracts. This means that the real investments, at least in that sample of enterprises, were two times as high as the guarantees. If we widen that figure to the total number of privatized enterprises, the share of investments due to privatization increases to 36 per cent of the level of investments into Estonian private and foreign enterprises.

In 1995, the total labor force of different types of enterprises was 442 108 persons. Of them, 76.5 per cent or 338 212 persons worked in Estonian private and foreign enterprises. Employment guarantees amounted during

1993–95 to 42 502 jobs. On the basis of these figures, the share of privatization in creating jobs in Estonian private and foreign enterprises is 13 per cent. This figure is probably at least two times lower than the real influence of privatization, because employment guarantees were not required in the process of small-scale privatization. Different data indicate that, in a direct sense, privatization played a minor role in creating the private sector. However, the role of privatization was much higher in other terms. Privatization confirmed the political will of different governments of Estonia to create a market economy based on the private sector and that very clear political signal promoted activities of various domestic and foreign economic agents in introducing their private businesses.

Private enterprises produced 66.8 per cent of net turnover in 1995. Additionally 15.5 per cent was produced by foreign enterprises, basically in private hands. The share of exports was 33 per cent of turnover in foreign enterprises and 20.2 per cent in Estonian enterprises. The last group of enterprises hired 69.5 per cent and foreign enterprises hired 7.0 per cent of the labor force. The per capita turnover was 258.1 thousand kroons in Estonian private enterprises and 581.1 kroons in foreign enterprises. The efficiency of enterprises diminished during the period of 1992–95 in all groups of enterprises. The net profit margin was 7.7 per cent in 1992, 1.7 per cent in 1993, 1.0 per cent in 1994 and 0.6 per cent in 1995. The return on total assets was respectively 16.8 per cent, 2.4 per cent, 1.7 per cent and 1.4 per cent. The return on equity had the same tendency: it was respectively 31.3 per cent, 3.9 per cent, 3.0 per cent and 2.3 per cent.

Foreign enterprises had a higher net profit margin than Estonian private enterprises in 1995 – respectively 1.0 per cent and 0.7 per cent. The return on total assets and equity was at the same time higher in Estonian private enterprises. The respective figures were 1.8 per cent and 4.7 per cent for Estonian private firms and 1.6 per cent and 4.1 per cent for foreign firms. Those financial indicators were lower in state and municipal enterprises. The return on total assets and the return on equity were negative in state enterprises – respectively –0.6 per cent and –0.9 per cent. Municipal enterprises had those parameters with a positive sign but lower than in Estonian private or foreign companies. The reason for this difference was partly the different branch structure in every group of enterprises classified by ownership. The state was still dominating in power engineering, where the prices were regulated by state administration, and this was the reason for modest economic results during those years.

A comparison of enterprises privatized between 1992 and 1995 shows that the economic results depend significantly on the type of new owner. The profit margin in enterprises privatized to the employees of the same enterprise was 2.6 per cent, privatized to other Estonian enterprises in the same field 1.2 per cent, privatized to a foreign company in the same field 8.8 per cent and privatized to a financial group 5.6 per cent. The return on total assets was in those groups of enterprises respectively 4.9 per cent, 2.9 per cent, 17.0 per cent and 7.9 per cent. The return on equity was respectively 11.3 per cent, 3.6 per cent, 30.7 per cent and 13.7 per cent. One explanation for these figures is that the foreign owners and the financial investors used the assets of enterprises more effectively. Another explanation is related to better access to markets in the case of foreign enterprises in the same field.

It is impossible to say on the basis of aggregate financial indicators that the two more efficient groups of enterprises had better access to loan capital, because the liabilities of long-term capital indicators were very close in enterprises privatized to their employees, in enterprises privatized to other Estonian companies and in enterprises privatized to foreign enterprises in the same field. On the other hand, the structure of liabilities was rather different, as case studies showed. The Estonian enterprises could pay the purchase price by installments to the Estonian Privatization Agency. The liabilities of companies privatized to the financial groups were much smaller than of other groups of owners.

The economic results of privatized enterprises seem to be better than the aggregate indicators of all Estonian private enterprises or foreign enterprises. That result could be caused partly by a statistical mistake because the analysed set was based on those enterprises whose balance sheets had been presented to the Statistical Office every year during the period. Most enterprises cut employment, especially during the period of economic decline and deep changes in foreign trade markets (1992–94). In 1995 and especially later, several enterprises started to increase employment. Sometimes it is hard to estimate the change in employment, because the company was split in the privatization process into several units. Enterprises significantly changed their production pattern. A major change was related to increasing subcontracting to Western companies. Since 1992 the profitability, in general, has decreased. The rapidly increasing input costs (especially wages and energy costs) were the main reason for that. The only way to avoid the influence of deteriorating economic conditions was to increase final products. The dominating price model for the clothing industry was cost-based pricing. Enterprises also followed the prices of their competitors and made some adjustments on that basis.

Companies sold their products either on Western markets, or on the Russian and Ukrainian markets. There was only one example of a company which managed to balancing the two types of markets producing, nevertheless, a major part of its production for the Russian market. The most profitable markets for several enterprises have been Russia and other CIS markets. However, Estonia has certain specific problems in trading with Russia. These are the so-called double customs tariffs. Estonian enterprises have to pay double tariffs because Estonia does not have the MFN status in trade with Russia and thus cannot have access to that market with preferential tariffs. Enterprises with foreign ownership received more credits and for lower interest rates from foreign banks, but also from Estonian commercial banks.

The structure of management was much clearer in companies with foreign ownership than in domestic private companies. Though the role of privatization has been formally rather modest in creating the private sector in Estonian economy, the applied privatization model made possible rather rapid privatization in industry, trade and the service sector. Some privatized assets have been sold to enterprises which have been outside the privatization scheme. The positive side of the privatization scheme was a fast change of ownership structure in economy and the clarification of ownership relations.

NOTES

1. The Estonian situation is different in this sense from developments in Hungary or Poland, where certain elements of the market regulation have been introduced already in the 1970s and 1980s. Though in the former Soviet Union a more centralized economic system existed, the Estonian economists watched very carefully what happened in Hungary. Particularly important have been the publications of Hungarian economists, from which some articles and books were also translated into Estonian. Ideas and publications of János Kornai have been very influential.
2. A privatization scheme – that in several aspects resembles the Treuhand-type privatization – has been applied in Estonia (together with consultants, know-how and funding from Treuhand).
3. The importance of privatizing SOEs and launching completely new private firms is a specific field for economic research. The role of the first phenomenon has been relatively modest in Estonia. However, we will concentrate here on the analysis of privatization in the more narrow meaning (that is, passing state enterprises into private hands). See the different definitions of privatization in the first chapter of this book by Dallago.
4. A more detailed discussion of the monetary reform is presented in Hansson (1995), Lainela and Sutela (1994), Saavalainen (1995) and Sepp (1995).
5. When parts of the state-owned property are sold for cash, 45 per cent of the received sum will go to the Compensation Fund, 25 per cent to the Government's Reserve Fund, 10 per cent to the Labor Education Fund and 10 per cent to the Pension Fund capital. When municipal property is sold then 25 per cent will go the Compensation Fund and 75 per cent to the local government. When land is sold, 50 per cent of the earnings will go to the Compensation Fund, 20 per cent to the local government and 20 per cent to the Government's Reserve Fund.
6. There is a dominating view in the Estonian Enterprises Register that mainly the private firms generated for short time activities or even for one business operation create the largest number of non-active entities still registered. It was not regulated very strictly how to abolish the firm's registration after liquidation or ending business activities. Since 1997 the new Business Law demands to follow more exactly determined procedures.
7. To avoid personal and especially social tax, some enterprises prefer to pay officially the minimum wage and add to their employees unofficially the so-called 'envelopes' with additional payment.

8. The business newspaper *Äripäev* reported that correspondent accounts of all Estonian commercial banks in Sankt Peterburg were blocked by local tax authorities from 31 July, 1997. The purpose was to force banks to pay the tax arrears of their clients, that is Russian enterprises, from their transfers to the correspondent accounts of Estonian banks (*Äripäev*, 6 August, 1997). The bank accounts were released ten days later.
9. If the GDP in real terms increased by 4.3 per cent in 1995 and by 4.5 per cent in 1996 and the GDP in current prices grew by 37.8 per cent and 26.3 per cent respectively, then the total amount of long-term credits (longer than one year) offered by commercial banks increased by 60 per cent in 1995 and by 90 per cent in 1996. Among them credits to enterprises increased by 55 and by 68 per cent respectively (*Eesti Panga bülletään*, 1997/2).

REFERENCES

Äripäev (1995), 'Erastamisprogramm valitsusse. Küsimustele vastab majandusminister Andres Lipstok', 13 December (The Privatization Program in Government. The Interview with the Minister of Economic Affairs).

Äripäev (1997a), 'Eesti pankade kontod on Peterburis blokeeritud', 6 August (Accounts of Estonian Banks are Blocked in Sankt Petersburg).

Äripäev (1997b), 'Hüvitusfond loobub lisaintresside maksmisest', 30 April (The Compensation Fund is Giving up Paying Extra Interest Rates).

Eesti ettevõtete finantsnäitajad 1995 I (1996), Tallinn, Eesti Statistikaamet (Financial Indicators of Estonian Enterprises).

Eesti erastamisagentuuri 1996 aata tegevusaruanne (1997), Tallinn. (The Report of the Estonian Privatization Agency 1996).

Eesti maksebilanss 1996. aastal (1997), *'Eesti Panga bülletään'*, No. 3, p. 22 (The Balance of Payments of Estonia in 1996).

Eesti Sónumid (1995), 'Müüki tuleb uus kogus Hüvitusfondi obligatsioone', 13 September (A New Amount of Bonds of the Compensation Fund is Sold).

Erastamisväärtpaberite väljaandmine ja kasutamine (1997), Eesti Vabariigi Rahandusministeerium. (Emission and usage of privatization securities. Ministry of Finance of the Republic of Estonia).

Estonian Statistics Monthly (1996), No. 12. Tallinn, Statistical Office of Estonia.

Estonian Statistics Monthly (1997), No. 2. Tallinn, Statistical Office of Estonia.

Frydman, R., Rapaczynski, A. and Earle, J. (1993), *The Privatization Process in Russia, Ukraine and the Baltic States,* 'Estonia', London: Central European University Press, pp. 130–93.

Hansson, Ardo (1995), 'Macroeconomic Stabilization in the Baltic States', Stockholm Institute of East European Economies, Working Paper No. 108.

Hänni, Liia (1993), 'Erastamisväärtpaberite kasutamise alused. Seletuskiri', *Rahva Hääl*, 5.aprill (The Concept for Using Privatization Securities. An Explanotary Letter Rahva Hääl, 5 April).

Klein, Alar and Tali, Veiko (1995), 'The Process of Ownership Reform and Privatization', in Lugus, Olev (ed.), *Transforming the Estonian Economy*, Tallinn: Estonian Institute of Economics, pp.140–68.

Lainela, Seija and Sutela, Pekka (1994), *The Baltic Economies in Transition,* Helsinki: Bank of Finland.

Purju, Alari (1996), 'Foreign Trade of Estonia: Factors Supporting Integration', Stockholm Institute of East European Economies, Working Paper No. 113.

Purju, Alari (1997), 'Estonia', in: János Gács (ed.), *Trade Growth in Transition Economies: Export Impediments for Central and Eastern Europe,* Aldershot, UK and Brookfield, US: Edward Elgar, pp. 61–86.

Reaalinvesteeringud 1993 (1994), Tallinn, Statistical Office of Estonia.

Reaalinvesteeringud 4/94 (1995), Tallinn, Statistical Office of Estonia.

Reaalinvesteeringud 4/95 (1996), Tallinn, Statistical Office of Estonia

Saavalainen, Tapio (1995), 'Stabilization in the Baltic Countries: A Comparative Analysis', IMF Working Paper 95–44, April.

Sepp, Urmas (1995), 'Estonia's Transition to a Market Economy 1995', *Review of Economies in Transition*, Bank of Finland, No. 5.

Statistical Yearbook of Estonia (1996), Tallinn, Statistical Office of Estonia.

Terk, Erik and Pihlak, Ülle (1996), 'Privatized Enterprises in Estonia: What Has Become of Them?', *The Baltic Review*, **10** (Summer), 23–24, 30–31.

5. Company Restructuring after Privatization in Hungary between 1988 and 1997

Iván Major, Cristiano Vezzoni and Andrea Szalavetz *

5.1 INTRODUCTION: ANALYTICAL FRAMEWORK

The formerly socialist economies of the Central and East European (CEE) countries suffered from inherent inefficiencies and the decay of the command economies was built into their economic systems. Consequently, the *raison d'être* of the transition process to a market economy based on private ownership has been that by accomplishing the economic transformation, the CEE countries will create an economy whose *allocative efficiency* on the macro level and its *productive efficiency* on the micro level will be significantly higher than what could be witnessed during the communist era. Instead of observing and comparing facts, many analysts are adrift on waves of disillusionment or euphoria. Disillusionment is widespread among those 'evolutionists' who are convinced that the CEE countries are heading nowhere or toward a special blend of 'state capitalism' that is loaded with massive corruption and with inequality between the poor and the rich (for example, Stark, 1992 and Murrell, 1992). On the other hand, a group of well-known scholars – who usually have acted as policy advisers to the governments of one or more countries in the region – triumphantly announce that 'the transformation is basically over' in CEE. These analysts point to the quantitative results of financial stabilization and privatization of the CEE countries and they also emphasize that after a short period of 'transformation recession', economic growth had already started in many of the formerly socialist

* Iván Major: Sections 5.1–5.6, and 5.8 and 5.10, Cristiano Vezzoni: Section 5.7, Andrea Szalavetz: Section 5.9. Mihály Laki conducted two case studies, which were utilized by Andrea Szalavetz in section 5.9.

economies in the mid-1990s (see, for example, Lipton and Sachs, 1990, Blanchard et al., 1991 and Aslund, 1994).

In our analysis we try to avoid both extremes. Notably, we do not share the view that privatization in CEE is nothing more than 'recombining' the state-owned property, as David Stark has formulated it. Nor do we believe that by adopting the prescribed measures of a radical price and trade liberalization, and by selling off or distributing more than 50 per cent of the state-owned property, the CEE countries have already arrived at the safe harbor of market capitalism. Our approach was constrained to the microeconomic and institutional aspects of the transformation. In our study we shall narrow down the scope of the analysis to what we believe is the main question of the economic transformation: has privatization of the state-owned property resulted in market-driven economic behavior and ultimately, in a higher level of productive efficiency of the companies in the CEE countries? The above question is complex enough in itself. Namely, it contains several sub-questions:

(1) Is privatization a *sufficient* condition for the companies' higher profitability and efficiency?

(2) Beside increasing the level of productive efficiency, can privatization bring about a complete change in the companies' financial behavior? Namely, will privatization result in the emergence of the *effective* (or hard)[1] budget constraint of the companies?

(3) Are there additional factors, beside privatization, that strongly influence the companies' adjustment to the new economic conditions of the CEE countries?

(4) Which are the main driving forces and the principal forms of company restructuring in CEE?

The first and last parts of this chapter – written by Iván Major (sections 5.1–5.6, and sections 5.9–5.10) – discuss the restructuring process as it has been reflected by the companies' balance sheets. Section 5.10 sums up the main conclusions. Section 5.7 by Cristiano Vezzoni is a multivariate analysis of the factors of the Hungarian companies' economic performance. Section 5.8 by Andrea Szalavetz is a summary of findings of the case studies, conducted at seventeen Hungarian companies.

In the balance sheet analysis we used two large samples of companies. First, we analysed the economic performance of all companies with double-entry book-keeping that operated in Hungary in the period of 1988–96. (So far, 1996 is the last year for which we have had company balance sheets data.) The group of these companies cannot be regarded as a standard sample, for their number exploded between 1988 and 1996. The reasons for the explosion were that many of the formerly state-owned enterprises (SOEs) were split up into dozens of smaller, legally and economically independent units, such as, for example, limited liability companies or joint stock companies. In addition, a great number of new, mostly private companies have been created via green field investments.

The second group of companies that was used in the analysis is a subsample of the larger sample discussed above. Notably, we analysed the change in economic performance of all those companies that belonged to one of the state privatization agencies.[2] The number of these companies – the companies that had been or which are going to be privatized fully or in part – was not the same for the years 1988–96 either, but it varied within a fairly narrow margin. The second sample of companies seems to be more adequate for the purpose of our research than the first one, because we attempted to outline the impact of privatization on the companies' economic performance. Nevertheless, the analysis of the first group is also useful since it makes feasible to compare the economic indicators of privatized, but formerly state-owned enterprises and those of the new-born private companies.

The structure of this chapter is as follows. In the second section we briefly describe the main institutions, the turning points and the actual results of the Hungarian privatization process. In the third section we present the database and outline the indicators and statistical methods that were used in assessing the companies' economic performance and structural change in different groups of companies. In the fourth section we shall outline the economic performance of the companies by branches and by regions. The fifth section discusses the companies' performance according to their ownership structure. The sixth section discusses the driving forces of the investment and export activity of the different company groups. The seventh section compares the performance of the state-owned enterprises (SOEs) and the private companies by using econometric methods. The eighth section sums up the main findings of the company case studies. The ninth section offers an explanation for the companies' low profitability and efficiency by analysing the *cost structure* of the different company groups. In the last section we sum up the main conclusions of the analysis.

5.2 PRIVATIZATION IN HUNGARY: TURNING POINTS AND RESULTS

The Hungarian privatization, its starting conditions, its institutional set-up, the initial principles and practical methods as well as the actual results have been extensively discussed in the literature.[3] Consequently, there is no need for a lengthy description of the Hungarian privatization process. By mid-1990, when the first democratically elected government assumed office, the basic institutions of a market economy and private ownership were in place in Hungary. The country had a liberalized price system and foreign trade regime, a two-tier banking system with an autonomous central bank and a dozen commercial banks, and a Western type personal income tax and value added tax system. In addition, the Hungarian Parliament adopted a legal act on foreign direct investment and profit repatriation in 1988, and the country had a currency that was *de facto* convertible on the current account transactions. The Commercial Code of 1875 was revitalized and upgraded in 1988 which provided the legal framework for establishing different kinds of private companies. The so-called 'Act on Company Transformation' set the stage for the corporatization of the SOEs in 1989. The State Property Agency (SPA) was established in early 1990 in order to guide and monitor the privatization process.

The Hungarian privatization process can be described as successive waves of centralization and decentralization of the privatization decisions. At the beginning the new Hungarian government and its agent, the SPA, intended to centralize all privatization decisions and SPA strove for actually administering every single privatization deal. However, it turned out very soon that the SPA was not capable of selling hundreds of medium- and large-sized companies and thousands of small shops and other businesses. Then in 1991, a wave of decentralization was initiated by the government that lasted until mid-1992. Actually, smaller and medium-sized companies got the right to search for a buyer with the assistance of a privatization adviser whom the companies had to select from the 'Register of Advisers' of the SPA. This period, then later the second half of 1995, can be considered as the most successful chapters of the Hungarian privatization process.

In 1992, the right-wing governing parties became dissatisfied with the speed of privatization and also with the composition of the new private owners. These parties believed that the share of foreign owners has grown too large in Hungary and they wanted to favor the Hungarian private investors instead. The government adopted a new economic strategy that advocated a massive decentralization of the privatization decision making. The new program argued that both the acceleration and the redirection of privatization toward domestic investors require a 'strong central hand'. As a part of this turn a new state agency, the State Assets Management Holding Ltd (SAMH) was established and the largest and most valuable 163 state-owned companies were transferred to the portfolio of the new agency. But despite all the rhetoric almost nothing happened in privatization until late 1993, when the SAMH and the government sold 30.2 per cent of the shares of the Hungarian

Telecommunications Company Ltd to a German–American consortium for $US 875 million. This sale – which was considered the largest of its kind throughout CEE by the Western governments and media – signaled a new turn in Hungarian privatization. But with the national elections of 1994 approaching, the former government acted as a lame duck and there was no continuation of privatization after the promising start.

The socialist-liberal government that was elected in mid-1994 and stepped down in mid-1998, launched an ambitious program of privatization very soon after its inauguration. Namely, it promised that it would submit a comprehensive Privatization Act to the parliament within weeks and most importantly, it would decentralize privatization decision making and finish the privatization process within two years. However, it took almost a year for the Parliament to adopt the Act on Privatization. Then, the two privatization agencies, the SPA and the SAMH, were merged into a single organization, the State Privatization and Asset Management Ltd (SPAM). But until November 1995 almost nothing happened in the field of privatization.

Then in an incredible rush, the government sold a minority share of the electricity distribution companies, some of the power plants, the Hungarian Oil Company Ltd and the National Savings Bank, and a majority share of the gas distribution companies and Budapest Bank, one of the largest commercial banks, and another 37 per cent of the shares of the Hungarian Telecommunications Company Ltd by late December 1995. The total value of these sales exceeded $4 bn out of which amount about $3.2 bn was paid by foreign investors in cash. Then in 1996, privatization slowed down again and SPAM has struggled with the problem of how to sell the 'leftover' of the state-owned property. It was not even clear for the SPAM or for the government what the realistic value of that 'leftover' was. We could witness a less robust acceleration of privatization in 1997 than that of late 1995. However, a few large state-owned enterprises from the vehicle and machinery industries have been privatized in this year. Moreover, the privatization of the Hungarian commercial banks was completed. Finally, 27 per cent of the shares of the Hungarian Telecommunications Company (HTC) was introduced in the Budapest and in the New York Stock Exchange. The HTC was the first Central and East European company whose shares have been traded on the New York Stock Exchange.

All in all, the Hungarian government privatized a sizable amount of the remaining state-owned property that was worth approximately $2.5 bn. But by mid-1997 the SPAM and the privatization minister were much more occupied with how to reorganize the agency after the privatization process was concluded than with actually selling the remaining state-owned assets. The share of the private sector increased to about 70 per cent in GDP production and employment by 1997. But we must keep in mind that privatization only affected 20 per cent of total productive assets in Hungary. The expansion of the private sector was much more fueled by the birth of new private businesses than by genuine privatization.

When privatization on a mass scale started in Hungary in 1990, SPA had 1857 SOEs in its portfolio. The actual total book value of the state-owned assets amounted to HUF 2600 bn.[4] In addition, there existed about 12 000 small businesses – retail stores, service units, restaurants, and so on – which were auctioned off, by the rules of a separate legal act of 1990. By 31 December 1995, 661 companies belonged to the State Privatization and Asset Management Ltd (ÁPV Rt., or SPAM), the sole privatization agency that had been born from the merger of the SPA and the SAMH in May 1995. Out of these 661 companies, 363 were owned in majority by SPAM, while the agency has held a minority share of the remaining 298 companies. The book value of the state-owned property amounted to HUF 1190 bn in current prices. Hence, more than 46 per cent of the former SOEs was fully privatized, about 20 per cent was liquidated and 34 per cent remained for future privatization. Measuring the scope of privatization in asset values, about 38 per cent of the state-owned assets was turned into private hands, about 8 per cent of the assets was subject to liquidation, and another 40 per cent of the assets remained state-owned.

A careful observer would notice that another 14 per cent of the assets is missing from the equation. This is due to the profit losses that incurred in the companies between 1990 and 1997. These losses reduced the companies' total asset value. However, if we measure the total value of the state-owned and the privatized or liquidated assets in US dollar terms, the picture is astonishing. Namely, the initial value of the state-owned assets that belonged to the privatization agencies amounted to $41 bn in 1990, using the actual average exchange rate between HUF and $US for 1990. By the end of 1995, the value of the remaining state-owned assets dropped to $9 bn in current $US, that is, to 21.9 per cent of the initial value.[5] It would imply that almost 80 per cent of the state-owned assets was either sold or liquidated between 1990 and early 1996. However, this share seems to be unrealistic if we take into account the size of the state-owned property still to be sold or 'managed'. But using the same exchange rate, that is, the average 1995 exchange rate between the $US and the HUF, which was HUF 132,2 per $US 1, for the 1990 asset value as well, we shall get a more realistic picture. Thus, the total value of the state-owned assets amounted to approximately $20 bn in 1990 (in 1995 $US terms) and it declined to $9 bn by the end of 1995. Consequently, the share of the privatized and liquidated state-owned assets would add up to 55 per cent and another 45 per cent still awaited privatization or liquidation in 1996. These figures are also much closer to the results we had obtained from the analysis of the company balance sheets. By late 1997, the total value of the state-owned property that could not be sold or will permanently remain state-owned, declined to about $5 bn. The number of companies that belonged to the SPAM was also reduced to 322.

It must be emphasized that the value of the privatized property was not equal to the amount of revenues that the state earned from the privatization transactions. In fact, the state's revenues from privatization were much less than the value of the privatized property. The gap can partly be explained by the *transaction costs* of privatization. But a large part – about 30 per cent – of the state-owned property simply vanished through subsidized loans and other privileges that had been granted to the buyers.

While the share of the privatized property barely exceeded 50 per cent by late 1996, the share of the *private sector* was much higher in Hungary. It amounted to about 70 per cent in the production of GDP, in employment and added up to 65 per cent of the total assets by mid-1997. The gap between the figures can be explained by the fact that *new* private businesses have been mushrooming in Hungary after 1989. The number of corporate entities increased to about 120 000 and the number of small private businesses exceeded 1 million by the fall of 1997. As regards the number and the share of private businesses in employment, capital and production it can be safely stated that the private sector dominated the Hungarian economy by 1997. However, it would be still premature to say that Hungary has become a fully fledged market economy where the institutions and the economic behavior and performance of the private firms match their Western counterparts. Hungarian companies, even the privately-owned ones have a long way to go until their restructuring and adjustment to the international economic community will be accomplished. In the following sections I shall present the data and analysis on how far the Hungarian companies have gone in restructuring and I shall explain what the driving forces and the stumbling blocks of their adjustment and restructuring have been. In addition, I shall address the issue why these companies have reached their particular point of transition. But first I shall describe the database and the methods of the analysis in the next section.

5.3 THE DATA AND THE ANALYTICAL METHODS

Our analysis of the economic transformation is based on a *microeconomic* approach, for we believe that the most decisive and long-lasting changes have occurred and will occur in the microsphere of the economy. Only these micro level changes can render long-term economic development and growth sustainable and ensure that the newly emerging institutions of a market economy and private ownership prove lasting. The adjustment and restructuring of the companies can be approached from many different angles and by many different methods.[6] But there is no more detailed and comprehensive statistical database on the companies' economic behavior and performance than the company balance sheets. In this study I shall use the balance sheets as a point of departure. In the next section I shall briefly present the characteristics of the company level database that has been used in the analysis and I shall also outline the economic indicators and the methods of the analysis.

5.3.1 The Database

The original data on all companies with double-entry book-keeping that have operated in Hungary between the period of 1988 and 1996 were provided by the *ECOSTAT,* Institute of Economic Analysis and Informatics of the Central Statistical Office. Because of confidentiality rules we could not obtain data on individual companies, only on company groups. The data was 'cleaned' by *ECOSTAT,* but we still had a few hundred companies each year that had not submitted all the data of their balance sheets. But the full database met the normality test, therefore we did not omit those companies which had not reported all the indicators. The company groups were assembled by using four criteria that I specified for the data provider. These criteria were as follows:

The first criterion represented the regional location of the companies. We specified six larger regions of Hungary and used the regional code for each company to form the six groups. Hence, each region consisted of three counties in average, since Hungary has 19 counties plus the capital, Budapest.[7]

Analysts of the East European countries are aware of the fact that regional differences matter a great deal. Those differences matter even more than in Western countries where one can find rich and poor regions, as well. For instance, in Hungary there are three large regions that have been much more affluent than the other parts of the country. These regions are: Budapest, the Western region that is close to the Austrian border and the so-called Hungarian 'Silicon valley', the mid-Western part of the country with Székesfehérvár, a larger city in the center. However, it would be a very superficial statement to say that progressive companies can only be found in those three regions. Other studies that focused on the issues of the labor market and unemployment and had been conducted in 59 sub-regions of the country (Fazekas, 1996) showed that even in regions that are considered very poor, such as, for example, the North-Eastern part of Hungary, there can be found prosperous sub-regions with flourishing companies. Our analysis arrived at a similar conclusion. Namely, the density of the viable companies is much higher in affluent than in backward regions, but those companies that survived in the poor regions seem to be as progressive and efficient as those that have the privilege to be located closer to Western markets and companies.

The second criterion reflected the branch affiliation of the companies, broken down to 78 sub-branches. We reduced the number of sub-branches to 22, for a very detailed breakdown of the companies' branch affiliation would have resulted in almost unmanageably large databases without adding substantial new information to our analysis.[8] The third criterion stood for the legal form of the companies. The total number of the company categories by legal form is 32. We formed ten groups out of the 32 categories.[9]

The fourth criterion we used reflected the ownership structure of the companies. It is not evident whether one should form only two groups of companies – state-owned and privately-owned – and then distinguish between the domestic and the foreign private companies, or is it more sensible to form clusters out of the sample of companies according to the actual share of private ownership within each company. In the analysis of the balance sheets data we decided to choose the latter rather than the former solution. Our reason for this was that by doing so we could get a finer picture about the companies' ownership structure. Hence, we first formed five company groups according to the share of private ownership within the issued capital stock. Then we used a second criterion (Code 1 or Code 2) to show whether the company had or it did not have foreign owners. We also gave a fantasy name to each group. The groups were as follows:

Group 11: Companies with state-ownership less than 5 per cent and with foreign (co-)owner (name: FORPRIV).

Group 12: Companies with state-ownership less than 5 per cent and with domestic owner only (name: DOMPRIV).

Group 21: Companies with more than 5, but less than 25 per cent of state ownership and with foreign (co-)owner (name: FORMOST).

Group 22: Companies with more than 5, but less than 25 per cent of state ownership and with domestic owner only (name: DOMMOST).

Group 31: Companies with more than 25, but less than 50 per cent of state ownership and with foreign (co-)owner (name: FORMIX).

Group 32: Companies with more than 25, but less than 50 per cent of state ownership and with domestic owner only (name: DOMMIX).

Group 41: Companies where the state had a more than 50 but less than 75 per cent share and with foreign (co-)owner (name: FORMORE).

Group 42: Companies where the state had a more than 50 but less than 75 per cent share and with domestic owner only (name: DOMMORE).

Group 51: Companies with more than 75 per cent state ownership and with foreign (co-)owner (name: FORSTAT).

Group 52: Companies with more than 75 per cent state ownership and with domestic owner only (name: DOMSTAT).

Here we must mention that especially domestic and foreign private ownership was not as obvious as was reflected by the codes. Namely, Hungarian citizens could illegally transfer money abroad and then buy into a Hungarian company by formally using a foreign investor. The opposite could also happen. Notably, foreign investors formally used Hungarian partners to acquire a piece of property especially in branches where the foreign citizens' rights to invest were restricted.

5.3.2 The Size and Representativity of the Company Samples

In tables 5.1 and 5.2 I provide some data on the group of all companies with double entry and on the group of companies that have been under the jurisdiction of the state privatization agencies, respectively. These data can provide the reader with an overview on how large the weight of these company groups has been within the nation-wide sector of all *registered* economic organizations. I must emphasize that the relative numbers do not reflect the real weight of our samples since we did not include the indicators of the unregistered economic activities in the basis of the comparison.[10] We avoided extending our comparison to the non-registered sector for we do not have reliable information about its size. Expert estimates about the relative size of the non-registered economy range between 20 and 50 per cent regarding employment and GDP production (Árvay and Vértes, 1995).

As can be seen from Table 5.1, the number of registered businesses more than tripled between 1988 and 1996. But out of them, the number of individual entrepreneurs was above 745 000, and there were only 304 000 economic organizations with or without legal entity. During the same period, the number of companies with double-entry book-keeping (CDEs), that is, our sample's size, increased more than tenfold.

Table 5.1. The share of the companies with double entry in the Hungarian economy between 1988 and 1996 (number of economic organizations or shares in per cent)

	1988	**1990**	**1992**	**1994**	**1996**
No. of companies with double entry (CDEs)	7 628	23 314	57 865	79 793	104 017
No. of all registered businesses	351 532	448 027	784 575	1 044 918	1 115 309
Of which: individual entrepreneurs	290 877	393 450	606 207	778 036	745 247
Share of the CDEs in employment	56.9	53.8	46.9	49.1	46.9
Share of the CDEs in total turnover	96.2	95.5	97.1	96.4	84.2
Share of the CDEs in total assets	51.3	59.0	81.1	90.5	83.8
Share of the CDEs in GDP production	65.5	63.2	64.3	61.0	60.3

Sources: Calculation based on own database and the National Bank of Hungary (1995), pp. 148, 163, 167; the National Bank of Hungary (1996), pp. 185, 201, 203, 218; *Statistical Yearbook 1991*, pp. 57, 62, 70; *Statistical Yearbook 1994,* pp. 2, 54, 65, 73 and 75; and *Statistical Yearbook 1995*, pp. 205 and 223, of the Hungarian Central Statistical Office.

It is also important to note that the share of CDEs was very high in the total turnover and in fixed assets. It usually surpassed 90 per cent for both indicators. Meanwhile, the share of the CDEs in employment and in GDP production was much lower. As regards employment the CDEs' share remained in the range of 46–57 per cent, and it varied between 61 and 67 per cent regarding the GDP. The huge difference between the CDEs' share in employment and in fixed assets, or between their share in turnover and GDP production points to the fact that the 'heavyweight' sector of the economy provided less and less jobs, while more and more people found their work as individual entrepreneurs. And since the largest part of the GDP is constituted by the total amount of wages and other remuneration, while the companies' turnover is determined in a large part by the cost of materials used in the production process, it can explain the gap between the CDEs' share in turnover and in GDP.

Another important fact is that the fixed assets were concentrated in the group of larger companies, while the small businesses mostly relied on labor. It can be noticed, too, that the share of the CDEs in total assets increased rapidly after 1991. This phenomenon can partly be attributed to organizational changes and to changes in the accounting system rather than to structural shifts in ownership or asset composition. First of all, the asset value of the real estates that the companies used had not been accounted for in their books before 1992, but it became an important part of their total assets afterwards. In addition, many of the municipal companies and budgetary organizations became 'normal' corporations during the 1990s and the value of their assets became an integral part of the companies' total assets during the 1990s.

In Table 5.2 I show the share of those companies that were subordinated to one of the state privatization agencies (SPACs), in employment, turnover, total assets and GDP, relative to the group of the CDEs. As can be seen in Table 5.2, the number of the SPACs first increased until 1992, then it started declining, while the relative share of the SPACs gradually decreased by every indicator for the whole period. What is striking: the SPACs' share in employment, in total assets and in GDP production was very similar, meanwhile their relative share in turnover was relatively low. The shrinkage of the SPACs' share in the national economy was largely due to the expansion of the new private businesses rather than to the change of the ownership title of the formerly state-owned companies.

Table 5.2. The share of the companies belonging to the state privatization agencies (SPACs) relative to the CDEs between 1988 and 1996 (number of economic organizations or shares in per cent)

	1990	1991	1992	1993	1994	1995	1996
No. of companies	1 773	1 775	1 881	1 813	1 602	1 468	1 403
Share of the SPACs							
– in employment	56.1	53.1	48.2	44.0	42.2	38.8	35.5
– in total turnover	63.8	55.0	47.1	40.8	35.6	32.2	54.7
– in total assets	62.3	58.3	44.6	45.5	41.4	36.5	45.3
– in GDP production	63.1	58.1	35.9	45.1	40.8	42.1	40.1

Source: Own calculations based on the companies' balance sheets.

All in all, the CDEs represent the Hungarian company sector very well. They account for at least 60 per cent of the registered Hungarian economy. SPACs, as a subsample of the CDEs, reveal similar characteristics as CDEs. However, a more rigorous statistical analysis of the representativity of our samples – using, for instance the Chi-2 test – would cast some doubt on representativity in a strict sense, for the samples do not incorporate small businesses.

5.3.3 Defining the Indicators

A company's economic performance is a very complex notion. Consequently, it cannot be described with one or with a few indicators. This is why I decided to analyse the companies' *profitability* and *efficiency* from many angles. It is a common mistake of many analysts that they make a sharp distinction between a company's so-called 'real activities' (that is, its production), and financial activities. I believe that a company's financial state is an integral part of its economic performance. To assess the companies' financial stability during transition is especially important since one of the main reasons for the SOEs' low efficiency had been that an effective budget constraint for the companies had not existed in the socialist economies. Thus, several indicators were used to assess the companies' financial state just before and during transition.

The results of our statistical and empirical analyses showed that profitability and efficiency are less important for the companies than expansion and the stabilization of their market position during the transformation period. Consequently, I had to use indicators that would reflect the change of the companies' market position and their changing attitudes toward expansion. To measure these changes I defined the indicators of investment and export activity just to show the differences between SOEs and private companies in this regard. In addition, I analysed the cost structure of the company groups with different ownership structures in order to trace the main factors of their diverging economic performance.

In the analysis I found that the different companies' economic performance has been affected much more by their branch affiliation, then by their regional location, than by their ownership structure. However, in this analysis most attention will be devoted to the interrelationship between economic performance and the companies' ownership. What interested me the most was whether there has been a significant difference between the economic indicators of the privately-owned and state-owned companies, and between the economic performance of foreign-owned companies on the one hand and companies with domestic owners on the other.

Profitability indicators

The success of the companies' adjustment to the new market environment can best be assessed by their profitability. The level of profitability is an important – and in the long run it is the most important – factor, but it is also the result of the companies' international competitiveness. In addition, profitability is closely connected to the companies' potential for expansion and structural change. But profitability is a complex notion. Consequently, it is not self-evident how to measure it. I used eight different profitability indicators in order to cover the numerous aspects of profitability. The indicators that have been used were as follows:

(1) NPROF: Profits after taxation (from 1992 retained profits) relative to the shareholders' equity.
(2) GPROF: Profits before taxation relative to the shareholders' equity.
(3) OPROF: Operating profits relative to the shareholders' equity.
(4) NICPROF: Profits after taxation (from 1992 retained profits) relative to the issued capital stock.
(5) GICPROF: Profits before taxation relative to the issued capital stock.
(6) NCEFF: Profits after taxation (from 1992 retained profits) relative to the total assets. (This indicator is also called ROA in the literature.)
(7) GCEFF: Profits before taxation relative to the total assets.
(8) TTA: Turnover per total assets.

I must emphasize that none of the indicators can be read as components of a time series without precaution. First, Hungarian companies had not reported their shareholders equity or issued capital stock before 1991, when the Act on Accounting was adopted by the Hungarian parliament. Consequently, the values for 1988–91 were *ex post* compiled by the statistical and financial agencies. Second, there had not been a continuous revaluation of the companies' assets that would have adjusted the asset values for the price changes and for the changes in the assets' composition. Third, the definition and content of profits have changed over time, too. The value of profits that has been reported by the companies after 1990 was dubious, because the companies made every effort to hide their profits behind costs in order to pay the very high taxes. Consequently, profitability indicators should be read as indicators of a cross-section analysis.

Indicators of efficiency

We deliberately decided to make a distinction between profitability and efficiency of the companies for one main reason. We believe that while profitability reflects the success level of utilization of a company's capital stock, efficiency is an indicator to show how successfully a company can utilize its flow expenditures. Thus, profitability is a long-term or 'stock' indicator of a company's competitiveness and business success, while efficiency is an indicator of short-term adaptability and adjustment. I used three indicators to measure a company's economic efficiency, which were as follows:

(1) NPM: Profits after taxation (after 1992 retained profits) relative to the company's turnover (Net Profit Margin).

(2) GPM: Profits before taxation (after 1992 retained profits) relative to the company's turnover (Gross Profit Margin).

(3) TLA: Turnover per liquid assets (net).

There is not an impermeable wall between profitability and efficiency as they have been defined above. While it can be asserted that a company's assets usually change over a longer period than other factors of production can, short-term changes of the components of a company's turnover can affect its profits and in turn, it can have an impact on the companies' profitability.

Indicators of productivity

There is one flow expenditure that has a special importance among the flow expenditure items. This is the efficiency of labor utilization, or as is called *labor productivity*. Labor productivity can be measured in several ways. One option could be to compare the amount of profits to the total labor costs. We calculated this indicator, too. But as a first approximation, we just simply calculated the companies' turnover and value added relative to the number of their permanent staff, respectively. (Each of the indicators is in thousand HUF per employee.) The productivity indicators were as follows:

(1) GPROD: The value of the companies' turnover relative to the number of their permanent staff.
(2) NPROD: The value of the companies' value added (GDP) relative to the number of their permanent staff.

Indicators of economic expansion

In a centrally administered socialist economy the companies were insensitive to the expenses of keeping huge and frequently unnecessary inventories. Hoarding was the usual – and under the conditions of central planning it was also the rational – way of avoiding shortages. Thus, the magnitude of inventories relative to a company's turnover shows how the company adjusts to the new economic environment. We calculated the share of inventories relative to the companies' turnover. We also measured the companies' export activity since we believe that the Hungarian market is too small for the companies as a long-term living space. Export is essential for the Hungarian companies to be integrated in the international economic community. Labor costs are one of the key factors of the companies' domestic and international competitiveness. Therefore, we separately measured the labor (total staff) costs relative to the companies' turnover. Thus, the indicators were the following ones:

(1) TINV: The total value of inventories bought and self-produced.
(2) SPINV: The value of inventories produced by the companies themselves.
(3) EXTR: the share of net export sales relative to the companies' turnover.
(4) LABC: The share of labor costs relative to the companies' turnover.

Indicators of investment activity
One of the main expectations toward the privatization of the formerly state-owned companies has been that the change of ownership will be accompanied or followed by a massive restructuring of the companies. Restructuring can mean several things in this context, but to restructure a formerly state-owned company cannot be successful without sizable investments. Consequently, the companies' investment activity is an important indicator of the restructuring efforts. We used three different indicators to measure the intensity of the companies' investment activities:

(1) UNIF: the value of unfinished investments relative to the companies' fixed assets. UNIF used to be an indicator of negative trends in investments during the period of the 'actually existing socialism'. This indicator reflected the dispersity and disorganized nature of the companies' investment activities. However, in a market economy, where companies cannot usually invest from state resources, UNIF gained a positive meaning. It means that the companies are very active in expanding their capacities and operation.
(2) FIF: The value of financial investments relative to the companies' fixed assets. We consider this indicator to be important since there has been a common belief in the economics profession that SOEs are systematically stripping their assets and they spend the money they receive for those assets on flow expenditures, especially on salaries. The data we analysed indicate that the above assumption is not true. Companies are not very active in investing into production capacities but the very same companies zealously invest in state bonds and in other securities. This fact indicates that interest rates are high and prospects for returns from investment are low in Hungary (as in the other Central and East European countries, too).
(3) ICR: Credits for investment relative to the short-term and long-term liabilities. This indicator shows whether a company takes debts upon itself in order to secure its future development, or the company's liabilities accumulate because of other reasons, such as, for example, covering old debts by new loans.

Indicators of financial stability and solvency
State-owned companies did not have an effective budget constraint, or to use János Kornai's terminology, they had a 'soft budget constraint' (Kornai,

1980, pp. 322–5). The general expectation of the economic profession and also the peoples of East Europe has been that the transition from a socialist toward a market economy – where the companies' financial autonomy and responsibility are the basic principles of the mode of operation of the economy – will result in the emergence of an effective budget constraint of the companies. Given the above arguments it seemed obvious that we devoted a lot of attention to the companies' financial state during and after the transition. We used seven indicators to describe the financial state of the companies. These indicators were as follows (all of them in percentages):

(1) FATA: The share of the company's financial assets relative to its total assets. This indicator shows – similarly to FIF – how large a part of the companies' assets are held in financial assets. FATA is composed from broader balance sheet items than FIF, since the former does not only include financial investments and fixed assets, but all financial assets and all company assets, as well.
(2) SOLV: Financial assets plus receivables relative to current liabilities. This indicator shows the companies' level of short-term solvency. The larger the value of this indicator the more solvent a company is.
(3) DEBT: Long-term liabilities relative to the shareholders' equity plus provisions. This indicator reflects the level of a company's indebtedness. The lower the value of DEBT the less indebted a company is.
(4) SIN: Shareholders' equity per fixed assets plus inventories. This indicator shows whether a company can finance its capital requirements from its shareholders' equity. The larger the indicator's value the more stable a company is in financial terms.
(5) EQU: The share of the trade creditors' claims (Accounts payable) relative to the amount of the company's receivables from its customers. This indicator reflects the extensiveness and depth of the well-known phenomenon of 'enterprise queuing' that has been one of the most serious problems of the socialist economies just before and after the initial phase of the economic transition. The larger the value of this indicator the longer a creditor must wait until it gets its money if it gets the money at all.
(6) LAT: Liquid assets (net) per total assets.
(7) LR: Liquid assets per cash-flow, or liquidity ratio.

All the indicators that have been described in the above sections are weighted averages of a group of companies. Consequently, an indicator tells something about a company group but it tells little about the behavior of an individual company. We could observe that the standard deviation or variance of the indicators around their averages were usually fairly large. This can cast doubt on the meaning of the averages that hide rather than reveal the specific features of a company group. This is why we conducted a cluster analysis for more homogenous groups of companies. In addition, we did a multivariate analysis and a multi-regression analysis on the interrelationship between the profitability indicators as dependent variables on the one hand, and the explanatory variables on the other. We also calculated the weighted standard deviations of the indicators for the whole set of the companies (WSDEV), and within a specific group of companies (wsdev), moreover, among the different company groups that had been formed by using the same type of criterion, for instance, we calculated the weighted standard deviation of the company groups that had been formed by using the regional criterion (wro).

A multivariate analysis was conducted by Cristiano Vezzoni on the Hungarian company sample and it will be presented in section 5.7. We also did a multi-regression analysis on the same database. It turned out that there is multicollinearity among the explanatory variables. Consequently, we had to do a factor analysis first, in order to determine the main factors that have the largest impact on the companies' profitability. Besides multicollinearity, we had to tackle the problem of the missing data. We decided to substitute the missing data of the companies for the group average of that individual indicator. The results of the analysis will be presented in section 5.5 below.

5.4 THE CDES' AND THE SPACS' ECONOMIC PERFORMANCE BY BRANCHES AND BY REGIONS BETWEEN 1988 AND 1996

First I shall show the indicators of profitability, efficiency and labor productivity by branches for the whole sample (the CDEs) and for the SPACs in selected years. Then I shall present the same indicators for the companies by regions. In the next section, a more detailed analysis of the companies' economic performance – including profitability, efficiency and labor productivity, moreover, financial stability – will follow by grouping the companies according to their ownership structure. In each section I shall present the results for the groups of the CDEs first, then I shall outline the results for the SPACs.

5.4.1 Profitability, Efficiency and Productivity by Branches

The capital to labor ratio of the companies varies from industry to industry and so does their market environment. The radical changes in the CEE economies' foreign trade pattern and especially the collapse of the CMEA markets in 1990–91 hit the companies very hard but the damage was not the same for each industry; the companies in different industries had very different chances to recover. In fact, the profitability and efficiency indicators of the companies varied much more by branches than by ownership as will be shown on the following pages. This is a very important conclusion of our research since it shows that privatization of the state-owned property in itself has a smaller impact on the companies' economic performance than the changes in market structure and in the competitive conditions of the companies.

Out of the eight profitability indicators defined above I shall present two indicators by branches and by regions: for OPROF, and for NCEFF or ROA. Since the indicators shown in the tables are weighted averages for the 22 branches, I also calculated the weighted standard deviation for each indicator. The weights were determined by factor analysis and they were combined from the data on net turnover, the shareholders' equity, total assets and the number of employees.

Profitability, efficiency and productivity of the CDEs by branches

We calculated the average profitability, efficiency and productivity of the companies with double entry book-keeping by branches for the period 1988–96. Table 5.3 shows these indicators of the CDEs by branches for 1988 (the year before the changes), 1990 (the year when transformation started, 1992 (the bottom of the 'transformation recession') and for 1996. It is important to note here, that the branch structure of the Hungarian economy radically changed between 1988 and 1996. The share of agriculture drastically declined and the share of industry also shrank, while the service sector rapidly expanded. The share of the service sector in employment and in GDP production amounted to about 60 per cent in 1996.

The tables provide a good basis for comparing the performance indicators of companies by branches. But these tables can be used as tools of a cross-section rather than a time-series analysis. It is important to note that most profitability and efficiency indicators had been positive before 1992, but then they went deeply into the red. Another important fact that can be observed is the growing magnitude of the weighted standard deviations within and between the branches and for the whole sample. The figures indicate that even within one branch, the distance among the different companies' profitability and efficiency became larger and larger.

Let us analyse the relative positions of the branches by profitability first! There were some spectacular changes in the ranking of the branches according to profitability between 1988 and 1996. An example is the vehicle industry which had ranked first in 1988, but it slipped back to the group of the largest loss-makers by 1992 and belonged to the middle-level profitability group between 1994 and 1996. The fairly poor performance of the vehicle industry is astonishing given the fact that major automobile producers, such as, the Japanese Suzuki, General Motors (Opel) and Volkswagen (Audi) set up new production plants in Hungary. The heavy losses were not incurred by these companies, but by the bus and truck production of the still state-owned Hungarian enterprises. Other similar examples are the financial services and domestic trade which had started as the most profitable industries but they became large loss-makers by 1992. It must be noted that the economic performance of the financial services was at least as much affected by government action as by the operation of those businesses themselves. Namely, the Hungarian government's so-called 'credit and bank consolidation program' of 1993 and 1994, that aimed at strengthening the banks' financial position and reducing the amount of inter-enterprise arrears, completely changed the banks' accounts independent of their own efforts. On the other hand, some service industries, such as, for example, telecommunications, culture, education and R&D, and healthcare, remained profitable even in the deepest recession period. The profitability of energy production and distribution widely fluctuated between 1988 and 1996.

It can be seen from the tables that the bottom of the Hungarian 'transformation recession'[11] occurred in 1992 when almost all branches generated losses in Hungary. By 1994 profitability somewhat improved and a few branches, such as, for example, the chemical industry, the construction materials industry or some of the service industries, showed decisive signs of recovery and a solid economic growth. Average profitability of the CDEs was even higher, that is, it was less negative than the 1994 indicator, in 1995. The machinery industry, the chemical industry, the construction materials industry and agriculture showed an amazing recovery by 1996. On the other hand, energy production, personal services, mining, and education and telecommunications services incurred heavy losses in 1995. Telecommunications showed a complete turnaround with high profits in 1996, just after the final stage of privatization of the Hungarian Telecommunications Company.

Efficiency – defined as the companies' profit margin – and especially labor productivity reveal relevant additional information about the companies' struggle for restructuring and adjustment. Notably, while the profitability indicators reflect, first of all, the companies' restructuring efforts of their fixed assets, the efficiency indicators show how successful they are as regards economizing with their flow expenditures, especially with wage costs and material expenditures. labor productivity narrows the focus of the efficiency analysis to the utilization of labor and how the companies have handled hidden unemployment, a leftover from the era of the socialist economy.

While the CDEs' efficiency indicators by branches showed a similar pattern between 1988 and 1996 to the profitability indicators, labor productivity followed a completely different trend. In 1988 all of the industries operated with positive profit margins. Postal and telecommunications services, healthcare, foreign trade and personal services, and also the computer industry, the construction materials industry, agriculture and the chemical industry had the highest net and gross profit margins in that year. The lowest profit margins could be observed in mining, in the energy production, in financial services and in metallurgy. The overall profit margins for all companies turned negative by 1992. It was only postal and telecommunications services and healthcare where the profit margins remained above zero. Mining, financial services and the machinery industry showed the lowest indicators, while postal and telecommunications services, healthcare and the energy production and distribution had the highest profit margins in that year.

The efficiency indicators by branches and for all companies considerably improved by 1994 and even more so by 1995. Although 13 industries out of 22 had negative net and/or gross profit margins, the magnitude of the losses substantially decreased. The largest lossmakers were the energy production and distribution, mining and business assistance. On the other hand, in some branches, such as, for example, in financial services, transportation, computer industry and healthcare, the profit margins were well above zero. The average efficiency indicator of the CDEs further improved in 1996. The financial services, the construction materials industry, the machinery industry, the chemical industry, agriculture, and the postal and telecommunications services had the highest and positive, while transportation, mining and energy production had the lowest, in fact negative, profit margins in that year.

As regards labor productivity, it fluctuated over the period of 1988–96, but it had an upward trend for all companies and for most branches. Gross labor productivity was the only indicator where we could observe a permanently increasing trend for the CDEs during the whole period. As to net productivity, that is, the companies' value added (GDP) relative to the number of their employees, the results were mixed. After a significant growth between 1988 and 1990, net productivity leveled out in 1992, then it started declining in 1993 and 1994. The trend would be even more decisive if we took into account the price changes over the period 1988–96.

Financial services, foreign trade, the chemical industry and domestic trade had the highest, while postal and telecommunications services, healthcare and mining had the lowest productivity indicators in 1988. It must be noted that labor productivity may be the most industry-specific indicator, not only in transforming economies, but also in advanced market economies. Consequently, the ranking of industries is very much influenced by the characteristic capital to labor ratio of the individual industries, beside the level of efficiency of the utilization of labor.

It is important to note that several of the traditional industries, such as, for instance, agriculture, light industry, the chemical industry, the construction materials industry, the electronics industry or the vehicle industry, had a higher than average profit margin in 1988. By 1990, all of these industries remained below average and the highest profit margins were generated by the service industries and by the energy production. The picture did not substantially change in 1992 either, although the CDEs as a whole and most branches produced negative profit margins. By 1994, the CDEs' average gross profit margin turned positive again, and apart from the service sector it was the construction materials industry and the chemical industry – especially the pharmaceutical industry – that substantially increased their efficiency.

As we have seen the highest indicators were achieved by the service industries, such as domestic and foreign trade, financial services or business assistance services in 1988. It was the chemical industry and energy production that showed relatively high productivity among the industrial branches in that year. In 1990, the relative position of the different industries did not change tremendously. It was only mining that could catch up with the other high productivity industries, and energy production improved its ranking substantially, while the chemical industry retained its good position. The service sector remained the leader in labor productivity in 1992, while energy production and the chemical industry could preserve its relative position and the ranking of the food industry – presumably as a result of sizable foreign investment – improved.

Apart from the chemical industry, it was the service sector, notably education, R&D and cultural services, foreign trade, telecommunications, business services and healthcare, that ranked the best in 1994. It is interesting to note that the relative position of the domestic trade deteriorated dramatically. This fact contradicts the common wisdom that retail and wholesale trading are productive 'by nature' because of the large turnovers these industries have. On the other hand, some traditional industries, such as, for example, the construction materials industry, the vehicle industry and the machinery industry, showed a higher than average labor productivity in 1994. These branches were the recipients of the largest amounts of foreign direct investment, beside telecommunications and the chemical industry.

We found the industries with the lowest productivity indicators among services and agriculture in 1995, while foreign trade, domestic trade, energy production and distribution and the vehicle industry had the highest level of productivity. But some of the services also belonged to the high productivity group. Notably, postal and telecommunications services and healthcare surpassed several traditional industries in productivity level. Foreign and domestic trade, energy production and distribution, the vehicle industry and education had the highest, while the community and healthcare services, transport and mining had the lowest productivity indicators in 1996.

Table 5.3. Profitability, efficiency (in per cent), and productivity (in '000 HUF) indicators of the CDEs by branches between 1988 and 1996

			1988				
Branch	**No. of CDEs**	**OPROF**	**NCEFF**	**GPM**	**GPROD**	**NPROD**	**Weight**
Agriculture	1 374	5.85	3.05	5.44	650.12	332.18	11.32
Food industry	247	9.15	3.26	3.90	1 695.29	569.53	8.34
Mining	30	2.62	0.46	3.01	617.17	275.83	1.86
Light industry	866	8.90	3.15	4.42	673.69	241.78	4.87
Chemical ind.	224	13.17	5.29	5.16	3 644.84	2 090.32	10.63
Construction materials ind.	52	5.26	2.68	5.43	982.09	358.11	1.06
Metallurgy	311	8.38	2.62	4.28	1 603.19	580.47	4.87
Machinery ind.	399	8.70	3.27	4.91	856.86	330.64	3.75
Telecom and computer ind.	189	9.58	3.32	6.20	837.86	369.17	1.65
Vehicle ind.	41	10.04	4.14	5.85	1 695.59	465.81	1.79
Energy prod.	203	1.27	0.86	1.40	2 909.08	1 858.20	8.72
Construction	1 384	11.94	3.82	5.35	729.26	389.87	4.34
Domestic trade	1 003	12.76	4.10	2.61	3 180.65	2 954.75	20.65
Foreign trade	121	25.26	2.86	8.55	6 064.41	5 571.86	3.06
Personal services	207	11.99	4.93	6.14	657.51	516.45	1.17
Transport	168	3.75	1.89	3.58	688.30	463.65	5.66
Post and tele-comm. serv.	3	7.75	4.03	15.18	439.51	335.74	1.45
Financial services	2	15.58	3.76	2.24	7 316.33	7 055.32	0.13
Business assistance	733	7.08	2.90	3.12	1 174.19	714.70	4.15
Public and community serv.	59	1.08	0.81	3.36	683.16	535.42	0.46
Education, R&D and culture	11	8.08	2.73	7.38	522.47	326.28	0.05
Healthcare and social serv.	1	7.77	6.42	8.75	914.75	449.47	0.01
All CDEs	7 628	7.88	3.11	4.12	1 353.28	846.00	100.00
wro		49.52	23.56	42.05	113.68	167.19	

Table 5.3 continued

				1990			
Branch	**No. of CDEs**	**OPROF**	**NCEFF**	**GPM**	**GPROD**	**NPROD**	**Weight**
Agriculture	1 956	3.03	2.17	2.32	970.63	511.23	11.05
Food industry	636	7.84	2.97	4.02	2 416.07	756.99	8.66
Mining	62	–0.34	5.47	–0.25	1 604.41	1 232.74	2.46
Light industry	2 039	2.90	1.29	1.67	878.55	356.99	5.22
Chemical ind.	609	17.64	5.42	11.14	4 456.84	2 493.47	10.73
Construction materials ind.	167	3.95	2.74	2.96	1 695.24	754.82	1.42
Metallurgy	863	0.93	0.03	0.51	2 420.61	907.17	4.83
Machinery ind.	1 050	0.31	0.49	0.18	1 113.40	451.52	3.64
Telecom and computer ind.	516	7.67	–0.15	–4.09	1 139.25	498.04	2.01
Vehicle ind.	112	–9.61	–3.65	–5.00	1 632.30	446.66	1.37
Energy prod.	97	7.02	4.19	6.39	3 891.90	2 494.34	8.77
Construction	3 342	1.40	0.67	0.77	851.89	493.87	3.97
Domestic trade	6 156	13.70	5.06	7.57	4 165.89	3 826.47	19.69
Foreign trade	1 298	17.80	3.14	5.03	7 689.85	7 019.23	3.58
Personal services	961	10.40	5.21	6.22	865.85	647.00	1.42
Transport	939	1.69	0.69	1.30	776.23	471.75	5.49
Post and tele-comm. serv.	18	9.55	5.05	6.32	538.68	407.18	2.06
Financial services	17	0.99	0.02	0.79	2 447.48	1 194.28	0.05
Business assistance	2 280	5.58	2.57	2.86	2 314.27	1 812.53	3.11
Public and community serv.	94	1.33	1.12	1.26	943.91	688.43	0.39
Education, R&D and culture	85	14.64	4.05	10.12	1 213.64	918.98	0.06
Healthcare and social serv.	17	6.37	5.71	5.33	1 283.40	715.36	0.01
All CDEs	23 314	6.65	2.91	3.32	1 874.73	1 195.48	100.00
wro		63.61	20.43	37.54	103.45	148.14	

1992							
Branch	**No. of CDEs**	**OPROF**	**NCEFF**	**GPM**	**GPROD**	**NPROD**	**Weight**
Agriculture	3 153	–5.34	–8.34	–12.35	1 132.36	549.94	8.66
Food industry	1 549	5.05	–4.90	–2.31	2 891.93	1 190.13	7.30
Mining	137	–8.23	–12.86	–22.59	1 470.77	749.82	0.94
Light industry	4 089	–4.19	–7.68	–5.98	1 243.08	605.07	5.59
Chemical ind.	1 041	1.18	–3.09	–2.96	4 211.05	2 153.13	8.00
Construction materials ind.	288	–4.19	–5.41	–8.78	1 888.98	846.09	1.14
Metallurgy	1 508	–13.07	–10.87	–9.42	1 904.89	767.37	2.99
Machinery ind.	2 102	–17.12	13.81	–13.44	1 509.06	745.24	3.01
Telecom and computer ind.	893	–8.09	–8.17	–7.64	1 699.91	945.27	1.41
Vehicle ind.	200	–7.41	–6.22	–10.86	2 163.34	848.33	1.49
Energy prod.	153	0.84	–0.34	0.02	4 782.29	3 004.69	15.97
Construction	5 561	–0.58	–5.65	–1.59	1 800.95	1 177.81	4.11
Domestic trade	15 199	2.22	–5.36	–1.21	5 201.73	4 802.58	13.43
Foreign trade	4 312	–15.63	–4.77	–1.91	11 607.99	10 613.95	2.78
Personal services	2 114	0.61	–3.29	–3.27	1 262.19	1 006.02	2.06
Transport	2 129	–4.87	–4.68	–5.16	1 345.96	927.04	5.78
Post and tele-comm. serv.	114	5.92	0.74	3.01	1 260.92	1 086.52	2.75
Financial services	617	–61.73	–0.41	–0.90	1 912.06	1 512.28	3.84
Business assistance	9 228	–0.17	–1.71	–1.75	2 770.50	2 314.29	6.85
Public and community serv.	887	–0.43	–1.29	–0.09	984.06	667.82	0.99
Education, R&D and culture	2 214	–1.97	–5.10	0.99	2 867.33	2 288.08	0.81
Healthcare and social serv.	377	29.81	2.17	9.88	2 472.15	1 975.04	0.06
All CDEs	57 865	–4.38	–2.58	–3.40	2 539.98	1 743.90	100.00
wro		12.77	3.95	4.61	86.62	55.67	

Table 5.3 continued

				1996			
Branch	**No. of CDEs**	**OPROF**	**NCEFF**	**GPM**	**GPROD**	**NPROD**	**Weight**
Agriculture	5 823	9.47	2.39	3.82	3 647.72	918.12	6.21
Food industry	2 694	14.70	–0.19	1.48	9 080.69	1 614.39	6.48
Mining	223	–3.19	–6.05	–5.64	3 940.71	1 732.83	0.77
Light industry	6 340	15.21	2.74	4.24	3 638.81	1 305.59	5.28
Chemical ind.	1 566	14.14	5.04	7.80	11 594.13	4 049.77	7.40
Construction materials ind.	427	11.34	4.52	7.70	5 999.42	2 121.91	0.88
Metallurgy	2 358	6.16	–1.86	0.14	5 906.07	1 515.15	2.73
Machinery ind.	2 926	26.56	6.67	7.80	5 074.61	1 778.63	3.44
Telecom and computer ind.	1 376	17.83	1.12	4.23	6 532.42	1 868.23	1.64
Vehicle ind.	290	21.16	0.17	6.80	12 865.79	3 330.62	1.98
Energy prod.	337	–0.35	–2.67	–4.09	10 144.40	2 472.77	13.15
Construction	8 681	9.79	–0.47	1.23	6 402.02	1 601.76	3.94
Domestic trade	28 702	13.18	–0.19	0.83	15 840.71	2 192.32	14.08
Foreign trade	7 231	13.51	0.44	2.61	24 000.14	4 057.43	2.57
Personal services	3 722	3.85	–0.80	1.38	3 287.17	1 511.02	1.76
Transport	3 690	–5.13	–5.34	–7.60	3 831.17	1 519.72	8.34
Post and tele-comm. serv.	273	12.83	1.58	3.66	4 703.08	3 538.20	3.67
Financial services	1 220	–35.85	0.96	35.27	4 584.65	3 231.99	5.04
Business assistance	19 780	3.88	–0.87	1.81	6 995.65	2 680.61	8.07
Public and community serv.	1 394	1.80	0.67	4.22	2 538.20	1 354.44	1.54
Education, R&D and culture	3 935	8.48	–2.57	1.04	8 202.18	4 371.80	0.86
Healthcare and social serv.	1 029	21.39	0.66	6.21	3 252.09	1 707.71	0.15
All CDEs	104 017	3.90	0.28	2.50	7 575.57	2 057.90	100.00
wro		32.65	22.90	28.59	65.04	45.12	

Note: wro of productivity indicators = (wro/All CDEs)*100.

Let us take a look at the weights of the different industries in 1988 and in 1996. There are some clear losers and winners as regards their weights during this period. Domestic trade lost its leading position to energy production and distribution by 1996. Agriculture, mining, the chemical industry and metallurgy also lost several percentage points of their relative weight between 1988 and 1996. Hence, the so-called 'strategic industries' of the socialist economy lost their importance during the transformation. On the other hand, financial services, business assistance, postal and telecommunications services and energy production and distribution have gained in weight to a considerable extent. It is also an indicator of the fact that the service industries are becoming a decisive sector and they have been the 'locomotive' of economic growth in Hungary.

Profitability, efficiency and productivity of the SPACs by branches

I conducted the same analysis for the companies that belonged to the state privatization agencies (the SPACs) by branches as I had done for the CDEs before. One of the main differences between the groups of CDEs and the SPACs was that the number of companies changed within a fairly narrow margin in the latter group while it substantially changed year by year in the former. As can be seen from Table 5.4, the composition of the SPACs changed between 1990 and 1996. Consequently, it cannot be argued that the data on the different branches are easily comparable over time. It is also impossible to follow the changes of the individual companies' restructuring. Still, we can get a good overview of the changes in the SPACs' economic performance by branches and we can also track the alterations in the branches' ranking in the selected years.

The SPACs' average *profitability* indicators were positive in 1990, and only six branches (mining, metallurgy, the electronics industry, the vehicle industry, the construction industry and transportation) went into the red. As compared to the CDEs, the SPACs' profitability indicators were somewhat higher than those of the CDEs in 1990. This fact indicates that those state-owned that were in a better position than the rest of the Hungarian economy companies had first been selected for privatization. When we turn to the analysis of the companies' profitability by ownership structure, we also see that at the start of the privatization process the SPACs' profitability indicators were usually higher than the newly established private businesses.

By 1992, the average profitability indicators of the SPACs turned negative, as did the CDEs' average indicators. Among the SPACs, mining, the machinery industry, metallurgy and the construction industry turned out to be the largest loss-makers in 1992. There were only five branches – mostly in the service sector, such as, for example, education, R&D and cultural services, postal and telecommunications services, personal services and business assistance services, and the energy sector – that produced positive, although very low, profitability indicators. The average profitability of the SPACs as a group was *lower* than the profitability of the CDEs in 1992. This fact signaled that the state was a poorer owner than the non-state owners. But many of the SPACs were also partially sold to private, mostly foreign, owners. Consequently, it cannot be stated that the private companies performed better than the state-owned enterprises as we shall see in later sections.

Table 5.4. Profitability, efficiency (in per cent), and productivity (in '000 HUF) indicators of the SPACs by branches between 1990 and 1996

			1990				
Branch	**No. of SPACs**	**OPROF**	**NCEFF**	**GPM**	**GPROD**	**NPROD**	**Weight**
Agriculture	136	3.94	2.50	3.47	971.42	458.36	4.99
Food industry	178	8.12	2.79	2.96	2 429.21	759.50	10.48
Mining	20	–3.40	–3.14	–3.85	771.06	418.02	3.24
Light industry	186	1.47	0.30	0.86	1 063.73	424.90	5.88
Chemical ind.	64	18.62	7.45	7.51	5 856.45	3 591.69	13.79
Construction materials ind.	30	2.34	1.30	2.58	1 544.17	758.20	1.76
Metallurgy	69	–0.82	–1.77	–0.30	2 855.08	1 261.80	4.58
Machinery ind.	119	–0.13	0.20	–0.07	1 182.64	475.13	4.69
Telecom and computer ind.	50	–13.90	–6.75	–9.07	783.11	343.36	1.69
Vehicle ind.	14	–13.02	–5.12	–7.65	1 821.61	464.85	1.89
Energy prod.	29	9.82	5.73	8.08	5 420.08	3 670.31	9.67
Construction	123	–1.76	–1.21	–0.87	1 025.95	583.04	4.13
Domestic trade	329	13.66	5.54	3.22	5 183.85	4 884.86	12.74
Foreign trade	38	13.80	2.40	5.66	6 736.99	6 301.59	2.33
Personal services	129	13.72	6.65	7.90	831.19	646.22	1.66
Transport	57	1.25	0.31	1.20	706.10	417.02	9.24
Post and tele-comm. serv.	3	9.63	5.07	18.39	525.27	399.44	4.32
Financial services	1	0.62	0.10	1.02	1 557.21	622.69	0.01
Business assistance	138	1.52	0.87	0.93	2 479.65	2 021.78	2.78
Public and community serv.	17	1.65	1.25	2.31	399.31	240.39	0.07
Education, R&D and culture	2	2.68	2.25	5.62	616.58	406.58	0.00
Healthcare and social serv.	1	7.02	5.84	6.46	1 305.25	659.01	0.01
All SPACs	1 733	7.16	2.81	3.61	2 129.38	1 336.41	100.00
Wro		1.45	2.74	1.41	108.88	81.22	

1992							
Branch	**No. of SPACs**	**OPROF**	**NCEFF**	**GPM**	**GPROD**	**NPROD**	**Weight**
Agriculture	132	–5.75	–8.63	–13.66	1 193.11	411.13	4.99
Food industry	177	9.95	–2.50	–2.86	4 410.25	994.04	10.48
Mining	30	–14.11	–20.16	–169.79	1 214.26	539.21	3.24
Light industry	207	–6.03	–7.14	–14.01	1 586.83	517.60	5.88
Chemical ind.	56	–1.78	–2.67	–10.31	6 882.09	2 729.98	13.79
Construction materials ind.	36	–9.38	–7.38	–38.00	1 465.98	657.24	1.76
Metallurgy	84	–23.94	–16.03	–18.80	4 878.67	476.16	4.58
Machinery ind.	125	–27.68	–17.85	–27.47	1 440.22	484.97	4.69
Telecom and computer ind.	57	–16.30	–10.15	–31.82	966.33	386.58	1.69
Vehicle ind.	17	–3.62	–5.13	–5.14	2 245.68	934.52	1.89
Energy prod.	28	1.15	–0.07	0.23	27 252.51	2 500.15	9.67
Construction	106	–18.54	–11.33	–17.19	1 928.47	554.36	4.13
Domestic trade	324	6.00	–5.62	–4.96	8 229.29	924.07	12.74
Foreign trade	40	–27.63	–3.45	–2.74	15 755.47	1 381.37	2.33
Personal services	121	4.12	–0.91	4.40	1 289.31	784.47	1.66
Transport	62	–6.78	–6.04	–10.87	1 109.42	533.33	9.24
Post and tele-comm. serv.	3	6.52	0.66	2.45	1 833.94	1 525.31	4.32
Financial services	20	–152.95	–1.83	–211.67	1 903.08	1 280.15	0.01
Business assistance	175	2.53	0.01	0.00	5 780.78	2 720.53	2.78
Public and community serv.	18	–4.80	–3.37	–5.74	698.50	358.36	0.07
Education, R&D and culture	60	0.65	–1.47	–6.13	4 619.72	3 865.81	0.00
Healthcare and social serv.	3	–8.70	–7.63	–7.44	727.35	411.15	0.01
All SPACs	1 881	–5.05	–3.16	–5.69	2 481.65	740.76	100.00
wro		19.09	6.23	31.51	360.81	100.21	

Table 5.4 continued

				1996			
Branch	**No. of SPACs**	**OPROF**	**NCEFF**	**GPM**	**GPROD**	**NPROD**	**Weight**
Agriculture	107	8.53	2.47	3.48	3 165.25	1 053.26	2.93
Food industry	136	16.04	–0.11	2.01	11 569.38	2 697.42	8.85
Mining	20	–211.79	–1.08	–107.45	4 374.00	1 756.93	0.49
Light industry	160	8.22	–0.18	–65.74	5 095.22	1 770.74	4.36
Chemical ind.	50	12.26	5.52	10.06	20 059.83	7 125.45	13.28
Construction materials ind.	35	22.70	11.85	15.85	19 305.93	6 705.45	0.70
Metallurgy	59	–166.99	–6.18	–90.81	5 723.98	640.29	1.44
Machinery ind.	86	21.97	10.54	8.41	6 388.26	2 057.53	4.11
Telecom and computer ind.	43	0.75	1.26	3.68	12 266.62	2 965.43	0.81
Vehicle ind.	10	–936.30	–5.21	–6.80	4 272.65	1 254.43	1.15
Energy prod.	28	–0.60	–3.50	–5.52	83 573.22	8 999.74	23.40
Construction	67	9.24	–2.82	11.59	9 616.98	2 064.71	1.96
Domestic trade	218	59.78	–1.96	–97.95	16 903.42	1 997.71	7.60
Foreign trade	29	–11.79	–1.74	–9.15	34 878.39	4 046.04	0.68
Personal services	75	7.49	4.09	–14.76	3 685.96	2 565.07	1.24
Transport	51	–6.89	–6.43	–26.09	2 886.97	1 621.36	11.39
Post and tele-comm. serv.	3	11.60	3.64	8.48	6 593.79	5 949.72	6.52
Financial services	18	–67.41	1.39	287.01	2 552.84	1 739.84	5.66
Business assistance	139	4.27	–9.73	–278.46	9 951.10	5 327.45	2.69
Public and community serv.	16	1.37	–4.97	–6.65	1 543.97	722.37	0.11
Education, R&D and culture	48	19.94	3.75	5.60	12 654.00	10 858.41	0.59
Healthcare and social serv.	5	23.24	11.08	10.92	1 880.67	1 276.24	0.02
All SPACs	1 403	–0.90	0.12	2.31	6 429.46	2 136.06	100.00
wro		109.69	4.75	90.13	858.36	336.32	

Note: wro of productivity indicators = (wro/All SPACs)*100.

1994 has brought about a complete turn in the SPACs' profitability. All average profitability indicators, except operating profits relative to the shareholders' equity, turned positive and only seven branches – mostly the branches of heavy industry – out of 22 remained in the red. But the SPACs as a group did not prove considerably more profitable than the CDEs. And a similar pattern can be observed in 1995, too. 1995 was the year when a strict stabilization and austerity program (the so-called 'Bokros-package', named after the finance minister Lajos Bokros) started in Hungary. Eight branches out of 22 had profitability indicators well above the overall average, while eleven branches still had negative indicators of net profitability relative to total assets (NCEFF). Education and culture, the machinery industry, the construction materials industry, the chemical industry, agriculture, personal services, transport and health care belonged to the group of the best performing industries among the SPACs in 1995. The largest loss-makers were the vehicle industry, energy production and distribution, the construction industry, mining and the business assistance services in 1995.

There was a radical change in the SPACs' profitability in 1996. SPACs in mining, metallurgy, the vehicle industry, transportation and in business services incurred heavy losses on average. On the other hand, the SPACs in agriculture, in the chemical industry, the construction materials industry, metallurgy, in education and healthcare achieved high profits relative to assets. The rest of the branches showed a modest performance. It was noticeable in 1996, that the variance of indicators within and among branches largely increased, implying a growing divergence among the companies. And the heavy loss-makers showed extremely negative results.

The *profit margins* and labor *productivity* of the SPACs were considerably lower than those of the CDEs in 1990. Interestingly enough, and even more so than what we had seen regarding the CDEs' indicators by branches, the traditional industries' efficiency among SPACs dropped deeply below zero in 1990. While the overall picture of the SPACs' efficiency and productivity was similar to that of the CDEs, the average indicators of the SPACs remained well below the CDEs' indicators in 1992. And this situation did not change for 1994 either. It is important to observe that while the average productivity was higher in the group of the CDEs than that of the SPACs in 1994, in the case of the leading industries, such as the chemical industry, telecommunications, education, R&D and cultural services, or energy production, the SPACs' labor productivity was much higher than the CDEs' relevant indicators.

The relative overall position of the CDEs' and the SPACs' profit margins and productivity indicators had not changed either in 1995. But it is important to note that some of the progressing industries, such as, for example, energy production, the chemical industry, the food industry and the machinery industry, as well as some of the advanced services, such as, for example foreign trade, education and healthcare, achieved impressively high productivity indicators. As to profit margins the machinery industry, the chemical industry, the construction materials industry and agriculture, as well as financial services, transport companies and healthcare services, performed the best in 1995.

The SPACs' efficiency indicators largely diverged in 1996. While financial services had extremely high profit margins, PTT and education, the construction materials industry and the chemical industry had respectable profit margins, mining, metallurgy, the light industry and domestic trade were on the other extreme end of the profit margin scale. As regards productivity, the indicators also varied extensively among the branches. The capital intensive industries, such as, for example, energy production and generation, the chemical industry, the vehicle industry, and additionally, education, had the highest productivity indicators in that year, while other services and agriculture lagged far behind.

Obviously, the weights of the different branches among the SPACs differed considerably from the branches' weights among the CDEs. But the trends and composition of industries showed a similar pattern in both company samples. Thus, SPACs in domestic trade, metallurgy, mining, agriculture and the computer industry lost the most in weight, while energy production and distribution, telecommunications services and transportation gained in weight between 1990 and 1996.

We can sum up the main results of the above analysis as follows: There has been a widening spread among the companies' profitability, efficiency and labor productivity by branches, both in the case of the CDEs and the SPACs. The ranking of the branches radically changed over time, while some of the service industries retained their leading position throughout the period of 1988–96 (or 1990–96 for the SPACs). The intra-branch and the inter-branch standard deviations were high and they grew over time, indicating a large diversity among the companies as regards their profitability, efficiency and productivity.

As a matter of fact, the inter-branch standard deviation was much higher than the interregional standard deviation of the companies, or the standard deviation among the companies with different ownership structure. This result points to the fact that a company's adjustment effort was very much affected by its branch affiliation independent of its ownership form. The explanation for this fact is fairly obvious: companies that have belonged to branches with well-established markets and with more extensive links to the international flow of technological and marketing know-how could survive the transformational recession with much more ease than those industries which had heavily relied on the CMEA markets and, first of all, on the Soviet market. When the Soviet Union vanished and the CMEA markets collapsed, most of the former 'flagships' of the Hungarian industry sunk into a hopeless crisis that could not have been quickly resolved even via privatization. Hungarian agriculture – one of the most important 'heavy industries' of the country that produced mass products, such as wheat and meat, first of all for the Soviet market – also lost its ground and struggled for survival.

An important aspect of the companies' adjustment effort from a branch perspective has been the successful operation and expansion of the service sector. There were, of course, branches within services, too, that suffered large setbacks during the transition period. One of them was domestic trade, which became 'overpopulated' by businesses and entrepreneurs by 1992–93. The other one was the financial services industry that carried a huge share of the burden of its loss-making clients. And transportation, especially railway traffic, has been a loss-maker, too. Hungarian transport, which depended heavily on transit freight traffic, was badly hit by the Yugoslav war. The losses in the transport sector were also connected to the collapse of the 'communist world market'. But services, such as, for example, education, telecommunications or healthcare, performed much better than most industrial branches. As a result of this, the share of the service sector in the Hungarian economy approached the level that is common in the advanced market economies. All in all, the service sector – including the energy networks and distribution – became the *locomotive* of the Hungarian economic recovery in the mid-1990s.

5.4.2 Profitability, Efficiency and Productivity of the CDEs and the SPACs by Regions

Although Hungary is a small country by territory, the regional location of its companies also strongly affects their economic performance beside the companies' branch affiliation. The economic transformation has brought about a vast differentiation among the companies' performance and changes in their ranking by their regional location. It is well known that the Northern and north-eastern parts of the country were the centers of the Hungarian industry – mostly heavy industry – beside the central region with Budapest, the capital in the middle. The Hungarian East and south-east were somewhat neglected although these parts of the country produced the bulk of its agricultural products. But the Western and south-western parts of Hungary were not rapidly developing either and they served as a *'cordonne sanitaire'* towards the West.

Liberalization of the Hungarian economy that started in 1968, but only accelerated in the late 1980s until it fully bloomed after the political changes in 1990, resulted in amazing changes of the development level of the different regions. In our analysis we only distinguished among six large regions, but other studies that mainly focused on labor market issues showed that dividing the country into 59 smaller sub-regions identified flourishing sub-regions even in the midst of a depleted region, depending on the activities of private businesses and on the level of infrastructural facilities (Fazekas, 1996). On the following pages I shall present the results of a similar analysis by regions as was just outlined above on the CDEs and the SPACs by branches.

Profitability, efficiency and productivity of the CDEs by regions

I calculated the same performance indicators for the CDEs by regions as for the branches before for the years 1988–96. As can be seen from Table 5.5, the central region of the country, including the capital, had shown the highest profitability indicators in 1988, before the economic transformation started. The profitability indicators of the other five regions ranged within a narrow margin. This result did not realistically reflect the companies' economic performance for the central region was the most densely populated by headquarters of the largest enterprises. And these enterprises had the easiest access to state subsidies and other resources that strongly biased their actual performance. In addition, the same companies that had their centers in Budapest were spread out in the country having a large number of factories in other regions.

The transition period has brought about remarkable changes in the ranking of the regional groups of the companies. First, the central region lost its leading position as regards the companies' economic performance by regions, and it was replaced by the western and north-western part of the country. This fact clearly showed that the relative closeness of the Western countries, first of all Austria and Germany, heavily influenced the development of that region. Nevertheless, the central region still remained the largest by the number of companies and the extent of the companies' economic activities, and its relative share further increased between 1990 and 1996.

Second, the disparity by economic performance among the regions became much larger than it had been before the changes. Although the companies' economic performance depended less on their regional location than on their branch affiliation, the average regional profitability indicators varied more than they had done before. Third, the Western and the Central regions attracted many more new investments and businesses than the other parts of the country. Consequently, these regions became overpopulated by businesses that put a tremendous burden on the infrastructure, while the neglected southern and eastern parts became more and more abandoned and depleted. But interestingly enough, there have not been sizable differences between the profitability indicators of the 'Western' or 'Central' companies on the one hand and the 'Eastern' companies on the other. Those 'Eastern' companies that survived the transition performed as well as the companies that had the privilege to be located closer to the Western border.

Table 5.5. Economic performance of the CDEs by regions, in per cent or in '000 HUF, between 1988 and 1996

				1988			
Region	**No. of CDEs**	**OPROF**	**NCEFF**	**GPM**	**GPROD**	**NPROD**	**Weight**
1	3 106	8.69	3.02	3.84	1 691.47	1 007.18	49.39
2	1 136	7.94	3.23	4.74	1 200.09	956.54	14.16
3	891	5.48	2.68	4.81	994.52	814.26	9.44
4	846	7.87	3.34	4.08	1 214.68	860.08	10.07
5	922	6.98	2.91	3.69	1 043.34	776.59	8.58
6	727	8.15	3.85	4.81	1 056.04	819.10	8.36
All CDEs	7 628	7.88	3.11	4.12	1 353.28	846 00	100.00
wro		9.77	2.86	9.44	49.96	44.92	

				1990			
Region	**No. of CDEs**	**OPROF**	**NCEFF**	**GPM**	**GPROD**	**NPROD**	**Weight**
1	11 281	8.15	3.50	3.71	2 223.66	1 438.53	47.68
2	3 222	3.16	1.72	1.62	1 655.24	1 237.70	14.29
3	2 283	5.64	2.75	4.15	1 529.01	1 053.85	9.85
4	2 073	10.95	4.12	5.47	1 763.15	1 405.50	10.57
5	2 611	4.82	2.16	2.25	1 550.23	1 010.66	8.75
6	1 844	2.90	1.04	1.52	1 610.75	1 117.21	8.87
All CDEs	23 314	6.65	2.91	3.32	1 874.73	1 195.48	100.00
wro		13.04	4.67	12.08	61.31	39.62	

All regions became loss-makers by 1992 as shown in Table 5.5. The largest losses incurred in the north-eastern and south-eastern regions in 1992. But by 1993 the central region closed up – or rather it 'closed down' – to the less-developed regions as one of the regions with the poorest performing companies. In 1994 the eastern part of the country resumed its rank as the region of companies with lowest profitability, but the ranking changed again in 1995. The central region, and the south west and south east hosted the heaviest loss-makers in that year. This tendency also continued in 1996. It is interesting to note, that the central region regained some weight in that year.

The *efficiency* indicators and the indicators of labor *productivity* by regions showed a diverging pattern, as was the case with branches. Notably, the average productivity indicator of companies in the central region was the highest in every year, but it was not the case for the profit margins.

Table 5.5 continued

1992							
Region	**No. of CDEs**	**OPROF**	**NCEFF**	**GPM**	**GPROD**	**NPROD**	**Weight**
1	29 697	–7.21	–1.97	–3.28	3 056.38	1 931.09	54.61
2	7 745	–0.68	–3.19	–2.12	2 314.36	1 796.16	14.97
3	5 538	1.11	–3.47	–3.04	2 107.01	1 598.05	4.98
4	5 032	–0.52	–5.95	–4.11	2 171.18	1 520.07	8.75
5	5 947	–0.80	–5.49	–3.86	2 117.19	1 498.85	7.98
6	3 897	–3.56	–5.52	–5.97	1 820.02	1 464.99	8.71
All CDEs	57 865	–4.38	–2.58	–3.40	2 539.98	1 743.90	100.00
wro		3.31	1.59	0.90	19.03	28.04	

1996							
Region	**No. of CDEs**	**OPROF**	**NCEFF**	**GPM**	**GPROD**	**NPROD**	**Weight**
1	53 192	0.16	–0.02	2.32	9 383.39	2 795.08	56.01
2	14 479	11.83	0.92	3.26	7 154.78	1 788.61	14.68
3	10 057	7.58	0.98	2.30	5 448.94	1 386.78	8.37
4	9 170	9.87	1.22	2.14	5 977.01	1 284.93	7.07
5	10 152	11.67	1.79	2.72	6 003.91	1 263.73	6.94
6	6 967	6.20	0.28	2.48	5 230.60	1 372.87	6.93
All CDEs	104 017	3.90	0.28	2.50	7 575.57	2 057.90	100.00
wro		15.03	6.12	13.44	52.74	43.36	

Note: wro of productivity indicators = (wro/All CDEs)*100.

The central region had ranked the fourth among six regions in 1988 for profit margins, and its relative position deteriorated even further over the years. For instance in 1992 it was only the northern region that had a lower average profit margin than the central region, and in 1993 the central region showed the poorest efficiency indicators among the six regions.

The relative position of the central region has not changed in 1994 and 1995 either. It had the lowest efficiency indicators in both years. Meanwhile the relative position of the other regions changed radically year by year. For instance, the northern region ranked in the middle in 1988, then it slipped back to the last place in 1990 and 1992. But from 1993 on, the relative position of the northern region gradually improved. And by 1995 it had the highest average profit margin among the regions, but the smallest number of companies remaining standing at the same time. The north-western region did not perform very well in 1988 and in 1990, but in 1992 when the whole economy suffered a huge setback, it hit the north-western region the least. When the economy started to recover in 1994 and 1995, the speed of recovery was fairly slow in that region, putting it in third place among the six regions in 1995. The least extreme shifts occurred in the relative position of the south eastern, south western and north western regions as regards profit margins between 1988 and 1996.

Labor productivity was the highest in the central region in 1988 and it remained so over the whole period. In 1988 the north-eastern region ranked second and the north-western region third by productivity. They were followed by the northern, the south-western and the south-eastern regions in that order. By 1992 the south-eastern and the northern regions showed the highest productivity indicators after the central region. South-west and north-west came next and the northern region occupied the last place in the row. In 1995 and 1996 the north-west took over the second place, the north ranked third, the south-west came fourth and north-west and south-west closed the line. It can be observed that the relative position of the regions by labor productivity closely followed the regional pattern of foreign direct investment in Hungary. This observation is in full accord with the results of our analysis by the companies' ownership structure as will be shown in the next section.

Another lesson that we learned was that the regional differences in overall economic development, in the provision of services and in the wealth of the local population, had a direct link to the number of companies and to the extent of economic activities in a given region, but they did not have a strong influence on the average level of profitability, efficiency and labor productivity indicators in the same region. Consequently, there is a potential for the more neglected regions to catch up since the relative costs of production are usually lower than in the more popular regions. What would be needed is sizable investments in infrastructure, financial support for entrepreneurs who would be willing to start businesses in the less favored parts of the country and a good information system that would provide the necessary and specific information on business opportunities for the potential private investors.

Profitability, efficiency and productivity of the SPACs by regions

The SPACs regional distribution was very similar to the distribution of the CDEs as regards the number and the magnitude of economic activity of the companies in the six different regions between 1990 and 1996. The profitability indicators of the SPACs also showed a similar pattern to the CDEs. The figures show that the SPACs mostly populated the central region, while the number of SPACs was close to each other in the other regions. As regards the profitability indicators, the SPACs in the central region did not have the highest indicators, even in 1990. The most profitable companies operated, somewhat surprisingly, in the north-eastern region of the country in that year. The companies of the central region ranked only second as far as their profitability was concerned. Companies with the lowest average profitability indicators could be found in the northern part of the country.

Table 5.6. Economic performance of the SPACs by regions, in per cent or in '000 HUF, between 1990 and 1996

1990							
Region	**No. of SPACs**	**OPROF**	**NCEFF**	**GPM**	**GPROD**	**NPROD**	**Weight**
1	647	8.35	3.70	3.81	2 449.75	1 736.23	51.18
2	288	3.15	0.80	1.63	1 719.53	850.19	13.76
3	228	5.00	2.06	4.39	1 638.01	951.69	10.46
4	179	15.44	4.84	7.32	2 348.84	1 401.82	8.91
5	209	5.09	1.42	2.12	1 770.94	938.82	6.45
6	182	2.70	0.45	1.48	1 858.91	875.05	9.22
All SPACs	1 733	7.16	2.81	3.61	2 129.37	1 336.41	100.00
wro		7.74	1.49	6.53	55.69	37.87	

1992							
Region	**No. of SPACS**	**OPROF**	**NCEFF**	**GPM**	**GPROD**	**NPROD**	**Weight**
1	792	−8.30	−3.05	−6.53	2 662.35	868.10	58.17
2	291	0.54	−2.56	−1.98	2 144.25	566.49	12.21
3	227	1.92	−3.23	−4.13	2 245.27	677.69	8.88
4	178	1.53	−6.59	−4.89	2 469.17	624.90	6.58
5	206	−0.27	−5.92	−5.02	2 115.58	479.21	5.60
6	179	−3.50	−6.11	−8.58	2 535.04	644.01	8.38
All SPACs	1 881	−5.05	−3.42	−5.69	2 481.65	740.76	100.00
wro		29.11	3.36	7.75	78.43	27.59	

By 1992, the level and the ranking of the SPACs' profitability by regions radically changed. First, all regional average indicators turned negative in 1992. The largest loss-makers could be found in the south-eastern, the northern and in the central region of the country. The western region also revealed losses, but the relative level of losses was the smallest there. The companies in the central region were loss-makers on average, too, and their level of negative profitability was close to the level of companies in the northern part.

1994							
Region	**No. of SPACs**	**OPROF**	**NCEFF**	**GPM**	**GPROD**	**NPROD**	**Weight**
1	672	–6.38	–0.44	0.98	3 838.06	1 367.12	59.74
2	269	2.83	0.74	2.85	2 437.49	670.71	12.43
3	190	2.72	–1.39	–0.80	3 398.14	1 053.59	9.44
4	157	6.08	–1.41	0.47	3 733.74	969.87	5.85
5	160	5.64	–1.41	0.21	3 723.59	850.41	5.11
6	154	4.30	0.12	1.41	3 788.76	1 127.34	7.43
All SPACs	1 602	–2.81	–0.45	1.01	3 530.07	1 136.85	100.00
wro		76.35	4.14	28.97	90.09	42.19	

1996							
Region	**No. of SPACs**	**OPROF**	**NCEFF**	**GPM**	**GPROD**	**NPROD**	**Weight**
1	625	–4.15	0.02	2.71	6 910.69	2 579.39	60.23
2	252	5.77	1.18	1.86	5 690.47	1 595.30	11.55
3	165	2.92	–1.65	–0.41	5 458.55	1 650.52	9.65
4	145	6.02	–0.65	0.61	5 761.87	1 452.80	5.88
5	143	8.57	2.57	1.94	5 862.28	1 310.06	5.15
6	138	12.24	4.74	4.65	6 661.49	1 903.70	7.54
All SPACs	1 468	–0.45	0.24	2.31	6 429.46	2 136.06	100.00
wro		157.18	153.26	8.23	32.61	24.23	

Note: wro of productivity indicators = (wro/All SPACs)*100.

Then another reranking occurred among the regions as regards profitability in 1994. The western region preserved its leading position, but the average profitability of the SPACs in the central region further deteriorated, while it considerably improved in the north-eastern region. The least profitable SPACs operated in the south-west. Most of their average profitability indicators remained below zero. The SPACs in the central region scored the second worst among the companies that belonged to the state privatization agencies. And the regional pattern of the SPACs' profitability remained almost the same in 1995, too. The most striking difference between the two last years was that the companies in the northern region ranked best in 1995, while the number of companies drastically declined in that region. Profitability of the SPACs in the central and in the northern regions was positive, while it was negative in the south-east and south-west in 1996. But the number of companies and their relative weight have not declined in the central region, while it shrank in the northern part of the country. In fact, the south-eastern and the northern regions lost the largest number of companies between 1990 and 1996.

The SPACs had an almost identical regional pattern of efficiency and labor productivity as we witnessed in the case of the CDEs. The north-east, the central region and south-west ranked the best regarding average profit margins in 1990. But by 1992 the north-west replaced the north-east as first in the line, while the central region ranked the second but last, just before the north-eastern region in the average profit margin of the SPACs. The relative position of the central region somewhat improved by 1995 and it ranked fourth out of the six regions in that year. At the same time, the north-west lost its leading position to the south-eastern and the northern region. There was a substantial deterioration of the SPACs' efficiency in some regions, while efficiency improved in the central region in 1996. It is interesting to observe that the northern region performed the best among the six regions, while the number of companies declined in that region. The relative position of the regions by labor productivity of the SPACs was almost the same as in the case of CDEs, with one important exception. The northern region showed the highest productivity level in 1995, while the central region ranked second, the south-west ranked third and the north-west was fourth in that year. The central region had the highest, while the south-west had the lowest productivity level in 1996.

What we learned from the former analysis was that both branch and region as selective variables matter in the economic success or failure of the companies. But we could also observe that the relative position of industries and regions changed over time which indicates that a company's adjustment and restructuring efforts are not absolutely constrained by those factors either. How branch affiliation, regional location and factors related to ownership and management interplay will be discussed in the following sections.

5.5 COMPANY RESTRUCTURING AND PERFORMANCE IN RELATION TO THE EXPANSION OF THE PRIVATE SECTOR IN HUNGARY BETWEEN 1988 AND 1996

One of the basic assumptions about the economic transformation has been that by replacing state ownership with private ownership and by creating the necessary institutions of private property rights the formerly socialist countries will develop advanced market economies with efficient private companies. The emergence of the private sector was envisioned as a two-track process. High expectations were attached to the privatization of the state-owned property, but it soon turned out that the birth of thousands of new private businesses may outweigh privatization in importance. Privatization still remained the focus of the transition and for good reasons. Namely, without privatizing the state-owned companies a 'dual economy' could have been developed where the co-existence of the private sector and the state-owned sector could have triggered 'abnormal' economic behavior on both sides. For instance, a sizable state-owned sector could have functioned as a leakage on the private companies' budget constraint giving the wrong market signals to the private businesses. In turn, the private companies would have accommodated the 'market-like' behavior of the state-owned enterprises without making them really accountable for their operation. A bizarre form of economic equilibrium could have occurred where each player would have been stuck in an undesired but unchangeable position. Such an equilibrium would not have been stable but it could have prevailed for a few years until the economy collapsed.

In addition to the economic considerations, political changes also called for privatization. Namely, state ownership was one of the main vehicles of the old socialist regime to exercise its political power in and outside the economic life. Consequently, privatization was inevitable in order to disentangle polity and economy and to remove a dangerous threat to the new and frail political democracy. Privatization of the state-owned companies had been a tolerated – though not very popular – idea among the people at the beginning of the process, but then it became increasingly unpopular for it has been accompanied by growing unemployment, by exploding diversity in people's incomes and wealth and by a very visible corruption. Moreover, the high hopes about the companies' economic performance that had been associated with the change of ownership gradually eroded. There has not been a consensus even among economic analysts as to whether the poor performance of many of the privatized companies was the symptom of the growing pains of the transition or it was organically connected to the emergence of a special blend of 'non-market capitalism' in CEE.

Privatization has had a distinctive feature in Hungary compared to most of the CEE countries. Notably, foreign investors – mostly from advanced market economies – played a decisive role in acquiring the state-owned property, and especially the larger state-owned enterprises. In principle, the dominance of foreign businesses in Hungarian privatization should have eliminated most of the teething troubles for those businesses have had a long record of operating under well-established market conditions all over the world. On the following pages we shall test the hypothesis of the private companies being more profitable, more efficient and more disciplined in financial terms than the state-owned enterprises in the case of the Hungarian economy during its transition. We shall also compare the investment and export activity of the private and the state-owned companies.

5.5.1 Profitability, Efficiency and Labor Productivity of the Companies with Different Ownership Structures

In the following sections we shall present only two profitability indicators (OPROF and NCEFF or ROA) out of eight, of the companies with different ownership structure in each year between 1988 and 1996 for the CDEs and between 1990 and 1996 for the SPACs respectively. We also analyse the efficiency (GPM) and the productivity indicators (GPROD and NPROD) of the CDEs and the SPACs, respectively. While NCEEF is neutral to, profit margins and labor productivity are sensitive to, the companies' branch affiliation and capital–labor ratio. We could have standardized the company groups by ownership and made them comparable if we composed those groups by keeping the shares of different branches identical for each group. However, such a transformation seemed unfeasible and it would have resulted in a bias toward the groups with less companies. What we have done instead was compare the average indicators of the companies with different ownership structure but with identical branch affiliation. We shall show the results later.

Profitability, efficiency and productivity of the CDEs

When we discuss the economic performance of the CDEs, we apply the notion of privatization in a broader sense of the word than usual. Now the term privatization stands for the expansion of the private sector whether the state-owned property was turned into private hands or the private businesses were established anew in the Hungarian economy. CDEs constitute a dominant share of the companies in employment, fixed assets and production, although they do not usually comprise the small private businesses. The indicators for 1988–96 are summed up in Table 5.7.

The first observation we could make was that the average profitability of the CDEs – by any indicator of profitability – gradually declined between 1988 and 1992 and it did not improve in 1993. After then we could witness an upturn in the profitability indicators between 1994 and 1996. We emphasize that the indicators cannot be read as time series, for their content has changed over the years. But the general trend of the indicators is still valid and it is compatible with the trend of the rate of economic growth in Hungary between the late 1980s and the mid-1990s. As can be seen in the tables, ownership had not played a role until 1990. Since then the number and share of the fully or in majority privately-owned companies has radically increased. A composite indicator of the share of companies with different ownership structure in employment, production and fixed assets is the relative weight of the company groups as given in the tables. If we just take the magnitude of the fixed assets into account, the share of the state-owned sector was larger than 50 per cent until 1994, but since then it has declined to less than 40 per cent.

Profitability indicators were positive between 1988 and 1990, but they turned negative afterwards. Fully private companies (*Forprivs* and *Domprivs*) had better profitability indicators than state-owned enterprises in 1990. The indicators of companies with majority private ownership but mixed ownership structure largely varied by ownership groups and it did not have a clear pattern. We could witness the lowest level indicators in 1992 and by then the ranking of the company groups by profitability substantially changed. As can be seen from the tables, the largest groups of the companies with majority private ownership, that is, the Forprivs, the Domprivs and the *Dommosts*, had lower level average profitability indicators than the enterprises with majority state-ownership. It is interesting to observe that within the large group of state-owned enterprises, the state-owned companies with less private ownership (the *Domstats*) performed better, or rather less poorly than the state-owned companies with a larger private ownership share (the *Dommores*) in 1992. The relative position of the private companies improved by 1993 and their profitability indicators showed lower losses than those of the state-owned enterprises, with the exception of the most relevant indicator: the net profits relative to total assets (NCEFF). The average indicator of the SOEs was higher than the indicator of the fully private companies in both years.

The profitability indicators slowly but steadily improved in every ownership group between 1994 and 1996. Regarding the gross profitability indicators, the private companies usually had higher average indicators than the SOEs. But in the case of the ratio of net profits relative to total assets, the private companies still had worse indicators than the state enterprises without foreign owners. And what was even more unexpected: according to their average profitability indicators, the private companies with foreign owners performed more poorly than the domestic private companies between 1993 and 1996. In previous studies I have already discussed the factors that can explain why private companies reported worse profitability indicators than the state-owned enterprises (Major, 1995a, 1995b, 1996a). It is in part connected to the fact that after the disintegration of markets and cooperation networks, the private companies have had more difficulties with establishing themselves on the new markets than had been perceived at the start of the transition. At the same time, the old state-owned enterprises could still rely on their former networks and administrative connections. Moreover, the transition process, that encompasses a radical restructuring of the companies, takes more time than had been expected. Also the private owners focus on expansion and stabilization of their operation first, and the profit motive can and will drive them only afterwards. But in addition to the reasons for low-level profitability mentioned above, there are other factors that cannot be neglected either. Notably, the old statistical and accounting system collapsed and it takes time for the government administration to build up new ones. And private businesses can hide their profits more easily than state-owned enterprises, for the latter ones can be and are being monitored by the former administrative routines. We shall see later that the international networks of foreign private owners can also be used as a channel to siphon off and reallocate profits from their Hungarian – or other CEE – businesses to their companies in other countries. As recent research indicates, foreign companies do not usually create production and marketing networks in CEE and they do not include their East European subsidiaries in their international networks (Comisso, 1997; Schwartz, 1997). They use their CEE companies as subcontracting partners instead. Hence, foreign owners have usually been seeking short-term returns on their investments in CEE. Domestic private owners are more constrained in channeling profits abroad but they also try to find ways to hide their profits behind costs. Whatever the reasons, it is still disturbing that the private sector has not shown its advantages over the state-owned companies in Hungary or in other CEE countries so far. It is unclear yet whether the formerly socialist countries will end up with an economic system of 'non-market capitalism' or they will be able to adjust their economic institutions to the institutions of the Western advanced market economies.[12]

The average indicators were accompanied by fairly large standard deviations. This fact indicates that each ownership group consisted of companies with very different profitability and efficiency. Sometimes the deviations were so large that the average indicator lost its meaning. Consequently, it was necessary to conduct an analysis on the companies' economic performance by using several clusters of profitability.[13] The results showed that there were fairly large sub-groups of companies within every ownership group that performed much better than average even in the worst years such as 1992 and 1993. And especially in the case of fully private companies with foreign owners the successful sub-group of the companies has gradually expanded over the past years, while the group of relatively successful state-owned enterprises has shrunk in size.

The indicators of *efficiency* and labor *productivity* show the success or failure of the companies' short-term adjustment efforts. Profit margins and productivity had very different patterns when we compared the companies in different ownership groups. Profit margins followed a similar trend as had been the case with the profitability indicators. Namely, the overall average and the group averages had been positive in the late 1980s and early 1990s until 1992. Then profit margins turned negative for each company group. A recovery of the indicator can be observed between 1994 and 1996. But comparing the group averages, foreign and domestic private companies had higher profit margins than SOEs, while the profitability indicators of the private companies had been lower than those of the SOEs, except for 1994. It is also interesting to note that the average profit margins of the domestic private companies have usually been higher than those of the foreign private companies.

Gross productivity, that is, turnover per the number of employees, perpetually increased while net productivity fluctuated between 1988 and 1996. A steady growth of the gross indicator is partly due to the shrinking employment. But it also shows, especially if we compare gross and net productivity, that the so-called 'transformation recession' did not result in a drop of overall production, only in the decline of the companies' value added. We shall discuss this important lesson in detail in the next section. Foreign private companies have had much higher, while SOEs much lower, productivity indicators than the overall average. The productivity of the domestic private companies was lower than that of the state-owned enterprises between 1990 and 1993, but it surpassed the average productivity of the state-owned sector between 1994 and 1996.

Table 5.7. Profitability, efficiency (in per cent) and productivity (in '000 HUF) of the CDEs by ownership between 1988 and 1996

				1988			
Ownership form	**No. of CDEs**	**OPROF**	**NCEFF**	**GMP**	**GPROD**	**NPROD**	**Weight**
Forpriv	0	n.a.	n.a.	n.a.	n.a.	n.a.	0
Dompriv	0	n.a.	n.a.	n.a.	n.a.	n.a.	0
Formost	0	n.a.	n.a.	n.a.	n.a.	n.a.	0
Dommost	0	n.a.	n.a.	n.a.	n.a.	n.a.	0
Formix	0	n.a.	n.a.	n.a.	n.a.	n.a.	0
Dommix	0	n.a.	n.a.	n.a.	n.a.	n.a.	0
Formore	0	n.a.	n.a.	n.a.	n.a.	n.a.	0
Dommore	0	n.a.	n.a.	n.a.	n.a.	n.a.	0
Forstat	0	n.a.	n.a.	n.a.	n.a.	n.a.	0
Domstat	7 628	7.86	3.11	4.12	1 353.28	846.00	100
All CDEs	7 628	7.86	3.11	4.12	1 353.28	846.00	100
wro		0.00	0.00	0.00	0.00	0.00	

Table 5.7 continued

1990							
Ownership form	**No. of CDEs**	**OPROF**	**NCEFF**	**GMP**	**GPROD**	**NPROD**	**Weight**
Forpriv	4 773	8.33	4.39	4.13	2 474.83	1 524.66	10.57
Dompriv	16 046	6.17	2.60	2.27	1 559.67	1 075.37	22.81
Formost	0	n.a.	n.a.	n.a.	n.a.	n.a.	0.00
Dommost	542	3.09	2.01	2.16	994.96	575.06	3.57
Formix	1	14.03	6.17	7.30	3 101.55	2 699.09	0.10
Dommix	154	1.26	0.81	0.81	950.33	575.56	0.72
Formore	5	−1.52	−1.20	−27.91	108.13	39.46	0.02
Dommore	50	1.58	0.62	0.72	1 079.82	768.94	0.24
Forstat	14	17.14	3.35	4.02	2 623.74	1 819.47	0.39
Domstat	1 729	6.82	2.77	3.72	2 081.26	1 294.15	61.64
All CDEs	23 314	6.65	2.91	3.32	1 874.73	1 195.48	100.00
wro		12.84	7.62	9.64	15.44	22.41	

1992							
Ownership form	**No. of CDEs**	**OPROF**	**NCEFF**	**GMP**	**GPROD**	**NPROD**	**Weight**
Forpriv	11 499	−3.42	−4.23	−1.91	4 514.33	3 275.08	11.78
Dompriv	39 850	−2.28	−4.35	−2.50	2 187.01	1 571.42	27.29
Formost	190	−15.16	−1.82	−0.08	3 763.68	2 755.62	1.30
Dommost	364	−12.63	−4.38	−6.69	1 678.85	1 193.30	0.79
Formix	342	−21.92	−1.70	−2.34	3 585.61	2 430.37	2.29
Dommix	563	−11.57	−1.31	−8.08	2 843.45	1 636.63	3.86
Formore	262	−3.89	−5.89	−7.74	2 931.82	1 597.45	1.76
Dommore	132	3.58	−2.70	−0.78	4 904.94	3 930.15	0.95
Forstat	71	5.10	−3.09	−3.33	2 171.56	1 222.32	0.80
Domstat	3 837	−3.60	−1.89	−4.57	2 263.67	1 470.62	48.97
All CDEs	57 865	−4.38	−2.58	−3.40	2 539.98	1 743.90	100.00
wro		4.08	1.82	16.99	12.77	21.15	

1996							
Ownership form	**No. of CDEs**	**OPROF**	**NCEFF**	**GMP**	**GPROD**	**NPROD**	**Weight**
Forpriv	19 651	9.82	0.91	4.06	12 513.96	3 503.05	28.33
Dompriv	81 778	11.80	1.17	2.55	6 776.55	1 492.90	33.23
Formost	110	–4.11	–0.83	3.16	6 920.31	2 162.10	2.43
Dommost	384	3.48	–0.98	0.10	5 381.76	1 285.25	2.05
Formix	95	–3.93	1.23	8.83	7 625.22	3 449.50	6.08
Dommix	232	6.37	–0.56	0.48	4 922.38	1 483.34	1.81
Formore	45	–5.95	0.41	2.23	16 661.46	5 383.01	5.46
Dommore	117	–3.15	–4.60	–3.86	3 957.43	802.87	0.24
Forstat	13	7.88	–4.82	–2.36	5 148.63	1 155.70	0.16
Domstat	1 592	–2.82	–3.27	–5.89	3 386.26	1 277.00	20.20
All CDEs	104 017	3.90	0.28	2.50	7 575.57	2 057.90	100.00
wro		47.12	17.84	42.11	51.89	60.81	

Note: wro of productivity indicators = (wro/All CDEs)*100.

We can conclude from the above results that the foreign private companies have been successful in their short-term restructuring efforts. They could reduce the number of employees more radically and increase the efficiency of labor utilization more successfully than either the domestic private or the state-owned companies. This is a striking difference from what we observed in the case of the profitability indicators. An obvious conclusion can be that foreign private companies have been focusing on short-term rather than long-term results. It was much easier for them to cut employment than to restructure companies by investing in new technologies and in new product lines.

Profitability, efficiency and labor productivity of the SPACs

We shall use here the conventional meaning of the notion of privatization in the analysis of the SPACs' economic performance by ownership groups. All the companies belonging to the SPACs have been subordinated to the state privatization agencies. Some of them will never be privatized and the state will retain a majority share in others. But the SPACs also consist of companies whose shares were sold to domestic or foreign private owners in majority. Consequently, we can assess the impact of genuine privatization on the companies' economic performance. In addition, we can also observe the influence of the state as an owner on the companies' economic indicators. (See the indicators in Table 5.8.)

The weight of the state-owned enterprises perpetually decreased while the relative weight of the private companies expanded between 1990 and 1996.

The composite weight of the Domstats was above 90 per cent in 1990 and it shrunk to 30.2 per cent by 1996. The share of private companies with foreign owners increased faster than the share of domestic private companies within the SPACs. The weight of the Forprivs stood at 4.9 per cent in 1990 and it grew to 18.3 per cent by 1995, while it increased from 3.7 per cent in 1990 to 11.3 per cent in 1996 in the case of the Domprivs.

A striking difference between the SPACs and the CDEs has been that, with the exception of 1990, both the foreign and the domestic private companies reported better profitability indicators within the SPACs while they had poorer results within the CDEs, as we discussed in the previous section. How can this diverging trend be explained? Did privatization itself have such a decisive and positive impact on the companies' performance? Or was there an inverse connection between performance and ownership change? Notably, was it not the case that those companies who were first bought by private, and especially by foreign, owners whose economic performance had been fairly good even before privatization? A large number of case studies that were conducted at foreign-owned companies support the above assumption. Otherwise the average indicators of the SPACs in different ownership groups followed the same trend as had been shown in the case of the CDEs. The SPACs could not escape the 'transformation recession' either, but their profitability indicators started to improve after 1993. And by 1995 the overall profitability indicators were above zero again. It was also true for 1996, although the SPACs' profitability indicators deteriorated somewhat.

The standard deviations of the profitability indicators were less extreme than in the case of the CDEs. But those deviations from the average indicators were large enough to call for precaution. As with the CDEs it was true for the SPACs that we could find companies with very different profitability indicators behind the averages.

The profit margins and labor productivity of the SPACs by ownership showed a similar pattern as had been the case with the CDEs. As can be seen in the tables, foreign private companies had higher profit margins than state-owned enterprises between 1990 and 1996. But domestic private companies performed more poorly than SOEs until 1993. It is important to note that SPACs reported lower overall profit margins than CDEs over the whole period. As regards labor productivity, the results were almost the same as in the case of profit margins. Foreign private companies operated with higher, but domestic private companies with lower, productivity than SOEs. What is worth noting is that the difference between the profit margin and the productivity level of the Forprivs and the Domstats has been smaller in the case of the SPACs than of the CDEs. This is an interesting contrast to the fact that the foreign private companies had better profitability indicators than the state-owned enterprises among the SPACs for the whole period, while the opposite was true in the case of the CDEs.

Table 5.8. Profitability, efficiency (in per cent) and productivity (in '000 HUF) of the SPACs by ownership between 1990 and 1996

1990							
Ownership form	**No. of SPACs**	**OPROF**	**NCEFF**	**GMP**	**GPROD**	**NPROD**	**Weight**
Forpriv	79	4.06	2.52	2.56	2 008.66	349.08	4.85
Dompriv	139	3.90	1.15	1.72	2 459.53	372.97	3.70
Formost	0	n.a	n.a	n.a	n.a	n.a	n.a.
Dommost	3	5.45	0.08	3.18	1 282.81	23.30	0.28
Formix	1	14.03	6.17	7.30	3 101.55	635.22	0.15
Dommix	4	10.31	4.65	3.65	2 542.28	327.82	0.11
Formore	1	–0.44	–0.40	–8.97	82.38	16.06	0.04
Dommore	3	25.08	6.26	4.32	2 706.74	356.02	0.03
Forstat	4	17.46	3.22	3.94	2 855.37	287.01	0.51
Domstat	1 499	7.41	2.91	3.73	2 121.12	440.23	90.33
All SPACs	1 733	7.16	2.81	3.61	2 129.37	431.50	100.00
wro		34.22	5.08	7.46	16.62	10.54	

1992							
Ownership form	**No. of SPACs**	**OPROF**	**NCEFF**	**GMP**	**GPROD**	**NPROD**	**Weight**
Forpriv	71	–0.37	–4.05	–1.21	3 345.14	910.52	4.03
Dompriv	167	–32.84	–21.09	–21.83	2 374.60	530.78	2.88
Formost	23	–31.83	–3.14	–1.80	3 557.86	1 435.50	1.67
Dommost	36	–18.32	–3.32	–6.02	1 988.10	490.29	0.65
Formix	43	–31.33	–2.01	–4.76	3 406.93	1 739.30	2.64
Dommix	41	–11.52	–1.12	–8.95	2 887.84	921.91	6.67
Formore	32	–6.24	–7.73	–12.46	2 682.30	852.94	2.43
Dommore	41	4.06	–2.16	–0.47	5 117.24	827.41	1.65
Forstat	12	8.62	–3.47	–2.59	2 060.93	909.19	1.28
Domstat	1 415	–2.80	–3.44	–5.18	2 327.36	679.27	76.10
All SPACs	1 881	–5.05	–3.42	–5.69	2 481.65	740.76	100.00
wro		8.83	2.87	22.02	29.81	24.94	

Table 5.8 continued

1994							
Ownership form	**No. of SPACs**	**OPROF**	**NCEFF**	**GMP**	**GPROD**	**NPROD**	**Weight**
Forpriv	124	13.51	0.99	3.63	5 262.49	1 605.05	9.02
Dompriv	379	3.00	−3.27	−0.78	3 036.11	744.20	4.12
Formost	54	−3.97	−0.95	1.04	2 842.24	1 248.15	3.76
Dommost	212	4.38	−1.00	0.65	3 426.60	926.26	4.02
Formix	43	−9.96	0.60	10.06	4 550.29	1 779.96	3.51
Dommix	78	1.75	−1.05	0.34	3 392.82	1 092.03	5.48
Formore	15	2.25	−0.17	0.45	5 081.89	3 125.61	6.52
Dommore	40	2.63	−0.60	−0.09	6 969.75	1 965.30	5.71
Forstat	12	−10.71	−0.07	1.33	9 655.75	3 424.50	7.49
Domstat	645	−5.17	−0.74	−0.26	2 659.31	729.62	5.04
All SPACs	1 602	−2.81	−0.45	1.01	3 530.07	1 136.85	100.00
wro		11.88	1.95	29.57	197.10	127.62	

1996							
Ownership form	**No. of SPACs**	**OPROF**	**NCEFF**	**GMP**	**GPROD**	**NPROD**	**Weight**
Forpriv	169	7.55	3.50	9.31	9 095.68	3 090.43	18.36
Dompriv	547	5.68	0.31	1.15	6 037.66	1 477.30	11.29
Formost	49	−4.79	−0.26	4.49	6 916.11	2 056.97	5.35
Dommost	184	4.41	−0.35	0.61	5 613.20	1 335.18	4.63
Formix	30	−4.00	1.12	8.00	7 591.48	3 529.92	13.33
Dommix	64	6.12	−0.25	0.87	4 744.46	1480.59	3.84
Formore	11	−6.12	0.37	2.10	17 352.71	5 752.89	12.03
Dommore	15	−9.97	−3.94	−5.17	6 870.51	1 447.38	0.71
Forstat	3	12.12	−0.33	1.42	5 167.80	1 038.99	0.27
Domstat	331	−3.60	−4.81	−7.88	3 537.20	1 259.03	30.20
All SPACs	1 403	−0.90	0.12	2.31	6 429.46	2 136.06	100.00
wro		5.46	3.12	6.76	66.97	71.53	

Note: wro of productivity indicators = (wro/All SPACs)*100.

The results support the assumption that foreign investors acquired those companies that had performed better before privatization, but those investors have usually not contributed a great deal to further improvement of the companies' economic performance after privatization. A factor behind this phenomenon can also be that restructuring and upgrading of a company's activities takes a longer time than had been expected.

As was mentioned above, the companies' branch affiliation may have a hidden impact on their efficiency and productivity indicators. To test this assumption we made an experiment with the CDEs. We recalculated the indicator of net profit margin for the foreign and the domestic private companies and for the SOEs in each year in the following manner. First we selected the weights of the branches within the group of the foreign-owned companies in each year and applied those weights for the domestic private companies and the SOEs. The result was that the gap between the Forprivs on the one hand, and the Domprivs and the Domstats on the other widened further. But when we chose the weights of branches within the group of the state-owned companies and applied those weights for the two groups of the private companies, the average net profit margins of the three company groups came very close to each other. In the case of the Domprivs and the Domstats, even their ranking changed for the benefit of the Domstats in 1990, 1992 and 1994. We can conclude that the branch structure of the company groups with different ownership structures does matter and it presumably favors the foreign private companies and it disfavors the state-owned enterprises. It is further evidence that foreign investors 'skimmed the cream' when they acquired shares in the Hungarian companies. Foreign investments targeted those industries that had been more successful and which had had well-established markets before privatization started.

5.5.2 The Financial State of the Companies with Different Ownership

Company adjustment and restructuring would be meaningless without the effective role of money and without an effective budget constraint of the companies in Central and Eastern Europe. But in a 'mixed economy' – as the CEE economies have been – the traditional functions of money, that are given in an advanced market economy, do not appear automatically. Since the state as an owner and the government as a regulator have a large influence on companies and markets, money and finances must undergo deep structural changes, too. These changes include a radical reform of monetary and fiscal policies and institutions on the macro level, and the emergence of an autonomous banking sector, the creation of financial and capital markets, and the reshaping of the company finances on the micro level. On the following pages we shall only focus on some crucial aspects of company finances in relation to the ownership change of the companies. We shall use five indicators to describe the financial state and behavior of the companies with varying ownership structures.

The indicator FATA stands for financial assets relative to total assets. This indicator shows how large a share of the companies' assets are held in – in other words, diverted toward – financial assets. The larger the indicator the most probable it is that the companies consider productive investments riskier than financial investments. Moreover, the companies may be forced to transfer resources toward financial assets if their net revenues are insufficient to cover the costs of their operation. Should this be the case, high indicators would signal an extensive asset stripping of the companies.

The other financial indicators – SOLV, DEBT, SIN, and EQU – were defined and explained in section 5.3 above. On the following pages we shall discuss the financial indicators of the CDEs first, then we turn to the indicators of the SPACs. The financial indicators, like the profitability indicators, can be applied for a cross-section analysis, but they cannot be considered as elements of a time series for the components of the indicators have changed in content during the past years.[14]

The financial performance of the CDEs

We outline five financial indicators for the groups of companies with different ownership structure for 1988 and 1990, that is, immediately before and after the start of the transition, and for 1992 – for the worst year of the recession – and for 1996 (Table 5.9).

Financial assets relative to total assets (FATA) were small on average in 1988. The indicator remained below 10 per cent, a magnitude not excessive compared to the companies' need for liquid money in order to pursue their production and marketing activities without too much friction. In fact, the magnitude of financial assets was even too low. Then FATA has perpetually increased over the last years and it exceeded 30 per cent in 1996. The indicator of the foreign private companies was the highest in 1990. It amounted to 20 per cent and it remained around 20 per cent in the following years, too. The indicator of the domestic private companies was much lower at the beginning, but then it started increasing and it exceeded 27 per cent in 1994 and 26 per cent in 1995. It declined somewhat to 25.9 per cent in 1996. The state-owned enterprises started with a fairly small indicator in 1990, but then it began to grow very fast. The Domstats had the highest indicator in 1994 and in 1995 with 31.1 per cent and 35.9 per cent respectively. Then their indicator shrank to 22 per cent in 1996.

The stability of the indicator of the foreign private companies implies that there is a 'normal' level of the financial assets relative to total assets that is compatible with the companies' need for liquid assets and also with their expansion. This level was around 20 per cent. Thus, the much higher level of the indicator of the state-owned enterprises showed that SOEs pursued a defensive rather than an offensive strategy. They kept their assets liquid and they also invested in financial assets rather than in productive assets for it was safer and more profitable to do. Consequently, it was not true that SOEs stripped their assets and spent the money on wages and other flow expenditures. They just reallocated their resources instead. This was a rational choice for them since SOEs have been in a fairly uncertain position. It was not always clear whether they would be privatized or not and if so, when the privatization would occur, and what would be the results of privatization on product structures, technology change and the size of the company.

Solvency of the CDEs declined until 1993, but it recovered between 1994 and 1996. It is interesting to note that the solvency indicator of the SOEs exceeded the indicators of the foreign private and the domestic private companies after 1991. This was in part due to the fact that the companies' solvency depended on the magnitude of their financial assets. And as we have just seen, the state-owned enterprises started accumulating large amounts of financial assets in the mid-1990s. But the relatively low level of solvency of the private companies also showed that they accumulated huge liabilities within a few years.

Table 5.9. Financial indicators of the CDEs by ownership categories in per cent between 1988 and 1996

			1988			
Ownership form	**No. of CDEs**	**FATA**	**SOLV**	**DEBT**	**SIN**	**EQU**
Forpriv	0	n.a.	n.a.	n.a.	n.a.	n.a.
Dompriv	0	n.a.	n.a.	n.a.	n.a.	n.a.
Formost	0	n.a.	n.a.	n.a.	n.a.	n.a.
Dommost	0	n.a.	n.a.	n.a.	n.a.	n.a.
Formix	0	n.a.	n.a.	n.a.	n.a.	n.a.
Dommix	0	n.a.	n.a.	n.a.	n.a.	n.a.
Formore	0	n.a.	n.a.	n.a.	n.a.	n.a.
Dommore	0	n.a.	n.a.	n.a.	n.a.	n.a.
Forstat	0	n.a.	n.a.	n.a.	n.a.	n.a.
Domstat	7 628	8.52	71.54	8.88	91.35	72.56
All CDEs	7 628	8.52	71.54	8.88	91.35	72.56
wro		0.00	0.00	0.00	0.00	0.00

Table 5.9 continued

1990						
Ownership form	**No. of CDEs**	**FATA**	**SOLV**	**DEBT**	**SIN**	**EQU**
Forpriv	4 773	20.07	76.86	18.35	87.07	96.17
Dompriv	16 046	14.40	69.69	8.56	87.81	94.40
Formost	0	n.a.	n.a.	n.a.	n.a.	n.a.
Dommost	542	10.91	75.10	8.22	91.89	63.73
Formix	1	5.92	116.23	5.04	150.20	84.82
Dommix	154	13.52	83.36	6.71	94.64	74.75
Formore	5	13.93	276.62	0.79	158.55	71.64
Dommore	50	7.77	69.67	6.14	88.38	97.00
Forstat	14	9.15	55.32	32.92	54.92	98.63
Domstat	1 729	10.38	69.94	9.22	93.59	70.72
All CDEs	23 314	12.56	71.32	10.00	91.48	81.03
wro		3.13	4.73	3.19	4.15	12.01

1992						
Ownership form	**No. of CDEs**	**FATA**	**SOLV**	**DEBT**	**SIN**	**EQU**
Forpriv	11 499	20.89	92.61	33.12	71.79	n.a.
Dompriv	39 850	18.27	82.67	16.81	80.91	n.a.
Formost	190	42.62	118.21	10.09	63.42	n.a.
Dommost	364	19.38	104.66	22.39	94.20	n.a.
Formix	342	30.09	117.47	107.33	53.87	n.a.
Dommix	563	16.31	125.60	40.90	85.99	n.a.
Formore	262	21.27	102.46	25.29	76.45	n.a.
Dommore	132	9.41	70.94	8.62	86.78	n.a.
Forstat	71	17.39	55.49	32.34	68.67	n.a.
Domstat	3 837	23.16	148.13	82.19	84.36	n.a.
All CDEs	57 865	22.06	123.32	56.53	80.54	n.a.
wro		3.85	30.67	31.10	14.86	n.a.

1996						
Ownership form	**No. of CDEs**	**FATA**	**SOLV**	**DEBT**	**SIN**	**EQU**
Forpriv	19 651	23.09	89.29	59.94	175.75	109.63
Dompriv	81 778	25.90	73.05	34.67	149.71	118.45
Formost	110	21.89	105.02	38.37	121.61	107.66
Dommost	384	18.51	71.35	7.46	122.45	91.95
Formix	95	20.86	82.24	50.34	130.35	73.30
Dommix	232	9.15	69.77	6.51	121.40	80.81
Formore	45	36.21	92.27	30.71	179.77	59.00
Dommore	117	13.66	60.79	6.79	122.78	120.00
Forstat	13	22.12	68.59	6.10	116.82	66.96
Domstat	1 592	21.46	94.29	8.57	107.59	68.67
All CDEs	104 017	24.16	84.80	34.22	143.74	103.17
wro		4.06	9.63	19.21	26.08	22.49

While the state-owned enterprises were in a better financial shape than the private companies in the short term, they have been much more in debt in the long run. This was due to the inherited debt of the SOEs from the socialist past and especially to the rapidly growing burden of servicing those debts. The level of indebtedness of the private companies also increased to a substantial extent, but they have had easier access to foreign loans with lower servicing burdens. As regards the indicator of financial stability, the state-owned enterprises performed better than the private companies until 1995, but since then they have fallen behind the foreign and domestic private companies. What is worth noting is that each company group had a high level of financial stability in 1995 and in 1996. This was a direct result of the so-called 'loan and bank consolidation program' of the Hungarian government in 1993–94.

It can be observed in the tables that private companies had a much higher level of arrears until 1991, and then in 1996 than SOEs. This is an unexpected result of the analysis that shows that private companies have not been more meticulous in paying their outstanding debt than state-owned enterprises during the last years. We can conclude that private ownership is not in itself a sufficient condition for the companies' higher level of financial discipline. Moreover, while the expansion of private ownership improved the financial performance of the companies, especially that of the foreign private companies, the process is controversial and it will take a long time until the private companies will operate under the same financial rules in Hungary as they do in advanced market economies.

The financial state of the SPACs

Now we turn to the financial indicators of the SPACs with different ownership structure. We present the same indicators for the SPACs as we did for the CDEs (Table 5.10).

Financial assets relative to total assets showed a similar pattern in the case of SPACs as it did for the CDEs. SOEs had much lower indicators than foreign and domestic private companies in 1990 and 1991. But then the SOEs' indicator started growing rapidly and it amounted to 31.1 per cent in 1995 and to 28.3 per cent in 1996. The indicator of the foreign private companies was somewhat higher than we saw in the case of the CDEs, but it remained in the 20–25 per cent range until 1995. Then it jumped to 28.7 per cent in 1996. The domestic private companies had a much lower indicator than Domstats or Forprivs and the indicator was also smaller than we had seen in the case of CDE domestic private companies.

The solvency indicators of the SPACs with different ownership structure behaved almost identically to the indicators of the CDEs. An interesting exception was the solvency indicator of the company groups in 1995. Domstats had a better indicator than Forprivs or Domprivs in that year. This fact indicates that state-owned enterprises belonging to the privatization agencies were more tightly controlled by those agencies than SOEs outside the jurisdiction of the privatization agencies.

Table 5.10. Financial indicators of the SPACs by ownership categories in per cent between 1990 and 1996

			1990			
Ownership form	No. of SPACs	FATA	SOLV	DEBT	SIN	EQU
Forpriv	79	19.05	81.58	10.08	94.51	67.69
Dompriv	139	14.17	76.46	20.09	80.67	70.43
Formost	0	n.a	n.a	n.a	n.a	n.a
Dommost	3	20.26	55.60	0.06	94.05	37.40
Formix	1	5.92	116.23	5.04	150.20	84.82
Dommix	4	9.15	78.65	20.51	83.92	44.27
Formore	1	9.83	212.88	1.01	165.47	63.56
Dommore	3	3.94	91.00	2.75	108.14	209.25
Forstat	4	9.15	55.06	35.05	54.01	99.05
Domstat	1 499	10.96	69.04	9.97	92.80	70.36
All SPACs	1 733	11.58	70.24	10.36	92.27	70.44
wro		1.76	26.11	2.62	5.69	24.20

1992						
Ownership form	**No. of SPACs**	**FATA**	**SOLV**	**DEBT**	**SIN**	**EQU**
Forpriv	71	22.49	106.49	9.05	93.15	n.a.
Dompriv	167	17.61	61.82	15.23	68.63	n.a.
Formost	23	58.24	137.99	7.35	47.77	n.a.
Dommost	36	19.60	98.71	31.04	80.50	n.a.
Formix	43	37.16	116.08	146.22	40.80	n.a.
Dommix	41	16.21	127.06	41.40	86.26	n.a.
Formore	32	23.18	87.65	27.49	65.59	n.a.
Dommore	41	9.20	73.58	6.26	90.64	n.a.
Forstat	12	6.86	75.25	13.44	77.79	n.a.
Domstat	1 415	28.79	83.56	10.02	85.21	n.a.
All SPACs	1 881	26.90	95.00	17.87	81.97	n.a.
wro		8.14	30.73	12.42	14.27	n.a.

1994						
Ownership form	**No. of SPACs**	**FATA**	**SOLV**	**DEBT**	**SIN**	**EQU**
Forpriv	124	25.76	91.85	17.59	71.17	n.a.
Dompriv	379	17.36	72.30	15.13	71.81	n.a.
Formost	54	31.80	86.31	10.17	68.61	n.a.
Dommost	212	16.03	80.12	5.82	86.18	n.a.
Formix	43	41.48	118.04	111.36	41.59	n.a.
Dommix	78	8.50	84.45	6.19	92.44	n.a.
Formore	15	14.73	100.38	22.79	78.84	n.a.
Dommore	40	2.54	64.27	9.09	86.60	n.a.
Forstat	12	21.52	112.37	42.37	77.73	n.a.
Domstat	645	34.78	87.49	26.36	75.79	n.a.
All SPACs	1 602	29.10	94.94	26.98	74.91	n.a.
wro		11.72	40.99	20.33	11.48	n.a.

Table 5.10 continued

			1996			
Ownership form	**No. of SPACs**	**FATA**	**SOLV**	**DEBT**	**SIN**	**EQU**
Forpriv	169	28.17	94.61	32.05	137.68	68.03
Dompriv	547	13.21	73.41	12.37	122.95	89.08
Formost	49	23.62	105.19	28.63	109.38	107.02
Dommost	184	18.63	71.18	7.67	122.72	91.32
Formix	30	19.12	80.91	47.27	125.02	72.02
Dommix	64	9.15	81.09	5.32	113.39	75.35
Formore	11	36.23	94.55	30.13	186.84	56.19
Dommore	15	3.57	57.58	75.27	196.00	81.61
Forstat	3	6.78	40.73	7.43	138.07	76.12
Domstat	331	28.13	95.27	9.92	109.82	64.07
All SPACs	1 403	25.36	89.09	23.75	129.57	70.97
wro		7.52	10.09	14.47	24.45	13.03

The level of indebtedness of the SPACs increased in each company group, but it was higher in the case of the Domstats than for the private companies. Financial stability oscillated in each company group over time. State-owned enterprises had a somewhat better indicator than private companies in 1995 and 1996, which also shows that control has been stronger and more effective within rather than outside the jurisdiction of the privatization agencies.

The overall financial performance of the SPACs has been poorer than the CDEs' performance. While the private companies achieved better indicators than the state-owned enterprises within the CDEs, the opposite was true in the case of the SPACs. An obvious conclusion from this fact can be that privatized companies that must tolerate the interference of the government administration also 'benefit' from this interference by being more lax in their financial activities. They can do so since they can count on the financial support of the government to a larger extent than other private companies can. Thus, the co-existence of private owners and the state as an owner reduces rather than increases the level of financial discipline of the otherwise privatized companies. A lesson can be drawn that clear and homogenous ownership is more favorable than mixed ownership in relation to the companies' financial performance.

5.6 EFFICIENCY OR EXPANSION? SOME PECULIARITIES OF THE TRANSITION

The socialist economy was a value distracting economic system by nature (McKinnon, 1993). A considerable share of its production could not be sold on the market because of quality reasons, or because of poor marketing and management. Factors of production were wasted to a large extent and economic growth was frequently accompanied by financial imbalances and by severe shortages of resources and consumer products. Dissatisfaction with the efficiency of the socialist economy had been prevalent even before the transition. The focus of the socialist governments' economic policy became efficient production instead of fast economic growth. The rate of growth decelerated in every socialist country in the early the 1980s, but the level of efficiency did not improve. Consequently, a general expectation about the economic transformation was that by replacing socialism with capitalism and state ownership with private ownership, the CEE countries will create an efficient market economy.

The transformation started with a huge recession in each CEE country. The setback was larger than during the world-wide crisis of 1929–32. Several analysts argued that the fall of production was unavoidable, for the 'moment of truth' arrived for the loss-making companies that had to be closed down or at least their production level had to be reduced. Consequently, the contraction of production was a part of the cure of the CEE economies' endemic inefficiency. However, in reality the recession did not only hit the loss-making companies or industries. Especially with the collapse of the CMEA trading system, whole market networks of the Hungarian companies disintegrated. The economy could not be divided into a healthy and an unhealthy sphere, but the transition undermined the stability of the whole company sector. Astonishing as it may sound, the state-owned enterprises coped with the crisis more easily – but only for a short period – than the privatized or newly-established private companies. The main reason for this was that the private companies had to create their marketing and production networks almost from scratch, while the state-owned enterprises could rely, at least to some extent, on their former connections with suppliers and customers and they were also supported by the government bureaucracy.

Stabilizing production and markets and restructuring the inefficient companies would have required sizable investments in production technologies, but also in management and organization. In addition, the loss of markets and the recession on the domestic market could only be counterbalanced by enhancing the companies' export activities on new markets. But did it all really happen? We analysed the investment and export activity of the companies with different ownership by using several indicators.

It is frequently argued that the low profitability level of the privatized and the newly-established private companies – which we also observed in the previous section – is a temporary phenomenon. It is due to the large investment and expansion efforts of the private companies that is necessary in order to restructure the companies and enlarge their market share. By comparing the indicators of investment and export activity of the private companies on the one hand, and the state-owned enterprises on the other, we can test the above assumption.

5.6.1 Investment and Export Activity of the Companies with Different Ownership Structures

First we shall discuss the investment activity of the companies. Then the analysis of the companies' export activity will follow. We used three indicators (UNIF, FIF and ICR) to measure the investment activity and two indicators (EXRT and LABC) were applied to measure the export activity of the companies. (The definition of the indicators is given in section 5.3.)

Investment and export activity of the CDEs

In this section we present first the three indicators of the CDEs' investment activity between 1988 and 1996. A more detailed analysis of the results will follow later in this section. Then we shall discuss the indicators of the SPACs in the next section (Table 5.11). As is shown in the tables, the ratio of unfinished investments relative to fixed assets (UNIF) increased with a few percentage points between 1988 and 1990, but then it started declining and it oscillated within the range of 4 to 6 per cent. Foreign private companies had a much higher indicator than domestic private companies and than state-owned enterprises. The indicator of the Forprivs exceeded the indicator of the Domstats two to six times during the period of 1988 and 1996. The indicator of the Domprivs was also somewhat higher than the indicator of the Domstats. These results clearly show that the private companies and especially the companies with foreign owners started more investments than the SOEs during the first years of the transition. It is also important to note that after 1990–91, the indicator of the Forprivs diminished, showing that foreign private companies have not continued to enhance their investments in later years.

The results are also compatible with the macro-level data on investment. The volume of finished investments substantially increased in 1993 and 1994. This implies that the average gestation period of the investments amounted to 2–4 years. Hence the new investments that had been started in 1990 and 1991 were put into operation in 1993 and 1994. But the volume of finished investments leveled out in 1995, which was a direct consequence of the decline of the volume of new, unfinished investments. We can conclude that a large part of the investment boom of the Hungarian economy in 1993–94 can be attributed to the dynamic investment activity of the foreign private companies at the beginning of the transition. But later on, the investment activity of the foreign private companies declined, while the domestic private companies and the state-owned enterprises have not started huge investments in a large number. As a result, the growth of investment decelerated. The same was true for 1996. A new upswing of investments did not occur until 1997.

The indicator of financial investments relative to fixed assets (FIF) showed a completely different trend from UNIF. The indicator was fairly high and growing over the past seven years. During the first years of the transition the Domprivs had the highest indicators, and they were followed by the Forprivs. But since 1992, the Domstats ranked first among the company groups with indicators around 30 per cent. The pattern was similar to that we had seen before in the case of financial assets relative to total assets. The results show that every company group favored financial investments for productive investments, but this trend was the strongest in the case of the SOEs.

Another indicator of investment activity was the ratio of investment credits relative to the companies' total liabilities (ICR). The average indicator of all companies diminished in the first years, but it increased again in 1995. This fact can indicate that a new upswing of total investment can be expected in the coming years. ICR was the highest in the group of Domstats until 1995, but then the foreign private companies ranked first. A part of the SOEs' investment credits could be carried over from the past, while private companies started borrowing only after the changes. Another difference between domestic and foreign companies was that domestic companies could usually borrow in Hungary, where lending rates have been fairly high, while foreign companies mostly borrowed abroad for lower lending rates. And a part of their credits did not show up in the books of the Hungarian companies.

We can conclude that the investment activity of the companies have not been very robust in Hungary since economic transformation started. Private companies, and first of all foreign private companies, had the lead in starting new productive investments, while state-owned enterprises increased their financial investments during the last seven years. The low propensity to invest contributed to the slow recovery of the Hungarian economy and a fairly low rate of economic growth even after the recession was over.

Let us turn to the analysis of the export activity indicators now. As a 'side effect' of the economic transformation, the former trade relations of the CEE countries disintegrated and their magnitude dropped to a minuscule level.

The collapse of trade among the CEE countries could have been avoided, but the actual system of trade – that was centrally planned, bilaterally regulated by CEE governments and used bartering procedures rather than money – had to be replaced by genuine markets. The collapse was fostered by political factors beside economic reality and political zeal pushed destruction beyond the level that would have been rational on economic grounds. Namely, the CEE countries had been and could still be natural trading partners to each other.

After the disintegration of CEE trade and the shrinkage of the domestic markets of the CEE countries that accompanied the 'transformation recession', these countries did not have other leeways than 'to escape forward', that is, to enhance their exports to, and imports from, the advanced market economies. Consequently, an obvious success indicator of the companies' adjustment and restructuring effort has been the level of their export activity. Export expansion can be regarded as an indicator of international competitiveness of the CEE countries. Since most CEE economies are small in size, their international competitiveness is the determining factor of the companies' overall competitiveness. It does not make sense to separate 'domestic' and international competitiveness in CEE, for CEE companies must either compete on international markets or on the domestic market with international competitors.

Table 5.11. Investment and export activity of the CDEs in per cent between 1988 and 1996

			1988			
Ownership form	**No. of CDEs**	**UNIF**	**FIF**	**ICR**	**EXTR**	**LABC**
Forpriv	0	n.a.	n.a.	n.a.	n.a.	n.a.
Dompriv	0	n.a.	n.a.	n.a.	n.a.	n.a.
Formost	0	n.a.	n.a.	n.a.	n.a.	n.a.
Dommost	0	n.a.	n.a.	n.a.	n.a.	n.a.
Formix	0	n.a.	n.a.	n.a.	n.a.	n.a.
Dommix	0	n.a.	n.a.	n.a.	n.a.	n.a.
Formore	0	n.a.	n.a.	n.a.	n.a.	n.a.
Dommore	0	n.a.	n.a.	n.a.	n.a.	n.a.
Forstat	0	n.a.	n.a.	n.a.	n.a.	n.a.
Domstat	7 628	7.78	8.40	10.81	12.15	11.50
All CDEs	7 628	7.78	8.40	10.81	12.15	11.50
wro		0.00	0.00	0.00	0.00	0.00

1990						
Ownership form	**No. of CDEs**	**UNIF**	**FIF**	**ICR**	**EXTR**	**LABC**
Forpriv	4 773	14.56	12.79	5.67	17.65	10.07
Dompriv	16 046	5.29	16.17	5.12	7.6	14.29
Formost	0	n.a.	n.a.	n.a.	n.a.	n.a.
Dommost	542	5.93	12.76	13.4	2.57	22.28
Formix	1	8.02	1.43	6.92	35.98	10.47
Dommix	154	4.16	12.77	8.59	2.88	22.1
Formore	5	0.19	2.63	0	1.6	31.84
Dommore	50	6.52	10.06	6.84	0.99	17.42
Forstat	14	1.51	11.45	4.97	22.23	6.88
Domstat	1 729	8.39	12.31	9.84	12.88	11.82
All CDEs	23 314	8.36	13.02	7.92	11.70	12.63
wro		2.60	1.67	2.43	3.71	2.58

1992						
Ownership form	**No. of CDEs**	**UNIF**	**FIF**	**ICR**	**EXTR**	**LABC**
Forpriv	11 499	8.44	16.2	n.a.	20.45	11.84
Dompriv	39 850	3.8	16.7	n.a.	9.99	17.25
Formost	190	2.49	42.2	n.a.	12.66	13.48
Dommost	364	3.76	21.76	n.a.	15.7	25.1
Formix	342	3.95	56.28	n.a.	14.72	16.3
Dommix	563	2.74	19.03	n.a.	8.9	19.95
Formore	262	5.4	22.96	n.a.	38.19	17.22
Dommore	132	14.41	6.69	n.a.	5.29	9.6
Forstat	71	4.73	22.54	n.a.	45.8	22.03
Domstat	3 837	3.33	29.46	n.a.	13.25	18.26
All CDEs	57 865	4.09	25.39	n.a.	13.92	16.64
wro		2.71	31.69	n.a.	5.46	2.44

Table 5.11 continued

		1996				
Ownership form	**No. of CDEs**	**UNIF**	**FIF**	**ICR**	**EXTR**	**LABC**
Forpriv	19 651	9.41	23.67	15.08	27.16	9.49
Dompriv	81 778	5.76	24.12	8.53	9.27	10.56
Formost	110	3.01	15	8.96	22.06	18.02
Dommost	384	3.89	17.61	6.39	6.81	15.25
Formix	95	6.7	14.3	9.94	12.49	18.39
Dommix	232	2.85	6.67	6.58	17.73	20.41
Formore	45	2.56	44.85	5.19	17.52	9.94
Dommore	117	16.26	5.71	8.47	9.34	19.91
Forstat	13	0.15	31.54	4.27	14.85	14.9
Domstat	1 592	4.15	18.63	14.81	10.54	26.05
All CDEs	104 017	6.14	23.43	11.38	16.72	12.10
wro		2.33	6.58	3.51	7.81	6.87

In an open economy, as most CEE economies are, the price of imported goods and relative labor costs are the most relevant factors of output prices and competitiveness. Therefore, we calculated the indicators of labor costs relative to the companies' turnover in the different company groups, too. As the data show there has not been a large increase of the export share of the companies since the transformation started. The little growth that we could observe was a result of the foreign private companies' moderate export expansion, while the export activity of the SOEs has not changed and the export activity of the domestic private companies has declined over the years. But the total turnover of the Hungarian companies expanded. Consequently, the total volume of exports has grown considerably over the last seven years. As regards relative labor costs, the foreign private companies operated with lower relative labor costs than the domestic private companies and the state-owned enterprises showed the highest relative labor costs. These results match our observation of the different levels of labor productivity according to ownership. There we could observe that foreign private companies operated with a much higher level of productivity than state-owned enterprises.

Investment and Export Activity of the SPACs

The analysis of the SPACs' indicators showed similar results as in the case of the CDEs (Table 5.12). As regards the indicator of unfinished investments relative to fixed assets (UNIF), the SOEs had higher indicators than the private companies in 1990 and 1991. But since then the private companies, and first of all the foreign private companies, have reported higher ratios of unfinished investments than the SOEs. But UNIF declined for all ownership groups between 1990 and 1992, and it started growing again only in 1993. It reached its peak in 1996.

The level of financial investments relative to fixed assets has been higher in every company group of the SPACs than in the case of the CDE groups. But there was no difference between the patterns in the two samples. Hence, the Domstats had the highest indicators and they were followed by the Domprivs, and the Forprivs came third. We can conclude that the state-owned enterprises that belonged to the privatization agencies diverted their investments toward financial investment the most, as was the case with the CDEs.

SOEs accumulated larger amounts of investment credit than private companies, but the accumulation process started well before transition. An overall conclusion can be that companies belonging to the privatization agencies did not show larger investment activity than other Hungarian companies. Foreign private companies were more active in starting new investment projects than state-owned enterprises, but their investment activity was not very large either. And after a few years, investments in production capacities decelerated and were replaced by financial investments in each company group. Consequently, privatization has not resulted in a breakthrough of investments in Hungary, although a short upswing could be witnessed in 1993 and 1994. But by 1995 the rate of growth of total investments leveled out. It even declined in 1996 and it only recovered in 1997.

Table 5.12. Investment and export activity of the SPACs in per cent between 1990 and 1996

			1990			
Ownership form	**No. of SPACs**	**UNIF**	**FIF**	**ICR**	**EXTR**	**LABC**
Forpriv	79	6.47	12.45	4.46	22.35	10.94
Dompriv	139	3.62	22.80	11.55	16.40	8.18
Formost	0	n.a	n.a	n.a	n.a	n.a
Dommost	3	11.62	20.50	0.00	18.36	24.97
Formix	1	8.02	1.43	6.92	35.98	10.47
Dommix	4	0.56	14.13	8.69	10.48	9.22
Formore	1	0.01	3.51	0.00	2.27	24.66
Dommore	3	1.48	0.00	0.00	0.00	8.12
Forstat	4	1.46	11.54	5.14	22.27	6.26
Domstat	1 499	8.53	13.89	9.59	13.15	11.53
All SPACs	1 733	8.21	14.14	9.22	13.75	11.37
wro		1.94	2.69	1.05	4.69	5.62

Table 5.12 continued

1992						
Ownership form	**No. of SPACs**	**UNIF**	**FIF**	**ICR**	**EXTR**	**LABC**
Forpriv	71	4.23	20.12	n.a.	20.02	15.58
Dompriv	167	5.53	19.57	n.a.	30.80	19.98
Formost	23	0.91	51.63	n.a.	7.71	13.27
Dommost	36	4.21	30.49	n.a.	23.65	26.20
Formix	43	2.21	66.5	n.a.	10.55	16.56
Dommix	41	2.6	19.21	n.a.	9.80	20.49
Formore	32	3.93	26.89	n.a.	45.08	17.15
Dommore	41	15.13	7.08	n.a.	4.27	9.39
Forstat	12	3.12	7.8	n.a.	54.92	22.80
Domstat	1 415	3.49	28.44	n.a.	13.45	17.79
All SPACs	1 881	3.49	28.81	n.a.	15.24	17.55
wro		0.69	8.69	n.a.	8.26	25.39

1994						
Ownership form	**No. of SPACs**	**UNIF**	**FIF**	**ICR**	**EXTR**	**LABC**
Forpriv	124	5.95	26.08	n.a.	20.88	15.31
Dompriv	379	2.19	18.81	n.a.	12.09	18.60
Formost	54	1.81	27.54	n.a.	16.18	15.82
Dommost	212	1.56	15.78	n.a.	10.31	19.31
Formix	43	1.78	66.55	n.a.	19.48	20.61
Dommix	78	2.9	5.13	n.a.	13.74	21.54
Formore	15	12.22	8.88	n.a.	34.53	19.20
Dommore	40	5.67	1.34	n.a.	4.98	13.98
Forstat	12	4.25	26.54	n.a.	17.81	12.18
Domstat	645	2.27	37.1	n.a.	10.80	22.40
All SPACs	1 602	3.61	31.08	n.a.	14.90	19.02
wro		2.32	14.41	n.a.	6.36	4.70

1996						
Ownership form	No. of SPACs	UNIF	FIF	ICR	EXTR	LABC
Forpriv	169	4.47	35.84	11.31	26.56	13.68
Dompriv	547	3.48	12.34	7.42	12.15	14.38
Formost	49	2.44	18.84	2.45	22.28	18.26
Dommost	184	4.05	17.81	6.41	6.58	14.94
Formix	30	7.32	6.72	8.68	10.92	18.66
Dommix	64	2.98	7.39	4.85	19.79	21.32
Formore	11	2.45	46.91	5.5	18.21	9.86
Dommore	15	0.88	0.59	64.94	4.73	14.34
Forstat	3	0.11	8.66	3.25	7.68	14.05
Domstat	331	3.71	28.22	14.77	13.62	24.75
All SPACs	1 403	4.08	27.07	8.94	17.27	16.49
Wro		1.46	13.04	6.21	6.05	5.45

Was there any difference between the CDEs and the SPACs as regards export activity? The ranking of the company groups were identical within the CDEs and the SPACs. The export activity of the foreign private companies among SPACs was higher than that of the SOEs throughout the whole period. But it is worth noting that the domestic private companies achieved high or even higher indicators than the Forprivs. The SPACs performed somewhat better than the CDEs between 1990 and 1996. As regards relative labor costs, the SOEs operated with the highest indicators and the foreign private companies had the lowest relative labor costs among the SPACs. This result is compatible with the fact that foreign companies proved to be more competitive and they were also more successful in penetrating international markets than SOEs in Hungary.

5.6.2 Investment and Export Activity: The Results by Clusters

The average indicators of the company groups provide a condensed picture of the companies' investment and export activity. A more refined description can be achieved by dividing the groups into clusters. I applied the cluster analysis for the three largest groups of the CDEs: for the Forprivs, Domprivs and for the Domstats. I defined six clusters by using the indicator of gross profit margin (GPM) within each group. The clusters were as follows:

(1) Companies with less than –5 per cent GPM,

(2) Companies with GPM between –5 and 0 per cent,

(3) Companies with GPM between 0 and +5 per cent,

(4) Companies with GPM between 5 and 10 per cent,

(5) Companies with GPM between 10 and 15 per cent, and

(6) Companies with more than +15 per cent GPM.

Table 5.13. The CDEs' investment and export activity in different clusters, in per cent, between 1990 and 1996

		1990				
	No. of CDEs	**GPM**	**UNIF**	**FIF**	**EXTR**	**LABC**
Forprivs						
Smaller than –5 per cent	327	–35.55	16.68	13.85	44.76	21.64
Between –5 and 0 per cent	249	–1.55	13.40	5.22	13.29	19.00
Between 0 and 5 per cent	1 345	2.72	5.69	11.95	12.02	9.98
Between 5 and 10 per cent	2 243	6.77	12.15	14.75	14.85	10.45
Between 10 and 15 per cent	315	12.05	4.33	33.91	13.15	10.18
Larger than 15 per cent	294	23.83	14.13	5.88	35.10	11.05
Total	4 773	2.82	9.48	14.44	18.83	11.80
Domprivs						
Smaller than –5 per cent	932	–5.45	5.94	11.58	12.87	20.31
Between –5 and 0 per cent	1 578	–1.68	6.32	17.61	11.31	20.32
Between 0 and 5 per cent	9 641	2.58	4.78	17.92	5.98	14.59
Between 5 and 10 per cent	3 143	6.78	5.94	13.20	15.41	17.47
Between 10 and 15 per cent	507	12.30	5.35	11.63	6.96	22.22
Larger than 15 per cent	245	29.67	6.70	9.60	7.63	24.01
Total	16 046	3.04	5.16	16.71	7.95	16.12
Domstats						
Smaller than –5 per cent	162	–15.05	11.45	16.09	27.73	29.70
Between –5 and 0 per cent	234	–1.27	5.20	12.59	23.36	27.87
Between 0 and 5 per cent	991	2.56	5.47	18.84	9.55	16.31
Between 5 and 10 per cent	274	6.28	7.72	13.74	14.42	11.27
Between 10 and 15 per cent	37	12.81	10.38	6.07	2.33	8.18
Larger than 15 per cent	31	20.35	15.92	5.03	6.95	25.82
Total	1 729	3.72	8.39	12.31	12.88	11.82

1992						
	No. of CDEs	GPM	UNIF	FIF	EXTR	LABC
Forprivs						
Smaller than –5 per cent	2 497	–53.34	7.11	13.91	19.90	21.17
Between –5 and 0 per cent	3 066	–1.78	7.75	26.02	22.20	15.41
Between 0 and 5 per cent	4 655	1.62	8.61	11.50	20.20	11.43
Between 5 and 10 per cent	779	7.36	5.96	14.28	20.06	16.36
Between 10 and 15 per cent	150	12.28	10.77	4.82	27.64	10.85
Larger than 15 per cent	352	27.55	9.50	20.81	25.92	24.95
Total	11 499	–1.91	8.44	16.20	20.45	11.84
Domprivs						
Smaller than –5 per cent	5 118	–19.30	2.94	12.85	7.68	39.87
Between –5 and 0 per cent	6 445	–1.94	4.69	14.08	6.59	22.72
Between 0 and 5 per cent	16 810	1.74	5.77	12.21	9.82	17.95
Between 5 and 10 per cent	8 937	7.22	7.28	20.62	11.43	22.46
Between 10 and 15 per cent	1 391	11.76	5.50	13.82	6.16	19.65
Larger than 15 per cent	1 149	46.31	4.80	38.35	4.48	37.84
Total	39 850	–2.50	3.80	16.70	9.99	27.25
Domstats						
Smaller than –5 per cent	1 590	–40.92	2.89	17.92	22.41	35.49
Between –5 and 0 per cent	790	–1.61	1.65	8.79	8.87	14.07
Between 0 and 5 per cent	1 189	1.95	4.54	24.71	9.04	15.71
Between 5 and 10 per cent	192	7.85	1.61	31.88	3.24	36.14
Between 10 and 15 per cent	33	12.15	1.08	18.26	4.78	39.35
Larger than 15 per cent	43	54.74	0.31	91.65	3.38	41.74
Total	3 837	–4.57	3.33	29.46	13.25	18.26

As shown in Table 5.13, the ratio of unfinished investments relative to fixed assets of the foreign companies was the highest in the clusters of lowest and highest profit margins in 1990, 1992 and 1994. But there was an inverse relationship between GPM and UNIF in 1995, and a similar pattern could be observed in 1996. In the case of the domestic private companies the level of the indicators was more even than for the foreign private companies, with a slight downward trend as GPM increased. The pattern of indicators was similar for the Domstats, as for the Forprivs in 1990–92, but the indicators of the state-owned enterprises showed a similar pattern as the domestic private companies in 1994–96.

Table 5.13 continued

1996	No. of CDEs	GPM	UNIF	FIF	EXTR	LABC
Forprivs						
Smaller than –5 per cent	2 758	–73.01	11.27	6.84	10.24	23.31
Between –5 and 0 per cent	2 725	–1.92	12.57	6.58	25.10	9.27
Between 0 and 5 per cent	10 657	2.12	6.52	13.25	24.42	9.64
Between 5 and 10 per cent	2 048	6.88	7.11	10.69	30.81	14.58
Between 10 and 15 per cent	956	12.41	13.36	8.71	48.31	10.61
Larger than 15 per cent	467	28.41	5.91	50.39	27.29	20.09
Total	19 651	4.06	9.41	23.67	27.16	9.49
Domprivs						
Smaller than –5 per cent	4 520	–31.67	4.46	27.59	5.31	19.44
Between –5 and 0 per cent	6 257	–1.64	7.92	14.51	10.66	15.20
Between 0 and 5 per cent	52 852	2.39	6.39	16.95	8.93	12.70
Between 5 and 10 per cent	11 925	6.78	5.29	12.32	9.54	18.39
Between 10 and 15 per cent	4 429	11.50	3.59	28.44	15.81	18.08
Larger than 15 per cent	1 794	73.12	3.00	54.77	8.66	41.06
Total	81 778	2.55	5.76	24.12	9.27	10.56
Domstats						
Smaller than –5 per cent	344	–127.71	4.56	27.17	12.09	52.04
Between –5 and 0 per cent	297	–2.37	3.03	1.98	3.18	26.49
Between 0 and 5 per cent	611	2.44	2.73	8.45	8.20	35.15
Between 5 and 10 per cent	169	6.74	2.67	7.65	15.76	35.76
Between 10 and 15 per cent	60	11.54	3.55	21.28	1.10	32.77
Larger than 15 per cent	73	115.10	3.81	33.17	1.28	101.15
Total	1 592	–5.89	4.15	18.63	10.54	26.05

The ratio of financial investments relative to fixed assets was usually the highest for the foreign private companies with high profit margins. This was also true for the domestic private companies and for the state-owned enterprises, but in these two groups the companies with very low and negative profit margins had fairly high indicators, too. We observed some fluctuation in the indicators in each company group. But the trend was fairly clear for the foreign private companies, while the domestic private companies and the state-owned enterprises showed a mixed pattern.

We can conclude that foreign private companies with low profit margins had more newly started investments than companies with higher profit margins in 1990. Thus, it can be assumed that a higher investment activity reduced the foreign companies' profit levels. But later on, more unfinished investment was accompanied by higher profit margins. Meanwhile, domestic private and state-owned companies showed the opposite pattern. The more unfinished investment they carried the lower profit margin they could achieve.

As regards financial investments, foreign private companies with high profit margins invested in financial assets more, showing that they usually did not reinvest their profits into their productive operation. Here again, domestic private and state-owned companies revealed a different attitude. The lower profit margins those companies had the more they invested in financial assets. It is probable that financial investment was a type of forced investment for those companies since they could not make sufficient profits on their productive operations.

The results of the analysis of the export activity indicators by clusters are fairly unexpected. One would have thought that the higher the average profit margin the larger the export activity indicator would be in a company group. But the relationship between export activity and profit margin is not so straightforward. In fact, we can observe high export activity indicators in the clusters of companies with the lowest profit margin in each company group.

It was only in 1995 that export activity indicators increased along with profit margins in every company group. The relationship between the profit margin and the export activity became much more mixed in 1996. As regards relative labor costs, companies with the lowest profit margin usually had the highest labor cost indicator. But there were exceptions from this rule, too. Especially in the case of domestic private companies and state-owned enterprises, companies with fairly high profit margins reported the highest relative labor costs. This result shows that several companies with large profits used their net revenues to pay high salaries instead of reinvesting their profits. In this regard, domestic private and state-owned companies followed more short-term goals than foreign private companies.

5.6.3 Factors of the Companies' Profitability and Efficiency: the Results of a Multi-Regression Analysis

After having presented the different performance indicators of the company groups we conducted an econometric analysis in order to trace the determining factors of profitability and efficiency of the companies with different ownership structure. According to the correlation coefficients, there was no sizable correlation between profitability and the financial indicators in the case of the Forprivs and the Domprivs. The correlation coefficients always remained below 0.10 and they usually did not exceed 0.05. According to the F-statistics, the connection was not significant between profitability and the financial indicators in these company groups. Interestingly enough, the correlation coefficient of the Domstats' operating profit indicator and indebtedness showed a fairly strong connection ($R^2 = 0.5134$), and the correlation coefficient between the operating profit indicator and financial stability was even higher ($R^2 = 0.8714$). These results show that the profitability of the SOEs is strongly related to their past financial state rather than to their actual operations. Both indebtedness and financial stability reflect a company's long-term financial obligations. Those SOEs that have been heavily indebted, mainly because of former large but unsuccessful investments, and also the companies whose stability has been undermined by the financial burdens they carried over from the past, were not capable of changing their product structure and technology in order to make their production activities profitable. These companies lack the financial means, but they do not have the energy either to engage in massive company restructuring. In the case of the SPACs we found a strong correlation between operating profits and financial stability in all the three groups. R^2 was equal to 0.8933 for the Forprivs, 0.7312 for the Domprivs and 0.9180 for the Domstats. But there was not a significant correlation between any other financial indicator and the companies' profitability.

We conducted the regression analysis for the profitability and investment, and export activity of the company groups. There was not even a medium level correlation between any of these indicators in any of the company groups. The correlation coefficients were somewhat higher in the case of the SPACs than in the group of CDEs, but still low. What only mattered was whether a company had foreign or domestic owner(s). Foreign companies showed higher export and investment activity than domestic private or state-owned companies. But the actual level of the so-called 'expansion indicators' has not had an impact on the companies' profitability. Nor were the regression results significant. Thus, the common wisdom, according to which the companies that expand their market share on foreign markets prove to be more profitable than the companies that are stuck to the domestic market, did not hold for the companies during the transition. Nor could we accept the assumption that the low or negative profitability indicators are connected to the investment boost of the companies. As is shown in the chapter on the multivariate analysis, rather the opposite seemed to be true. Notably, those companies showed a higher investment activity that reported higher profitability indicators, irrespective of their ownership structure.

It is frequently mentioned by analysts of the transition economies that the strength of the private sector is clearly reflected by its higher productivity level than that which can be found in the state-owned enterprises. But does productivity affect the companies' profitability? According to the regression analysis, it does not, or productivity has an influence on profitability only to a limited extent. In the case of the CDEs the correlation coefficients between profitability and productivity were very low and not significant. The same was true for the Domprivs among the SPACs. The correlation between profitability – measured by gross profits relative to total assets – was significant on the 0.05 level in the case of Forprivs and the coefficient was equal to 0.2965. The same relationship was also significant for the Domprivs, but the coefficient amounted only to 0.1044. Consequently, we could not find an unambiguous relationship between the profitability and the productivity of the Hungarian companies during the transformation. The results are very similar to those found by Bai, Li and Wang for the Chinese companies (Bai, Li and Wang, 1997). These authors argue that the Chinese state-owned enterprises are not profit maximizers – those companies rather strive for expansion – and this is why their profitability and productivity do not change in a parallel way. We could observe something similar in the case of the private companies during transition. After having lost their former markets, these companies concentrate their efforts on expansion rather than on efficient operation. If this is a temporary phenomenon, then it can be regarded as the cost of the transition.

We can conclude that the regression analysis has brought negative results; except for the relationship between profitability and the financial indicators of the state-owned enterprises, we did not find even a medium–strong correlation between the companies' profitability and the other indicators of their economic performance. This fact casts some doubt on the measurement of profitability. That is, we can suspect that the profit or loss statement of the companies reflects the skills of accountants and book-keepers rather than the actual results of the companies' economic operation.

As was outlined in the first section, we also conducted a multi-regression analysis to determine the nature of relationship between the CDEs' profitability and efficiency on the one hand, and the other indicators of the companies' economic activity on the other for the period of 1990–95. (We did not have the data for 1996 when the computation was done.) Since we found multicollinearity among the explanatory variables, we had to transform them into independent factors in order to achieve sensible results. The tools of the factor analysis were used to determine the main factors that can exhaustively explain the changes in the profitability indicators. We present the results of the factor analysis in Table 5.14.

As is shown in Table 5.14, three to four main factors explain the variance of the dependent indicators between 1990 and 1995. Thus, the first main factor is the 'inventories' variable that comprises the indicators of the self-produced and the purchased inventories of the companies respectively (TINV and SINV). The second main factor is the liquidity indicator that includes the share of the liquid assets relative to the total assets (LAT), the liquidity ratio

(LR) and the indicator of solvency (SOLV). The third main factor is the financial factor that consists of the share of financial investments and financial assets relative to total fixed assets respectively (FIF and FATA).

Table 5.14. A summary of the results of the factor analysis

Year	Main factors	Explanatory force of variable	Economic meaning of main factors
1990	F1 = 0.50721 TINV + 0.50721 SINV	97.2%	Indicator of inventories
	F2 = 0.28355 LAT + 0.44381 LR + 0.44067 SOLV	70.1%	Liquidity indicator
	F3 = 0.61506 FIF + 0.61506 FATA	66.1%	Financial indicator
1991	F1 = 0.57327 FIF + 0.57327 FATA	76.1%	Financial indicator
	F2 = 0.65456 SIN + 0.65456 LAT	58.3%	Indicator of financial stability
	F3 = 0.50010 TINV + 0.50010 SINV	100%	Indicator of inventories
1992	F1 = 0.50008 TINV + 0.50008 SINV	100%	Indicator of inventories
	F2 = 0.38647 LAT + 0.45909 LR + 0.38574 SOLV	65.5%	Liquidity indicator
	F3 = 0.51674 FIF + 0.51674 FATA	93.6%	Financial indicator
1993	F1 = 0.52883 TINV + 0.52883 SINV	89.7%	Indicator of inventories
	F2 = 0.5004 SOLV + 0.5004 LR	99.8%	Liquidity indicator
	F3 = 0.57317 FATA + 0.57317 FIF	76.1%	Financial indicator
	F4 = 0.57878 SIN + 0.57878 LAT	74.6%	Indicator of financial stability
1994	F1 = 0.51961 TINV + 0.51961 SINV	92.6%	Indicator of inventories
	F2 = 0.5 likvráta + 0.5 SOLV	100%	Liquidity indicator
	F3 = 0.54951 FIF + 0.54951 FATA	82.8%	Financial indicator
	F4 = 0.6097 SIN + 0.6097 LAT	67.3%	Indicator of financial stability
1995	F1 = 0.5924 TINV + 0.5924 SINV	71.2%	Indicator of inventories
	F2 = 0.29534 LAT + 0.44565 LR + 0.43711 SOLV	69.9%	Liquidity indicator
	F3 = 0.53708 FIF + 0.53708 FATA	86.7%	Financial indicator

Finally, the stability factor is a composite of the liquidity ratio (LR) and the indicator of financial stability (SIN). The explanatory relevance of the main factors ranges between 70 and 100 per cent, that is, those are good explanatory variables of the indicators' variance. This fact is shown in the third column of Table 5.14. The last column gives a summary name to, and some explanation for, the content of the individual main factors.

Next, we conducted the multi-regression analysis for each year between 1990 and 1995. We present the some of the results in Table 5.15. The explanatory and the dependent variables in the tables below are defined either in the third section, or in Table 5.14, when we describe the main factors. There is one explanatory variable, named OWN which is new. It is a dummy for the ownership groups starting from 11 and ending with 52.[15] Three types of explanatory variables were used in the multi-regression analysis. First, we used the main factors as explanatory variables. Second, we selected those individual indicators – as they had been defined in the first section – which had a significant impact on the companies' profitability and efficiency. Third, we also used those original items from the balance sheets (such as, for example, the number of employees) that also had a significant connection to the indicators of profitability and efficiency. As can be seen from the tables in the Annex, not all of the profitability and efficiency indicators had a systematic relationship with the explanatory variables. The indicators of turnover relative to total assets and relative to liquid assets respectively, moreover, the indicator of net profits (losses) relative to total assets and the ratio of gross profits relative to the shareholders' equity, proved to be relevant.

First, we should note that the correlation coefficients show a medium–strong regression fit between the dependent and the explanatory variables. (The correlation coefficients are given in the last row in each table below.) In the case of such huge samples and with so many variables, a medium level correlation indicates a relevant and significant relationship. Thus, the selected variables decisively influence the companies' profitability and efficiency. As regards the specific relationship between the individual profitability or efficiency indicators on the one hand, and the explanatory variables on the other, we obtained some expected but also some unexpected results. It is small wonder that the indicator of inventories has an inverse relationship to profitability and efficiency. It was also a reasonable expectation that the larger the share of the private ownership in a company, the higher its profitability and efficiency will be. The financial stability of a company positively correlates to its profitability, too. More profitable companies invest more intensively, and larger investments usually result in higher profits in a market economy.

Table 5.15. The results of the multi-regression analysis between 1990 and 1995

1990	TTA	TLA	ROA
Constant	0.366 (3.10)	0.367 (3.16)	0.379 (8.71)
Inventories	–0.542 (–5.76)		–0.146 (–3.47)
financial ind.			0.079 (2.40)
liquidity indicator		0.309 (2.73)	0.603 (7.32)
UNIF			0.097 (3.71)
EXRT	–0.090 (–3.21)		
LABC	–0.765 (–7.07)		–0.283 (–3.02)
DEBT	–0.048 (–3.62)		
SIN	0.081 (7.71)		
ICFOR	–0.790 (5.76)		
OWN	–0.050 (–4.12)	–0.061 (–2.84)	–0.163 (–11.3)
EMPLOYEE	–0.102 (–2.74)	–0.103 (–2.74)	
inventories2	0.029 (4.60)		
EXRT2	0.019 (2.33)		
LABC2	0.032 (6.89)		0.011 (2.87)
inventories-financial ind.	–0.049 (–2.39)		0.026 (2.26)
inventories-EXRT	0.0653 (3.91)		
EXRT-LABC	0.125 (2.49)		
liquidity ind.2		–0.016 (–2.63)	–0.040 (–7.09)
DEBT-SIN		–0.018 (–5.27)	
financial ind.2			–0.020 (–2.93)
R^2	0.18	0.08	0.24

1992	TTA	TLA	ROA
constant	–0.093 (–3.11)	–0.452 (–2.81)	–0.157 (–3.89)
inventories		–0.555 (–31.57)	
financial ind.		–0.154 (–3.25)	–0.129 (–3.36)
liquidity		0.131 (4.12)	0.264 (3.30)
UNIF	0.273 (5.74)		0.071 (3.17)
EXRT	–0.050 (–2.31)		
LABC	–0.600 (–8.16)		
DEBT			0.013 (3.96)
OWN	–4.782 (6.02)	–3.255 (–4.81)	6.318 (6.67)
EMPLOYEE		0.120 (0.28)	
financial ind.2	–0.034 (–11.97)		
LABC2	0.039 (7.41)		
UNIF2	–0.055 (–5.76)		
EXRT-LABC	0.189 (3.79)		
LABC-UNIF	–0.062 (2.03)		
SIN-EXRT	0.298 (3.07)		
LABC-SIN	0.488 (6.88)		
R^2	0.26	0.36	0.11

Table 5.15 continued

1995	TTA	TLA	ROA	GPROF
constant	0.62 (11.6)	0.071 (2.15)	–0.0004 (–0.03)	0.059 (1.98)
ICFOR	–0.548 (–13.36)		–0.144 (–2.69)	
inventories	–0.427 (–13.45)		–0.166 (–5.30)	
liquidity			0.506 (6.82)	
financial ind.				
UNIF	–0.042 (–2.48)			
ICCOOP	–0.714 (–5.74)			
EMPLOYEE				
OWN	–0.222 (–13.15)	–0.034 (–2.89)		–0.041 (–2.21)
inventories2	0.016 (11.6)		0.006 (5.22)	
financial ind.2	–0.05 (–9.57)			
inventories-liquidity	0.006 (3.02)		–0.011 (–3.22)	
inventories-financial ind.	0.046 (2.01)			
LABC2		0.023 (24.05)		
UNIF-LABC		–0.081 (–2.49)		
liquidity ind.2	–0.025 (–4.63)			
EXRT2			0.062 (3.97)	
financial-DEBT				1.003 (3.91)
R^2	0.20	0.65	0.15	0.63

The number of employed and the companies' efficiency has an inverse connection, as can be expected. However, it was somewhat surprising that foreign ownership negatively relates to the companies' profitability and efficiency. It was unexpected, too, that the indicator of the export activity (EXRT) and the combined indicator of export activity and relative wage costs (EXRT-LABC) showed an ambiguous relationship to profitability. It needs further analysis as to why the companies' liquidity had an inverse relationship to their profitability.

Other studies showed that the size of the companies has had a larger impact on their profitability than the different indicators of their economic performance (Halpern and Körösi, 1998). This fact, along with our findings, should warn us that past behavior of the formerly state-owned companies does not fade away as fast as one would like to think. The economic transformation is a longer process on the micro level, than what we had expected at the start.

As was shown above, we could find a decisive relationship between the companies' profitability and efficiency on the one hand and the indicators of their economic activity on the other, when we applied the tools of the factor analysis and multi-regression analysis. In this case, the structure of ownership had a significant impact on the companies' profitability. But most of the results of the multi-regression analysis comply with the findings of the pair regressions. The most important ones among these results were that foreign ownership is not a remedy for all the illnesses of the CEE economies. It is also doubtful whether the private sector could prove its higher efficiency as compared to the SOEs, or the most successful SOEs had been turned into private hands first and this resulted in the better performance of the private companies. A robust economic growth started in Hungary in 1996, and it had already begun in 1994 in Poland. This gives us some hope that the most painful part of the transition is over.

5.7 A MULTIVARIATE ANALYSIS OF THE ECONOMIC PERFORMANCE OF HUNGARIAN COMPANIES DURING THE TRANSITION

This section shows the results of a multivariate analysis of the economic transition of Hungary from 1990 until 1995.* In the first section we present the database and the variables, while in the second section the hypotheses of the analysis are made explicit. After a sketch of the structure of the Hungarian economy, presented in section 3, in section 4 we define the concept of the companies' economic performance (profitability and productivity). In sections 5, 6 and 7 we test our hypotheses on property rights, foreign investment and on the attitudes towards investment. The results are not exhaustive, but represent an original empirical approach by means of statistical modeling of the companies' financial data during the transition process.

* Special thanks to Christine Willems, who constantly encouraged me in the development of my work.

5.7.1 The Data, the Variables and the Methods

The database used in the following analysis is identical to the one described in section 5.3. Thus, the first group (BLOCK 1) consists of all the companies with double-entry book-keeping (the CDEs) Their number was 23 314 in 1990 and it grew to 90 204 by 1995. In this block, former socialist enterprises and the green field – that is, newly established – companies are presented together. The second group (BLOCK 2) contains the balance sheet data of the companies that were owned by one of the two privatization agencies, at least for a while. The number of these companies ranged between 2900 and 3500 in the period of 1990–95. As already specified, the most variables were derived from the balance sheets of the companies. Another group of variables gives the share of issued capital stock in the hands of different owners.[16] Finally, three category variables define the groups of companies: the region where their headquarters are located, the branch of their main activity, and the legal form of the companies.

As was mentioned before, the balance sheet information is not related to single companies but to groups that are defined by crossing the three category variables described above (Region, Branch and Legal Form). This has substantial consequences for the data analyses and for the conclusions drawn from these data. First of all, the infra-group variability is eliminated because of the lack of information on the real distribution of the companies within the groups. From a statistical point of view, the assumptions are partly violated. Although no analyses are inhibited, the results must be interpreted with caution. The characteristics of the data do not allow standard econometric analyses to be run except the use of aggregate figures, given by the sum of all groups across the years. But that is not the aim of this study. This is the reason why we decided to choose a more fuzzy approach, utilizing the analysis of variance. This could seem a quite simple approach to the data but the complexity and the huge number of observations suggested a strategy that allowed some comparison to be made – based on statistical assumptions – between the different groups of companies.

We follow a top-down strategy, which means that first all the groups are considered together and afterwards they are verified for each discriminatory variable which is available. Other ways could seem more sophisticated and elegant but it was not up to us to choose the data and we have to cope with them. A big task was to clean the data in order to make them meaningful for the analysis. Once this has been done, the analytical force of this method lies in the possibility of giving some statistical support to our hypothesis.

5.7.2 The Hypotheses of Research

The analysis in this study tries to clarify some aspects of the economic performance of the companies during the transition process, focusing on the significant differences between the groups. But first of all, the concept of economic performance should be defined or, better, operationalized. So the question is how to measure it. The economic performance is a multidimensional concept: several aspects are connected with each other, but sometimes there are trade-offs between them. At the beginning, we will try to clarify which dimensions could be considered here and which indicators are reliable, being in possession of the balance sheet data. We suggest two dimensions, profitability and productivity, that are supposed to have different trends across the years. The first step of the analysis is checking this assumption. After having defined our idea of performance, we will test the classical property right hypothesis. According to the general statements about the effects of property rights on performance, the private companies should act better than the others. The hypothesis is formulated as follows: the kind of property affects the economic performance of the companies: the private behave better then the state-owned companies; the intermediate situations (from 5 per cent to 75 per cent of state property) are more confused and more difficult to generalize.

On the other hand, the property rights do not exhaust the field of research. Other conditions could have an impact on the performance. Therefore we will consider even the role of the foreign capital and the attitude towards investment of the companies, the main sign of restructuring. Before developing the arguments about the previous questions and to check how the data fit the exposed ideas, a more detailed picture of the Hungarian situation drawn from the data should be presented.

5.7.3 A Sketch of the Economic Structure of Hungary in Transition

In this section we try to describe the economic structure of Hungary, as allowed by the data. The transition process is a very complex situation. The magnitude of the phenomena overwhelms any comparison with developed capitalist countries. For example, the rate of growth of the number of companies in five years is more than 1000 per cent. Hence, the aim of the next section is to deal with an introduction of the context, by means of a structural presentation of the Hungarian economic situation, as presumed from the data. The main aim of this presentation is a descriptive one; using some categorical variables, we even try to discover if the process could be considered continuous or would present strong fractures during its development.

From an empirical point of view, it is clear that the situation has changed radically after 1989. But following such a passage, which is often traumatic, what has been the evolution of the economic structure in the various countries? We ask whether during the years following the political and economical liberalization in the CEE countries there have been ulterior transformations which cannot be reduced to a progressive process, even if the fundamental elements of the economic structure have remained the same through the years. The answer to these questions is not unequivocal and can be different according to the countries and the implemented economic policies. So we will try to understand what kind of transformation there has been in some important aspects of the economic structure, especially in the distribution of the companies and their employees according to ownership, size and region of origin, in the years from 1990 to 1994. The variables used in the analysis are: (1) the type of ownership structure, defined according to the percentage of state ownership (OWN); (2) the size of the companies, based on the number of their employees (SIZE); and (3) the region where the company is located (REGIO).[17] The theoretical question of our research was whether the transformation of the Hungarian economic structure has permanently progressed since 1989 or whether it has become stable after a while. According to the considered hypothesis, we have tried to formulate some expectations about the frequencies inside each company group (cell). For this purpose it seems appropriate to use log-linear modeling techniques which supply an adequate answer to this type of question.

Before starting the exposition of the analysis and the results, it is worthwhile to clarify how the concept of economic structure is used in our context. Economic structure is not considered in an abstract way, rather the empirical aspects of it are pointed out. The economic structure will therefore be defined as the result of the interactions between different economic variables. Then, its dynamic aspects will be estimated. Of course the survey does not pretend to be exhaustive and as a matter of fact it examines only some specific aspects of the companies' performance. Our investigation goes in the direction of specifying in an explicit way some of the tendencies of company transformation which are often assumed but never empirically checked in the academic analyses. Moreover, the applied methods are not standard and can supply an original approach in the analysis of the economic data regarding the CEE countries.

The passage of 1989

At the beginning of the transition Hungary was in an advantageous situation with respect to the other CEE countries because of the reforms which, since the end of the 1960s, resulted in a flexible economic structure (Adam, 1989) and because of the fundamental laws passed during the 1980s (see Dallago,

1995). Even before the changes in 1989, a first spontaneous privatization process was already taking place. The year 1989 nevertheless marks a radical transformation in the economic structure with respect to ownership and size as illustrated in Table 5.16. Table 5.17 shows the structure of companies by employment. The spontaneous privatization (or privatization of the 'nomenklatura', see Dallago, 1995) has brought a redefinition of the ownership structures. The medium and large-sized companies were the majority – about 60 per cent of them had more than 100 employees – before the transition.

Table 5.16. Distribution of companies by ownership (in absolute numbers) and by size (in per cent) before and after 1989

	OWN				
	Private	Mostly private	Mixed	State	**Total**
1988	0	0	0	7 628	7 628
1990	20 658	540	155	1 791	23 314
			SIZE		
	1–25	26–100	101–1000	1001–5000	>5000
1988	9	32	49	9	1
1990	57	23	18	2	0

Source: Computation of the author based on the available data.

By 1990 the situation had reversed: 80 per cent of companies had less than 100 employees in that year. This phenomenon can partly be seen as a result of the split of the big SOEs into companies with a smaller size. (The same phenomenon occurred in the Czech Republic, see Sereghyova, 1996). Moreover, a considerable impact on the number of companies can be ascribed to the rise of the so-called 'green field' firms, the new companies that have been founded after the liberalization of the economy.

Table 5.17. Employees by size of company before and after 1989, (per cent)

	1988		1990	
SIZE	per cent	Cum (per cent)	per cent	Cum (per cent)
1–25	0.2	0.2	4.9	4.9
26–100	4.3	4.5	8.3	13.2
101–1000	43.2	47.7	46.8	60.0
1001–5000	38.2	75.9	27.2	87.2
>5000	14.0	100	12.9	100
Total (in absolute numbers)		3 150 000		2 940 000

Source: Computation of the author based on the available data.

To sum up, it can be affirmed that the political and institutional revolutionary process which took place in 1989 has been accompanied by important transformations on the micro level, but features of the former system can also be traced, partly attenuated, in the new economic order. Therefore, it can be pointed out how important the inherited characteristics of the past are to determine the fundamental elements of the new situation.

After 1989: permanent transformation or stabilization?

From 1990 on, the transformation process seems to become stable and it goes in the direction of a new equilibrium. Private ownership proves to be clearly dominant, and large-sized companies tend to disappear, leaving room for a great number of small new businesses. Connected to this last phenomenon, particularly important is the increase of the absolute number of companies which multiply by ten (from 7600 to almost 80 000) within the span of five years. These trends are shown in Table 5.18. Now our question is: has the economic structure of Hungary – and especially some of its elements on the level of the considered companies – continued to transform after 1989 or can it be asserted that it remained almost unchanged, apart from the changes in the number of companies?

The first analysis is developed to establish the structure of interactions between ownership and size of the companies in the years between 1990 and 1994. The hypothesis we test is whether the interaction between ownership and size has undergone some modification, given the changes in numbers through time. Therefore the basic model considers already these changes and on this basis the next steps will be developed. The base model is as follows:

$$\text{(BASE) } 1 + \text{YEAR} + \text{OWN} + \text{SIZE} + \text{YEAR}^*(\text{OWN}+\text{SIZE}) \qquad (5.1)$$

The total deviance (dev) is 43 087 with 120 degrees of freedom (d.f.). With respect to this model the successive improvements will be evaluated. The first hypothesis to be tested is whether there is one single structure of OWN and SIZE that remains unchanged throughout the years. In order to test this assumption, a model will be fitted with a different parameter for each combination of OWN and SIZE but it is assumed to be constant for that specific combination in all the years.

$$\text{BASE} + \text{OWN}^*\text{SIZE} \qquad (5.2)$$
$$\text{dev.} = 3003 \quad \text{with d.f.} = 96$$

The introduction of the new parameters significantly reduces the deviance (reduction of about 40 000) and the R^2 assumes a value of 0.930. Interactions exist, therefore, between OWN and SIZE which remain stable across the years. The model however is not satisfactory, and the goodness of its fit is very low ($\chi = 3003$ with d.f. = 96). The likelihood to obtain the observed frequencies, given true to the model, is p = 0.0000. The evaluation of standardized residuals shows how the expected values are still rather approximate. In addition, a contrast is delineated between the first two years and the last three. For the first years the greatest part of the residuals is negative (this means that less companies are observed than had been expected according to the model) and those residuals are distributed quite homogeneously over the cells. The most evident exceptions to this statement are the medium-sized companies of mixed ownership (according to the definition, 'Mixed' and 'Mostly private') in the two first years. This phenomenon could be interpreted as the process of splitting up and gradual privatization of the big SOEs, that have been divided into several little companies, then those were partly taken under private control. Once the anomaly is noticed, the hypothesis of two structures of interaction, one for 1990–91 and another for 1992–94, will be tested. The model is:

$$\text{BASE} + \text{OWN}^*\text{SIZE} + \text{OWN}^*\text{SIZE}^*\text{PERIOD} \qquad (5.3)$$
$$\text{dev.} = 943 \quad \text{with d.f.} = 72$$

with PERIOD as a dichotomous variable, 1 for 1990–91 and 2 for 1992–94. The reduction of the deviance is considerable (reduction is equal to 2059) and the coefficient of determination is very high ($R^2 = 0.978$). But the adaptation is still not satisfying ($\chi = 943$ with d.f. = 72 and p = 0.0000) and the residuals remain elevated, above all in 1992. This situation can be considered as an effect of the ratification in 1992 of the law about bankruptcies and of the realization of the distributive privatization programs, that started in 1991. Moreover, in the same year a new phase of decentralized privatization started (see Dallago, 1995) which left the initiative with the investors and with the companies themselves.

Consequently it will be checked if it is necessary to consider three structures instead of two, and specifically one for 1990–91, one for 1992 and one for 1993–94. In this case we could conclude that an ulterior transformation after 1989 took place in 1992, while in the two years before and after there have not been evident breaks. But the reduction of variance due to the introduction of new parameters (24, one for each interaction OWN*SIZE in 1992) turns out to be small, and therefore the above formulated hypothesis is refused. The last model which *a priori* could be postulated consists of the consideration of different structures which evolve in a linear way through the years. The model which expresses this hypothesis eliminates the interaction introduced at the preceding step (model III) and introduces a linear time variable which can be applied to the structure OWN*SIZE. The model is:

$$\text{BASE} + \text{OWN*SIZE} + \text{OWN*SIZE*TLIN} \qquad (5.4)$$
$$\text{dev.} = 1905 \quad \text{with d.f.} = 72$$

Table 5.18. Distribution of companies by ownership and by size between 1990 and 1994 (absolute number and percentage)

	1990		1991		1992		1993		1994	
OWN	sum	per cent	sum	per cent	sum	per cent	sum	per cent	sum	per cent
Private	20 658	89	35 436	94	51 062	90	65 232	94	75 427	95
Mostly private	540	2	517	1	527	1	640	1	603	1
Mixed	155	1	145	0	860	1	667	1	483	1
State	1 791	8	1 738	5	4 230	8	3 143	4	2 300	3
Total	23 314		38 041		57 865		71 503		79 793	

	1990		1991		1992		1993		1994	
SIZE (by number of emloyees)	sum	per cent	sum	per cent	sum	per cent	sum	per cent	sum	per cent
1–25	13 169	57	28 707	76	47 203	83	60 261	87	69 009	88
26–100	5 286	23	5 007	13	5 383	10	6 532	9	7 438	9
101–1000	4 169	18	3 808	10	3 848	7	2 704	4	2 192	3
1001–5000	490	2	295	1	231	0	165	0	157	0
>5000	30	0	19	0	14	0	20	0	17	0
Total	23 314		38 041		57 865		71 503		79 793	

Source: Computation of the author based on the available data.

An evident result of this last model is that the fitting is worse than the preceding one even if the degrees of freedom remain unchanged. We can conclude that the previous parametrization was better, consequently, the last modification of the model is rejected. We can try to synthesize the results. With regard to the considered variables, the hypothesis that after 1989 the Hungarian economic structure has maintained stable components is not rejected, but is not sufficient in itself to express in a satisfying way the variability of the data. A dichotomy is found between the first two years after the changes (1990–91) and the successive three (1992–94).

Size and region: physical constraints and stability

As shown in Table 5.17, the changes in the distribution of employees seem to be less considerable than those for companies. However, if we consider the dynamics of the total number of employees for the different types of companies, we notice that the process of reduction has been important and continuous. Only in 1994 can signs of a revival be observed, however those are very small. The reduction of employees peaks in 1991, with a fall of almost 20 per cent in employment, but it also continues in the successive years.

Several analysts assumed that after 1989 the labor market would witness a huge increase in unemployment, due to the expulsion of many workers from the SOEs, which were in crisis or in a phase of reorganization in order to maintain their competitiveness. Afterwards the persons who had lost their job would have been slowly taken up by the private sector which was in expansion. As a result, the unemployment rate would get close to that of the Western countries. The path followed by the rate of unemployment would have assumed the shape of a reversed parabola: low in the beginning, high in the middle, and descending in the final phase of the process. It is not possible to observe this trend in the present data, but it became clear how the most widespread phenomenon observed in the trends of employment has occurred in the direct passage of workers from the state sector to the private economy, without a longer or shorter absence from work (see Boeri, 1993). Considering these two sectors we notice how the shrinking of the first one is complementary to the growth of the second one (see Figure 5.1). The other two types of ownership form have a marginal role, in the same way as is shown in Table 5.18 with respect to the distribution of the companies by ownership form. Thus we can point out a polarized situation where the declining state ownership is accompanied by a rising share of private ownership.

The last aspect taken into account is the distribution of employees by the size of the companies. In the small companies the relative number of employees has grown. In the companies with 100 to 5000 employees there is a substantial decrease. The splitting up of the big companies, the development of the 'green field' firms and the emergence of the hidden economy partly explain these trends. However it seems interesting to notice the stability of the relative weight of companies with more than 5000 employees. This result underlines the existence of physical constraints to the change. The legal creation of a company takes a small period of time, so the total number of companies can easily grow. The restructuring or splitting up of old big companies is a complex process which requires great investments in time and in money. Hence, changing actual characteristics of companies is slower and gradual. With regard to this, one can compare Table 5.19 with Table 5.17.

After 1989 the distribution of companies by size and by ownership form has undergone considerable changes. Moreover, the number of companies has grown dramatically. Even in the occupational sphere transformations have taken place: a considerable decrease in the number of employees could be observed. But as already noticed before, in the latter sphere the dynamism has been less than in the former, because of physical constraints to a considerable modification of the set of inherited factors.

Figure 5.1. Employment by ownership form between 1990 and 1994 (in per cent)

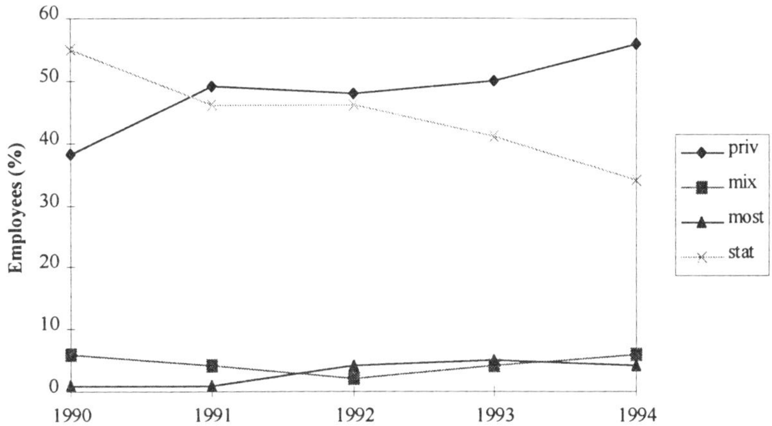

Source: Computation of the author based on the available data.

Table 5.19. Distribution of employees by the size of firms between 1990 and 1994 (per cent)

Year	SIZE				
	1–25	26–100	101–1000	1001–5000	>5000
1990	5	8	47	27	13
1991	12	11	46	19	12
1992	17	12	41	17	12
1993	23	17	33	14	13
1994	27	19	28	15	11

Source: Computation of the author based on the available data

In this section we outline how the regional distribution of companies and employees has changed. Our main argument considers an important aspect that is not so easy to change in a small period of time, that is, the influence of regional location as a deep trait of economic structure. The variable for region is taken as dichotomous: Budapest, the capital, versus the rest of the country.

In the past, the center of the Hungarian economy has been Budapest and its neighborhood. In 1989, almost 40 per cent of the companies and employees were located here. After the changes of 1989, the state stopped intervening in smoothing out the regional inequalities. Thus, a stronger concentration around Budapest has taken place. Employment has declined more slowly in Budapest than outside the capital city, so the weight of the capital has shown some growth (from 42 per cent to 45 per cent). The share of Budapest as regards the number of companies has remained astonishingly stable over the years. It changed from 47 per cent in 1991 to a peak of 52 per cent in 1993. Thus Budapest has not found itself in a far better position as regards the development of new companies and private ownership. It seems clear that a 'structural inertia' due to the former system's characteristics is embedded in the set-up of the Hungarian economy, and it functions as a physical constraint to change.

5.7.4 The Definition of Economic Performance

The concept of a company's performance is very wide and can be applied to several aspects of a company, which not always derive from the same root. In this study, we focus on the economic aspects of the performance and we compare different groups of companies in this respect and across time. Two important dimensions are used to evaluate the outcomes of a group of companies: their profitability and their productivity. These indicators are not directly observable from the data and a work of operationalization is necessary. One of the main tasks is to find reliable indicators which reflect the real trend of the investigated dimensions. For this reason, it could be dangerous to consider just one indicator for each aspect of economic performance, because some variables that are not within a company's control can affect its results. Therefore many indicators are selected and their trends are checked across the years. We selected three indicators for each dimension of the performance.

(a) *Profitability indicators*
ROI (return on investment): the operating profit relative to the total assets;
GROSPROF (gross profitability rate): the profit before taxation relative to the total assets;
NETPROF (net profitability rate): the profit after taxation relative to the total assets.

The first one is a classical indicator in the balance sheet analysis and it is used to measure the efficiency of the utilization of all the accumulated assets in the typical activity of a company. The other two indicators focus on the profit of a company and try to evaluate the impact of the taxation on it.

(b) *Productivity indicators*
GDPn (per capita productivity): the company's value added (GDP) in relation to the number of its employees;
PRODUC (labor productivity): turnover relative to the total staff costs;
PRODWA (wage productivity): the turnover in relation to the amount of total wages and salaries.

Here the focus is on the wage dynamics that is a very important factor in the transition process (see Kornai, 1995).[18] The indicators show different aspects of the two dimensions of performance. Analysing the means across the years, we determine if there is some parallel trend between them. One of the problems we encountered during this computation was the presence of outlying values for each indicator. These outliers would strongly have affected the estimates, which are not robust in comparison with them. So, considering the large number of observations and the huge dimension of the databases (it was not possible to verify where each outlier was placed), the values which strongly differed from the characteristic range were excluded in order to get more reliable estimates.

We also must point out that the number of outliers was little compared to the total number of the data. The results computed in BLOCK 1 (all groups of companies) for all indicators are shown in Table 5.20. It is not easy to evaluate the results in a direct way. As a matter of fact the trends could be determined by composed effects that disappeared when we control the other category variables. But it is possible to draw some general conclusions from the results.

It is clear that the values for all the profitability indicators decreased until 1992 and then they remained stable in 1993. From 1994 ROI started growing again, while GROSPROF and NETPROF were late and their growth started only in 1995. Moreover for the last two indicators the results in 1995 are worse than the values observed in 1990. The decrease of the profitability for the first years of a transition is an expected result. It is known that the profitability of capital tends to go down, because large investments in restructuring and re-orientation are needed. Another reason for the observed trends is the presence of the green field in the considered database (BLOCK 1). Generally, these new companies are in a situation where the profitability is lower, due to the takeover of a new activity.

Finally, it is not easy to explain the late growth of the last two indicators. We have to consider that profit before and after includes the financial transactions of the companies, which are heavily affected by the bad loans that the companies had accumulated in the past. Whereas in the operating profit (used for the computation of ROI) only the results of the company's typical activities are considered with no regard to financial aspects. This means that the companies have produced more in a more efficient way since 1994 but they have to pay for the previous bad performance and accumulation of loans.

The trend of productivity indicators seems to be more varied. Moreover it is not the same for all the three indicators. On the one hand, GDPn grew constantly between 1990 and 1995. This growth is strongly linked to the adjustment, especially the restructuring of production and the re-orientation of foreign trade, that occurred during this period. At the same time the companies not involved in the privatization process, namely those left in state ownership or the new ones, found themselves in an increasingly dynamic and competitive environment. Therefore they were forced to behave in a more efficient way and to adopt new technologies, now more easily available.

On the other hand, PRODUC and PRODWA followed almost the same trend as the profitability indicators, but for both productivity indicators the upswing had already started in 1994 and the absolute value in 1995 was better than for all the others. But the reasons which explain this situation seem to be very different from those exposed for the profitability indicators. To understand what has happened, it is necessary to take into account the changes in wages and salaries that were the center of attention even in public discussions (see Kornai, 1995).

Table 5.20. Means for the indicators of economic performance of the groups of companies between 1990 and 1995

DIMENSION OF PERFORMANCE	YEAR	1990	1991	1992	1993	1994	1995
PROFITABILITY	ROI	0.06	0.01	–0.01	–0.01	0.01	0.05
	GROSPROF	0.06	0.01	–0.02	–0.03	–0.02	0.03
	NETPROF	0.04	0.01	–0.04	–0.04	–0.04	0.01
PRODUCTIVITY	GDPn	5.6	5.8	6.4	6.6	6.8	6.8
	PRODUC	1.8	1.8	1.6	1.6	1.8	1.9
	PRODWA	2.3	2.3	2.1	2.2	2.3	2.4

Source: Computation of the author based on the available data (BLOCK 1)

The results for BLOCK 2 confirm the observed trend in BLOCK 1, even though here the values for PRODUC and PRODWA are lower in 1995 than in 1990. In this case it becomes necessary to verify the effects of the type of property, because we may suppose that the state-owned firms present strong constraints to restructuring and, mainly, to the dismissal of redundant labor. So the bad performance of these companies could strongly affect the general means in some years.

These remarks underline the existing differences among the trends of the considered indicators in the two dimensions of performance. Even in the case of parallel trends, the reasons for their shape seem to be substantially different.

The variety of indicators helps to reduce the distortions and the bias in the evaluation of the data. The result seems to support our argument that the economic performance of a company is not unidimensional and it has at least two aspects. In addition, we can conclude that a few indicators could be chosen as representative ones: ROI for profitability and PRODWA for productivity. This choice simplifies the presentation of the results and it is supported by the evidence. As a matter of fact, as far as profitability is concerned, all the indicators (ROI, GROSPROF and NETPROF) behave in the same way and the presentation of ROI alone avoids redundancies of information.

As regards productivity, there is no coherence in the trends of indicators but the productivity of wages seems to be a more relevant aspect because it is directly linked to the real cost of labor. Therefore we have chosen PRODWA, in conformity with the previous argument. Further steps of the analysis will furnish other elements to support our choice. Hence, the next step is the construction of an analysis of variance (ANOVA) where our first aim is the evaluation of the impact of property rights on the economic performance.

5.7.5 The Property Rights Hypothesis

In this section, Hypothesis 1 (difference in performance due to the type of property) is tested. The type of property is defined by the share of the property of the state in relation to the issued capital stock, as explained in the previous chapter. But here we define five types of ownership (that is, STATE, more than 50 per cent of property of the state, was divided in two groups: MORE and STATE again). The distinction among the five groups is sufficiently articulated to cover the differences which exist among the companies in reality.

After the definition of the independent variable (the type of property in five categories), the analysis of variance will be conducted, taking all the indicators as dependent variables, one at a time. This time the results refer to the data in BLOCK 2. Our choice of the database is based on the idea that, at least at the beginning of the transition and privatization, the status of these groups was more similar hence it is meaningful to compare the evolution of the groups of companies according to their performance. The results of the analyses of variance are shown in Table 5.21.

It is clear from the data that the type of ownership affects the performance across the different groups of companies. The probability (p) is often equal to 0, which means that the differences are statistically significant (at the level of 0.001 per cent, as specified in the table's notes). But once again the two aspects of the performance show some differences.

Table 5.21. Results of the analysis of variance (test F and significance p) by type of ownership for all indicators

YEAR	total d.f. (a)	ROI F Ratio	ROI p(b)	GROSPROF (c) F ratio	GROSPROF (c) p(b)	NETPROF F ratio	NETPROF p(b)
1990	589	4.8	0	4.8	0	7.5	0
1991	651	13.4	0	13.4	0	7.8	0
1992	980	3.8	0.005	4.0	0.003	3.7	0.006
1993	1049	9.0	0	9.9	0	9.8	0
1994	938	11.4	0	6.0	0	7.2	0
1995	893	6.1	0	3.7	0.005	3.4	0.009

YEAR	PRODUC F-ratio	PRODUC p(b)	PRODWA F-ratio	PRODWA P(b)
1990	1.4	0.241	1.6	0.176
1991	1.1	0.371	2.3	0.057
1992	2.9	0.020	3.4	0.010
1993	7.2	0	7.4	0
1994	15.9	0	15.4	0
1995	15.7	0	14.43	0

Notes:

a. The total number of degrees of freedom (d.f.) represents the number of groups of companies per kind of property minus one.
b. P represents the probability that the difference found between groups of companies by kind of property would be random; p = 0 indicate a probability lower than 1/1000. Hence, the probability that the difference found would be random is always less than this threshold, in each year.
c. In the first two years, the data for GROSPROF are the same as ROI.
d. In BLOCK 2 the figures for GDP are not available.

Source: computation of the author based on the available data, BLOCK 2 (d).

Table 5.22. Means of the groups of companies by type of ownership between 1990 and 1995

	ROI means across YEARS					
STATE2	1990	1991	1992	1993	1994	1995
PRIV	0.08	0.05	–0.01	0.00	0.03	0.06
MOST	–0.02	0.02	–0.02	–0.02	0.02	0.01
MIX	0.08	0.06	0.00	0.02	0.02	0.02
MORE	0.04	0.00	–0.05	0.00	0.00	–0.02
STATE	0.04	–0.02	–0.06	–0.06	–0.07	–0.04

	PRODWA means across YEARS					
STATE2	1990	1991	1992	1993	1994	1995
PRIV	2.5	2.3	2.0	1.9	2.0	2.1
MOST	2.7	2.8	1.9	1.8	1.9	2.0
MIX	2.9	2.3	2.1	2.0	2.0	2.1
MORE	2.1	2.7	2.0	2.0	2.2	2.2
STATE	2.3	2.2	1.8	1.6	1.5	1.6

Source: Computation of the author based on the available data (BLOCK 2)

As to the profitability indicators, the effect of ownership starts almost from the beginning and remains significant until 1994. In 1995 we observe a little change in the results concerning GROSPROF and NETPROF. But without the values for the next years, it is not possible to determine if there is a change in the trend or if something special has happened in 1995. However, as to the productivity indicators, the differences start to be significant from 1993.In the first two years of the transition, there are no significant differences in productivity due to the type of ownership (the probability of random differences is not greater than 0.05) and in 1992 the values of F determine a probability of random effects too high to be considered significant, according to this kind of data. After 1992, however, the differences between groups became highly significant (the probability of random differences is not less than 0.001). It seems that the effects of the transition due to the change of property rights on productivity are not immediate and they need some time to emerge. To test this assumption, and to see the difference between state-owned and private companies, the means for ROI and PRODWA for all kinds of property across the years are shown in Table 5.22 above.

It is easy to notice that the private companies are generally better than the state-owned ones (STATE with more than 75 per cent of state ownership), both for profitability (ROI) and for productivity (PRODWA). But the trends for PRIVATE and STATE are parallel, even though there is a difference between their levels. The trend already observed for the general means is typical even for these groups. A more complex task is to explain the trends for the other three intermediate groups (MOST, MIX, and MORE). But we have to keep in mind that, above all in the first years, the small number of companies in these categories makes the estimates less reliable.

To sum up: the property right hypothesis does not seem to be falsified by the data: private companies (PRIVATE) behave better than the state-owned companies (STATE). It is difficult to understand the position of the intermediate groups and many questions remain still open. Other factors could affect the economic performance. So we continue to test the second hypothesis.

5.7.6 The Impact of Foreign Investment

Another factor seems relevant to determine the performance of a company: the presence of foreign investors that acquire a share of the issued capital stock. The arguments in this respect could be discussed from many points of view. First of all, experience suggests that the foreign investors who buy a part of, or all, the assets of a company, take over the management, and this is not linked to the size of their share in the firm. Once the company has passed into their hands, restructuring becomes easier because the political and social constraints are weakened and the structural resistance has been overcome. Actually the choice of the foreign investors is not unrelated to the characteristics of the company: the most familiar situations, where the constraints are already weak, are privileged. This happened above all in the first years of the privatization process when the best companies with good forecasts for the future were sold and passed into private or foreign hands.

Another relevant aspect of the presence of foreign investors is related to the possibility for the Hungarian companies owned by them to be supported by the international network of the mother-company. This is true above all in the case of the multinationals and it provides several advantages. Indeed, for the companies with interests spread all over the world it is easier to obtain loans at better conditions than those offered on the Hungarian market to the domestic investors. In this way the financial costs for loans are diminished and the profits grow. The international experience of the mother-company also allows the Hungarian companies access to advanced technology and the advantage of the knowledge acquired elsewhere. This is very important in the

Hungarian case where the previous technology cannot compete on the international market, but the skill level of human capital is quite high, compared to countries at the same degree of development (see Swaan, 1997).

Following these arguments, we test the first part of HYPOTHESIS 2, namely if the presence of foreign capital affects the economic performance of the companies, and we try to determine what is the direction of the differences. The methodology used is the same as the previous one, that is, an analysis of variance where the dependent variables remain the performance indicators and the independent variable (factor) is a dichotomous one, FOREIGN ('yes' or 'no' according to the presence of foreign capital). In Tables 5.23 and 5.24, the result of statistical tests and the means for ROI and PRODWA are shown.

The effect of foreign investments is not always significant. However, as far as productivity is concerned, only in the first year are there no significant differences and afterwards the groups with foreign investors have higher productivity than the others. On the other hand the differences in profitability (ROI) are not so strong and, from a statistical point of view, they are not significant in 1990, 1992 and in 1995. (The probability of random differences is greater than 0.05 in the first two years and it is about 0.04 in the third one.) In the other years the probability is less than 0.001. So it is not possible to draw an incontestable trend for the results of profitability, even if the ROI means of the groups of companies with foreign investors are higher than the means of the other groups.

We observed clearly significant differences due to foreign capital only in productivity since 1991 and not for profitability. The reason for that could be the higher level of investment made by foreign owners that reduce the profits even though it prepares a better situation for the future. But it is not a completely convincing argument. In the first place, the productivity data do not follow the same course in either of the two databases. As a matter of fact, as far as productivity is concerned, significant differences exist between the groups of companies, with a better course for the ones with foreign capital. Therefore, in this case it seems that a higher quality of the new management produces immediate results and it does not require a period of consolidation. Otherwise the data we have at our disposal do not seem to show that the companies which are partly or completely owned by foreign investors have a stronger disposition to investments. Thus, the decision to undertake investments does not seem to be particularly connected to the presence of foreign capital and therefore it cannot give an explanation for the lower level of profitability for the groups of companies which reveal this characteristic. Moreover, Gáspár (1996) emphasizes how most multinationals – who have invested in CEE – use their positions as bridgehead in order to be able to enter the markets of the region. Therefore, the question of the commercial reconversion has not always been relevant for companies with foreign property and the acquisitions have even represented a strategic move towards the creation of outlets in the markets which previously belonged to the CMEA.

Table 5.23. Results of the analysis of variance (test F and significance, p) relative to the groups of companies by FOREIGN for the ROI and PRODWA indicators

		ROI		PRODWA	
Years	**Total d.f.**	**F-ratio**	**p**	**F-ratio**	**P**
1990	589	2.6	0.105	5.9	0.016
1991	652	12.9	0	7.8	0.005
1992	980	3.8	0.051	17.0	0
1993	1 051	13.3	0	26.0	0
1994	938	14.5	0	21.9	0
1995	893	4.2	0.042	19.4	0

Source: Computation of the author based on the available data (BLOCK 2)

Finally, another argument which does not seem coherent with the observed results in terms of profitability concerns the time horizon of foreign investors in CEE. CEE presents a higher risk not comparable, for instance, with that of the countries of the European Union. Thus the foreign investors count upon the realization of considerable profits within a short period, which compensates them for the undertaking of higher margins of uncertainty. Many researchers have presented hypotheses about the transfer pricing practices of particular Hungarian companies owned by multinationals. Even though it is an almost natural process, no previous research about the explanation of this point has been able to obtain definitive results supported by empirical verifications. The aggregated data at our disposal do not allow us to check if this practice can be actually verified and is more prominent for the companies with foreign investors. The only observation one can make is a result of the comparison of the two dimensions of the companies' performance which present trends which are not coherent with the factor FOREIGN. As a matter of fact, the absolute values of operating profits, or of GDP or total turnover, can be altered in the book-keeping of the companies and therefore they do not show completely the actual situation of the companies.

Table 5.24. Means of the groups of companies by FOREIGN across years

INDICATOR	FOREIGN	1990	1991	1992	1993	1994	1995
ROI	yes	0.07	0.05	–0.02	0.01	0.04	0.04
	no	0.05	0.00	–0.05	–0.04	–0.02	0.01
PRODWA	yes	2.6	2.4	2.1	2.0	2.1	2.2
	no	2.3	2.2	1.8	1.7	1.8	1.9

Source: Computation of the author based on the available data (BLOCK 2).

However, the number of employees and the amount of the expenses in wages are more reliable and these are more difficult to manipulate. Therefore, even if the absolute value of the indicators of productivity can be insignificant, the consideration of it in relative terms for groups of companies, seems to be more reliable than the other indicators of profitability, which are exclusively based on financial variables of the balance sheets. The better performance in terms of productivity of the companies wherein foreign enterprises have invested seems a more relevant and attested aspect compared to the substantial lack of differences in the profitability within the groups of companies determined by the factor FOREIGN.

5.7.7 The Role of Investments

Foreign investment is an explicit variable that affects the economic performance of a CEE company. It is very important to estimate this aspect in order to check if there actually exist differences between companies which invest and those which do not, assuming that the investments require an initial financial effort but that they lead to better results over the mid and long term. Unfortunately, only one variable in the database at our disposal has been connected to the investments and through this one we can obtain only an indicative and rather approximate idea of them. The variable represents the absolute value in HUF of the unfinished investments. These are examined with comparison to the general value of the tangible assets, generating in this way the indicator INVESTRATE. This is considered as a dichotomous variable (INVESTRATE other than 0 or equal to 0).[19] The results are presented in Tables 5.25 and 5.26.

The results of the profitability for the first two years do not show particular differences in the two groups and only from 1992 do the groups of companies with unfinished investments behave in a better way. The most natural interpretation for this could be given by the consideration that in the first phase of the transition and of restructuring, some investments which will reap results in the future are charged to the companies as expenses and, finally, as losses. And so we return to the argument of the necessity of a period of balance in order to be able to overcome the first difficulties connected to the industrial restructuring and/or the commercial re-orientation. As a matter of fact, until 1992 the amount of the unfinished investments did not simply concern the new investments undertaken in the course of the previous year, but also all those accumulated before. This problem had been solved in 1992 when the accounts of the companies had been set to zero by law through a redefinition of their legal form and the calculation has started from scratch. Leaving out of consideration the first two years, it is interesting to estimate the averages of the indicators of performance once INVEST and OWNER (type of ownership) cross, which is considered in this context as dichotomous, that is, less than 50 per cent of state ownership, and more than 50 per cent. In this case, the effects of the two categorical variables are summed up and a particular and rather interesting situation is determined, where the groups of better companies seem to be the private ones with investments and the worst ones are the state companies without investments, while the other two groups behave in the same way.

Table 5.25. Means of the groups of companies by INVESTMENT (yes or no) between 1990 and 1995

INDICATOR	INVESTMENT	1990	1991	1992	1993	1994	1995
ROI	yes	0.05	0.01	–0.03	0.00	0.02	0.03
	no	0.06	0.01	–0.08	–0.08	–0.04	–0.02
PRODWA	yes	2.41	2.27	1.95	1.86	1.95	2.05
	no	2.21	2.04	1.69	1.54	1.60	1.79

Source: Computation of the author based on the available data (BLOCK 2)

Table 5.26. Cross effects of ownership and investment

OWNER INVEST	Private +	State –
yes: +	+ +	+ –
no: –	– +	– –

The above observation is confirmed by the course of the averages of ROI and PRODWA from 1992 on. Especially as far as PRODWA is concerned, these courses seem to be strictly confirmed. Therefore it is possible to synthesize in a descriptive way the two variables for ownership and investments in one single typology of three categories, wherein, as far as performance is concerned, there exists an order from the best to the worst. The new variable presents the three types of groups of companies according to the crossings of the previous table: type 1 (+ +), type 2 (– + or + –), type 3 (– –). The results in terms of averages are presented in Table 5.27. We observe that from the starting point of 1990 all the groups of companies for each indicator (ROI and PRODWA) have shown declining results. But from 1994 on a quite strong upswing for companies Type 1 and 2 began. Meanwhile, Type 3 continued to show a very low performance and, for ROI, its outcome became even worse. So, what could we deduct from the typology?

If for a group to be or not to be private is not a sufficient condition to determine the performance (in Type 2 we have both private and state-owned companies that behave in a quite similar way), the composition of the positive effect of investment with private ownership brings higher outcomes than the others. Symmetrically, the state groups which do not undertake any kind of investment survive adrift but with very low results. If the Hungarian economy is going to be exposed to increasing international competition, these latter companies have to change their behavior or they are doomed to disappear.

Otherwise, Type 2 shows that the effect of private ownership without investment is in some way counterbalanced by the attitude towards investment in the state-owned groups of companies. So once again, it is shown that the simple ownership type is too poor a discriminant to judge and to forecast the performance of a company and we have to pay attention to many other factors, such as the behavior in the given institutional framework, the attitudes of its management and the presence of foreign investments which affect strongly its strategy.

Table 5.27. Means for the three types generated by crossing STATE and INVESTMENT

INDICATOR	OWNERSHIP BY INVESTMENT TYPOLOGY	1990	1991	1992	1993	1994	1995
ROI	TYPE 1 (++)	0.07	0.04	0.00	0.02	0.04	0.04
	TYPE 2 (–+ OR + –)	0.05	0.01	–0.03	–0.03	–0.01	0.02
	TYPE 3 (—)	0.01	–0.09	–0.12	–0.11	–0.11	–0.14
Ln (PROWA)	TYPE 1 (+ +)	2.6	2.4	2.0	1.9	2.0	2.1
	TYPE 2 (– + or + –)	2.4	2.2	1.9	1.8	1.8	1.9
	TYPE 3 (– –)	2.0	1.9	1.5	1.2	1.2	1.4

Source: Computation of the author based on the available data (BLOCK 2)

By analysing the economic performance of the companies, we have seen that the kind of property affects in a significant way both profitability and productivity. But the analysis showed that there are other relevant variables explaining the outcomes of the restructuring process. We have considered the presence of foreign investment and the attitude towards investment of a company. These factors determine significant differences in the performance of the companies, even though not always in the expected direction. Then the empirical results underline that the type of ownership is not a sufficient condition to forecast the restructuring success or the lack of it. This result is especially relevant in the context of Central Eastern Europe where many scholars and politicians often press for privatization, believing that the transfer of the state property into private hands could be enough to improve the efficiency of the whole economic system.

5.8 WHERE HAVE THE PROFITS GONE IN HUNGARY?

The above analysis showed that the expansion of the private sector in general and privatization in particular have not yet resulted in a considerable improvement of the companies' economic performance in Hungary. Private companies as a group did not generate profits – nor did state-owned enterprises, but the latter has been expected while the losses of the private sector has not – and foreign ownership has not turned the companies into efficient agents of a market economy. These phenomena can partly be explained by the collapse of traditional markets and by the disintegration of the former production and cooperation networks of the Hungarian companies. In addition, private companies had to invest first in order to restructure the company and to reshape its management and marketing systems. Still, the question remains, where have all the profits gone in Hungary over the past seven years? Most analysts argue that the overall fall of production can be made responsible for the company losses. In addition, the changing rules of accounting and taxation of the companies also contributed to the vanishing of profits.[20] The impact of a disintegrating statistical and accounting system of measuring profits cannot be denied. But was it the drop of production that played the main role in pushing most companies into the red?

In order to test this assertion, we calculated the real value of total turnover of the CDEs between 1988 and 1996. We used the GDP deflator as an implicit price index to recalculate nominal values into real values. Since the total turnover of the CDEs accounted for more than 90 per cent of the gross production of the Hungarian economy, we can safely say that the results of the following analysis are valid for the whole economy. As a next step, we also outline the cost structure of CDEs between 1988 and 1996. The results are shown in Table 5.28.

Table 5.28. The structure of expenditures of the CDEs relative to turnover between 1988 and 1996, in per cent

		1988	1989	1990	1991	1992
1.	Number of CDEs	7 628	12 353	23 314	38 041	57 865
2.	Cost of materials and semifinished products	37.5	36.3	36.2	38.2	31.4
3.	Purchase price of products resold	42.4	42.4	42.2	40.9	40.5
4.=(2.+3.)	Cost of materials and resold products together	79.8	78.7	78.4	79.1	71.9
5.	Staff costs, including social security exp.	11.5	11.9	12.6	14.7	16.6
6.	Depreciation	2.3	2.2	2.1	2.3	4.6
7.	Overhead and miscellaneous costs	2.3	2.6	3.1	4.5	7.0
8.	Banking costs	1.7	2.5	3.0	3.6	9.8
9.	**Total costs**	97.6	97.9	99.2	104.2	109.9

Table 5.28 continued

		1993	1994	1995	1996
1.	Number of CDEs	71 503	79 793	90 224	104 017
2.	Cost of materials and semifinished products	29.7	28.3	29.3	28.6
3.	Purchase price of products resold	41.7	43.7	43.9	44.2
4.=(2.+3.)	Cost of materials and resold products together	71.4	72	73.2	72.8
5.	Staff costs, including social security exp.	16.3	15	13.2	12.1
6.	Depreciation	4.2	4	3.7	3.8
7.	Overhead and miscellaneous costs	7.5	7.8	7.8	7.8
8.	Banking costs	6.7	4.9	5.8	2.3
9.	**Total costs**	106.1	103.7	103.7	98.8

The first important observation from the table is that the total real turnover of the CDEs has not declined since 1988. The only exception was 1991, the year of the Hungarian 'shock therapy', when the volume of Hungarian foreign trade with the former CMEA countries dropped most drastically. In other years, the volume of the companies' total sales substantially increased. This was true despite the fact that both industrial and agricultural production shrank in the 1990s, until 1994. But the drop of industrial and agricultural production was counterbalanced by the expansion of services. The service sector became the 'locomotive' of the Hungarian economy.

If it was not production decline that could explain the company losses, then it could only be the case that the increase of costs exceeded the growth of revenues of the companies. We could observe that total costs relative to total turnover have been higher than 100 per cent since 1991. This is why the companies have generated losses since then. It is also interesting to follow the changes of the cost structure since 1988. There were two types of costs that have had a rising trend: the 'purchase price of products resold' and the 'overhead costs'. The first item consists of products that had been bought, mostly imported by companies and then resold without substantially altering those products in the production process. In addition, this cost item incorporated the expenses paid to the companies' subcontractors. The second cost item, overhead costs, included those expenses of a company that could not be directly related to individual products or services. Such expenses were, for instance, the administration and organization costs of a company and the salaries and other benefits of the top management.

Total wage costs relative to turnover also increased until 1993, but they have declined since then, mostly due to the austerity program of the Hungarian government (the so-called 'Bokros package'). Another cost item that largely contributed to the company losses until 1992–93 was the banking costs, that is, interest payments and other debt service obligations of the companies. The ratio of the banking costs has shrunk since then, due to the so-called 'loan and bank consolidation program' of the Hungarian government that cleaned up the books of the companies and the banks from a large part of their arrears. Finally, depreciation also showed a growing trend.

We can conclude that it was a cost explosion rather than a huge decline in total production that has resulted in the large losses of the companies since 1991. The fast increase in costs was in part fueled by a radical change of the currency regime of the Hungarian economy, and also by the liberalization of prices and by the elimination of production and consumption subsidies. But the cost explosion was also a symptom of the low level of efficiency and adaptability of the companies and a sign of the lack of efficient markets. There can be another factor behind the cost explosion. Since the old accounting and reporting system of the companies disintegrated, several companies found it tempting to apply different 'tricks' and hide their revenues behind costs in order to avoid paying taxes. Consequently, we cannot be certain that most of the CDEs were really loss-makers, or they just reported losses.

So far we have discussed the cost structure of all CDEs. But we had seen before that there were sizable differences of profitability among the companies with different ownership structures. Thus, it is an obvious question to ask whether there was a difference in the cost structure of those companies, too? We analysed and compared the cost structure of three groups of companies: the foreign private companies (Forprivs), the domestic private companies (Domprivs) and the domestic SOEs (Domstats) (see Table 5.29).

Table 5.29. Turnover and profits in bn HUF, and the cost structure of the companies relative to turnover, in per cent, between 1990 and 1996

		1990			1992		
		Forprivs	**Dom-privs**	**Domstats**	**Forprivs**	**Domprivs**	**Domstats**
1.	No. of companies	4 773	16 046	1 779	11 499	39 850	3 969
2.	No. of companies without fin. serv.	4 771	16 043	1 777	11 409	39 371	3 949
3.	Turnover	563	1 400	3 328	992	1 850	2 272
4.	Turnover, without fin. services	563	1 400	3 328	969	1 850	2 250
5.	Profits before tax	23.3	31.7	123	–19	–46	–101
6.	Profits before tax, without fin. services	23.3	31.7	123	–19	–46	–110
7.	Profits after tax	26.2	24.6	74	–30	–64	–124
8.	Profits after tax, without fin. services	26.1	24.6	74	–29	–62	–130
9.	Cost of materials and semifin. products, %	38.4	31.1	37.8	25.4	28.2	34.5
10	Purchase price of products resold, %	41.2	46.0	40.5	46.8	45.4	36.8
11.= (9.+10.)	Cost of materials and resold products, %	79.6	77.1	78.3	72.2	73.6	71.3
12.	Staff costs, inlc. social exp. %	10.1	14.3	11.8	11.8	17.2	17.9
13.	Depreciation	1.3	1.2	2.5	3.4	3.3	5.8
14.	Overhead	3.4	2.7	3.2	10.3	6.7	5.4
15.	Bank costs	4.5	5.2	4.9	5.3	6.1	10.6
16.	**Total costs**	98.9	100.5	100.7	103.0	106.9	111.0

Table 5.29 continued

		1995			1996		
		Forprivs	Dom-privs	Domstats	Forprivs	Domprivs	Domstats
1.	No. of companies	18 740	68 638	1 692	19 651	81 778	1 592
2.	No. of companies without fin. serv.	18 629	68 368	1 683	19 475	80 764	1 575
3.	Turnover	3 670	4 430	1 310	5 133	5 802	1 215
4.	Turnover without fin. services	3 597	4 392	1 190	4 921	5 741	1 212
5.	Profits before tax	57.6	89.5	–1.7	208.5	147.8	–71
6.	Profits before tax, without fin. services	54.3	88	–25.3	147.2	141.8	–66
7.	Profits after tax	–22	24.2	–25	55.4	50	–82
8.	Profits after tax, without fin. services	–21.8	23.5	–42.8	20.5	49	–79
9.	Cost of materials and semifin. products, %	29.6	24.2	38.2	30.9	24.9	32.5
10.	Purchase price of products resold, %	43.9	53.1	26.3	41.1	53.1	29.7
11.= (9.+10.)	Cost of materials and resold products, %	73.5	77.3	64.5	72.0	78.0	62.3
12.	Staff costs, inlc. social exp. %	9.5	11.5	24.7	9.5	10.6	26.1
13.	Depreciation	3.4	2.4	5.6	3.4	2.3	8
14.	Overhead and other, %	9.1	6.7	6.3	8.8	6.5	6.8
15.	Bank costs	4.0	3.7	11.5	2.5	1.6	2.9
16.	**Total costs**	99.5	101.6	112.6	96.2	99.0	106.1

It is shown in the table that the total turnover of the foreign private and the domestic private companies has increased over the years as it did for all the CDEs. But the turnover of the SOEs showed a declining trend. Thus, production decline could not be a reason for company losses for all CDEs, but it could be a factor that contributed to the decline of profits in the group of the Domstats. Our second observation was that while private companies hit the bottom as regards profits in 1992, the worst year for SOEs was 1993. But if we exclude financial services, the total loss of the SOEs was also highest in 1992, and it was lower than that of the private companies in 1993. This large change in the relative position of the SOEs can be attributed to the so-called 'bank consolidation program' again. Namely, the state-owned banks acquired the majority of the bad debt of the SOEs by 1993. While private, non-financial companies had higher total losses than SOEs in 1993, the bulk of the losses was generated by the Domstats in 1995 and also in 1996.

We observed obvious differences among the cost structures of the foreign and domestic private companies and the SOEs. First, the relative costs of materials and semi-finished products was the highest in the group of the SOEs. This was due to the fact that a fairly large number of the SOEs operated in material-intensive branches, moreover, they have not been efficient. As regards the relative costs of products resold, the private companies, and especially foreign private companies, had the highest and increasing indicators, while SOEs had the lowest and decreasing indicators. This is a very important difference between private and state-owned companies, because it indicates that private companies probably extensively followed the practice of 'transfer pricing'. This could be a way of transferring profits from their Hungarian subsidiary to one of their other foreign subsidiaries.

Relative wage costs were the highest in the group of the state-owned enterprises. This result showed that wages and wage costs were fairly rigid in the state sector, while private companies, in particular foreign private companies, were much more flexible and efficient in reducing wage costs. It is interesting to note that depreciation was also the highest in the group of the state-owned companies and the lowest in the domestic private companies. This could have indicated a relatively fast replacement of obsolete equipment in the state sector, but this was not the case. SOEs usually channeled depreciation toward financial investments.

There has been a real gap between foreign private companies on the one hand, and domestic private companies and SOEs on the other as regards relative overhead costs. It was much higher in the first group than in the other two groups. This fact can partly be explained by the foreign companies spending more on changing company management, upgrading the statistical and the accounting system of the company and reshaping the company's marketing and logistics activities than domestic private or state-owned companies did. But the gap is due in part to the spending of foreign companies on expensive cars and other benefits for top managers, and hiring expensive 'consultants' and subcontractors from abroad. As regards banking costs, the state-owned enterprises ranked first again. It is small wonder, for state-owned enterprises had been in debt to a large extent from the time before the transformation and they had to service the debt. Their debt mostly stemmed from government loans for huge investment projects that could never be realized or that could not pay reasonable returns after their completion.

In conclusion, we could see a characteristic difference between the cost structure of the private companies on the one hand, and state-owned enterprises on the other. While private companies, and especially foreign private companies, have spent relatively more on products that they resold, and also on overhead expenses, state-owned enterprises have had relatively high wage costs and banking costs. In other words, private companies could flexibly use those cost items that are not easy to account for and control to hide their profits, while state-owned enterprises remained on a forced track to cover wage costs and debt service. Hence, state-owned enterprises have usually been loss-makers by heritage and because of the way they regularly functioned, private companies could 'choose' to become loss-makers in order to conceal their profits.

5.9 COMPANY RESTRUCTURING IN HUNGARY: A CASE STUDY ANALYSIS

5.9.1 Introduction

Evaporating profits, diminishing investments and asset values on the one hand; soaring productivity, spectacular betterment of export capabilities, and rapidly improving indicators of corporate indebtedness on the other. These are the initial, rough impressions gained from the national statistics (balance-sheet data of all firms using double-entry book-keeping) on Hungary's industrial transformation. Attempts to assess corporate performance immediately face terminological problems. Under what conditions can a company be called restructured? What kind of performance and what indicators of it attest to this?

The *definition of restructuring* can be approached by considering it as the result of a dynamic process, which was the approach I took in an earlier study (Szalavetz, 1997a). There I defined restructuring as a complex transfer mechanism that includes the financial consolidation of a company and the introduction of smoothly functioning financial management. Besides the financial aspects, restructuring includes the modernization of various fields of the corporate activity, the introduction of organizational and production best-practice methods, and at least some technological upgrading. The term 'transfer mechanism' implies the existence or emergence of an exogenous source, such as a new, decisive owner or a new, creative management team.

But can it be claimed that privatized and new private firms perform better than state-owned firms?

An attempt to define what exactly is meant by 'performing better' leads to a second possible definition. A company is restructured if its performance indicators have sufficiently improved and it keeps gaining or at least maintaining its market share. Financial requirements must also be included. A restructured company can have no liquidity problems. This definition leaves open several questions. What should the indicators of the restructured company show? At what stage can a firm be said to have improved *sufficiently*? What is the order of priority among the indicators that attest competitiveness?

While the first of the definitions implies the introduction and the successful enforcement of a more or less standardized set of measures, the second examines their effect on the various factors of the company's performance. According to the first definition, if a predetermined set of modernization measures is adopted and introduced, the company is considered as restructured. According to the second definition, it is restructured if its performance indicators surpass a certain threshold. The value of the threshold is greatly influenced by branch-specific and overall macroeconomic factors (see Szalavetz, 1997b).

The discussion can be concluded by introducing another term: long-term (dynamic) competitiveness. With adequate caveats and reservations, the 'restructured' label is appropriate for any company if the various restructuring measures are adopted and introduced, and/or if the effect of these measures is reflected by an improvement of *some* of its performance indicators. If, however, the term restructured is tied to sustained competitiveness, the priority list of performance indicators is clear: profitability comes at the top.

The empirical research sought to examine the relationship between the various balance-sheet items and the restructuring performance in a pre-selected group of companies. We had three aims: (i) To complement the rough picture of Hungarian firms' restructuring suggested by the statistical analysis of the national database, by obtaining detailed insight into individual companies' business activities. (ii) To compare the conclusions drawn from the statistical analysis of the balance sheets with the experience of individual firms. (iii) To discover how the analysis of the balance-sheet data at a more or less aggregate level yield too general conclusions by analysing the multiplicity of effects that can distort the individual balance-sheet items.

The research method we applied included in-depth interviews with various representatives of the companies in the sample as well as an MC analysis of the individual balance-sheet data of the firms in the sample.[21] The interviews were intended to reveal the reasons and concrete strategic steps behind the changes in the individual items of the company balance sheets, and also the traps the conclusions drawn from the analysis of pure balance-sheet data bear.

This section summarizes the results of field interviews conducted with a sample of 16 companies. These explored the strategic steps that explain the results of each sample company, the driving forces behind its restructuring, and the inherent obstacles to it. A further aim was to establish whether ownership can be seen as the main explanatory factor behind performance differences. The next section defines the working hypothesis of the research. This was tested through a predetermined set of open-ended questions, put during field interviews.

5.9.2 The Hypothesis

Research on industrial transformation usually addresses the question whether performance can be tied to ownership, and especially to privatization.[22] Empirical surveys or statistical analyses use samples of various sizes to test the hypothesis that the performance of private companies exceeds that of state-owned ones.[23] This research took a different starting point: it is not corporate performance as such whose correlation with ownership needs to be examined, but *various aspects* of that performance. There is a strong correlation of some performance indicators (for example, operating profit relative to equity or to sales, or turnover relative to the number of employees) with private ownership, and still more with foreign private ownership. With other indicators (notably profits before taxation relative to equity or to sales) the correlation is rather weak and sometimes inverse. The various ownership categories characteristically show different sets of strongly correlating performance indicators during the various phases of industrial transformation (Szalavetz, 1996). As time goes by, one sees a clear convergence of these sets of strongly correlating indicators among the various ownership categories.

5.9.3 The Sample

We conducted interviews and case studies at 16 firms. Nine of the firms surveyed were in mechanical or electric *engineering*, and seven in *textiles* or clothing. Apart from branch affiliation, the following criteria affected selection:

Three groups were singled out according to different *ownership* categories for a simple majority of the shares, as decisive factors in the specification. So the sample includes companies in (i) majority private Hungarian ownership (four companies), (ii) majority foreign ownership (four), and (iii) majority state ownership (eight). We selected firms that had been *converted* from state-owned enterprises (SOEs) into company forms well before the change of the ownership. The sample contains companies that have inherited an important (favorable or negative) legacy from past activities, which has influenced their restructuring history and the outcome of the restructuring process. The average age of the firms in the sample in 1997 was 78 years (since foundation or foundation of a forerunner). We selected *medium-sized and large* companies. The average turnover of the companies in the sample was HUF 5104 million ($US 34 million) in 1996. The average payroll was 1307 full-time employees, (1776 for the engineering and 776 for the textile and clothing companies; N = 15, as one company undergoing liquidation was excluded from the calculation). Seven companies in the sample are successors of SOEs that received *privileged*, special treatment under the socialist system (Major, 1997b). We also tried to include in the sample companies in different *regions*: the capital (six companies), developed, industrialized and prosperous areas (six), and underdeveloped areas (four). Because of confidentiality rules, the companies in the sample are numbered instead of using their original name.

Besides general conclusions, the present study contains several specific case-study examples. The case-study examples included are not intended to support or refute the general conclusions, simply to illustrate specific types of corporate strategy and adjustment mechanism.

5.9.4 Rationalization

Assets

The majority of the transformed companies in our sample inherited a highly distorted asset structure that hindered the improvement of corporate efficiency and profitability. The distortion was twofold. There was an excessive share of invested assets relative to that of current assets, so that the current asset position was dangerously low. In the kind of credit squeeze that occurred in the early 1990s, this prevented companies from increasing their output, engaging in extensive R&D, and expanding marketing and distribution activities. The lack of current assets sometimes forced the companies to reduce the local value added and resort to outward processing contracts, where the foreign partner financed the necessary input of materials. Distortions also arose because the maintenance costs of the superfluous invested assets have been too high to allow for an efficient operation.

Rationalization implied selling off superfluous assets, closing loss-making plants, and writing off frozen, unfinished investment. The reduction of the stock of invested assets has in most cases led to an improvement in asset-based profitability indicators. Furthermore, the value of the indicator showing the share of the invested assets, covered by the company's equity, converged on the value shown for companies in market economies. However, a reduction in the stock of invested assets is not a virtue in itself. Asset sales led to an overstated improvement in efficiency and profitability indicators, by diminishing the denominators of these indicators. The other drawback of asset sales is that the breathing time earned with the extraordinary income from asset sales can be used to postpone other, cumbersome adjustment measures.

In terms of asset rationalization, a clear difference between state-owned firms and private ones can be seen. Asset sales and rationalization continued at state-owned firms during the whole period examined. The importance of rationalization through asset sales (the income generated from this source) is well demonstrated by the *unusually huge yearly amounts of extraordinary revenues and extraordinary expenditures at the surveyed companies.*

Although asset sales proved to be very important at the surveyed foreign-owned firms as well, in their case however we can observe a turning of the tide towards the mid-1990s. By that time defensive adjustment had given way in their case to offensive steps (new investments and expansion of activity). As time went by, the sale of invested financial assets became an increasingly conspicuous item within the reduction of the stock of invested assets. This reflects a clear trend of decentralization: demergers of various companies from the parent, or sale of the headquarters premises. Demergers accelerated the transformation of the market structure in the various branches.

The reduction in the stock of invested assets tended to accord with the following pattern. Firms in which there was foreign investment would usually sell superfluous tangible assets (sites, buildings, workshops, warehouses and superfluous machinery) within one to two years of acquiring the firm, so as to recover some of the purchase price quickly. Such sales were characteristically made between 1991 and 1993. Sales of superfluous assets, plants and so on, were also characteristic of state-owned firms that participated in the 1994 debt-consolidation program. Selling various provincial plants to offset part of the rescheduled debt was one of the stipulations of the consolidation agreement.

Other state-owned companies decided not to sell superfluous assets, but to transfer them to legally independent, wholly-owned subsidiaries. This caused the stock of invested financial assets to increase. Companies might later decide to sell off these subsidiaries, so actually, instead of just formally, outsourcing some of their production. It is very difficult to follow and identify these moves simply by looking at hard data on the balance sheet, which are hopelessly misleading in relation to ownership-specific patterns of asset management. Apart from the measures described already, other factors can influence the value of specific balance-sheet items. These include (i) write-offs (due to the closing down of under-performing plants), (ii) revaluations of company assets, which make the data for consecutive years incomparable, and (iii) heavy investment that increases the stock of tangible assets.

Rationalization also included improving the current asset structure. Some of the frozen inventories were written off or sold well below their price on the books. This brought considerable immediate accounting losses (extraordinary expenditures), but provided some immediate income, with which some liquidity problems could be eased. The medium- to long-term effect of this rationalization measure was that (i) less operating capital was tied up in inventories and (ii) it provided a good starting point for redesigning the inventory–management system (introducing appropriate software, stipulating new management criteria, and so on) to prevent future inflation of inventory stocks. The management of trade receivables as reflected by its share in the stock of current assets shows an ambiguous performance. At a national level of aggregation the stock of trade receivables rose rapidly in the first phase of industrial transformation (Szanyi, 1994b, 1997).

The time series of national average value of trade receivables over net sales (calculated from a sample of all firms with double-entry book-keeping) reflects the degree of market clearing. This indirectly records the existence of the key institutional and legislative requirements for a market economy, and the efficiency of enforcement. At company level, however, an increase in the stock of trade receivables may be a 'normal' accompaniment to corporate growth. The ability to cover longer payment deadlines reflects an improving liquidity position. A rising trend in trade receivables over net sales at national level suggests that overall financing opportunities have improved: it has become easier to draw commercial credit and finance the payment terms required. This is true to some extent, by comparison with the first phase of industrial transformation, which was close to a 'credit crunch'. The flipside of the coin is that there remains a huge difference between the average payment deadline for domestic transactions (15–30 days) and foreign transactions (60 or 90–120 days). This may damage Hungary's foreign-trade balance, by encouraging companies to procure inputs from abroad (with longer payment deadlines) and target the domestic market, where they can recuperate their money more quickly.

Ambiguity around the evaluation stems from the fact that although the share of trade receivables within current assets increased, the stock of doubtful and overdue debts decreased at the surveyed companies. And a diminishing value for the indicator of trade receivables over net sales is not a virtue in itself. A growing value can also reflect an improved capacity to finance longer payment terms favorable to the company's customers. The ability to afford long payment deadlines reflects an improving operating-capital position.

Redundant labor

The shedding of redundant labor in Hungary began well before the change of regime in 1989–90, due to a number of factors. Empirical research suggests that the Soviet market did not collapse overnight, as claimed. The volume of orders was already falling steadily in the late 1980s.[24] The shedding of labor was already occurring in parallel with the market reorientation in the second half of the 1980s. Also over by the mid-1980s was the period of extensive growth marked by an ever-growing payroll. Demergers became increasingly frequent in the second half of the decade, which reduced the companies' average payroll. Downsizing became more pronounced after 1989 and peaked in 1991–92 (Szanyi and Szemlér, 1997). This applied to the companies surveyed, whose payrolls began to fall in the second half of the 1980s.

We compared the figures by which the payroll was reduced during the examined period, with the payroll of the base year. The example of the companies show how hard it is to establish the base point for comparison. The chosen year was in most cases 1990 (or 1992 if no earlier data were available), not the peak year in the 1980s. The average reduction was 44 per cent. Some companies postponed the cumbersome measure of firing people as long as they could, while in other fields of the corporate activity the management adopted decisive and offensive restructuring steps. In other companies the payroll reductions were paralleled by a change in the organizational structure. Some of the activities were taken over by legally independent entities (out-sourced), distribution was assumed by self-employed agents, and so on.

We also examined whether (and when) the restructuring histories of the companies attest a reversal in the downsizing tendency. In the first phase of industrial transformation, for example, the extent to which labor is shed used to be considered as one of the success indicators of restructuring. In the second phase the indicator of success is already the increase in employment. Although half of the sample consisted of cases of successful restructuring,[25] only three of them showed a reversal of the downsizing tendency at a certain juncture. There are several reasons for this. Meanwhile the tide may have clearly turned in the profitability and productivity indicators, some of the companies reached a balanced level of payroll only in 1996. With others, expansion led to an increase not in the number employed by the company itself, but in a contracted (self-employed or externally employed) workforce.

The companies where a clear reversal of the downsizing could be seen were either acquired by foreign investors and/or took up subcontracting for foreign clients. Their contribution to the collaboration was of a high quality and reliability, so that the foreign contractor or investor kept increasing its orders. This allowed its Hungarian partner to hire new employees and expand its activities.

Organization

Rationalization included (i) flattening a highly hierarchical corporate organization, (ii) reducing the number of decision-making levels, (iii) abolishing parallel functions, (iv) creating transparent divisional structures, and (v) introducing new functions while phasing out or abolishing others. Organizational modernization was paralleled by the introduction of computerized control and production-management systems. The creation of new departments and new functions was due to the introduction of these computerized systems, and to qualification of the company for a standardized international quality certificate.

Companies acquired by foreign multinational investors managed to carry out organizational changes quite rapidly (compared with the state-owned firms). This was because the well-run systems (the organizational pattern) of their foreign owners were installed at the Hungarian subsidiaries during integration into the multinational's global organization. With the state-owned companies, the redesign and simplification of the corporate organization followed some time after the spin-offs and divestment. Surprisingly, it was not only downsizing that called for organizational renewal, but also corporate growth. Organizational changes at companies in parallel with considerable downsizing were not once-and-for-all changes. The modernization tended to take place by trial and error, which left some scope for feedback and modifications if the original circumstances changed (for example, the company started growing again).

5.9.5 Cost Policy

The first thing both a Western and an Eastern company looks at when entering on a restructuring program is the scope for cost-cutting. This is easier and has faster effects on the profit-and-loss account than any so-called offensive steps (improving the order-acquiring capability, launching new products, discovering new markets, and so on). Easy as it seems, cost-cutting still proved very difficult in the first phase of the restructuring process, for two reasons. (1) The whole period of restructuring was characterized by a significant increase in the various cost factors of the companies. (2) The majority of cost-cutting measures led to an initial worsening of the indicators. The positive effects of cost-cutting could be felt only after some delay.

Material costs increased because of price increases on the world market, successive devaluations of the Hungarian currency, and the introduction of an 8 per cent import surcharge in 1995. Another factor that pushed material costs up was the substitution of domestic for foreign suppliers. A third factor was the low capitalization of the companies, especially, but not exclusively, the state and privately-owned Hungarian ones. This prevented the companies from making strategic purchases of material inputs at times when they were trading at low prices on world commodity exchanges. Furthermore, companies were obliged to resort to the suppliers offering the easiest payment conditions. Indeed payment conditions became one of the main factors determining factors the selection of suppliers. Foreign companies could therefore benefit from their good current account positions and build the highly favorable payment conditions into the price of the inputs they supplied. In an era where the usual payment deadline for domestic transactions was 8–15 days, Hungarian companies did not care much if the price was higher, so long as the foreign supplier gave them a much longer period of 90–120 days' grace.

Energy costs increased through significant price increases.[26] Although still considerably lower than the Western average (one sixth or one seventh of it), labor costs increased because of accelerating inflation, considerably increased social charges, and new incentive systems. The costs of financial transactions increased to unprecedented heights due to the sudden, significant increases in interest rates and the accumulation of punitive interest on overdue debt. National statistics show a rapid rise in the share of 'other costs' and 'other expenses'. Development of the two cost items in the companies is more ambiguous.

The increase of the 'other costs' item is in principle not necessarily bad. Certainly other costs include management fees paid to third parties, which considerably increased at the companies surveyed, irrespective of ownership form. But a closer look at these services shows that they were related either to management consultancy services (audits and elaboration of strategic plans) or to acquiring international quality certificates. These items were necessary criteria of the restructuring process, rather than parts of simple-transfer pricing mechanisms. Another considerable sub-item of 'other costs' was the cost of non-material type services, especially advertising. This also attests to an offensive restructuring, rather than a simple consumption of profit. Nonetheless, indirect costs and 'other expenses' are the usual targets of cost-cutting programs. The restructuring experience of the companies in the survey showed that arbitrary cost-cutting does more harm than good.

Another common target of cost-cutting programs is labor costs. Firing employees believed to be redundant is, however, not necessarily the best solution. Sometimes better production organization is what can solve productivity problems. Analysts may therefore conclude that the company (or industry or country) still has reserves of labor for further downsizing. However this may only be partly true. In most cases the firm will already be over the necessary downsizing period, so that a further improvement in productivity depends on improving production management (Hammer and Champy, 1993).

Downsizing is a prime example of the time lag before the effects of cost-cutting appear in the profit-and-loss statement. Redundancies and the accompanying severance payments bring enormous labor cost increases in the short run. Managements have to draw up any downsizing plan carefully, calculating its long-term benefits and short-term costs, as well as the growth potential that may soon require the company to hire new labor again. The downsizing dichotomy of short-term costs versus long-term benefits points to another characteristic of cost-cutting programs: high cost/low cost solutions. Initially, costs can be cut relatively easily, rapidly and with little additional investment, but a second (qualitative) step of cost-cutting requires tremendous initial investment. It immediately involves costs, but the benefits only appear in the long run.

Some energy costs, for instance, can be cut by installing better insulation or introducing energy-saving methods of production, but to redesign its energy system, a company would have to invest in completely new heating and lighting systems. There is a similar dichotomy with material costs. The costs of material inputs can be cut without additional investment if companies make suppliers compete for orders, if they seek alternative quotations before each purchase, or if they replace some material inputs with cheaper alternatives. To modernize production technology so that less waste is produced or less material is required is a much more expensive solution. With banking costs the first step usually taken by privatized companies (acquired by well-capitalized, well-known foreign investors) is to make a better choice of banks and open negotiations on obtaining better credit conditions. The second, costlier step is to restructure the debt portfolio and reorganize production financing.

Our empirical investigations revealed that changes in the activity or in the main parameters of the companies frequently distorted not only the composition of costs but also various other items of the annual report. At a national level, many undercapitalized companies (especially in textiles, clothing and engineering, and to a lesser extent chemicals and metallurgy) lacked the operating capital to finance their production and exports. They had to resort to processing work, where material inputs and even production equipment were supplied by a foreign partner. This had multiple effects on the balance sheet. Material costs fell rapidly which was not due to any efficiency increase or elimination of waste, but only to the fact that the foreign contractor paid for and delivered the material to be processed. Indirect costs have also diminished spectacularly, but this again was not due to a rapid efficiency increase but rather to the fact that foreign partners took over the pre-production and post-production activity. The value of net sales also diminished (even if the volume of production increased) because the contractor paid only the processing fee, not the price of the whole product. Outward processing has accounted for about a quarter of Hungary's exports, in every year since 1992 (Sass, 1997). This has a very significant distortive effect.

However, offensive management strategies and improved financing capabilities gradually widened the scope for outward processors to increase the complexity of their production and undertake backward integration through independent procurement of inputs. So at sub-branch level, if the effects of price and tariff changes can be estimated, an increase in the material intensity of production could mean that the proportion of firms engaged in simple outward processing is falling again. Inventory management methods as well as distribution activity have also become different due to the change in the main parameters of the activity. In established market economies such changes in core activities are exceptional, but in transition economies they would significantly distort the time series of specific income statement items.

5.9.6 Financial Management

One aspect of the burdensome legacy from the past that firms remaining in state ownership during the transition find it hardest to shed, is corporate indebtedness. Most firms had built up a huge stock of debt, mainly from earlier investments financed with soft loans. With the liberalization of the economy, the majority of these projects turned out to be irrational, and those offered no return. Meanwhile interest rates increased considerably and financing conditions worsened, so that the cost of debt servicing became prohibitive. This coincided with a rapid contraction in the demand for many companies' products. Profitability indicators turned negative, and the debt burden built up very rapidly. Meanwhile companies that were undercapitalized had to face debt arrears from their partners, which added to their own liquidity problems. The obvious assumption is that financial consolidation would be most efficient at companies privatized by foreign investors. However, in the surveyed companies, the financial consolidation under foreign ownership did not involve huge additional investment. Let us enumerate some common methods of privatizing and consolidating ailing companies without any (significant) additional investment. One common method of privatizing ailing firms involved liquidating the hopelessly indebted firm. The investor, the new owner would take the assets and the workforce of the liquidated firm over and create a new legal entity. Since the new company is not the legal successor of the liquidated company, it escapes taking over its obligations (see, Szalavetz, 1998).

Another way of avoiding past obligations was to create a (joint venture). Indebted companies would be separated into two parts. This usually happened in the same way as described by the IMF prescriptions concerning the bailing-out method of ailing banks. In those cases the IMF recommendation prescribed the creation of a good bank and a bad one. As far as the indebted Hungarian companies were concerned, where the entry method for foreign investors was through a joint venture, the procedure was to divide the indebted company into (i) a good company without obligations and with profitable activities, a stock of profitable orders and the necessary inventories, and (ii) a bad company with all the existing stock of obligations, the superfluous assets, the frozen inventories, and so on. The good company was privatized (partly) to the foreign investor, with the 'bad' company as co-owner. The share held by the bad company was soon bought out by the foreign investor, either directly or indirectly, through successive capital increases performed unilaterally by the foreign owner, which the bad company could not afford to match.

Some ailing companies have been bought up or bought out from liquidation by a financial investor, the Hungarian Investment and Development Bank. A takeover by the bank does not simply mean the appearance of a well-capitalized new owner. The bank as a financial investor has a well-founded reputation in corporate restructuring. As the takeover increases the chance that the company will remain a customer for its suppliers and its banks, able to service its debts, pay taxes and social-security contributions and so on, creditors are likely to forgive some of the debt (or at least the punitive interest charged on it). With state-owned firms, the most frequent method of financial consolidation was to rationalize to improve efficiency and sell superfluous assets. These steps resulted in a spectacular turnaround in some of the companies. Others, however, are still on the verge of liquidation or at least facing day-to-day liquidity problems.

Some of the foreign-owned companies – the ones that were fully integrated into their multinational owners' production network – relied on internal financing. They were financed from credit pools available for the various subsidiaries of the multinational owner. Others could get access to commercial loans at terms more favorable than the average, because of the 'letters of comfort' by the mother companies. The subsidiaries that exported their products using the channel of intra-firm trade, were financed by their owner that granted them favorable payment conditions.

State-owned or Hungarian private firms could also achieve very favorable payment conditions. Still in their case this did not reflect a good bargaining position. Instead, it pointed to the exposed position of the company, for which payment deadlines were the only factor when selecting suppliers. In cases where the customer simply could not afford to pay for material inputs supplied (could not afford to pre-finance its production) favorable payment terms were built into the price of products supplied. However, the fact that companies could discover forfeiting possibilities and organize forfeiting contracts or the construction of consignment stores attests to an offensive adjustment. Hungarian-owned companies would rarely try to soften the budget constraints by increasing their indebtedness to their suppliers, which can cause a rapid deterioration in relations. If materials are withheld by an unpaid supplier or transportation company, it may cause unwanted idle production periods. Patience may be lost altogether, so that new suppliers have to be found. If liquidity constraints forced the companies to choose potential 'victims' of their liquidity problems, they preferred to become indebted to the state authorities.

The results of financial management can be measured with two indicators. The results of financial consolidation and improvement of the capital structure are best reflected by the profits on financial transactions as a proportion of operating profits. The efficiency of financial management is reflected by the current ratio (current assets over short-term liabilities). The balance sheet data of the surveyed companies showed that irrespective of ownership form, operating profits have been partly or completely 'consumed' by the excessive expenses on financial transactions.

The current ratio is influenced by the original capital structure of the companies. The interest conditions have rarely allowed the companies to overcome being heavily undercapitalized initially. The composition of the companies' liabilities reflect an interesting characteristic of companies in transition economies: *short-term liabilities dominate their liabilities*, accounting for over 80 per cent. This can be ascribed partly to the reluctance of banks to provide long-term commercial loans or to lack of sources of investment and development credit. Another reason is that even creditworthy companies would rather resort to short-term loans and roll them over because they are somewhat cheaper than long-term loans. Even the long-term liabilities do not usually consist of investment, development or other long-term loans, but in many cases obligations to founders or other long-term liabilities.

Foreign owners have not been interested in allocating sufficient working capital to their Hungarian subsidiaries through capital investment – a cash injection or an increase in issued capital stock – either. Capital investment has strict return (ROI) requirements. So multinational investors prefer financing the activity through commercial loans, even if it seems more expensive and the loss on the financial transactions 'consumes' the operating profits of the company.

5.9.7 Market Reorientation

Recent literature on Hungarian companies' spectacular market reorientation in 1992–93 does not omit to say that some of their export performance was due to forced exports with a very low or even negative return. Companies sought Western export markets at any price (Szanyi, 1994a). The companies in the sample also had to reorient much of their exports during the period examined. There was a considerable loss of traditional Eastern markets both in volume terms, and according to the geographical structure of sales. Empirical evidence suggests, however, that the reorientation of sales from Eastern to Western markets is not a necessary criterion for restructuring. There were several cases where the offensive restructuring strategy of the management focused on retaining customers in the former Soviet Union or regaining the company's former Eastern markets under the changed – and much hardened – circumstances of competition. The profitability of sales to the CIS market promised such a high return compared with Western markets that some managements did their utmost to preserve or regain these traditional markets.

Of course it cannot be claimed that the Soviet (CIS) market has always offered a much higher profit margin than Western or domestic sales. There were companies that reported good profitability on the Soviet market before the change of system. However, this was due to governmental subsidies tied to Soviet sales. Once subsidization was abandoned – in the second half of the 1980s – and ruble export even attracted fiscal discrimination, the profitability conditions changed considerably. However, in the mid-1990s the companies that were still exporting to any of the successor states of the former Soviet Union had reported higher profitability than Western sales, for various reasons. One was the fact that the profitability of Western sales tied to specific export channels (outward processing, intra-firm trade and subcontracting) kept declining over time, with the rapidly increasing costs of domestic producers. Another was the fact *that sales to the former Soviet Union had a higher average local value added than sales to Western markets*. Furthermore, the relatively high margins reflected higher risks associated with the CIS market. Otherwise, hardly any geographical patterns could be found among the explanatory factors for export profitability. This seemed to depend less on the geographical location of the foreign customer than on the product itself (value added, innovative character, quality and so on) and on the marketing channel. Profitability correlated strongly with the company's marketing input.

The period of forced exports with a minimal or negative return did not last long. As the budget constraints hardened, companies unable to carry out the restructuring measures required for a positive return had to exit from the market. By the mid-1990s, forced exports had ceased to be a characteristic adjustment measure. The export patterns of most of the surveyed companies reflected the results of a different type of adjustment: a step (or several steps) back along the value chain. To carry on exporting and survive under the altered competitive conditions, they had to incorporate themselves into the global development trends in their industries. This meant switching to the production of parts and components with a lower added value, rather than finished products. Hungarian players were not able to compete head on in a highly concentrated worldwide market dominated by a few multinational manufacturers of original equipment. This was not, or not only, because their products and marketing skills were of a lower quality and they had a minor presence in developed markets. It was also due to the general characteristics of industrial production and trade in the manufacturing industries in which they were trying to compete.

Some companies that failed to find a foreign investor that would incorporate them into the globalized patterns of production, were squeezed out of the domestic market, and also of their traditional export markets (developing countries), by multinational competitors. Since many of the companies had a traditional, outstanding stock of human capital – as successors of large, priority enterprises – some were able to survive, but the price was painful adjustment measures in the management of the product range. Even companies able to find foreign investors willing to incorporate them into their global production and distribution network did not always fare better than Hungarian-owned firms struggling to find their own market for their products.

The share of exports relative to company turnover, and the geographical distribution of sales, is one of the most widely used soft indicators to measure restructuring performance. This reflects a hidden assumption that the ability to find export markets attests to a relatively high performance, production quality and efficiency, marketing skills, and so on. Although in some cases we could discover a marked increase in export intensity, *it is misconceived to measure restructuring performance with changes in export intensity*. The relationship is much more complex, for the following reasons:

(i) In the second phase of industrial transformation, the share of Western exports compared with exports to Eastern Europe or to domestic sales not necessarily reflects the performance of a company. This indicator, or rather time series of changes in the geographical distribution of sales, could represent a company's adjustment capabilities and speed of export reorientation in the first phase of industrial transformation, when the Eastern markets collapsed. Once this phase was over, success in any market, domestic, Eastern or Western, may have required similar capabilities, given that once the domestic market was liberalized, companies faced similarly intensive competition on the domestic market as on Western markets. (ii) Sales to some Eastern markets proved in most cases extremely difficult, as capital was required to finance the exports. (iii) A spectacular increase in export intensity usually reflects a change in the product mix. A company can dramatically increase the export intensity of its production if it is acquired by a foreign investor that makes it specialize on a part or component of the end product it used to manufacture. Instead of exporting end products in the frame of arm's-length trade, it exports components in the frame of intra-firm trade, with a much lower local value added than its production used to be characterized by. (iv) Given that domestic sales are usually more profitable than average, since they tended to contain more local value added, in some cases it is the reduction of export intensity (of course if accompanied by an increase in sales), that reflects the results of a successful restructuring.

5.9.8 Investment Patterns

The wide disparity between the companies' investment patterns shows some correlation with their ownership form. The successful restructuring pattern of former SOEs shows clearly distinguishable sequences of divestment, rationalization and investment. With companies acquired by foreign investors, the defensive and offensive restructuring measures would usually go on almost parallel to each other. Our empirical investigations did not support the assumption that income from the necessary rationalization measure would enable the company to accumulate enough capital for new machinery and expanded and modernized activity. *Rationalization in itself is not sufficient to achieve the goal of becoming competitive and profitable.* Offensive steps (in the field of marketing and sales) seem indispensable. New markets are to be acquired. This, together with the necessary capital investment, makes external financing inevitable. The income stemming from the rationalization measures usually proved to be insufficient to finance the investment into marketing and into the modernization of capital equipment.

Even if downsizing is assumed to restore profitability, restructured state-owned firms prove unable to accumulate sufficient capital to allow for large-scale investment activity. One aspect of the 'restructured' label is that the growth path of a company turns upwards. However, the turnaround will not bring a steep enough increase in profitability to allow for spectacular growth. The typical growth path of a successfully restructured, but still unprivatized former SOE is a slow increase, so that capital accumulation is also very slow. Restructured state-owned firms cannot usually engage in comprehensive investment activity that would propel them into a steeper growth path. Their managements cannot and must not 'think big', especially not under the credit conditions prevailing. Accumulation of retained profits is the common financing method, because a rapid expansion based on commercial credit would threaten the firm's very existence. With a stock of commercial credit larger than necessary just for financing production, the companies will be unable to withstand consecutive bad years.

These characteristics – very slow expansion, slow accumulation, cautious investment – apply only to large, traditional, successfully restructured companies still in state ownership. The pattern can be partly explained by the fact that the typical export channel of these companies is arm's-length sales. (This applies to engineering and textiles, but not to clothing.) With subcontracting, even if the purchasing is done by the Hungarian partner, the foreign contractor may contribute to financing the pre-production and production activities, as well as financing the post-production activities totally. So the financing period for companies that manufacture finished products and sell them by arm's-length trade is much longer than is the case with subcontracting. Furthermore, the production runs are much shorter than with companies making parts and components. So the average profitability of the companies that manufacture finished products is higher, but their gross stock of profits is often lower than with subcontracting companies. The need to grant favorable payment conditions to customers, as one of the main explanatory factors behind competitiveness, lengthens even further the average financing cycle. The length of the financing cycle and the greater than average operating capital requirement account for the slow growth and slow accumulation characteristics of these companies. Usually, these companies can only move onto a steeper growth path after privatization, if they are acquired by a foreign professional investor or are listed on the stock exchange.

As far as investment in capital equipment is concerned, companies acquired by a foreign investor are usually allowed much greater play. The target and volume of investment usually correlate strongly with the export-channel characteristics and with the local added value. Intra-firm trade and a relatively low local added value correlate with high investment in capital equipment aimed at increasing the Hungarian subsidiary's production capacity. Arm's-length trade and independent market-seeking activity by the subsidiary correlate with relatively lower investment in production equipment. The investment is aimed not at a capacity increase, but at increasing productivity. The volume of investment, relative to the existing stock of production equipment is smaller on the average than it is in the capacity-increasing (efficiency seeking) cases.

If the products of the Hungarian subsidiary are sold through *intra-firm trade*, the investment pattern is decided by the multinational owners. Parallel to necessary rationalization measures ('investment' in severance payments and so on) and some basic maintenance work (to improve working conditions for manual and clerical workers alike), the foreign parent will invest in new capital equipment to create and increase capacity. Intra-firm trade thus correlates with investment into capacity increase. In these cases of efficiency-seeking investment, there are several waves of capacity increases, as the multinational owner relocates steadily more production to its Hungarian acquisition.

We could observe the clear correlation of investment patterns with the type of the products manufactured by the Hungarian subsidiary. With companies that manufacture finished products, or at least products with a higher than the average local added value, the purpose of the foreign owners' investment was to increase productivity, efficiency and quality rather than capacity. The foreign owner would introduce a control system, investing in computer-controlled inventory management, in information technology that accelerates control of the production process, in quality control, and so on.

Indicators obtained from surveys based on standard questionnaires would try to quantify the results of the investment activity by comparing the time series of the *average vintage of capital equipment.* Changes – the decline of the vintage – would reflect restructuring in terms of technological modernization. This indicator, however, is misleading from several points of views. (1) Before the transition, SOEs were manufacturing with obsolete, several decades old machinery. Inconsistent asset-development activity under the socialist system bred investment cycles, with investment peaks lasting two to four years and eight to twelve years of minimal investment.[27] The investment cycles and lack of consistent asset development led to technological bottlenecks that decreased efficiency, and to an average age of capital equipment that masked great differences of age among various production lines. The average equipment vintage may vary for each type of production line, irrespective of the value added or share of the product group in the firm's turnover or profits. Beside such 'horizontal' differences, there are many cases of several technological lines of different ages being integrated into a single vertical chain of production. In addition, we formulated the hypothesis that products with a higher local added value would usually be made on relatively older capital equipment. In other words, the correlation between local added value and 'average age' of capital equipment was inverse.

(2) Investment in technological upgrading may produce a spectacular increase in the efficiency and profitability of production, even if the average age of capital equipment is little changed. This happens if the machines remain in place, but some key functions are given new parts and components. On the other hand, technological development sometimes brings qualitative changes. New generations of equipment allow greater flexibility, incorporate features that hitherto required accessory devices, slash the costs and increase the speed of production, and so on. Some firms, however, would not benefit from a new generation of technology at all. They may not need the additional functions the new technology offers, or they may be unable to match the requirements on the market side. Using such machinery might require higher production runs, or a different role from the one the company currently plays in its business relations.

Similarly the time series of the annual stock of non-financial unfinished investments do not unambiguously reveal the volume of investment undertaken by the company in the year. Conclusions may be distorted, because in the first phase of industrial transformation several companies had huge stocks of unfinished, frozen investments. The sale of an unfinished plant or workshop contributed to the success of restructuring, helping to raise funds by which some of the company's debts could be repaid, or new investment in modernizing production could be financed. In many cases, several years elapsed before an unfinished investment could be sold. During those years, the stock of 'investment in progress' remained high. This did not reflect a heavy investment activity year-by-year, but the carrying forward of unfinished, frozen, useless investment that burdened the balance sheet.

As far as investment in financial assets is concerned, state-owned firms show a clear trend towards divestment and selling off their subsidiaries. However, this again is reflected ambiguously by the time series of the appropriate data in the balance sheets. The data are distorted by cases where the newly spun-off companies were appropriated by the State Privatization Agency (SPA, later the State Property and Asset Management Holding Ltd), and their assets simply deducted from those of the converted SOE. If the spun-off subsidiary was appropriated by SPA this appeared in the item of extraordinary expenditures. If the subsidiary was sold the result of the transaction appeared in the item of extraordinary revenues. In some cases the spun-off entities were swapped for some of the headquarters' outstanding debt, which again meant that they did not increase the stock of invested financial assets. Ad hoc increases in the time series of the stock of invested financial assets do not necessarily reflect expansion. They do not always mean that other companies were taken over by the company or new subsidiaries created. In the majority of the cases the increases referred to the emergence (and later sale) of spun-off subsidiaries.

5.9.9 Company Performance in the Light of Balance-Sheet Indicators

This section returns to the issue raised in the introduction: the various aspects of corporate performance. Notably, to what extent did the performance indicators improve as a result of the restructuring measures? Was the improvement sufficient to label the company a restructured one? Are there any differences between the various ownership categories? Rationalization led to spectacularly improved productivity under all forms of ownership.

Table 5.30 sets out to quantify the productivity improvement at each company. In some cases the improvement was really spectacular. However, the question remains whether the improvement was due (1) to a low basis of comparison (for example, the companies' average performance in 1992 was inferior to the Western average in the same industries), (2) high inflation that exaggerated the improvement in net sales, or to (3) a real performance improvement. Although we lack the adequate data for the productivity of each company's competitors, it is still possible to test the hypothesis that the spectacular improvement of productivity was mainly due to a low basis of comparison and high inflation. It can be done by examining the changes (in per cent) in the numerator and the denominator of the productivity indicator, using constant, 1992 prices[28] (see Table 5.30).

Table 5.30. Productivity at the companies surveyed: net sales/employee (HUF million) between 1992 and 1996

Company	1.	2.	3.	4.	5.
1992	1.8	0.5	0.9	2.2	1.5
1994	3.0	0.8	2.1	2.4	3.1
1996	4.4	1.2[a]	3.3	5.0	5.6
Ownership[b]	S	S	S	F	F

Company	6.	7.	8.	9.	10.
1992	1.2	2.7	1.1	0.6	2.7
1994	4.0	8.3	1.8	0.7	3.2
1996	11.5	2.0	3.4	1.0	4.6
Ownership[b]	F	HP	S	S	F

Company	11.	12.	13.	14.
1992	0.3	1.5	1.2	0.5
1994	0.9	1.6	1.6	0.6
1996	0.6	3.1	3.0	0.8
Ownership[b]	S	S	HP	HP

Notes

a 1995

b S = State-owned, F = Foreign, HP = Hungarian private

Table 5.31 provides evidence that in most cases changes in the denominator (resulting from defensive restructuring measures such as layoffs) exert a stronger effect on the indicator than changes in the numerator (as a result of offensive restructuring steps such as acquiring new markets and customers). As far as the numerator is concerned, the 1996 figures for net sales at constant, 1992 prices are astonishing. Column A shows that despite a sharp increase in net sales at current prices, calculations at constant prices show no expansion in most cases. Indeed there is a marked decline. The improvement in productivity becomes less spectacular as well (column C). The table also indicates the contributions by the two components of the productivity:

$$C = A * 1/B,$$

Where:

A = net $sales_{1996}$ /net $sales_{1992}$ * 100 (measured at constant (1992) prices),
B = number of $employees_{1996}$ /number of $employees_{1992}$ * 100,
C = (net $sales_{1996}$/number of $employees_{1996}$)/(net $sales_{1992}$/number of $employees_{1992}$) * 100 (measured at 1992 prices).

Table 5.31.The two components of productivity improvement

Company	Net sales increase (1996 constant price/ 1992) per cent A	Payroll reduction 1996/1992 per cent B	Productivity change 1996/1992, C=A*1/B*100 per cent C	Ownership
1.	72.6	66.0	110	State
2.	n.a.	61.0	na	State
3.	14.6	8.4	174	State
4.	106.7	105.0	102	Foreign
5.	205.7	123.9	166	Foreign
6.	135.6	31.0	438	Foreign
7.	26.7	80.8	33	Hungarian private
8.	89.8	63.8	141	State
9.	47.4	57.9	82	State
10.	86.6	113.3	76	Foreign
11.	29.1	36.1	80	State
12.	86.9	96.4	90	State
13.	91.1	84.0	108	Hungarian private
14.	65.4	89.1	73	Hungarian private

If the productivity increase was due to an offensive restructuring whose effect was to expand output and sales, the values in column A would be above 100 (which means net sales, measured at constant, 1992 prices have increased). Values below 100 attest to a reduction in net sales, which should be compensated for by the defensive adjustment of reducing the payroll. The reduction of the payroll would play a neutral role if the values in column 1/B*100 were 1. If they exceed 1, the effect of defensive adjustment predominates. There is a clear disparity among the various forms of ownership in this respect. Most of the SOEs experienced a defensive adjustment strategy. The foreign-owned firms mainly attained an improvement by finding additional sales opportunities. Similarly revealing results emerge from examining changes in the components of the indicator that quantifies the financial stability of operations: equity over invested assets (Tables 5.32 and 5.33). Table 5.32 quantifies the changes in the financial stability of the companies (equity over invested assets). Data in the table show that half the companies surveyed experienced some improvement or stagnation in the indicator for equity over invested assets. The figures for the rest show that their financial stability worsened. The indicator shows that ownership again has a strong explanatory power.

$$Z = X * 1/Y,$$

Where:

$X = (\text{equity}_{1996}/\text{equity}_{1992}) * 100,$

$Y = (\text{invested assets}_{1996}/\text{invested assets}_{1992}) * 100$

$Z = (\text{equity}_{1996}/\text{invested assets}_{1996})/(\text{equity}_{1992}/\text{invested assets}_{1992}) * 100$

With SOEs it was typically a decline in the stock of invested assets that improved the indicator (values of 1/Y * 100 well above 1). The tables provide some evidence for the claim that ownership shows a weaker correlation with the performance indicators themselves than with the two components of the indicators. The correlation between ownership and performance was even looser in the case of the various profitability indicators (operating profit or gross profit over net sales, over total assets, and over equity). These exercises show it is time to modify the preliminary working hypothesis. The soft information gathered during the field investigations supports the hypothesis that the improvement in the individual performance indicators[29] has a different pattern and extent in each ownership category. There is empirical evidence that the effects of offensive adjustment are better reflected by the performance indicators of companies in foreign than in domestic ownership. The foreign companies are the ones that spectacularly improve sales, and they can boast of good or outstanding operating profits. (Gross profits depend rather on the arbitrary decision of the owner, who decides on fiscal grounds where the profits should appear.)

Table 5.32. Equity over invested assets (per cent)

Company	1992	1994	1995	1996	1996/1992 in per cent Z	Ownership[b]
1.	79.8	102.5	127.0	131.4	164.6	S
2.	52.2	−138.3	−345.5	n.a.	−662.1[a]	S
3.	144.0	74.1	46.6	100.2	69.6	S
4.	136.0	73.6	58.9	41.3	30.4	F
5.	25.2	22.0	113.4	124.7	494.9	F
6.	198.0	113.5	32.5	n.a.	16.4[a]	F
7.	259.8	81.8	−759.8	−379.0	−145.9	HP
8.	57.2	60.8	57.3	61.1	106.8	S
9.	120.8	129.4	126.4	134.8	111.6	S
10.	135.9	150.2	144.8	114.0	83.9	F
11.	n.a.	n.a.	n.a.	95.0	n.a.	S
12.	57.1	45.8	47.1	3.1	5.4	S
13.	121.5	123.8	122.9	116.2	95.6	HP
14.	145.7	142.4	141.5	140.0	96.1	HP

Notes
[a] 1995/1992
[b] S = State-owned, F = Foreign, HP = Hungarian private

However, even in the second half of the 1990s there are too many company-specific, path-dependent factors that influence or distort the data. The initial distortive changes contributed to a gradual improvement in the quality of balance-sheet data of transformed SOEs. As the main events distorting the balance sheet cease, a rising proportion of the national sample will consist of firms with ‘normal’ indicators, so that conclusions drawn from analysing the national sample become increasingly reliable. The flipside of the coin is that once these indicators reflect what they normally would in established market economies, the first chaotic phase of industrial transformation can be said to be over.

Table 5.33. The two components of improvement in the financial stability of operations

Company	Equity over invested assets 1996/1992 in per cent, Z=X*1/Y	Equity growth 1996/1992 in per cent	Reduction in invested assets 1996/1992 in per cent	Ownership*
	Z	X	Y	
1.	164.6	125.9	76.5	S
2.	–662.1	–370.2	55.9	S
3.	69.6	54.2	77.9	S
4.	30.4	81.2	267.4	F
5.	494.9	531.8	107.5	F
6.	16.4	17.0	99.1	F
7.	–145.9	–220.7	151.2	HP
8.	106.8	86.9	81.3	S
9.	111.6	89.2	79.9	S
10.	83.9	148.5	177.0	F
11.	n.a.	n.a.	n.a.	S
12.	5.4	4.8	88.8	S
13.	95.6	101.9	106.6	HP
14.	96.1	102.2	106.4	HP

Note: * S = State-owned, F = Foreign, HP = Hungarian private

The convergence of the performance indicators characteristic of companies in specific forms of ownership was also supported by the results of the field investigations. Convergence can be observed less in the value of the indicators than in their tendency to improve, for instance in the steepness of the curve. If the reasons for this convergence are examined more closely, it turns out that ownership correlates with the way the indicators improved during the restructuring process. The initial hypothesis was that ownership correlates with some individual performance indicators that together, in a specific order of priority, constitute *corporate performance*. Statistical analysis of the hard indicators leads to a conclusion that complements the preliminary hypothesis. In the first and the second phases of industrial transformation, ownership showed a stronger correlation with the individual components of the performance indicators than with the various individual performance indicators. The ownership factor correlated with whether this convergence was achieved by offensive adjustment measures, or by defensive measures of rationalization.

5.10 PRIVATIZATION, CORPORATE GOVERNANCE AND COMPANY RESTRUCTURING IN HUNGARY: CONCLUSIONS

Privatization is loaded with political considerations and it is subject to the active participation of the state agencies, as was discussed in section 5.2. CEE countries have gone a long way in dismantling the centralized political and administrative regulation of the economies. State ownership does not dominate these economies anymore. But it would be premature to say that the CEE economies are dominantly regulated by markets. Governments and central agencies still have a strong influence upon the companies' operation in several CEE countries. Political interference in economic matters cannot be regarded as non-existent. It is partly so because these countries witnessed chaos and a vacuum of regulatory forces after the disintegration of the socialist economic regime. The old routines gradually died but markets have not emerged fast to replace the socialist rule. In addition, political groups and governing political parties also wanted to use their leverage on the economy for their own political and/or economic benefit.

In this chapter we wanted to test the assumption that turning the state-owned property into private hands would considerably improve efficiency on the macro level and on the level of the companies, as well. In addition, we addressed the issue of whether the actual methods of privatization have a decisive influence on the companies' performance after the change of ownership occurs. Our analysis showed that privatization has proved to be a mixed blessing in Hungary (and in the CEE countries) so far. What were the reasons for the mixed results? Was it the overall framework or the concrete methods of privatization that had a controversial impact on the companies' economic performance? Do the achievements and the shortcomings of the private sector have to do with the new governance structures of the private companies? Or is it just a matter of a time lag until the change of ownership reaps tangible results on the level of companies and for the economy as a whole? In the next sections I shall address these issues in detail.

5.10.1 Possible Links Between Privatization and Economic Performance of the Companies

Experience showed that state agencies have not been very efficient in selling the state-owned property. Moreover, government bureaucracies could not be immune from political interference which can further distort the privatization transactions on the seller's side, but also on the side. Evidence also shows that company performance after privatization is not neutral to the way the company had been privatized. The more government bureaucracies were involved in the transaction the larger the chance that the company will not survive privatization and go bankrupt, or it will need a longer time to stabilize itself financially and on the market. Government involvement usually gives the wrong incentives to the private investor, too. If the privatization agency strives for a high sales price, the investor will try to recover her investment as soon as she can by squeezing the profits of the company. If the seller wants to impose several commitments on the buyer, such as, for example, preserving jobs, making new investments, improving the surrounding infrastructure, the buyer will use much of his energy to find the escape routes from his commitments. We can conclude that more rather than less government intervention carries privatization further away from regular and economically rational market transactions which, in turn, lowers the future efficiency of the privatized company.

As regards the speed of privatization, there has been a lot of misunderstanding about this issue. It seems obvious that the faster the privatization transaction of a company starts the shorter the period of uncertainty for the company will be. And waiting for privatization enhances the chance of rent seeking and creates the problem of moral hazard within the company management. It can easily result in forced asset stripping since the company must stay alive but it is demobilized and demoralized.

A usual argument about the speed of privatization is that the free distribution of the state-owned property on a mass scale is the solution for it can reduce the time requirement of privatization the most. It is true that free distribution avoids much of the problems of asset evaluation, governance, the evaluation of the financial, environmental and other aspects of the companies' operation during the initial period, but those issues will emerge later and they may turn out to be unmanageable for the institutional owners of large groups of companies. As evidence shows, the privatization methods that are closer to conventional sales are 'front loaded' as regards the time requirement and the necessary amount of bureaucratic and managerial energy, while the free distribution techniques are 'rare loaded'. We can conclude that it is crucial to turn the state-owned property into private hands as fast as possible in order to cut the ties of the new economic system to the previous regime of political regulation and, to create a firm basis for private property rights. But 'speed' without 'sense' can result in more chaos and disintegration of the economy than what is manageable.

Apart from compensation as a form of restitution for the confiscated property, Hungary opted for a case-by-case sale of the state-owned property and it aimed at attracting foreign investors as new private owners of the privatized companies. Foreign owners dominate the large company sector and they are in the majority in several branches, such as, for example, in the food industry, vehicle industry, telecommunications, banking and financial services. Even in industries where foreign owners only have a minority share, they usually have controlling positions in the companies' management. Selling the state-owned property to foreign investors resulted in a substantial amount of inflow of cash and investment. Consequently, the Hungarian government was able to reduce the country's foreign debt to a large extent. Moreover, foreign direct investment made the deficit of the balance of payment manageable. In addition, it contributed to the growth of total investment in Hungary and to the upgrading of industry and services. But has foreign capital been efficient in the sense that it increased the profitability of the companies and it restored the companies' financial stability? As we saw before there is not a clear answer to this question.

The economic performance of the foreign companies as a group has usually been better than the performance of the domestic private companies, and the foreign companies have been more successful than the state-owned companies in many respect. But not in every respect. As was discussed in the previous sections, the profitability of the foreign companies was the poorest among the CDEs even in 1995. Their ranking only changed in 1996. When we analysed the SPACs, we got different results though. The foreign companies had the highest profitability among the SPACs by 1994 and also in 1995 and in 1996. The profit margins of the foreign companies were also lagging behind the domestic private and the state-owned companies in some years. These results are fairly disappointing, although one can argue that foreign investors had to make sizable investments in their acquired new ventures. Moreover, they had to restructure the companies, to build up new market networks and reshape the staff and management. But these changes had to be made in most domestic private companies, too. It is true that foreign investors have usually been active in larger businesses where investments and restructuring may take a longer time and need larger expenditures. But it seems also true that many of the foreign companies still think short-term and they do not expand their operations, which could explain the temporary losses.

Domestic private companies performed even worse in average than foreign companies. We can list three factors that explain this phenomenon. Domestic private companies are usually small in size and they lack the network of extensive connections to foreign markets. These companies usually produce for domestic markets where demand has been subject to the overall recession. In addition, Hungarian companies must compete with foreign companies for a contracting aggregate demand on the domestic market. And they are outcompeted in most cases. Another alternative would have been if domestic private companies could have joined the large production and marketing networks of multinationals and other foreign companies that have been operating in the Hungarian economy. But research showed that production networks created by foreign investors have been the exception rather than the rule in Hungary and in other CEE countries (Comisso, 1997; Schwartz, 1997). Foreign companies have rarely used Hungarian suppliers or sub-contractors. They preferred to ship even raw materials and spare parts from abroad. The transfer of technology and know-how from foreign companies to Hungarian partners was rare, too. Consequently, foreign investors built up, then lived on, a fairly isolated island within the Hungarian economy.

Another factor that contributed to the poor performance of many domestic companies was that political interference and adverse selection was the strongest when state-owned assets were privatized to domestic investors. The political elite frequently used privatization to 'buy' loyal supporters. Or the elite converted the state-owned property into private companies for their own benefit. And evidence showed that political figures or their clients are not necessarily the most skillful owners or managers.

Finally, Hungarian private investors did not usually have sufficient means even to buy a part of the state-owned assets, let alone to invest into the acquired company. Consequently, they had to draw credits and pay high interest rates in order to be able to pay for the company. Servicing the debt bled most Hungarian investors dry. Since profitability of the companies was low while interest rates were high, even the debt service was more than an investor could bear. Nothing was left for upgrading the company's technology and product structure. This has become a vicious circle for many companies. Ultimately, the company went bankrupt.

We need also to explain how many of the state-owned enterprises could remain standing during the period of an overall recession? SOEs were usually large in size, they employed thousands of people. Consequently, they have received a lot of attention from the government. Sometimes government attention meant subsidies, but it also meant information, marketing support and networking for the benefit of the SOEs. In addition, SOEs could rely, at least to some extent, on their former trading links inside Hungary and with other formerly CMEA countries. Hence, the connections to their former markets have not disintegrated to the extent they did for the reorganized or newly-created private companies.

The Hungarian privatization law requires that the sale of an SOE should occur by an open tender. A transparent tendering and contracting procedure without manipulation is very important in order to create the credibility of institutions and markets and to enforce private property rights. It can also contribute to the companies' improved performance in the long run. But it does not have a direct positive impact on the companies' profitability in the short run. An in-depth analysis of the 50 largest Hungarian companies revealed that less bureaucratic intervention from the government in the companies' privatization went along with more successful operation after the ownership changes (Major, 1997b).

There is no simple conclusion from the balance sheets analysis about the links between privatization and company performance in Hungary. Private companies, and first of all foreign companies, are becoming the dominant players in the Hungarian economy. Foreign companies dominate foreign trade and investment and they are producing with the highest labor productivity. The international competitiveness of the foreign companies is also the strongest as regards relative labor costs. But private companies have not become decisively more profitable than state-owned enterprises so far.

5.10.2 Corporate Governance: How Does It Work in Hungary?

State ownership, or rather 'collective' ownership in a socialist economy was frequently described as a system of 'collective irresponsibility'. Different level organizations of the communist party and branch ministries acted as owners of the state-owned enterprises, but these bodies also delegated a part of the ownership rights to the managers of the companies. Anyone who was in a decision-making position could abuse property rights. A general expectation from the economic transformation was that privatization will put an end to the former practices. Collective irresponsibility will be replaced by the individual responsibility of private owners. Moreover, property rights and management rights will be clearly defined and separated.

Numerous and radical changes have occurred in the companies' corporate governance on the legal level since transformation began.[30] State-owned enterprises were converted into corporations and many of them were privatized. Even if the state remained the owner of a company, it could not arbitrarily impose decisions on a company anymore. It also had to honor and obey the law. Consequently it seems that there is no substantial difference between the CEE countries and the advanced market economies as regards corporate governance. But how can we explain the relatively poor performance of the private companies in CEE if we assume that the owners of the companies act like their Western counterparts? The balance-sheet data of the companies do not provide us with sufficient information to conduct an in-depth analysis of the companies with different corporate governance structures. Such an analysis was done on the basis of the case studies. Using the results of the current analysis and additional information on the companies' operation suggest that private ownership, even foreign ownership, is not a sufficient condition for an efficient system of corporate governance in a company.

The results of the balance-sheet analysis indicate that many of the private owners have short-term interests in their newly acquired company. This fact in itself creates serious conflicts between owners and managers of the companies. Interestingly enough, managers of formerly state-owned companies are usually much more interested in the long-term viability of the companies than the owners. This is a peculiar and unexpected phenomenon since it is assumed that owners represent the long-term and 'strategic' thinking in a company, while managers are more short-sighted and they focus on details. This unexpected phenomenon can be the consequence of the uncertainties and risks that are directly connected to the transition period in CEE. Namely, private owners frequently take a 'wait and see' position and, moreover, they strive for a quick return on their initial investment, while company managers are interested in maintaining employment and they identify with their company.[31] This is another factor that can explain why privatization was the most successful when it was carried out by, or with the active participation of, the management of the relevant company. And in companies where the new private owners regard managers as their partners, the economic performance of the companies are usually much better than in companies where the new owners act as unchallengeable 'warlords'. These findings contradict the common wisdom about 'spontaneous privatization', at least in Hungary.

It is common knowledge that institutional or financial investors pursue different goals and they have other perspectives than 'core investors' who have a solid background in the type of business their company is active in. While financial investors think in the short term and they want to have immediate and regular returns on their investment, core investors usually have a long-term perspective and they think in terms of market expansion, strategic alliances among companies and long-term technological development. Such a distinction is not obvious in the CEE countries yet. It is not so much the time horizon that makes a difference between financial and core investors, but the effectiveness of management control. Institutional investors are fairly weak in enforcing corporate governance strategies at companies, while core investors are much more successful in controlling the company's operation. A well-known example of the weakness and inefficiency of the institutional investors is the case of the Czech privatization funds.[32] But there is one exception to this rule. Notably, the banks that hold the debt of several companies can fairly effectively control a company's activities.

We can conclude that formally the legal framework of an effective corporate governance and a large variety of governance structures already exist in several CEE countries. But the actual functioning of those governance structures is not very efficient yet. The regulatory and disciplining function of well-established markets is also necessary for the CEE countries to have an efficient governance system.

5.10.3 Company Restructuring after Privatization

When economic transformation started in CEE most politicians and analysts believed that privatization of the state-owned property would not only change the ownership title of companies but it would take care of the restructuring of those companies, too. After eight years of the transition we already know that privatization is just the first step, and it is not even the most difficult part, of the necessary changes within the formerly state-owned companies. Restructuring is a very complex and frequently cumbersome process that takes a fairly long time. But what does company restructuring exactly mean in CEE?

According to several analysts, restructuring basically means that the new private owners of the companies erase 'hidden unemployment', and by doing so they increase the companies' productivity and they decrease relative wage costs. Consequently, the companies' competitiveness will improve. An even narrower approach measured company restructuring by the number of managers who had been replaced or sacked (see Janackova and Janacek, 1992). I do not think that restructuring can be sensibly interpreted and carried out in such a narrow sense. Companies are like living organisms whose different parts and functions are interrelated. Consequently, company restructuring means that the *incentive system*, the *management*, the *accounting* and *book-keeping system*, the *technology* and the *product structure*, the *employment structure* and, in addition, the links between the company and the outside world, are changed in a holistic, comprehensive way.

The results of the balance sheet analysis indicate that companies with different ownership structures adopted different restructuring patterns during the transition. Foreign private companies immediately focused on increasing the efficiency of employment and labor utilization. In addition, they have been active in investing into the companies and expanding the share of exports within the companies' total sales. On the other hand, foreign private companies have not shown a superior performance as regards profitability. It is interesting to note that foreign companies with a higher than 5 per cent stake of the Hungarian state within the companies' assets (the Formost and the Formix companies) have been more profitable than fully private foreign companies. Usually those companies belonged to the two groups which had been more successful even before the transition.

Low profitability of the foreign private companies could have different causes. Those companies that became loss-makers because of extensive restructuring efforts in the first period, gradually reversed this trend afterwards. But we could also find a fairly large group of foreign private companies that have remained chronic loss-makers for several years. This group is not homogenous either. Several companies can be found that are parts of huge multinational conglomerates and their net revenues may be reallocated to other parts of the parent company abroad. In this case, the Hungarian subsidiary and the Hungarian economy at large lose, but it can still be a rational strategy from the multinational company's point of view. Another case is when the foreign investment turns out to be miscalculated and the company will be abandoned by its owners. Finally, several companies that report negative profits are not real loss-makers, but they hide their profits behind costs.

Domestic private companies have a more limited access to markets and know-how and modern technology than foreign firms do. Many of these companies have been struggling for survival or they are becoming bankrupt. Domestic private companies are very sensitive to branch affiliation, for they usually produce for the domestic market. And the Hungarian market is not only small but it is also very uneven as regards demand and import competition. In addition, domestic private companies are much more exposed to the general climate of the Hungarian economy than foreign companies. Uncertainty and frequent changes in the government regulations further shorten the time horizon of the domestic companies. A usual escape route for domestic private companies is to convert their assets into financial investments. Productive investment is much more rare in domestic private companies than in the case of foreign companies. It is small wonder, since the profitability of the domestic companies is usually much lower than the interest rates on bank loans are. Moreover, domestic private companies frequently lack the information on, and the necessary channels to, foreign markets.

The prospects for state-owned enterprises are not very bright although they have shown an amazing vitality since the transition began. What explains the vitality of many state-owned enterprises? Strange as it may sound, it can be because of the expansion of the private sector. Hungary has been a 'mixed economy' in the sense that the state sector softened the hard constraints of the private companies. But the presence and activity of the private sector imposed many of the rules of a market economy on the SOEs. These companies compete on the same markets as private companies. In addition, the SOEs' market network has not deteriorated as rapidly as had been expected. But they are not actively expanding their production capacities and market share. They usually convert their assets into financial investments and live from the earnings on those investments. This can allow survival for them in the short run, but it cannot be a basis for a viable strategy for the future.

Ultimately, does ownership matter in relation to company performance? As we showed before, there are aspects of the companies' economic performance where the type of ownership does make a difference. But in other parts of the companies' economic activities it does not. What we could observe in the econometric analysis was that it is not private or state ownership that has the largest impact on the companies' economic performance, but the fact of whether the company is dominated by foreign or by domestic owners. In addition, the company's branch affiliation and its market position have a more substantial impact on the company's profitability and other indicators than its ownership structure. It is frequently argued that the success of the economic transformation of the CEE economies mostly depends on the *stabilization* of state finances, on the *liberalization* of domestic markets and foreign trade and on the *privatization* of the state-owned property. But without a massive profitability and expansion of the companies and without an effective budget constraint on the companies' financial operation there is no sustainable economic growth. Consequently, there cannot be long-term financial stability of the economy. The broad issues of the economic transformation may be solved in several CEE countries by now, but the hard part comes after. It is the successful restructuring of the companies and their adjustment to the requirements of the domestic and international markets. And as we could observe, this part of the transformation is far from being over in the CEE countries.

NOTES

1. The term 'hard budget constraint' was introduced by János Kornai (1980).
2. Hungary used to have three different state agencies to deal with the privatization and management of state-owned property. The first one, the *State Property Agency* was created in 1990, just before the political changes. The second agency, the *State Assets Management Holding Ltd* was founded in 1992. There existed a third agency, the *Asset Management Holding of the Treasury*, whose functions were gradually distributed among the local governments and the Ministry of Finance. The municipal governments themselves created their own local asset management companies, too.
3. See, for example, Frydman, Rapaczinski and Earle (1993), Kornai (1990), Laki (1993), Major (1993, 1994a), Mihályi (1998), Stark (1996), Voszka (1995), Borish, Long and Noel (1995).
4. The above figures do not include the companies that belonged to the municipalities and they also exclude the asset value of the arable land and the value of land and real estates that were transferred to the local governments by successive legal acts in 1990.
5. The sources of the above data are the *Privatization Monitor,* ÁPV Rt., Budapest, January 1996 and Mihályi (1998).
6. One approach is presented by Janackova and Janacek (1992) where the authors 'measure' restructuring with the frequency of replacement of the company managers. Another analyis, based on company case studies, was conducted by Szanyi (1994b).
7. The six regions were as follows: (i) Center: Budapest and Pest county, (ii) West and Mid-West: Fejér, Győr-Sopron-Moson, Komárom-Esztergom, Vas and Veszprém counties, (iii) South West: Baranya, Somogy, Tolna and Zala counties, (iv) North East: Hajdú-Bihar, Szabolcs-Szatmár and Bereg, and Jász-Nagykun and Szolnok counties, (v) Bács-Kiskun, Békés and Csongrád counties, (vi) North: Borsod-Abaúj-Zemplén, Heves and Nógrád counties.
8. The 22 branches that we worked with were the following ones:
   (1) Agriculture, (2) Food Industry, (3) Mining, (4) Light Industry, (5) Chemical Industry, (6) Construction Materials Industry, (7) Metallurgy, (8) Machinery Industry, (9)

Telecommunications Equipment, Precision Engineering and Computer Industry, (10) Vehicle Industry, (11) Energy Production, (12) Construction Industry, (13) Domestic Wholesale and Retail Trade, (14) Foreign Trade, (15) Personal Services, (16) Transportation, (17) Postal Services and Telecommunications, (18) Financial Services, (19) Business Assistance Services, (20) Public Administration and Community Services, (21) Education, Research and Cultural Services, (22) Healthcare and Social Services.

9. The groups were as follows:
(1) Traditional state-owned enterprise, (2) Municipal and self-governing company, (3) Other non-corporatized economic organizations, (4) Economic associations, (5) Limited liability companies (LLC), (6) Joint-stock companies (JSC), (7) Cooperatives (agricultural, industrial and services), (8) Economic organizations without legal entity, (9) Individual entrepreneurs, (10) Budgetary organizations.

10. The different guesstimates on the size of the hidden sector vary greatly and those are not justified by solid information and analysis. According to these estimates the hidden economy can be as large as 20 to 40 per cent of the registered economy.

11. The term 'transformation recession' was first used by János Kornai (1993).

12. Aslund (1996) arrived at the same conclusion in the case of Russia.

13. Such an analysis can be found in Major (1995a).

14. A detailed description of the technical problems with the financial indicators, moreover, an analysis of the companies' financial performance in Hungary during transition is given in Major (1997a). In that study I also discuss the financial indicators by industries and by regions extensively.

15. The computations were made by Norbert Maier (1997).

16. The ownership groups are distinguished as follows: (1) property of the state, (2) property of private owners, (3) property of employees, (4) property of foreign investors, and (5) cooperative property.

17. OWN has four levels according to the share of state ownership:

Label	priv	most	mix	stat
State ownership (%)	<5	5–25	25–50	>50

SIZE has nine levels according to the number of staff employees (see Sereghyova 1996): 1–25, 26–50, 51–100, 101–200, 201–500, 501–1000, 1001–2000, 2000–5000, more than 5000. However, in the tables SIZE has five levels, in order to synthesize and clarify the presentation. The levels are: 1–25, 26–100, 101–1000, 1001–5000, more than 5000. REGIO has six levels but here only two levels will be considered: Budapest and the Others. Hereinafter the variables will be mentioned by their labels.

18. The indicators relative to the productivity show a strong asymmetric distribution, with several observations near to zero and a long tail on the right side, representing the extreme values. To obtain a distribution consistent to the assumptions of the analysis of variance, we used for all three indicators the natural logarithm which produces like-normal distribution in the computations.

19. Analysing the groups of companies which have an INVESTRATE other than 0 by means of a regression analysis, one can notice that in these groups there are not significant differences in profitability and productivity due to the level of INVESTRATE. So it is allowed to distinguish only the differences between groups that have any possible level of unfinished investments as long as they are different from 0 and the rest.

20. The most comprehensive explanation for the economic decline is given by Kornai (1993).

21. MC analysis, commonly applied by management consultancies, entails analysing in detail each row of the balance sheet (separately and in the context of other rows), and assessing the reasons behind the values and the changes compared with the base year.

22. See, for example, Aghion, Blanchard and Burgess (1994), Amsden, Kochanowicz and Taylor (1994), Brada (1996), Carlin, Van Reenen and Wolfe (1995), Estrin, Gelb and Singh (1995), Pinto (1995a, 1995b), and Pinto, Belka and Krajewski (1993).
23. Kuznetsov and Kuznetsova (1996) provides a clear categorization and an accompanying list of references to the various theories defending the critical importance of privatization. The categories they set up are those of the political theory, the competence theory and the microeconomic theory (the efficiency argument) (see p. 1173). Dallago in the first chapter gives a comprehensive list of references to the existing relevant quantitative analyses, and quotes authors who review a sample of such studies and draw ambiguous conclusions about the superiority of private over public enterprises.
24. Empirical research has provided evidence against the widespread assumption that Hungarian firms turned their back to the Russian market. Instead, they were crowded out by Western competitors (Szalavetz and Réthi, 1998).
25. Defined as sustained viability achieved without regular government support. See Major (1996b).
26. Surprisingly the prices calculated in US dollars show a declining trend. However, the $US data conceal the rapid devaluation of the Hungarian currency. Average electricity prices for the industry: ($US/kWh) were 0.060 in 1990, 0.068 in 1991, 0.066 in 1992, 0.049 in 1994, and 0.049 in 1996. According to the author's calculations (using company data) the price of electricity for industrial usage increased by 40 per cent between 1994 and 1996. Of course it is not only electricity that matters. The price of steam increased by 47 per cent, that of industrial water by 76 per cent, and that of gas by 23 per cent.
27. The phenomenon, first described by Bauer (1981) and Soós (1986), is treated at length in Mihályi (1992).
28. We deflated the 1996 turnover data by the cumulative value of the GDP deflator between 1992 and 1996, which was 222 per cent according to data from the Central Statistical Office.
29. Productivity indicators, indicators on financial management, indicators on cost-cutting, and profitability indicators.
30. Different governance structures in CEE are extensively discussed by Frydman and Rapaczynski (1994).
31. Kornai (1980) argued that an important factor of the SOEs' overinvestment was in the socialist economy that enterprise managers identified with their job. While this was a dubious assumption in an economy of 'collective irresponsibility', it has become a relevant one under a dominant private property rights regime.
32. The experience of the Czech privatization funds is extensively discussed by Mertlik (1996).

REFERENCES

Adam, Jan (1989), *Economic Reforms in the Soviet Union and Eastern Europe since the 1960s*, London: Macmillan.

Aghion, Philippe, Blanchard, Olivier and Burgess, Richard (1994), 'The Behavior of State Firms in Eastern European Pre-Privatization', *European Economic Review*, **38** (6), 1327–49.

Amsden, A., Kochanowicz, J. and Taylor, L. (1994), *The Market Meets Its Match. Restructuring the Economics of Eastern Europe*, Cambridge, MA and London: Harvard University Press.

Árvay, J. and Vértes, A. (1995), *The Share of the Private Sector and the Hidden Economy in Hungary,* Budapest: GKI Economic Research Co.

Aslund, Anders (1994), 'Lessons of the First Four Years of Systemic Change in Eastern Europe', *Journal of Comparative Economics,* **19** (1), 22–38.

Aslund, Anders (1996), 'The Russian Economy: Where Is It Headed?' SAIS, John Hopkins University, The Ernest Sturc Memorial Lecture.

Bai, Chong-En, Li, David D. and Wang, Yijiang (1997), 'Enterprise Productivity and Efficiency: When is Up Really Down?' *Journal of Comparative Economics,* **24** (3), 265–80.

Bauer, Tamás (1981), *Tervgazdaság, beruházás, ciklusok* (Planned Economy, Investment, Cycles), Budapest: Közgazdasági és Jogi Publishing Ltd.

Blanchard, Olivier, Dornbusch, Rudiger, Krugman, Paul, Layard, Richard and Summers, Lawrence (1991), *Reform in Eastern Europe,* Cambridge, MA: MIT Press.

Boeri T. (1993), 'Transitional Unemployment', OECD, *Economics of Transition*, **2** (1), 1–25.

Borish, Michael S., Long, F. Millard and Noel, Michel (1995), 'Restructuring Banks and Enterprises: Recent Lessons from Transition Countries', World Bank Discussion Papers, No. 279, Washington, DC.

Brada, Josef C. (1996), 'Privatization is Transition – Or is it?', *Journal of Economic Perspectives*, **10** (2), 67–86.

Carlin, W., Van Reenen, J. and Wolfe, T. (1995), 'Enterprise Restructuring in Early Tansition: The Case Study Evidence', *Economics of Transition*, **3** (4), 427–58.

Comisso, Ellen (1997), '"Implicit" Development Strategies in Central East Europe and Cross-National Production Networks' Paper prepared for *Foreign Direct Investment and Trade in East-Central Europe: The Creation of a Unified European Economy.* Vienna, Austria, June 5–6, mimeo.

Dallago, Bruno (1995), 'La Privatizzazione in Ungheria', Trento: Euroest Working Paper University of Trento.

Estrin S., Gelb, A. and Singh, I. (1995), 'Shocks and Adjustment by Firms in Transition: A Comparative Study', *Journal of Comparative Economics*, **21** (2), 131–51.

Fazekas, Károly (1996), 'Types of Microregions, Dispersion of Unemployment, and Local Employment Development in Hungary', *Eastern European Economics,* **34** (3), 3–48.

Frydman, Roman, Rapaczynski, Andzrej, Earle, John (1993), *The Privatization Process in Central Europe, Vol. 1,* London: Central University Press.

Frydman, Roman and Rapaczynski, Andzrej (1994), *Privatization in Eastern Europe: Is the State Withering Away?* London: Central European University Press.

Gáspár, Pál (1996), 'The Changes in the Financial Sector in Hungary in the Transition Process', in B. Blaszczyk and R. Woodward (eds), *Privatization in Post-Communist Countries – Volume II,* Warsaw: CASE, pp. 181–212.

Halpern, László and Körösi, Gábor (1998), 'Corporate performance in the transition – the case of Hungary: do new structures help create efficient ownership control?', in László Halpern and Charles Wyplosz (eds), *Hungary: Towards a Market Economy,* Cambridge: Cambridge University Press, pp. 159–84.

Hammer, M. and Champy, J. (1993), *Reengineering the Corporation,* New York: Harper Collins.

Janackova, Stanislava and Janacek, Kamil (1992), 'Privatization Strategy in International Comparison', *Prague Economic Papers,* **1** (1), 73–84.

Kornai, János (1980), *The Economics of Shortage,* Amsterdam: North Holland.

Kornai, János (1990), *The Road to a Free Economy,* New York, NY: Norton.

Kornai, János (1993), 'Transzformációs visszaesés' (Transformation Recession), *Közgazdasági Szemle,* **XL** (7–8), 569–99.

Kornai, János (1995), 'Lasting Growth as a Top Priority: Macroeconomic Tensions and Government Economic Policy in Hungary', *Acta Oeconomica,* **47** (1–2), 1–38.

Kuznetsov, A. and Kuznetsova, O. (1996), 'Privatization, Shareholding and Efficiency Argument: Russian Experience', *Europe-Asia Studies,* **48** (7), 1173–86.

Laki, Mihály (1993), 'The Chances for the Acceleration of Transition: the Case of Hungarian Privatization', *East European Politics and Societies,* **7** (3), 440–51.

Lipton, David and Sachs, Jeffrey (1990), 'Privatization in Eastern Europe: The Case of Poland', *Brookings Papers on Economic Activity,* No. 2.

Maier, Norbert (1997), 'A magyar vállalatok hatékonyságát befolyásoló tényezõk becslése 1990–1995-ös vállalati mérlegadatok alapján' (Estimating the Efficiency of the Hungarian Companies on the Basis of the Balance Sheets Data), manuscript, Budapest.

Major, Iván (1993), *Privatization in Eastern Europe: A Critical Approach,* Aldershot, UK and Brookfield, US: Edward Elgar.

Major, Iván (1994), 'The Constraints on Privatization in Hungary: Insufficient Demand or Inelastic Supply?' *Moct-Most,* **4** (Special Iussue), 107–45.

Major, Iván (1995a), 'A magántulajdon terjedése és a vállalatok gazdasági teljesítményei 1988 és 1992 között' (The expansion of the private sector and corporate performance between 1988 and 1992), *Közgazdasági Szemle,* **XLII** (2), 139–73.

Major, Iván (1995b), 'Hová lett a profit?' (Where have the profits gone?), *Külgazdaság,* **5** (9), 20–9.

Major, Iván (1996a), 'What Comes After? The Expansion of the Private Sector and Its Impact on the Corporate Sector's Economic Performance in Hungary', *Euroest,* Working Paper No. B–96/5, University of Trento.

Major, Iván (1996b), *A vállalati tulajdonosi szerkezet változásának hatása a versenyképességre* (The Effect of the Change in Corporate Ownership Structure on Competitiveness), Research report, Center for Institutional Studies, Institute of Economics, Hungarian Academy of Sciences, Budapest.

Major, Iván (1997a), 'Financial Performance of the Hungarian Companies during Transition', Phare ACE Programme, Budapest, mimeo.

Major, Iván (1997b), 'Az 1972-ben kiemelt 49 nagyvállalat életútja a mérlegadatok tükrében' (The Saga of the 49 Hungarian 'Strategic' Enterprises from 1972 as Reflected in Their Balance Sheets between 1990 and 1993), in Éva, Voszka (1997), *A dinoszauruszok esélyei* (The Chances of Dynosauruses), Budapest: Pénzügykutató Rt.-Perfekt Publishers, pp. 239–92.

McKinnon, R.I. (1993), 'Liberalizing Foreign Trade in a Socialist Economy: The Problem of Negative Value Added', in K.Z. Poznanski (ed), *Stabilization and Privatization in Poland: An Economic Evaluation of the Shock Therapy Program,* Norwell, Mass. and Dordrecht: Kluwer Academic Publishers, pp. 125–47.

Mertlik, Pavel (1996), 'Czech Privatization: From Public Ownership to Public Ownership in Five Years?', in B. Blaszczyk and R. Woodward (eds), *Privatization in Post-Communist Countries, Vol. 1*, Warsaw: CASE, pp. 103–22.

Mihályi, Péter (1992), *Socialist Investment Cycles – Analysis in Retrospect*, Dordrecht: Cluwer Academic Publishers.

Mihályi, Péter (1998), *A magyar privatizáció krónikája, 1989–1996* (The History of Hungarian Privatization: 1989–1996), Budapest: Közgazdasági és Jogi Könyvkiadó.

Murrell, Peter (1992), 'Evolutionary and Radical Approaches to Economic Reform', *Economics of Planning* (1), 79–95.

National Bank of Hungary (1995), *Annual Report*, Budapest.

National Bank of Hungary (1996), *Annual Report*, Budapest.

Pinto, B. (1995a), 'A Primer on Enterprise Adjustment and Governance in Transition Economies: What Poland has Taught Us', Working Paper, Munich: Osteuropa Institut.

Pinto, B. (1995b), 'Ownership and Corporate Control in Poland: Why State Firms Defied the Odds', Discussion Paper No. 1273, London: CEPR.

Pinto, B., Belka, M. and Krajewski, S. (1993), 'Transforming State Enterprises in Poland, Evidence on Adjustment by Manufacturing Firms', *Brookings Papers on Economic Activity* No. 1, pp. 213–70.

Privatization Monitor (1996), Budapest: ÁPV Rt.

Sass, Magdolna (1997), 'A bérmunka és a vállalatközi kapcsolatok' (Contract Processing and Inter-Company Relations), mimeo, Budapest: Institute of Economics, H.A.S.

Schwartz, Andrew (1997), 'Privatization, Foreign Direct Investment, and the Possibility of Cross-National Production Networks in Europe', Paper prepared for *Foreign Direct Investment and Trade in East-Central Europe: The Creation of a Unified European Economy*, Vienna, Austria, June 5–6, mimeo.

Sereghyova, J. (1996), 'Decentralization and Centralization in the Enterprise Sphere of Czech Republic', in B. Dallago and L. Mittone (eds), *Economic Institutions, Markets and Competition*, Cheltenham, UK and Brookfield, US: Edward Elgar, pp. 241–51.

Soós, K. Attila (1986), *Terv, Kampány, Pénz* (Plan, Campaign, Money), Budapest: Közgazdasági és Jogi Publishing Ltd

Stark, David (1992), 'Path Dependence and Privatization Strategies in East Central Europe', *East European Politics and Societies*, **6** (1), 17–53.

Stark, David (1996), 'Recombinant Property in East European Capitalism', *American Journal of Sociology*, **101** (4), 993–1027.

Statistical Yearbook 1991, 1994, and *1995*, Budapest: The Hungarian Central Statistical Office.

Swaan, Willem (1997), 'Tacit Knowledge and Post-Socialist Transformation: Results of a Comparative Study', in *Economic Systems*, **21** (4), 375–9.

Szalavetz, Andrea (1996), 'Measuring the Restructuring Performance of Firms in Transition Economies', Working Paper No. 69, IWE.

Szalavetz, Andrea (1997a), *Reorganizáció pénzügyi befektetõ irányítása alatt. Az MFB Rt. szerepe, a portfóliójába tartozó cégek reorganizációjában* (Reorganization under the Direction of a Financial Investor. The Role of the Hungarian Investment Bank PLC in Reorganizing the Firms in Its Portfolio), Budapest: MBV.

Szalavetz, Andrea (1997b), 'The Reliability of Hard Indicators for Measuring Restructuring Performance', Working Paper No. 82, Budapest: IWE.

Szalavetz, Andrea (1998), *Az energetikai gépgyártás privatizációja* (The privatization of energetic engineering companies), Budapest: ÁPV Rt.

Szalavetz, Andrea and Réthi, Sándor (1998), *Visszatérés az orosz piacra, érvényesülési stratégiák, esélyek és buktatók* (Returning to the Russian Market, Success Strategies, Opportunities and Traps), Budapest: ITD Hungary.

Szanyi, Miklós (1994a), 'A Transitional Assessment', Working Paper No. 42, Budapest: IWE.

Szanyi, Miklós (1994b), 'Magyar iparvállalatok alkalmazkodási törekvései az átalakulási válság során' (The Adjustment of the Hungarian Industrial Companies during the Transformation Crisis), *Közgazdasági Szemle,* **XLI** (11), 1036–50.

Szanyi, Miklós (1997), 'Market Exit in Hungary, 1990–1994', CASE Working Paper, Warsaw: Center for Social and Economic Research.

Szanyi, Miklós, and Szemlér, T. (1997), 'Investment Patterns in Hungary 1989–1995', Working Paper No. 79, Budapest: IWE.

Voszka, Éva (1995), *Az agyaglábakon álló óriás* (The Gholem), Budapest: Pénzügykutató Rt.

Voszka, Éva (1997), *A dinoszauruszok esélyei* (The Chances of Dynosauruses), Budapest: Pénzügykutató Rt.-Perfekt Publishers.

6. Privatization and Company Restructuring in Poland

Barbara Blaszczyk, Grazyna Gierszewska, Michal Górzyñski, Tytus Kamiñski, Wojciech Maliszewski, Richard Woodward and Aleksander Zolnierski

6.1 PROGRESS OF PRIVATIZATION AND THE RESULTING OWNERSHIP STRUCTURE IN POLAND: A GENERAL OVERVIEW

6.1.1 Introductory Remarks

Together with the stabilization and liberalization of the economy, privatization was one of the underpinning principles of the reform program launched at the end of 1989. Under the program, privatization is to be a tool for increasing the efficiency of enterprises and bringing the ownership structure of the economy into line with market economy norms. In the first privatization program, overly optimistic assumptions were made whereby approximately half of all national assets would be transferred to private owners in the course of the initial three years of the reform.[1] The reality of privatization proved to be much more difficult. From the beginning of the transition the Polish privatization concept was burdened with too many different expectations and important goals competing among each other.[2] It was not immediately evident to all Polish reformers and politicians that some of those privatization goals were partly contradictory and could not be achieved simultaneously. (For instance it is impossible to gain high revenues from privatization for the state budget and to maintain a rapid speed of ownership transformation.)

On the other hand, privatization was seen as a very controversial political topic by the public. Social mistrust of privatization arose from different reasons. Fears of radical changes were linked with resentments of a historical nature (for example fears of losing working places and of 'selling out' enterprises to foreigners)[3] and strengthened with bad examples of asset stripping by the new-old owners (the so-called 'nomenklatura'). Last but not least, influential groups of the population were interested in keeping the state-owned sector unchanged and felt threatened by privatization (Macieja, 1997). The consolidation of these groups led to pressures on the government, in order to obtain preferential treatment instead of fast privatization and radical restructuring. The politicians were unable to play against these groups, being anxious about losing large parts of their constituency.

However, during the eight years of reforms public opinion on privatization changed slowly. Experience with privatization taught many people that privatization results in benefits to the enterprises and employees and to the economy as a whole. Moreover, many of the enterprises' managers learned that privatization is an unavoidable step for the future development of their enterprises. Additionally, the public now is much more aware of the necessity of deep restructuring of each enterprise and of the economy as a whole in order to compete on the domestic market and on the future European market. This results in a more positive attitude to foreign investors than at the beginning of reforms.

In this chapter, the privatization of the economy is not regarded as just the privatization of the state sector. The former notion refers to the increase of the private sector share in the economy, whereas the second denotes the transfer of assets from the former state, or public, sector to private owners. Privatization of the economy is not achieved exclusively through the state sector privatization but also – and, in the Polish case, actually to a far greater extent – through the spontaneous emergence of new private companies. Similarly, state policies on the privatization of the economy focus on encouraging new private domestic and foreign businesses to enter the market and establishing an environment which facilitates their development, while policies on public sector privatization aim at replacing the state as an owner with other entities. Both groups of policies are equally important and closely linked with each other.

6.1.2 Privatization Concept and Legal Framework

The Act of 13 July, 1990, on the Privatization of State Enterprises constituted a compromise between a number of different concepts. While adopting the flotation of shares (which provides the greatest revenues to the budget) as the primary privatization method, the law also gave substantial privileges to employees and laid the groundwork for a future mass (voucher) privatization program.[4] On the other hand, the law failed to settle the problems of restitution and/or compensation for previous owners whose property had been nationalized by the Communist regime. Two main privatization methods were provided for under the act. The first, called capital (or indirect) privatization, is used for large state enterprises and consists of two stages: first, the enterprise is 'commercialized' (that is, transformed into a joint stock company wholly owned by the State Treasury), and second, shares in the newly established companies are made available to private investors through public offerings, tenders or negotiations following a public invitation. The second method, referred to as liquidation (or direct) privatization, involves transfer of a given enterprise's assets or an organized portion thereof to private investors. Under this method three options are available, namely: (i) sale; (ii) in-kind contribution to a company; and (iii) leasing. The last method is targeted at acquisition of small enterprises by their management and employees. State enterprises in the agriculture sector are privatized according to different principles, provided for under a separate law. (The Act of 19 October, 1991, on Management of Agriculture Property of the State Treasury.)

These new privatization methods were supplemented by liquidations conducted under the State Enterprise Law of 25 September, 1981 (applicable to enterprises with poor financial standing) as well as bankruptcy and various types of debtor–creditor arrangements. In April 1993, following lengthy discussions, the Act on National Investment Funds (NIF) was finally adopted. This law formed the basis for the mass privatization program, allowing every adult Polish citizen to acquire a portion of national assets for a nominal charge. The NIF program was supposed to accelerate the pace of privatization, at the same time providing for restructuring of enterprises prior to their privatization, facilitated by the expertise of the professional management companies employed by the NIFs. There were 512 enterprises selected for the program, in which 15 NIFs were to participate.

In 1993 two other laws of crucial importance for the privatization process were adopted. The first law referred to financial restructuring of enterprises and state-owned banks and enabled such banks to launch debt reduction proceedings which allowed for conversion of debt into equity (the Act of 3 February, 1993, on Financial Restructuring of Enterprises and Banks). The second exempted a group of enterprises considered to be of strategic importance for the state from privatization based on generally applicable rules (155 enterprises were selected from the coal, power and defense industries, for which special privatization procedures were to be applied).

In the first half of 1993, due to the slow pace of privatization and various constraints hampering the process, work began on amendments to the 1990 Act. In August 1996, lengthy debates were brought to an end and a new privatization law was adopted. This law gives employees a more privileged position with respect to acquisition of shares in their companies and establishes special privatization procedures for indebted enterprises and those of strategic importance.[5] As for so-called direct privatization, the new law allows 'outsiders' to put forward privatization initiatives without the need for seeking approval of the 'insiders'; however, it also reduces the number of enterprises eligible for this type of privatization by introducing very low ceilings on the size of enterprises considered eligible.[6] Additionally, while the employees of the enterprises privatized according to this method do not receive 15 per cent of the shares for free, as in the case of capital privatization, under the new law they may receive the equivalent thereof paid to their accounts in the company's social fund.

The new law, by itself, is in our view not likely to change the privatization practice in any dramatic way. However, on 1 October, 1996, implementation of the reform of the central government administration began which included, among others, important changes in the institutional order in the area of privatization. A new Ministry of the Treasury has been established, which has assumed the responsibilities of the former Ministry of Privatization. The new Ministry is responsible for the supervision of all state-owned assets and only one of its functions will be privatization. Smaller enterprises will be privatized by the local governments (voivods) by the use of direct privatization methods. From the latter change a more efficient privatization may be expected, due to the decentralization of the privatization process (Balcerowicz, Blaszczyk, and Dabrowski, 1996).

6.1.3 Privatization Tracks and Their Results

Implementation of the privatization programs in accordance with the principles discussed above started in August 1990. By the end of that year six large enterprises had undergone capital privatization in the form of initial public offerings. The scale of capital privatization operations was broadened in 1991. Nevertheless, every enterprise was privatized on an individual basis, applying lengthy and complicated procedures, which considerably slowed down the entire process. Direct privatization of small and medium-sized enterprises, usually by leasing to employees and management, proved quicker and more effective. The NIF program was designed to speed up the privatization process, but its implementation did not begin until the end of 1995. In the first half of 1997, the NIF program entered a more advanced stage, with shares of the 15 funds being listed on the Warsaw Stock Exchange.

Table 6.1 depicts proportions between the group of enterprises having initiated privatization processes between the end of 1990 and December 1996 and those in which privatization has been completed.

Table 6.1. State enterprises which have initiated ownership transformation procedures, by type of privatization (December 1990–96)

Number of state enterprises (In parentheses: as per cent of state enterprises existing on 31 December, 1990)		Share of completed cases	
Existing on 31 December, 1990	8 441 (100)	Comments	in per cent of started transformations in the group
Transformed into companies wholly owned by the State Treasury	1 227 (14.5)	183 privatized; 512 transferred to the NIF Program	14.9 41.7
Of which: Transformed into companies under Law on Ownership Transformation of Enterprises of Special Importance	160 (1.9)	Temporarily not subject to privatization	–
Liquidated under Law on Privatization of State Enterprises (direct privatization)	1 247 (14.7)	1 221 projects completed	97.9
Liquidated under Law on the State Enterprise (liquidation)	1 464 (17.3)	494 projects completed; 441 went into bankruptcy procedures	33.7 30.1
Taken over by the Agency for Agriculture Property of the State Treasury	1 654 (19.5)	Leased, subject to management contract or sold	
Insolvent or in liquidation under the Bankruptcy Law	662 (7.8)	304 ongoing bankruptcy procedures	
Turned over to local governments under the Law on Municipalization	263 (3.1)	May undergo further transformations	
Total number of enterprises subject to ownership transformations*	5 592 (66.2)		
of which: Privatization completed	1 898 (22.4)		

Note: *From December 1996 (including transfer to local governments and all forms of liquidation).

Sources: Central Statistical Office (1997), *Privatization of State Enterprises as of 31 December, 1996*, Warsaw, *Small Statistical Yearbook 1997,* pp. 360–2 and author's calculations.

Out of 1227 enterprises transformed into companies wholly owned by the State Treasury, only 183 have completed the capital privatization process; while 512 of these companies were included in the NIF program, their complete privatization will take a few more years. Almost all direct privatization projects have been completed (1221 out of 1247), whereas less than one third (494 out of 1464) of the liquidation projects commenced under the State Enterprise Law have been completed. Thus, between December 1990 and the end of 1996, 5592 (66.2 per cent) of the total of 8441 state enterprises existing at the outset of the process had initiated the transformation processes, but only 1898 (22.4 per cent) had managed to complete it.

With respect to the sectoral breakdown of transformed enterprises from 1990 through June 1996, the relative importance of ownership transformations is much greater in the manufacturing sector than in other segments of the economy. Within the manufacturing sector, in turn, the largest number of transformed enterprises are active in the processing branch, which by far outperforms the other sectors (mining, power, gas and water supply) in terms of transformation pace (Figure 6.1). As of the end of 1996, the majority of large enterprises in such utilities as power, gas and water supply, as well as in transportation and telecommunications, were excluded from the ownership transformation process. The numerical data illustrating the privatization progress in various parts of the economy need to be supplemented with a brief description of the qualitative effects encountered on the individual paths of privatization.

Capital privatization has been applied in 183 large companies, mostly from food and beverages, tobacco, chemicals, electrical appliances, machinery and the garment industry, moreover a few large banks were included. Though limited in quantitative terms, this type of privatization has been of great importance for the economy in view of the size of the enterprises concerned, their market positions, number of employees and the fact that they represented important branches of the economy. Due to resource limitations of potential domestic investors, around 50 per cent of the capital privatization projects involved foreign capital. The sale of shares in these enterprises facilitated the establishment and development of the Polish capital market and was the main source of privatization proceeds to the state budget. In qualitative terms, the majority of enterprises privatized through capital privatization – in particular those with foreign capital involvement – are showing high growth; they have engaged in deep restructuring (Dabrowski, 1995). The high degree of centralization of the administrative procedures applied in capital privatization and its strong sensitivity to political constraints are among the main weaknesses of capital privatization.

Different measures need to be used when assessing the effects of commercialization in cases in which this was not followed by privatization (approximately 400 cases). One has to be extremely cautious in evaluating the significance of this process for the progress of ownership transformations, since commercialization is primarily a formal and legal stage which does not automatically lead to further changes in a given enterprise. In spite of this reservation, it should be added that in our opinion, given the current situation, commercialization – even without subsequent privatization – may have certain disciplining effects due to the increased transparency and improved control mechanisms which follow from the introduction of new accounting rules and standards in the commercialized enterprises as well as the obligation to publish their financial results.

Figure 6.1. Industrial enterprises in the transformation process by branch

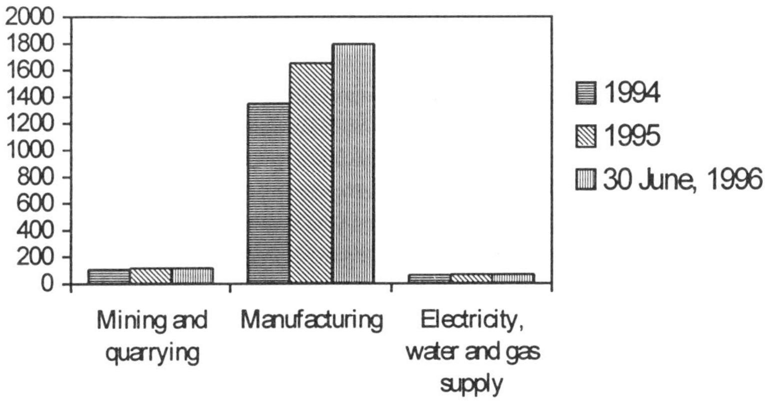

Yet another set of considerations applies to the companies included in the NIF program. After the special Government Selection Committee had selected supervisory board members and managers of the funds, paired the funds with management companies and completed negotiations on the funds' management, the operating phase of the program began in June 1995 with allocation of company shares to the funds. Ultimately, majority stakes in 512 companies wholly owned by the State Treasury were turned over to the 15 National Investment Funds, whose tasks included restructuring and privatizing those companies.[7] The management companies which manage the funds are responsible for improving the financial results of the companies held by the funds, which they may do by directly or indirectly participating in the companies' restructuring or by supporting the privatization process and seeking strategic investors; they may also sell or liquidate the companies. Portfolio investment will be one of the important features of the NIFs' activities.

Certificates for shares in the NIFs were distributed to the public between November 1995 and November 1996 and, according to official data, the vast majority of eligible Poles (25.7 million) purchased the certificates, paying a registration fee which by the end of the distribution period was seven to eight times lower than the market value of the share certificate. A half year later (June 1997) 15 millions of certificates were dematerialized (put into the computerized system of the Warsaw Stock Exchange).[8] The certificates may be freely traded on the over-the-counter market and the stock exchange. Since the shares in the NIFs have been listed on the Warsaw Stock Exchange since May 1997, every certificate is convertible into 15 shares, one in each NIF. At the end of June 1997, 5 million certificates had been converted already into the NIF shares. The funds started their operations with analyses of their majority holdings in order to prepare restructuring or sale plans. The funds were also obliged to present their consolidated balance sheets for the first year of operation (1995) as well as the adjusted balance sheets of their companies in order for the Securities Commission to approve trading of those companies' shares on the stock exchange. The first year has shown that the funds have been active and varied in the character of their activity, developing restructuring and investment plans adjusted to the unique characteristics of their portfolios. Plans have been made to sell off enterprises with good financial standing while restructuring others which require more profound preparation for privatization. By August 1996, the funds submitted projects which planned the sale of 76 of the 512 companies. One year later, the sale of 21 companies out of 31 prepared transactions was already completed. The stock exchange listing of some 60 to 70 companies was also planned and eight of them entered the Warsaw Stock Exchange. In spring 1996, the sale of minority stakes commenced, in particular those of cement industry companies. On the average, NIF companies are of medium size (200–1000 employees), and operate chiefly in the manufacturing or construction sectors. The manufacturing companies are dominated by machinery and equipment, foods and beverages, and the chemical, construction materials, metallurgy and garment industries.

Over recent years the overall financial standing of NIF companies has deteriorated in comparison with companies not participating in the NIF program, generally due to the following reasons: first, while waiting for implementation of the program, many of the most financially sound companies attracted strategic investors for capital privatization and left the NIF program; second, a large number of enterprises selected for mass privatization spent two or more years in a state of uncertainty and idleness, without any restructuring effort. Finally, the funds, in order to meet the new accounting rules and prudential standards which follow from the 1994 accounting law, introduced high reserves backing every expected kinds of risks, at the enterprises level and at the funds level, which proved to be costly.

Through 31 December, 1996, *direct privatization through liquidation*, designed for small and medium-sized enterprises, had been launched in 1247 enterprises and completed in 1221. The fastest and the most popular method for transfer of ownership rights in Poland, direct privatization, may often be classified as a quasi-sale method due to the payment deferment and the existence of various regulations facilitating purchase on favorable conditions.

Most cases of direct privatization involve leasing of assets to a company established by the employees of the 'liquidated' state enterprise; there have been fewer enterprises sold or contributed in kind to a company.[9] Despite serious concerns about the future of the so-called employee-owned companies, their financial results so far are generally better than expected, although investment volume is still insufficient. The research conducted so far proves that these enterprises currently have very diversified ownership structures, ranging from very concentrated to highly dispersed (Jarosz, 1996). When negotiation of the State Enterprise Pact began in 1992, the pace of the direct privatization process decreased substantially. While this could possibly be a result of the shrinking of the pool of financially sound small and medium-sized state enterprises, it appears that the overwhelming factor was the decision of enterprises to wait for the adoption of a new privatization law, expected to provide better financial conditions for this type of privatization. It is not yet possible to assess to what extent further direct privatization operations will be impacted by the new (1996) law. One may reasonably assume that the pace of the process will largely depend on the determination of the voivods (to whom the power to privatize most small enterprises has been transferred), the capacity of voivodship institutions and initiatives of the regional offices of the Ministry of the State Treasury. As the results show, privatization slowed down even more in 1997.

Liquidation under the State Enterprise Act is triggered by poor financial standing of the enterprise concerned; privatization should therefore be viewed as a 'byproduct' of the process. Nonetheless, any liquidation under the provisions of article 19 of this law materially supports privatization by enabling small private companies to purchase the assets of the enterprise under liquidation at a relatively low price. Although these enterprises cannot continue to function in their current form, their assets and labor force may be effectively used by others. However, the procedure is much more complex and lengthy than direct privatization. As of December 1996, liquidation had been initiated in 1464 state enterprises, but only 494 (33.7 per cent) of these liquidations had been completed, with the rest still in progress. Another group of 441 enterprises being in liquidation went into bankruptcy procedures.

Since 1990 a large number of SOEs have been declared bankrupt or have had to engage in arrangement proceedings. As of December 1996 around 662 state enterprises had been declared bankrupt or subject to court arrangement proceedings. In some cases creditors took over the enterprises and became their new owners. Moreover, between 1993 and 1996, under the Act on Financial Restructuring of Enterprises and Banks, state banks launched conciliatory proceedings involving 196 indebted state enterprises and companies wholly owned by the State Treasury. The law provided for the following methods of enterprise restructuring: bank conciliatory agreements, public sale of debts owed to banks, conversion of debt into equity and liquidation or receivership. In December 1996 the files maintained by the Ministry of Privatization contained 128 cases of debt-equity conversions. Only 13 bank conciliatory proceedings have been fully completed at that time.[10] The conversion procedures, in addition to reducing financial tension in the firms involved, may lead to partial, and in some cases complete, privatization.

6.1.5 *De novo* Private Sector Development

De novo privatization, that is, private sector development through the establishment of brand new companies, proved to be of particular importance in Poland. The spontaneous expansion of the private sector has been the most dynamic phenomenon in the entire transition to a market economy. The *de novo* private sector has also been the one with the fastest growth of production, sales and investments. This generated a large number of jobs, thus counteracting the rise in unemployment. If we look at the rates of growth of the numbers of enterprises in the private and public sectors, we note that the fastest growth was in the number of private companies and companies with foreign capital. Between 1989 and 1996 the number of private businesses owned by individuals more than doubled, from 813 000 to 1.95 million.[11] Starting up small private businesses was made relatively easy by the liberal, straightforward registration requirements and commercial regulations as well as the availability for buying, at relatively low prices, assets formerly belonging to state enterprises. This is evidence that effective privatization methods, decentralization of decision-making regarding disposal of state enterprise assets and other favorable systemic solutions were all important factors in private sector revival.

The so-called small privatization process, affecting the retail trade, catering and service sectors, also proved extremely successful in the process of ownership transformation in Poland. During the operation, conducted between 1990 and 1992, approximately 97 per cent of retail and small service outlets and restaurants were privatized (Earle et al., 1994). As a result of small privatization, by the end of 1992 over 90 per cent of the domestic trade sector labor force worked in private companies, with this share increasing to 94 per cent by the end of 1995. Between 1990 and 1995 the number of private shops doubled (from 223 113 to 419 313), and their sales increased almost tenfold (from PLN 16 926.0 million to PLN 157 025.5 million in current prices). Today the vast majority of small shops and businesses are private, although most of the real estate on which they are located is owned by the local authorities. A similar development occurred in the wholesale trade sector, where sales increased almost 17 times (from PLN 10 477 million in 1991 to PLN 176 555 million in current prices in 1995).

6.1.6 Foreign Investment

The ability to attract foreign investment to enter the Polish market was limited in the initial stage of transformation, due to high risk resulting from the high inflation rate, the immense and unsettled foreign debt, the disastrous situation of numerous enterprises following the stabilization shock, and the unpredictable effects of the reforms and prejudices of a part of the society and certain politicians against foreign investors. This changed over time, and in particular after 1993, when the pace of the Polish economy's growth accelerated and the foreign debt had been successfully restructured. The general reception of foreign investors has also gradually improved. These factors encouraged foreign investors to expand their operations on the Polish market. In addition to the incentives associated with the high growth rate, Poland's international treaties (World Trade Organization, European Treaty and other) are an important factor in ensuring economic stability.

The Act of 14 June, 1991, on Companies with Foreign Capital is the legal basis for foreign investment. In adopting this law, the Polish Parliament decided that the same regulations should apply to foreign and domestic investors; tax allowances or other special incentives for foreign investors were therefore dropped, with the exception of large-scale investment projects implemented in regions with high rates of structural unemployment or those of exceptional scientific and technical value. However, the principle of equal treatment of Polish and foreign investors is still not applied consistently. Restrictions affecting land acquisition, remaining following liberalization of relevant legislation in April 1996, still constitute the main legal barrier to foreign investment. On the other hand regulations requiring foreign investors to obtain permits in order to operate in certain business areas were lifted. The introduction of tax exemptions linked with exports and investments and promotion of special economic zones protecting investors were further measures, taken in 1993–94 in order to attract investors – both domestic and foreign. Nevertheless, a general opinion exists that the greatest existing barrier for foreign investments in Poland results from bureaucratic procedures and frequent local hesitance with respect to foreign investments. As for large-scale infrastructure projects, the government has not shown a consistent strategy, no transparent and effective procedures have been put in place and certain areas lack adequate legislation (Carter et al., 1996).

Under the relevant legislation, foreign direct investments may take the form of a capital share in an already existing or newly founded joint-stock or limited liability company. A foreign investor may also extend a long-term loan to a company. The profits on direct investments may be re-invested or transferred outside Poland without restriction. By the end of 1996 roughly 28 000 enterprises with foreign capital participation were operating in Poland. However, according to the data of the State Foreign Investment Agency, only in 492 such enterprises did the value of foreign inputs exceed $US 1 million.[12] By the end of 1995 large scale foreign investments (valued at more than $US 1 million) in Poland totaled $US 6.8 billion (PAIZ, 1996), and smaller scale investments were estimated at $US 1.8 billion. Therefore, the total investment volume totaled $US 8.5 billion. The total value of additional commitments relating to the investments was estimated in 1995 at $US 5.2 billion.

In 1996, there was again a high increase of the foreign investment inflow, reaching more than $US 5 billion. Altogether a total of $US 12 227 billion in foreign direct investments (large scale investments) flowed to Poland between 1990 and 1996, increasing steeply every year. From 1993 through 1996, the inflow of foreign direct investments doubled each year. According to the most recent estimates of the State Foreign Investment Agency, it is expected that in 1997 such investments will grow in a slower pace and their inflow will reach approximately $US 3.5 billion (*Rzeczpospolita*, 16 April and 9 September, 1997). One may suggest that the reason for this is the slower pace of structural reforms in Poland during the most recent years and in the lack of large privatization projects, especially in infrastructural sectors.

If we consider the largest foreign investments in Poland in terms of branches, the manufacturing sector leads the list, followed by the financial, construction, services and power sectors. 1995 saw a relatively rapid increase in investments in manufacturing, as a result of which this sector accounted for 63.3 per cent of the total value of foreign investments (data from State Foreign Investment Agency). With respect to nationality, the foreign investors' group is led by Americans, followed by multinational companies,

Germans, French and Italians. In terms of single investors, the largest amounts in the period were invested by Fiat, the EBRD and the Polish–American Enterprise Fund.

6.1.7 Macroeconomic Results and Changes in the Ownership Structure

Following eight years of transformation, the extent of privatization of the economy – in the broad sense – is significant. The private sector share in GDP grew from 30 per cent in 1989 to around 60 per cent in 1995.[13] By the end of 1996 the private sector's share in total industrial output was 51.7 per cent; corresponding figures for construction and domestic trade were 87.9 and 92.9 per cent respectively. In the transport and communication sector the share of the private output remained at a lower level of 39.5 per cent. The private sector's share in foreign trade amounted to 62.8 per cent of exports and to 75.6 per cent of imports. Additionally, the sector (including agriculture) employed 65 per cent of the entire labor force (Central Statistical Office, *Small Statistical Yearbook* 1997, pp. 351–6) (see Tables 6.2 and 6.3).

Together with the changes in the ownership structure, important changes in the physical structure of the economy emerged. The share of the industrial sector in GDP declined from 44.9 per cent in 1990 to 27.5 per cent in 1996. The share of agriculture (together with forestry, fishing and hunting) fell from 7.2 per cent to 5.8 per cent and that of construction from 9.2 to 5.3 per cent. The share of retail trade and repair services was estimated in 1996 at 14.3 per cent (estimates of the Central Statistical Office, *Small Statistical Yearbook* 1997, p. 341). However, despite these massive changes, from the point of view of GDP production, industry is still the dominant sector.[14] The second most important place belongs to the trade and repair sector. Agriculture, though employing 28 per cent of the total workforce, produces only 5.8 per cent of GDP, which is evidence of very low labor productivity in this sector. It should be noted that the public sector, despite the drop to 35 per cent of the total labor force employed, continues to hold over one half of national assets (59.7 per cent of book value in 1995) and still has a high share in total investment, 55.8 per cent in 1995 (*Small Statistical Yearbook* 1997, p. 351).

There are substantial differences between the composition of production in the private and public sectors. In the public sector, industry is responsible for the majority of value added, with the remainder produced by services, transportation and a very small share of other sectors. In the private sector it is trade that contributes the most to value added, followed by manufacturing and services; agriculture and construction are less significant. This also means that the private sector performs an important role in modernizing the structure of the economy (through the gradual reduction of the significance of manufacturing). The private sector has become the Polish economy's engine of growth. Between 1991 and 1995 the annual increase in value added in the sector was between 7.0 per cent and 26.7 per cent, whereas in the public sector value added declined continually until 1994, when slight (2.8 per cent) growth was reported (Blaszczyk, Bratkowski, and Dabrowski, 1996). For example, in 1995 value added in the private sector increased by 15 per cent compared with only 3 per cent in the public sector.

Table 6.2. The private sector's share in output and employment, 1989–95

Branch		**Dec. 1989**	**Dec. 1991**	**Dec. 1992**
Industry	a	16.2	24.6	31.0
	b	29.1	35.8	41.4
Construction	a	25.5	62.2	77.7
	b	37.4	59.5	71.8
Transport	a	11.5	25.2	39.3
	b	14.3	26.0	23.1
Domestic trade	a	59.5	NA	86.1
	b	72.7	88.3	90.5

Branch		**Dec. 1994**	**Dec. 1995**	**Dec. 1996**
Industry	a	38.3	44.0	51.7
	b	44.8	50.5	55.2
Construction	a	85.0	87.0	87.9
	b	79.3	80.9	85.0
Transport	a	45.1	45.0	39.5
	b	28.1	26.6	28.8
Domestic trade	a	91.5	92.0	92.9
	b	92.0	94.1	94.8

a: private sector share in output, % b: private sector share in employment in the sector, %

The growth of private investment was remarkable, too; its share in total investments rose by more than 40 per cent in 1996 (*Koniunktura gospodarcza Polski*, 1997). During the time under consideration massive shifts in employment among sectors emerged as well. The rising share of employment in the private sector illustrates its scale in the economy. Together with private agriculture, employment in the private sector reached 50 per cent of the total workforce as early as 1990 and at the end of 1996 amounted to 65 per cent.

Table 6.3. Employment in the national economy by sectors, in millions

SECTORS	1989	1996
PRIVATE SECTOR	4.0	4.2
– non-agricultural	1.8	5.2
Total private sector	5.8	9.4
'SEMI-PRIVATE' SECTOR		
– cooperatives	2.2	0.6
– other 'socialized' entities	0.2	NA
TOTAL NON-PUBLIC SECTOR	8.2	10.0
PUBLIC SECTOR	9.3	5.4
of which:		
– state ownership	9.3	3.9
local government ownership	–	1.2
TOTAL EMPLOYMENT IN THE NATIONAL ECONOMY	17.5	15.4

Sources: Central Statistical Office, *Statistical Yearbook*, 1991, and *Small Statistic Yearbook 1994–97*.

If we look closer at the structure of employment (excluding agriculture) in the private sector in Table 6.3, we can see other important shifts. Here we can see that employment in the remaining private sector (without cooperatives) rose from 1.8 to 5.2 million between 1989 and 1996. This figure includes persons employed in all private companies and partnerships, but primarily consists of the large number of self-employed. At the same time employment in the cooperative sector shrank from 2.2 to 0.6 million. Altogether employment in the private sector rose from 8.2 to 10.0 million. On the other hand, the workforce in the public sector shrank from 9.3 to 5.4 million, that is by 3.9 million, and total employment in the economy declined from 17.5 to 15.4 million, that is by 2.1 million. This means that the private sector employed a significant number of former public sector employees and also a large number of former employees of the 'socialized' cooperative sector, which became private and underwent serious restructuring.

The share of private employment in different sectors of the economy remains uneven. In industry, this share was 29.1 per cent in 1989 and it rose very gradually, not reaching the threshold of 50 per cent until the end of 1995 and amounting to 53.4 per cent in 1996. In construction it rose very steeply from 37.4 per cent in 1989 to 85 per cent in 1996. In domestic trade as early as 1989 private employment (including cooperatives) accounted for 72.7 per cent, and its share increased to 94.8 per cent by 1996. Among the sectors of material production and trade shown in this table, transportation is the only one where the share of the private sector is still lower than 30 per cent (due to the state-owned railways, ports, airlines, postal service, telecommunication, and so on, belonging to that sector). If we included in this table other infrastructural sectors and showed the structure of industrial employment in more detail, the uneven degree of privatization among sectors and branches would be much more evident.

The share of private employment was over 80 per cent in construction and over 90 per cent in agriculture and trade in 1996. In some kind of services (such as real estate) it amounted to more than 60 per cent, but it was almost absent in some other services, such as education (3.4 per cent) or health and social services (4.5 per cent). In the three main divisions of industry the share of the private sector is very uneven. On average, industry is 55.2 per cent privatized. But as we can see in the table, whereas private employment reached 64.9 per cent in the manufacturing sector, in both remaining sectors of industry (mining and quarrying and electricity, gas and water supply) it stands at 3.3 and 4.5 per cent respectively[15] (Figure 6.2).

Figure 6.2. The share of the private and the public sector in employment by branches

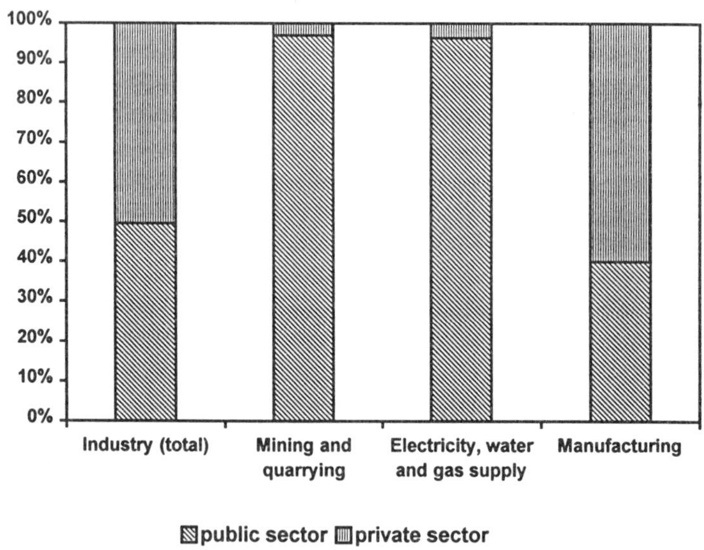

It is important to note that the impressive structural shifts between the public and the private sectors described above have not been achieved in the way that was expected at the beginning of the reform process. The explosion of newly-founded private firms was the main driving force behind ownership transformation, followed by the decentralized 'bottom-up', or direct, methods of privatization of state property. The contribution of centralized, 'top-down' privatization methods controlled by the government and much more under the influence of political fluctuations has been much smaller. An important factor in changing the whole economic structure was also the systematic contraction of the public sector. Evidence for these claims can be found in the fact that former public enterprises comprise only a small part of the private sector with regard to their share in employment and the employed assets.

This is illustrated by the following facts: As of the end of 1996, in the 'privatized' sector (that is, formerly state-owned enterprises) over 400 000 persons were employed, whereas the entire private non-agricultural sector employed over 5 million persons (out of 15 million employed persons in the entire economy, of which 10 million were in the non-agricultural sector). Thus, employment in the 'privatized' sector represented 8 per cent of private sector employment and 2.6 per cent of total employment (see Tables 6.2 and 6.3). The entire group of enterprises which had initiated ownership transformation processes (whether completed or not) employed slightly less than 1.5 million persons, or about 10 per cent of the national labor force (and 30 per cent of employment in the private sector). Although this figure indicates that while this group of enterprises constitutes an important element of the Polish economy, it does not alter the fact that the vast bulk of Poland's private sector (in terms of human and productive potential) is made up of *de novo* private enterprises rather than privatized ones. It is the *de novo* private sector which was responsible for the high rate of economic growth in Poland in recent years. The sector's growth can be seen not only in the rapid expansion of the number of enterprises, but also in the rates of growth of production, sales, and investment, which are higher than those for any other sector of the economy. In short, the expansion of the *de novo* private sector has been the most dynamic phenomenon in the entire market transformation of Poland.

We may conclude that, for numerous reasons, the privatization approach in Poland has been pluralistic. Some of the methods used have proved successful, some have failed. Poland is behind other countries in terms of privatization of the largest heavy industrial enterprises and infrastructure. On the other hand, impressive results have been accomplished in development of the *de novo* private sector. The small and direct privatization programs used for small and medium-sized state enterprises and driven by bottom-up initiatives, have also been successful. The rate of inflow of foreign direct investments to Poland is increasing, bringing obvious benefits for the restructuring process. The figures and statistical analyses cited above constitute strong evidence that private sector growth in Poland has to be attributed primarily to the spontaneous development of new firms under liberal systemic conditions, aided by the decline and partial disintegration of the state sector. However, despite this impressive spontaneous private sector development, the extent of privatization of the economy, measured by the private sector's share in GDP, employment and assets, is still unsatisfactory. In reviewing the qualitative effects of privatization we have to admit that only some of the targeted goals have been met.

Through privatization a rapidly developing capital market was established in Poland. Many hold that the Polish securities market is the best organized, most transparent and promising in Central Europe.[16] The State Treasury was strengthened with direct proceeds from privatization, which, though moderate in volume, have been important for the consolidation of the budget.[17] One may expect that in the future the state budget will indirectly benefit from privatization, for example due to reductions in subsidies to the public sector and increasing tax revenues from private enterprises.[18] The eight years of transformation have proven beyond doubt that privatization supported with competition stimulates the increase of enterprise effectiveness. Significant accomplishments have been recorded in the restructuring of large enterprises through commercial procedures, particularly with foreign investors' participation (Kaminski, 1996).

The state sector has diminished, though to a lesser extent than originally planned. The overall result of the privatization process is unsatisfactory due to the continuing large number of state enterprises, the substantial value of assets still within the public sector and the uneven pace of privatization in certain sectors, especially in infrastructure, which so far has been excluded from privatization. Additionally, there is still insufficient popular support for privatization, because many hopes and expectations linked with it have not been fulfilled.

6.1.9 Results of Previous Research on Enterprise Restructuring in Poland

During the seven years of transformation in Poland described above (1990–96), deep changes occurred in the behavior of enterprises. These changes have been described in numerous empirical and statistical studies. The best known statistical research is the ranking of the 500 largest manufacturing enterprises, led by the Institute of Economics of the Polish Academy of Sciences since the early 1980s. Its scope has been broadened during the 1990s, so that besides the largest manufacturing companies in the public sector, lists have been prepared on the largest companies in the public and private sector and separately on other sectors outside manufacturing. On the basis of the company level data numerous papers and books on different aspects of enterprise restructuring have been published (for instance, Mujzel, 1997).

Among the most important empirical research on enterprise restructuring during the early transition in Poland are studies by Pinto, Belka and Krajewski (1993), followed up in later years with research in a larger group of enterprises (Belka et al., 1995), and empirical research conducted by the Gdansk Institute of Market Economics since 1990 in both state enterprises and a group of enterprises (starting from 60 and finishing with about 150) undergoing different types of ownership transformation.[19]

It is very difficult to compare or to generalize the outcomes of these empirical studies since none of them is based on a representative sample and are related to different groups of enterprises. On the other hand, the statistical research, which is more representative, may not answer many interesting questions because of the massive changes in the statistical methodology which occurred during this period of time. One should also realize that all ranking lists with their rich information include changing samples of enterprises, so that it is not possible to observe changes in the same sample. (An exception is Grosfeld and Nivet, 1997.) In many cases, a large amount of quantitative information is accompanied by a deficit of qualitative information, necessary in order to explain the reasons behind observed changes. Therefore, it is possible to conduct econometric analyses, but it is very difficult to interpret the results of these analyses. However, all these studies and available official statistics allow us to draw a general picture on the adjustment behavior and restructuring effects on enterprises:

1. The adjustment behavior of all types of enterprises has shown many similarities during consecutive stages of transformation. Most authors distinguish two (Belka et al., 1996) or three such stages (Maczyñska and Zawadzki, 1997).

The first stage (1990–91 or 1990–92) was a period of severe crisis caused by external shocks linked with the systemic change. While in 1990 many enterprises could still allow themselves a 'wait and see approach' because of accumulated financial and other reserves, 1991 was a year of a sharp decline. At that time the enterprises made intensive efforts to find short-time survival strategies, mostly by employment cuts, sale of non-productive assets and so on, and tried to establish new markets for their goods. Production and sales, as well as all other economic indicators, fell sharply. The real indebtedness of enterprises was growing. *The second stage* of adjustment identified in the three-stage approach was in the years 1992–93 when the enterprises tried to halt the decreasing trend of production and sales. In this stage they introduced new sale strategies.

Table 6.4. Economic relations in companies of different types as of 31 December, 1996

Specification	Employment (in thousands)	Cost indicator[a]	Net profitability[b]	Current ratio[c]
Enterprise sector, total[d]	4 626.0	97.1	1.6	22.2
Enterprises which have begun ownership transformation[e]	1 496.3	97.9	0.9	19.8
Companies wholly owned by the state treasury, of which:	1 064.3	99.0	0.4	16.4
– prepared for individual capital privatization	396.9	97.8	1.8	22.9
– prepared for NFI	358.5	100.2	– 1.6	13.5
– others	308.9	100.2	– 1.4	9.9
Companies in which capital privatization was completed, of which:	175.1	95.6	2.3	31.5
– with foreign capital	68.9	96.4	1.8	24.9
Companies established from liquidated state enterprises, of which:	58.2	99.7	– 0.9	23.1
– with foreign capital	21.9	99.1	– 1.0	28.9
Employee–owned companies	186.2	94.0	3.4	22.4
State enterprises in liquidation, of which:	12.5	110.1	– 5.8	9.3
– under the state enterprise law	6.3	131.4	– 16.3	8.8
– under the privatization law	6.2	99.0	– 0.3	10.9
State enterprises not having begun ownership transformation	771.6	98.4	0.4	25.2
Public enterprises, total	2 619.9	97.8	1.0	23.1

Notes

[a] Ratio of costs to total revenue; [b] Ratio of net profit or loss to total revenue;
[c] Ratio of current assets to current liabilities; [d] All enterprises employing over 50 employees;
[e] Including those which have completed privatization.

Source: Central Statistical Office, 'Financial results of economic entities, January–December 1996,' in *Privatization of State Enterprises as of 31 December, 1996*, Warszawa 1997.

The first sign of recovery was the rise of labor productivity in 1992 accompanied by production increase, but the profitability indicators of enterprises were still decreasing. Investment stagnated. 1993 was the first year when the financial performance of enterprises recovered and when investment rose (although net profitability was still negative). *The third stage* of adjustment, starting in 1994 (or the second stage, beginning in 1993 in the two-stage approach), was characterized by steady production growth, improvement of profitability, rising net profitability and investment spending. In 1996 the overall financial performance of enterprises deteriorated again, but investment and labor productivity continued to rise.

2. A surprising result of research conducted during the first two stages of transition was that privatization seemed to have little influence on the adjustment and restructuring patterns of enterprises. All enterprises, whether privatized, state-owned or commercialized seemed to react in similar ways to the hardening of budgetary constraints and increasing competition.[20] In the next stages of reforms, especially since 1994, a gradual differentiation between restructuring patterns of enterprises was more and more visible. It is now clear that privatization matters. With respect to deep (strategic) vs. defensive restructuring (Grosfeld and Roland, 1996), most research has shown that the strategic restructuring process, involving large investments and innovative technological changes, was possible only in privatized enterprises, mainly with the participation of a foreign investor. Moreover, the behavior of enterprises of different ownership types in the wage setting process has been investigated. The non-privatized enterprises have a tendency to consume the largest part of labor productivity increases in wages while the privatized enterprises use it for further investment (Grosfeld and Nivet, 1997). A similar conclusion was made in an international comparative World Bank study (Pohl et al., 1997). The differences between privatized and state companies measured by the indicators of financial and economic performance are becoming striking (see Table 6.4). The only difference between the conclusions of the World Bank study and most research done in Poland is that, in our view, not only privatization by itself but also the methods of privatization have a strong influence on the quality of the restructuring process.

6.2 A SHORT DESCRIPTION OF THE INDUSTRIAL BRANCHES REPRESENTED IN THE SAMPLE

Here, we provide a comparative background to the analysis of the companies in our sample by investigating economic indicators of the relevant industries. We start from a brief description of production dynamics in manufacturing and in all branches under investigation. Then, changes in average employment and wages are investigated. Finally, aggregated data concerning the financial indicators of enterprises in these branches are presented. These indicators include gross profitability, the investment to revenue ratio, and the quick ratio. Table 6.5 contains basic statistics for the year 1995 on production, employment, wages, and investment for the branches represented by the companies in our sample.

Table 6.5. Basic 1995 statistics for branches represented in sample

	Production sold (million PLN)	Average employment (thousand)	Average monthly wage (PLN)	Investment outlays (millions of PLN)
Manufacturing	211 533.1	2 616.0	699.27	11 732.7
Apparel, dressng and dyeing of fur	6 338.5	240.0	499.56	232.5
Food products	51 629.7	452.0	683.81	2 694.6
Machinery and equipment	13 689.3	292.0	682.93	584.4
Electrical machinery and apparatus	6 179.4	87.0	747.51	381.4
Fabricated metal products	9 367.5	87.0	683.89	325.8
Radio, television and communication equipment	3 348.0	43.0	754.68	151.2

Source: Central Statistical Office, *Monthly Statistical Bulletin*

6.2.1 Production in the Manufacturing Sector, 1990–96

Production in the centrally planned economy was not governed by market demand but determined by supply conditions. Relative prices were distorted by the widespread control and persistent shortages resulted in forced substitution. Moreover, the administrative allocation of capital and labor was inefficient, magnifying distortions in the production structure. Heavy industry was overdeveloped, mostly for political reasons.

Transformation to the market economy required fundamental changes in the structure of industrial production. The first two years of transformation (1990–91) were characterized by a severe recession. Industrial production fell by ~20 per cent in 1990 and by ~10 per cent in 1991. The reduction was caused by the shock therapy necessary for macroeconomic stabilization, but also by the process of production restructuring in response to market signals. The dynamics of sold production of manufacturing branches (NACE Divisions) are reported in Figures 6.3 and 6.4.

The initial decrease was not identical across the branches. Figure 6.3 shows that the production of 'consumer goods' fell significantly less than the manufacturing average. It is obvious that initially repressed demand gave way to relatively higher consumption and less output fall. The opposite is true for producers of 'investment goods' (with the exception of one branch). A clear-cut difference between the decrease in 'investment' and 'consumer' goods production may be difficult to establish because the latter did not necessarily reflect consumer needs. The opening up of the Polish economy and large-scale import of consumer goods extended consumer choice and allowed for substitution of unwanted products. On the other hand, the decrease in production caused by the process of restructuring was 'cushioned' by the initial devaluation of *zloty*, which made Polish imports expensive and exports highly competitive in 1990. In mid-1991 domestic prices adjusted and true competitiveness began to determine trade flows.

In 1991 the dissolution of the CMEA produced another large negative demand shock. Trade with the USSR and other countries of the Eastern block dropped significantly. Economic links with Western countries were not established yet and the shock exerted considerable influence on the Polish economy. Production in branches exporting to the CMEA countries decreased. Recession ended in 1992, which was the first year of production growth.

Since 1993 production has been increasing by 10 per cent per year. Enterprises began to adapt to the new, market environment. The expanding private sector constituted a considerable part of the economy. Initially, increasing exports to the European Union (especially to Germany) boosted demand. Then, the domestic demand recovered and the production growth was fueled mainly by domestic absorption. It is important to note that the structure of production growth in manufacturing has changed in last two years. Figures 6.3 and 6.4 indicate that the dynamics of the 'consumer goods' sectors declined, while the production growth in the 'investment' branches increased relative to average growth in manufacturing. Thus, the process of restructuring seems to positively affect investment demand, which is fairly obvious in transforming economy.

Figure 6.3. Dynamics of sold production – 'consumer goods'

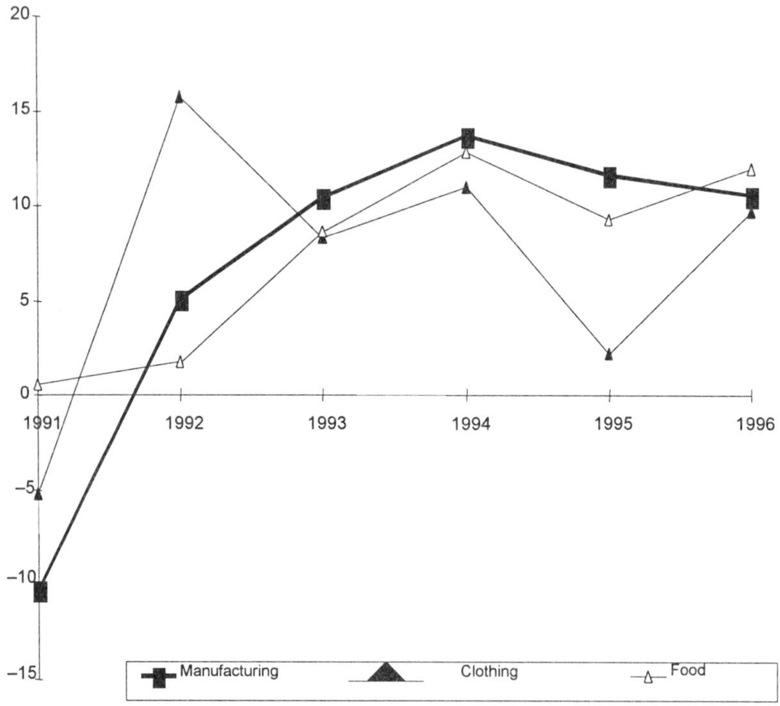

Source: Central Statistical Office

Lipowski (1998), discussing changes in the structure of the manufacturing sector in 1990–95, observes that pre-transformation manufacturing production in Poland was extremely material intensive and its competitiveness was relatively low. It follows that the production of raw materials and low-processed goods should gradually fall with the progress in restructuring and adopting new technologies. There is only one division producing low-processed goods in the sample under investigation, namely Manufacture of Fabricated Metal Products. This is one of the fastest growing branches so the data do not seem to confirm this supposition.

Figure 6.4. Dynamics of sold production – 'producer goods'

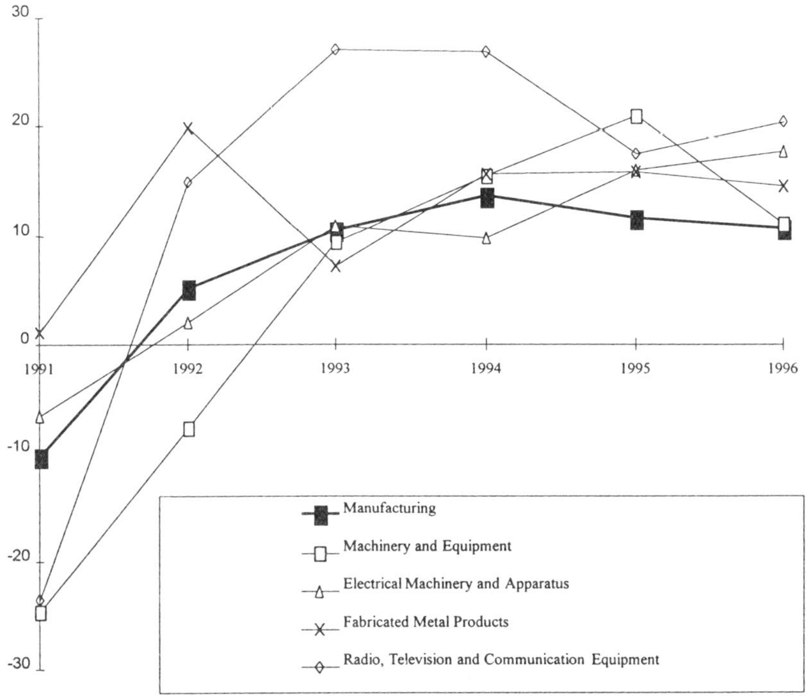

Source: Central Statistical Office

6.2.2 Employment Dynamics and Average Salaries

In 1990–94 average employment in industry was continuously falling. The exact estimation of employment dynamics is impossible because of changes in industrial classification but it is justifiable to use the available figures for rough comparison. In 1990 average employment in industry (KGN classification) was 4 620 000 while in 1994 it dropped to 3 641 000 (NACE classification). Enterprises in the pre-transformation period were plagued by a substantial overmanning. The process of adjustment was painful and labor hoarding remained a considerable problem even after four years of reforms. Results from a broad survey of Polish enterprises indicate that the issue of overmanning was certainly unsolved in 1993 (Belka et al., 1995). The last year of employment decline was 1994, followed by growth in 1995.

The dynamics of employment showed a declining trend both in the consumer goods and in the investment goods production between 1993 and 1996. It is clear from the data on employment that the average employment growth differs across branches. The most noticeable 'outlier' is very high employment growth in the clothing industry in 1993 but growth in the food industry is also substantial. As was already shown, the food industry did not experience production decline at the beginning of the transformation. A decrease in the production of clothing was lower than the manufacturing average. These observations seem to confirm the supposition that the consumer goods sector was less influenced by the stabilization shock and demand contraction. The pressure on restructuring might have been lower than in other branches. However, the food industry experienced decline in employment in 1994, indicating that employment was excessive.

A situation in the investment goods sector was different although one branch had also experienced high employment growth already in 1993 (Production of Fabricated Metal Products). In other branches employment was significantly reduced at the beginning of the transformation. Two branches were capable to increase employment in 1994–95 (Fabricated Metal Products and Electrical Machinery and Apparatus). The Production of Radio, Television and Communication Equipment experienced persistent decline in employment. These results confirm that the pressure on restructuring was stronger in the investment goods sector due to demand contraction. The situation of the consumer goods sector was better at the initial stage of transformation since demand for these products was repressed in the planned economy and the demand contraction due to transformation was less severe. To fully assess the employment decisions of the firms, we also analysed the salaries in branches under investigation relative to the manufacturing average.

Salaries in the food and clothing industry were generally below the manufacturing average (although close to average and, in 1992, higher in the food industry). Moreover, salaries in the clothing industry are declining relative to the average in manufacturing. Two branches in the investment sector had considerably higher salaries than the manufacturing average – Production of Electrical Machinery and Apparatus and Production of Radio, Television and Communication Equipment. These branches (especially Production of Radio, Television and Communication Equipment) are certainly the most human-capital intensive in the sample. The positive difference between salaries in these branches and the manufacturing average may be explained by the fact that highly skilled labor is employed in both industries. On the other hand, severe and persistent employment decline in Production of Radio, Television and Communication Equipment may suggest that the average salaries paid in this branch is too high, making the manufacturing of high-tech products too expensive.

6.2.3 Enterprise Profitability and Liquidity

In the previous two sections it was shown that the enterprises restructuring in manufacturing, combined with demand contraction, resulted in a substantial decline in production and in employment. In this section an influence of these factors on profitability will be investigated. Figures 6.5 and 6.6 compare gross profitability of branches with gross profitability in manufacturing. Gross profitability in the consumer goods sector was higher than the manufacturing average in the 1992–93 period and lower afterwards. The profitability of the food industry is gradually increasing after a decline in 1993. The clothing sector obtained the highest profitability in 1993–94.

Figure 6.5. Gross profitability – consumer goods

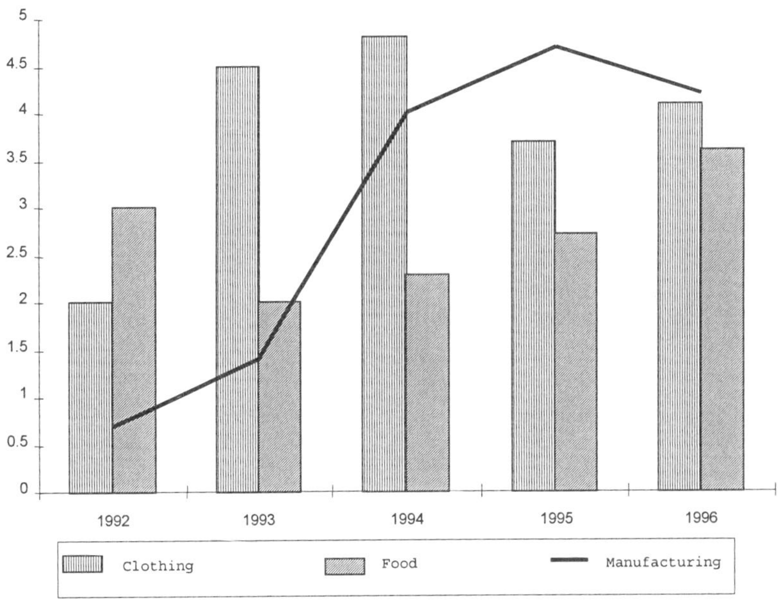

Source: Central Statistical Office

In the investment goods sector gross profitability was continuously above the manufacturing average in two branches: Production of Fabricated Metal Products and Production of Electrical Machinery and Apparatus. In Production of Machinery and Equipment, profitability became positive in 1994 and higher than the manufacturing average in 1996. Production of Radio, Television and Communication Equipment generated losses and became profitable only in 1996. These facts confirm our hypothesis that the situation of the consumer goods sector was relatively better at the beginning of the transformation process. The profitability of the investment goods sector gradually improved, although in some branches it was very high from the beginning of the period.

Figure 6.6. Gross profitability – investment goods

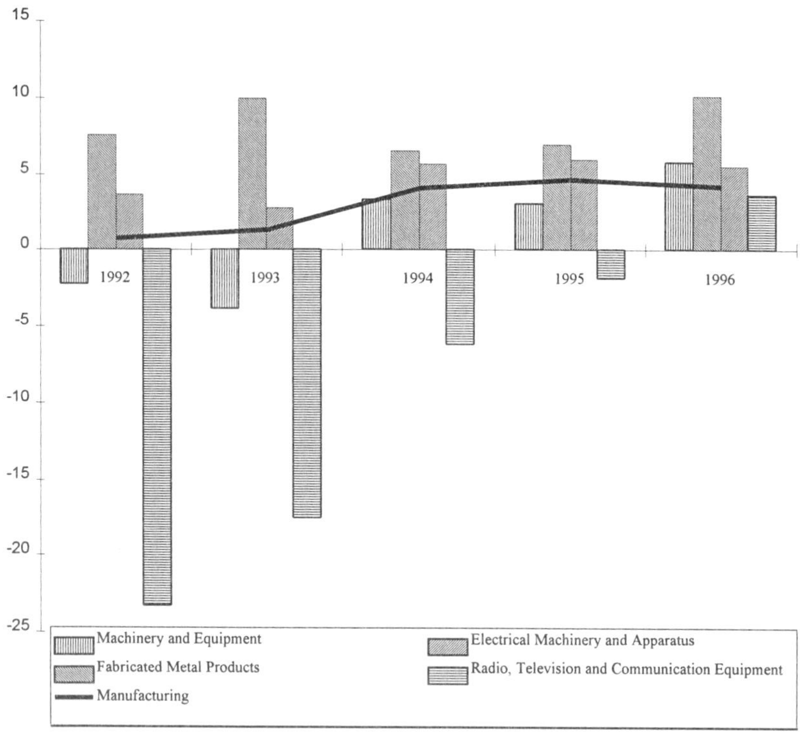

Source: Central Statistical Office

In further investigations of the financial situation in manufacturing we analyse liquidity in enterprises. Quick ratio indicators largely differed between the consumer goods and the investment goods sectors. The figures do not reveal any clear patterns in changes in liquidity or in differences between the groups. Liquidity remained roughly constant in the consumer goods sector and was slightly increasing in the investment goods sector. Within the consumer goods sector, wearing apparel had an above-average indicator with 80 per cent, while food production showed a below-average liquidity with 50–60 per cent between 1993 and 1996. Within the investment goods sector, it was only machinery and equipment production, plus the telecommunications equipment production that had a below-average quick ratio, with 60–70 per cent, and 45–55 per cent, respectively. The quick ratio of fabricated metal products, manufacturing and electrical machinery amounted to 100–120 per cent, 90–100 per cent and 65–80 per cent, respectively.

Figure 6.7. Investment to revenue ratio – consumer goods

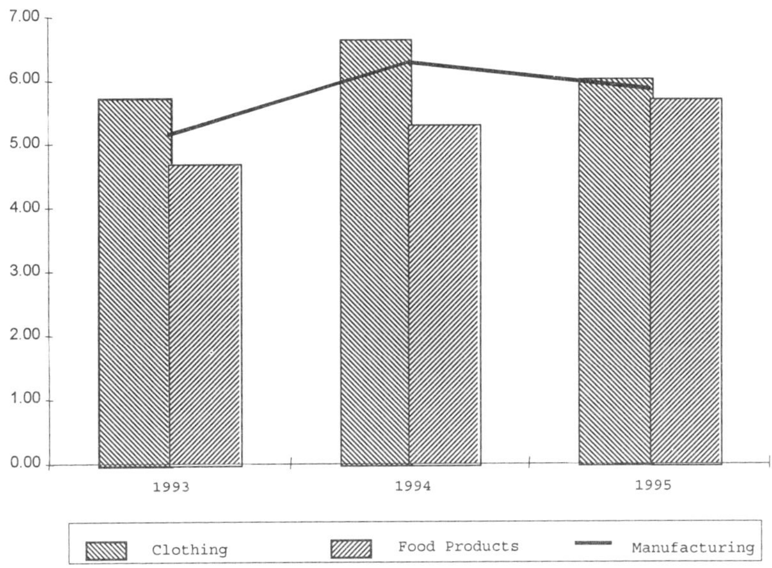

Source: Central Statistical Office

The differences between branches seem to be caused by persistent branch-specific effects, that is, differences in the 'normal' liquidity level for branches. Figures 6.7 and 6.8 present investment to revenue ratios for the branches under investigation. Investment patterns reflect the current situation of the enterprises but also expectations concerning future demand for products and profitability of the industries.

Investment outlays (as percentage of revenue) were increasing in the Manufacturing of Food Products and remained constant (and higher than manufacturing average) in Production of Wearing Apparel. In the investment goods sector the investment to revenue ratio decreased in almost all branches except Production of Machinery and Equipment. The reduction of investments may indicate a gradual decline in the initial growth potential in these industries.

Figure 6.8. Investment to revenue ratio – investment goods

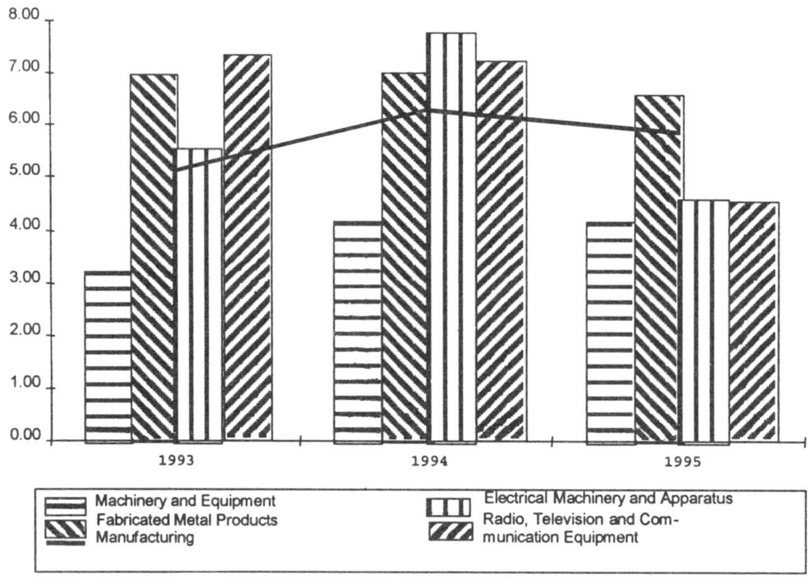

Source: Central Statistical Office

The main conclusion from our investigation is that the branches producing consumer goods faced less demand contraction at the beginning of the transformation process than the industries producing investment goods. The less severe initial conditions were reflected in lower output and employment decline, as well as in higher profitability in the consumer goods sector. After the initial restructuring, the situation in the investment goods sector improved and the economic performance of these branches became better than the manufacturing average. However, the other financial indicator – liquidity – does not follow this pattern and seems to be determined by branch-specific characteristics. Investment outlays recently decreased in the investment goods sector, which may indicate a decline in the growth potential of these industries.

6.3 OWNERSHIP TRANSFORMATION AND ORGANIZATIONAL TRANSFORMATION

The purpose of this section is to paint a fairly detailed picture of the various types of ownership transformation processes which all the firms in our sample have undergone, and then to examine the results of restructuring in order to determine whether there is any relationship between such restructuring processes on the one hand, and the nature of the ownership transformation process or the branch in which the enterprise operates on the other.

6.3.1 Description of the Sample

The firms are divided into two broad groups: those producing consumer goods and those producing investment-type goods (one firm producing household appliances has been included in the group of investment goods' producers due to the nature of the production technology). Our sample of 24 firms includes 11 enterprises producing mostly investment goods and 13 consumer goods' producers. Companies in the consumer group represent the food and clothing industries. Enterprises in the investment group are more diversified but most of them may be classified in the machinery industry. The sample contains only six firms that have not been fully privatized: three state treasury companies – that is, companies which have undergone so-called 'commercialization' but have not advanced beyond wholly state-owned status – and three companies participating in the National Investment Fund (NIF) program. One firm in the sample is also treated as a privatized firm although it is still majority owned by the state treasury and its strategic investor is also a state agency. The vast majority of privatized firms in our sample were privatized on the basis of conventional methods (for example, initial public offerings and trade sales) referred to in Poland as 'capital' or 'indirect' privatization; only three were privatized on the basis of employee leasing (the most popular of so-called 'liquidation' or 'direct' privatization). One very interesting and exceptional case is that of an employee-owned company which was created by being separated from a company which had earlier been commercialized and then sold to a foreign investor. All the enterprises in the sample but three (employee-owned) underwent commercialization. The timing of the commercialization does not seem to be correlated with the size of firm and does not differ significantly across the two industrial groups.

6.3.2 Initiators of, and Motives for, Transformation

In most cases, when we asked respondents who had initiated the ownership transformation process, they named the director (sometimes jointly with the employees' council; in one case, a third party – the Solidarity trade union – was mentioned). In three cases – a state treasury company, an NIF company, and a privatized firm with a large foreign shareholder – the initiator named was an outsider (the ministry). Another state treasury company named the state treasury, insiders and a bank as initiators. The founding organ (voivode) was named in one case as an initiator. Four companies provided no answer.

As regards the motives, seven firms provided no answer. The firm which had still not been privatized five years after commercialization stated that it had chosen commercialization in order to avoid the *dywidenda* tax.[21] Motives of commercialization were named in five other cases. The most popular motive was making privatization possible (commercialization being the necessary first step of 'capital' privatization). This motive was named by four companies (all privatized), although one of them also mentioned the desire to avoid the *popiwek* tax.[22] One company stated that its motive for commercialization was the ability to create a holding company and carry out other organizational changes and improve decision-making process.

The most popular motive of privatization named by the companies was the desire to acquire investment capital. There were two variants of this motive. One was the acquisition of a strategic investor who would provide these funds (named by three firms, all owned by strategic investors – two foreign and one a Polish individual). In the other variant the strategic investor does not appear as a source of funds. This variant was named by five firms. (Interestingly, all of them but one have strategic investors.)

6.3.3 Ownership Structure – Past and Present, and Employment Restructuring

All firms in the sample were still 100 per cent state-owned as of the end of 1990. By definition, all state treasury companies continue to be 100 per cent state-owned. The NIF firms in the sample still have a relatively uniform ownership structure: in each of them 33 per cent of the shares belong to the leading fund and 27 per cent to the other 14 funds. As two of the firms are food processing firms, both employees and farmers supplying the firms are entitle to free shares, giving these two groups a combined share of close to 30 per cent in both firms; the remaining approximate 10 per cent is held by the state treasury. In the other firm, employees hold 15 per cent, and the state treasury holds 25 per cent.

If we turn to other firms acquired by Polish owners but not employees we note, first, that only in one case out of seven was the purchaser an individual. In all cases (four) in which there is a strategic investor (holding 30 per cent or more of the shares), it is an institutional investor – in two cases a financial investor (bank) and in two cases a non-financial investor (a holding company and a state-owned agency).

A question often posed in discussions about the role of privileges for employees in the privatization process concerns the shares which employees acquired at preferential prices or even for free (in the case of 'indirect' privatization, the employees are given such privileges): Have they simply sold them to make a quick and very large profit, or do they appear to be genuinely interested in being co-owners of the firms in which they work? In cases of publicly traded companies, it is often very difficult, if not impossible, to determine how many shares are held by employees (five companies were unable to provide data on what percentage of shares was held by employees – although one of these was not publicly traded), but the information provided by our respondents concerning the number of shares held by employees in firms privatized by so-called indirect methods (in which employees acquired shares at half their face value or for free) indicates that employee shares in those companies were between 1 and 7.5 per cent in 1996. Given the fact that in all these companies 20 per cent of the shares were originally reserved for the employees on preferential conditions, it seems that employees have in fact generally been quick to dispose of their shares, often realizing impressive gains. Another important issue is the state share maintained in companies privatized by indirect methods. This share was generally low in the companies in our sample. In seven companies the state treasury held no shares whatsoever; in the others, the state shares – as of 1996 – ranged from 0.2 per cent to a majority share. All three of the firms in the sample privatized by employee leasing have undergone further ownership transformation, becoming non-leasing firms before the expiration of the leasing contract. This is indicative of a trend occurring throughout the economy with respect to better-performing companies privatized by this method. In one case, all shares were sold to a foreign owner; in two other cases, additional capital has been obtained by means of quotation on the Warsaw Stock Exchange.

Some of the most important questions surrounding the influence of ownership transformation processes on employment are: Does privatization (commercialization) change the pace of employment reduction? Or does employment reduction follow industrial patterns irrespective of ownership form? Or does it vary from case to case, depending solely on the financial health of the firm? Does the type of ownership matter (for example, are firms owned by strategic investors more willing to cut employment than firms owned by employees)?

Before examining the evidence from our sample, it is worth noting two things. First, in the state and former state sector in 1990 and 1991 – in the depths of the transformation recession (which ended in 1992) – the pace of employment reduction was much slower than the rate of production decline; however, this pace continued relatively unabated (or even accelerated) into the period of recovery. Second, a belief very widely held in Poland is that privatization is followed by accelerated employment reduction, despite the fact that several empirical studies have concluded that this is not the case and that employment reduction generally begins well before privatization. Does the evidence from our sample shed any light on these problems?

First, we must note the unfortunate number of companies (seven) in our sample for which we have no data on employment or for which the data are only from a single year, not allowing for an analysis of employment dynamics. In addition, there are six companies for which there are no data from recession years and seven firms for which there are no data before privatization/commercialization.

Having noted that, we can state what we found in those companies for which we have data. We might start with the good news: three enterprises had no significant drops in employment during the period for which we have data. Turning to the worst news, the most drastic drops in employment during the entire period of the 1990s were found in four companies. In the first two cases, the biggest drops occurred after privatization, whereas in the second two (commercialized, EO), they occurred before privatization. Looking at the best and worst cases, there is certainly no obvious correlation between type of ownership and employment policy. As for less extreme cases: for three companies (an NIF company, a publicly-traded company, and a state treasury company), the largest drops occurred in the same period (covering more than one year) as privatization, and we cannot determine whether this was before or after actual privatization. Finally, in four companies (an NIF company, a publicly-traded company, a foreign-owned company, and a company owned by a Polish strategic investor) the most dramatic drops occurred after privatization.

Three companies experienced their most dramatic drops in employment during the recession. Four companies' most dramatic drops occurred after the recession. It is interesting to note that we observe companies from the same branch (clothing) and ownership groups (NIF, publicly traded) in both categories (employment drops before and after recession).

Clearly, the evidence here is very mixed. The size of the sample and the gaps in the data suggest the utmost caution, but there is certainly no evidence in our data that ownership transformation is related in any deterministic way to employment policy: we can find companies with identical ownership forms and very different employment patterns. There may be a certain branch relationship: the three companies that managed to avoid large employment drops were all food producers and the four companies which shrank drastically were all machine producers.

6.3.4 Labor Costs and Changes in Pay and Other Motivation Systems

Following the analysis of employment, the next task is to analyse the extent to which employment rationalization affected labor costs and the relationship between labor cost growth and ownership transformation vs. other factors (for example, branch) dealt with above in the employment analysis. Once again, we must begin by noting the fairly large gaps in the data. No data at all were received from seven firms. No data on recession years were received from eight firms, and five firms failed to provide data from the period preceding privatization. (Additionally, data for five firms prior to privatization is lacking because they were privatized so early.)

The first observation seems to be that in the recession years firms tended to keep the growth of their wage bills well below the growth in the producer price index. Seven firms showed an increasing trend following privatization; two firms did not. In the end, six firms (from every ownership category except publicly traded firms) had wage bill growth lower than the growth in the producer price index during the entire period for which they provided data. Two of these six provided no data on employment, but the other four showed the biggest employment reductions in the sample.

As a sort of check on the comparison between employment data and wage bill data, we gathered information on average monthly wages in the firms. (Here too there are large gaps in the data.) An interesting contrast to the data on the total wage bills is noted here: while total wage bill growth tended to stay well below producer price index growth during 1991 and 1992 (as the recession was coming to an end), average monthly wage growth in this period exceeded consumer price index growth with only one exception. In the first year of growth, wage growth in the foreign-owned firms was – with one exception – above consumer price index growth, while in the other firms the situation varied. In the following years, characterized by steady growth, wage growth has been consistently above consumer price index growth.

However, the large gaps in the data suggest great caution in the interpretation of these results.

Changes in pay systems, especially if they are designed to increase the motivation of employees, often constitute an important aspect of organizational change. Close links between performance and pay are often considered especially important for management. We therefore sought information on changes in pay systems, with an emphasis on motivational elements – both for managerial and non-managerial employees. It should be noted, however, that in some cases it is difficult to determine the nature of the motivational element of pay for non-managerial employees. In many cases a bonus is referred to, but in some cases this is a bonus linked to the financial performance of the company and thus having the incentive effects of a profit-sharing arrangement; in other cases, it is simply a fixed bonus which is withheld in cases of absenteeism or discipline problems and therefore has a more disciplinary than motivational character. We are not always certain to which type of bonus a given correspondent was referring.

Four firms (one NIF firm, one employee-owned firm, and two with Polish strategic investors) reported no changes in their pay systems. Eight companies, from all ownership types and branches, reported using a bonus system for their employees. However, the direction of developments with respect to bonuses is not the same throughout the sample. While three firms noted that the weight of the performance-related component of pay had increased, and one reported a planned increase, three firms (all foreign-owned) reported a decrease in the weight of the performance-related component of pay.

The principles determining base pay also differ quite widely. For example, while six firms reported using fixed daily or monthly rates (and two of them had switched from piece rates), four reported the use of piece rate wage systems for production workers, and two others reported the use of both (although one of these is gradually shifting from a piece rate system to daily rates). Here too there appear to be no patterns with respect to ownership type, although there seems to be a shift away from piece rate systems in companies producing investment goods.

6.3.5 Training and Organizational Changes

Firms generally provided little information about training activity. Aside from health and safety training, which is required by the law, our evidence seems to indicate that Polish firms generally tend to underestimate the importance of investment in human capital regardless of their ownership status, unless they are owned by foreign investors or have introduced an ISO certification program.

In the area of organizational changes, three firms reported that no changes worth mentioning had occurred. Five companies reported that the only change had been the creation of one department or division; in two cases, this was a marketing department. (Creation of a marketing department was one of a number of changes made in five other firms.) The development of two or more new departments and divisions was mentioned by four firms.

Spatial expansion of various kinds was reported by six companies. In contrast, spatial concentration was mentioned by six companies. Plant closings occurred in two firms, and one plant was sold by another. Apartments, holiday camps, and other employee service facilities were sold by four firms, and other real estate (buildings and land) by three others. Strictly organizational measures took place in five firms. Employment restructuring was mentioned by two firms. A holding structure was created by another. An employee-owned firm introduced cost and profit centers, meaning that the firm's six plants (corresponding to six product groups) are highly autonomous, with each having its own design, sales, marketing, quality control, personnel management, and accounting. Divisions were reorganized by two firms.

6.3.6 Company Presidents, Directors and Supervisory Board Members: from Where, by Whom and for How Much?

Managerial continuity is observed very generally in our sample and seems to be independent of the mode of ownership transformation. Our data indicate that there have only been eight cases of management shake-ups in the 1990s. Six of these were cases with strategic investors (five of them foreign, the other a case in which the owner took over the position of president shortly before our research was conducted), and two employee-owned companies. Generally, however, today's managers were also the managers of yesterday's state-owned enterprises under socialism.

Asked who determines membership of the board of directors and the supervisory board, most respondents simply answered in accordance with the commercial code that the membership of the board of directors is determined by the supervisory board and that of the supervisory board by the shareholders' assembly. Only a few companies went into more detail about the 'politics' behind these personnel decisions, providing some insights into how these decisions are made in reality, 'behind the scenes'. A number of responses indicate that while the president is chosen by the supervisory board, the other members of the board of directors are usually hand-picked by the president.

Who sets the remuneration for members of the two boards? Eleven firms reported that management's pay is determined by the supervisory board.

Seven firms reported that supervisory board members' pay is determined by the shareholders. One NIF firm said that the NIF determines pay for both boards, and two firms with strategic owners (one domestic, one foreign) said that the owner determines pay for both boards. In two foreign-owned companies, representatives of the owners on the supervisory boards are not paid. A respondent from one publicly-traded firm said that management base pay was set not by the supervisory board but by the shareholders' assembly, and that the supervisory board set the bonuses for management. Finally, eight firms provided no information on this subject.

Possibly the two most interesting observations concerning supervisory board membership in our sample are that the boards of firms owned by strategic investors tend to include employee representatives and that there is a strong outsider presence on employee-owned firms (in at least two cases representing a source of technology transfer). Thus, it seems that insider-dominated firms often appreciate the contributions that outsiders can make, and that outsider-owners often continue to find value in the employee representation which originated before they acquired their firms. In firms owned by Polish strategic investors, representatives of the owners dominate the supervisory boards but are not the exclusive members. By contrast, three foreign-owned companies' boards consist exclusively of representatives of the strategic investors. (The same situation exists in the former employee-owned company which is now foreign-owned.) The boards of the other four all include employee representatives, and the board of one in which the state treasury still maintains a significant stake also has one member representing the state treasury.

There is wide variation in the frequency of supervisory board meetings. The frequency named by the largest number of firms (11) is once a month. In five firms, the board meets every two to three months; in four (all foreign-owned), every three months, in two, two to three times a year, and in one (foreign-owned), once a year. Only in one foreign-owned company do meetings occur once a month; in all other foreign companies, they occur every three months at best. Apart from this, however, we do not observe any correlation between the type of ownership and the frequency of board meetings. Even more interestingly, frequency does not appear to be very strongly linked to whether or not the board in a firm is involved in strategy formulation, as one of the three firms meeting less than once every quarter is described as a strategy-maker, and two of the four boards meeting once every quarter are strategy-makers (although the board that meets only once a year is also the only one described as a passive organ). There does, however, appear to be a strong connection between frequency and whether a board is described by the respondents as an active one. Of the eleven boards described as active, only two have boards which meet less than once a month.

In evaluating the role of supervisory board in Polish companies, one must first be careful to distinguish between the role of this organ in the European two-tier management system and the role of the board of directors in the Anglo-Saxon system, where corporate executives sit beside outside monitors on one body. Generally speaking, the role of the supervisory board in the European system is to monitor the performance of management – and, when the need arises, to discipline or even replace management – and not to manage the company. Of course, in practice, the actual range of activities in which the supervisory board engages may span a wide spectrum, depending on numerous factors, of which the ownership structure is undoubtedly one. But it would certainly be a misunderstanding to judge a supervisory board to be unduly passive if it evaluates plans developed by the board of directors without, for example, developing alternative plans of its own. The need for caution is further underlined by the highly subjective, and therefore often vague, nature of the respondents' evaluations of the supervisory boards' role in the decision-making process.

Respondents tended not to express negative opinions concerning the role of the supervisory board. There were only two cases of unambiguously negative evaluations of the supervisory boards' performance. In one firm owned by a Polish individual investor, the supervisory board (which meets every two to three months) was described as playing no role in the decision-making process. (Accordingly, the owner was named as the only strategy maker in this firm.) Furthermore, we asked respondents whether the supervisory board was a passive or active organ, and in only one case – that of a foreign-owned firm – was passivity indicated. (This was also a firm in which the board of directors alone was named as the strategy-maker and the one in which the board meets least frequently – only once a year.) Turning to more indirect measures, we asked whether the board was rather a consultative or a decision-making organ. These were not necessarily seen as mutually exclusive categories, as two boards (in an NIF company and an employee-owned company) were described as both.

Just as a decision-making character and a consultative character are not mutually exclusive, neither is an active role necessarily associated with a decision-making, or strategic, role. While boards of a decision-making or strategic character are described as active, the reverse is not necessarily the case. Most descriptions (16) of the supervisory boards' activities listed those which are statutorily required: the boards of four companies of diverse ownership types, including two foreign-owned companies, were described as consultative organs, those of five companies as monitors and advisors to the board of directors, and those of seven were described as both (the latter two groups were also of diverse ownership structures, although neither included foreign-owned companies). While seven boards described as active were described as having monitoring and advisory roles, only four were described as decision-making organs, and two were described as strategy-makers.

We asked the respondents to identify the most active members of the supervisory board. Although we received very few answers (five), they indicate an interesting diversity. In four companies (two foreign-owned, one NIF, and one in which the state and a state agency hold the majority of shares) whose supervisory boards include employee representatives, the representatives of the owners were said to be the most active, whereas in one company owned by a Polish individual, the employee representative was the most active.

6.3.7 Who Determines the Company Strategy?

Respondents were asked who formulates the company strategy. Four companies (all foreign-owned) provided no answer. The answers received indicate that the board of directors usually plays the crucial role here, with the supervisory board usually taking the back seat. Interestingly, there seems to be no correlation between the type of ownership and the location of strategy-making responsibility, as all ownership types are represented both in the group of firms in which supervisory boards play a small role in strategy-making and in the group where they play a greater role. (Neither is there a correlation between branch and the location of strategy-making responsibility.) Another interesting observation is that owners – even in cases of strategic investors – seldom play a direct role (although the lack of answers from four foreign-owned companies may distort this picture). Six companies indicated that the board of directors alone determined strategy. Two (an NIF company and one with a Polish institutional strategic investor) indicated that the owner and the board of directors did so together, and one owned by a Polish individual investor indicated that the owner alone determined company strategy. Four indicated that strategy was formulated by the board of directors, with review and advice by the supervisory board. Six respondents stated that their firms' strategies were worked out by the board of directors and supervisory board together. Finally, in one foreign-owned firm, strategy is developed by the owner's representatives on the supervisory board.

6.3.8 Views on Corporate Governance and How to Improve it

The response rate to this question was quite good; only one firm failed to provide an answer. Nineteen companies' respondents said that there were no problems in relations between the two boards. Conflicts between the boards were only mentioned in two cases. In an NIF company, disagreement arose because the supervisory board did not agree to a share issue intended by the board of directors to increase investment funds, due to the fact that the NIF wants to maximize the price of the company's shares. In a state treasury company, the respondent state that the first supervisory board had tried to force a certain strategy on management, but that the second supervisory board works 'better' with management and problems have been eliminated.

In keeping with the generally positive evaluation of relations between the two boards, a large number (11) of respondents saw the corporate governance structure seen as adequate and did not mention any changes they believed would be desirable. Four firms did not indicate whether they saw the governance structure as adequate or in need of change.

Only five respondents commented on the role of trade unions in corporate governance. One of these did so only indirectly by saying that there were no bodies beside the two boards which had any influence on governance. Another (from a foreign-owned firm which experienced drastic employment reduction) said that trade unions in the firm had dissolved themselves in 1995. Two others (in an employee-owned company and one in which the state treasury and a state agency have controlling shares) said that trade union representatives were pragmatic and did not cause any conflicts with management. Only in one company (an NIF company) did the respondent remark that the role of trade unions was excessive and should be reduced.

Nine respondents either stated what they thought should be done to improve corporate governance or reported what was being done to improve it. One managing director of an NIF firm said that he believed the company would be better off without a supervisory board. As mentioned above, in another NIF firm, the respondent felt that the role of trade unions should be decreased. One state treasury company representative said that in his opinion supervisory board members should have capital links to the company to increase motivation. The managing director of a publicly traded company said that he was considering adding a new member to the board of directors (which had three members at the time of the interview). The director of an employee-owned company said that the decision-making process would be improved if share ownership were concentrated, with a controlling package of shares in the hands of a small group of people; he also said he would like to expand the board of directors from 2 to 3 persons. The respondent from the company owned by a Polish individual investor said that the company needs a 'new, intelligent investor' with a different development vision than the current owner's. One employee-owned company representative said that control over the firm's wholly-owned subsidiaries is to be tightened. Another respondent from an employee-owned company said that there should be an advisory body for production/quality control matters and market research. Finally, a representative of a foreign-owned company reported that corporate governance was to be improved by the introduction of computerized information systems, which should improve information flow.

6.3.9 Respondents' Overall Evaluation of Restructuring and Challenges for the Future

We asked the respondents to evaluate restructuring efforts in their companies to date by identifying the most important successes in restructuring, the deciding factors in those successes, and the problems that had not yet been addressed in the restructuring process. Eight firms provided no answer to this group of questions. In general, producers of consumer goods stressed market-oriented and production measures, while investment goods producers were more strongly represented in the groups emphasizing organizational and cost-reducing measures, as well as those emphasizing ownership transformation itself. As for restructuring problems not yet dealt with, two noteworthy observations are that companies are generally satisfied with their market-oriented measures of the past and seem to want to concentrate on production issues – especially investment – in the future and that employee-owned companies are interested in further ownership transformation.

We asked the respondents to identify the biggest challenges facing their firms in the future. Six firms provided no answer to this question. Three respondents saw their biggest challenges in the area of cost reduction, seven mentioned market-oriented measures, six mentioned production-oriented measures, and four mentioned ownership transformation itself (six provided no answer). It is interesting to note that while some employee-owned companies indicated their desire for further ownership transformation, none indicated that this area would be the most important challenge in the future.

6.4 INVESTMENT AND TRANSFORMATION OF THE PRODUCTION PROCESS

The research presented in this section is concentrated on the following issues: (1) Changes in the product range accomplished over the last six years, including main and secondary items manufactured by the enterprise. (2) Changes in the market position of enterprises measured by the share in the market. (3) Industrial adjustments of enterprises to customers' expectations and market requirements involved with the shortening of life cycles of products. (4) Methods of modernization of production. (5) Transformation of production processes, including changes to production cycles, productivity, production capacities in enterprises and their utilization over the last six years. (6) Changes in the composition of suppliers.

6.4.1 Production

Changes in the product range

Changes in the basic and secondary product range are of very different nature and scope depending on the ownership form of the analysed firm and the branch in which it operates. Very substantial changes were found in nine enterprises, of which four were privatized firms with a majority stake held by foreign owners, four were privatized firms with a majority stake held by Polish owners, and one is an NIF company. Small changes in the product range were introduced in five enterprises, of which three were privatized firms with a majority stake held by Polish owners, one was a privatized firm with a majority stake held by foreign owners and one was an NIF company. No changes were introduced to the basic product range in nine of the analysed enterprises, of which two were NIF companies, one was a state treasury company, two were privatized firms with a majority stake held by foreign owners and four were privatized firms with a majority stake held by Polish owners. Privatized enterprises having introduced no changes to their product range explained that in terms of continued requirement for items manufactured by them the problem was not the product range but product quality. Consequently, these enterprises, following their privatization, concentrated on modernization and improvement of product quality. The changes in the structure of production in surveyed enterprises were aimed at: launching new products, limiting the output or discontinuing the production of previously produced items, and increasing the production of supplementary items.

The share of newly-launched products in surveyed enterprises can be estimated at 10 to 45 per cent in most firms. The furthest-reaching changes were found in two firms having replaced as much as 90 per cent of the assortment of production (interestingly, both these enterprises are manufacturers of capital goods). The data concerning the share of new products in total production are estimates, as such records are rarely kept by companies themselves. In many cases the problem lies in classifying a product as 'novelty'. It is justified when new products require introduction of completely new technologies, different from those applied so far. The launching of new products was accompanied by the withdrawal of unprofitable and hardly marketable items from the market. Most enterprises which have not implemented any major changes to their product range embarked on product quality improvements (these issues are to be discussed later on).

Changes in the market position of enterprises

It is difficult to evaluate the market position of enterprises due to lack of complete data concerning market shares of an enterprise and its major competitors at two points in time, that is, in 1990 and 1996. Five enterprises failed to provide any data on their and their main competitors' market positions in 1990 and 1996, and four respondents were unable to specify market shares in 1990. The analysed sample included three firms currently holding monopolistic position on the market – manufacturers of capital goods, and one food-processing firm having lost its monopolistic position to foreign competitors.

The market position of the remaining surveyed enterprises for which data were available is considerably diversified. Some firms formerly held monopolistic positions and have lost them. We observe other firms with market shares as low as 0.7 per cent. Four firms dominate in their sectors over their main competitors in terms of the value of sales, although their market shares do not exceed 30 per cent. These are sectors of the engineering industry, in which the pattern of competition changed over the last six years due to the entry of foreign firms either with their finished products (imports) or through capital investment in Polish enterprises.

Two surveyed firms (both of them NIF companies) compete on local markets, with their shares in the value of sales reaching 50 per cent and showing sustained growth over the past six years. For the near future, these enterprises do not plan to undertake actions towards a substantial expansion and are still going to consolidate their position exclusively on the local market. Their long-term strategy assumes penetration of markets of the former Soviet Union.

Industrial adjustments of enterprises to customers' expectations

Industrial adjustments in the surveyed enterprises were aimed at: launching new products and new assortments of goods, introducing new products and new assortments of goods to new market segments, modification of products manufactured so far involving their modernization, improvement of quality, user's features, appearance, and so on. In addition, firms targeted the expansion of production capacities – construction of new production plants, purchase of technology lines, purchase of state-of-the-art machinery and equipment. In only 5 out of 23 surveyed enterprises were no new products introduced to the market. In the remaining firms the changes were the following: in 10 enterprises the scale of changes was very large – new production was started and products were introduced to the market, in three enterprises the scale of changes in the portfolio of goods was limited – the so-far assortments were supplemented with new items, and in two enterprises product changes were manifested by an improved appearance of products or packaging.

The already mentioned candy sector provides a good example here. These firms managed to enhance their productivity and to increase their capacities in view of a soaring market demand for their products. Polish manufacturers managed to maintain or even strengthen their position on this difficult, highly competitive and open to foreign companies market. Undoubtedly, the standing of privatized firms with a majority stake held by foreign owners is the best. Small firms operating on this market chose a strategy of copying the already established, well-selling products. Large firms in this sector stepped up their exports to the difficult markets of the European Union, the US and the former Soviet Union. Small firms enjoyed the booming market and based their exports on cross-border deals.

Engineering industry enterprises, manufacturing capital goods and so-called consumer durables did not restrict their industrial restructuring to the widening of the product range by the introduction of new products based on state-of-the-art technologies, adding new functions to their products, modification of technical and quality specifications, as well as modernization of the already manufactured products. Market changes in this sector have also resulted in undertaking new follow-up services, the extension and improvement of the maintenance network and offering financial assistance to customers. Foreign-owned firms gained competitive advantages thanks to making special offers to customers, that is offering products closely following customers' specifications and satisfying particular requirements.

Market adjustments in surveyed enterprises also covered such activities as: improvement of product quality, improved appearance of goods and packaging, new patterns (clothing sector), implementation of ISO 9000 quality standards, extension of products' storage life (foodstuffs). They also aimed at the introduction of new standards in the field of production preparation, product adjustments to individual tastes of customers, filling in market niches, the implementation of new production technologies, outward processing traffic, the creation of new enterprise structures aimed at vertical and horizontal integration, reconciling interests of suppliers and producers in achieving better quality of final goods, and channeling production to higher market segments (better product quality, higher price, more well-off but at the same time more demanding customer).

Methods of production modernization

The main ways of modernizing production by the surveyed enterprises included:

- working out their own research and development (R&D) base – in 19 surveyed enterprises;
- know-how transfer – in 17 surveyed enterprises;
- studies provided by research institutes or specialized R&D units operating in some sectors – in 5 surveyed enterprises;
- cooperation with suppliers in the field of improving the quality of final goods, in two surveyed enterprises.

Undoubtedly, the own research and development (R&D) base is of crucial significance in the product modernization in surveyed enterprises. In recent years, many firms operating on highly competitive markets have established their R&D departments, scientific laboratories and design departments. Fierce rivalry results in innovativeness, while catching up with technological and organizational progress requires regular implementation of new solutions not only in production, but also in company management processes. In some enterprises the strengthening of R&D departments brought about original patents. Know-how transfer takes various forms, including new technologies of production, new products, state-of-the-art organization and management techniques. This was the case in both the food sector and the engineering industry.

In the clothing sector, more significance is attached to the experience gained by Polish enterprises within the framework of the so-called outward processing traffic (OPT). This form of cooperation has been developed by some firms for more than ten years. Two surveyed enterprises producing finished clothing employ foreign designers. These firms argue it is a very efficient way of improving the quality of products, expanding the product range and working out features distinguishing the firm among its market competitors.

Transformations in production processes of enterprises

The modernization of production, introduction of new products and changes in the assortment structure find their consequences in changes to labor productivity and to the life cycle of products. In some of the surveyed enterprises (five firms) no relevant information was obtained, while in three firms it was stated that productivity changes and life cycle duration had not been monitored. In one enterprise the life cycle was extended by some 30 per cent, and labor productivity declined, as the output had been reduced. Fourteen surveyed enterprises saw various changes to labor productivity and to the production cycle.

Labor productivity soared (in one enterprise it went up ten-fold). The level of capacity utilization increased, also a consequence of the sale of non-productive fixed assets. (In some of the surveyed enterprises, transformations in production processes adversely affected capacity utilization. Usually, the production of unprofitable assortments was canceled, closing down entire production lines, while fixed assets remained, as their sale was not easy.)

Transformations in production processes often result from the more effective utilization of working time in firms characterized by attractive wages coupled with new work discipline standards. This refers, in particular, to enterprises privatized with a majority stake held by foreign owners, in which foreign strategic investors introduced new organization and different patterns of employee attitudes. As a result of industrial restructuring, production capacity increased in 10 enterprises, remained unchanged in seven firms, and fell in three, three enterprises failed to provide explicit information (for example, seasonal fluctuations of production and difficulties with specifying the level of capacity utilization were stressed, the scale of plant modernization was too large to compare 1990 with 1996).

Privatized firms, both those with a majority stake held by foreign owners and those with a majority stake held by Polish owners, associate changes in production process with ownership transformations. The problem lies not only in the fact of production modernization, launching new products, the acquisition of know-how, but also in genuine interest of employees in labor productivity growth (the distribution of company shares among employees contributed to improvement of the quality of work according to one respondent).

Changes in cost structure and cost management policy

We asked respondents about changes in cost structure; that is, changes in the share of various items in total costs. One firm (a foreign one) provided no information at all on this subject. There were six firms whose cost structures were fairly stable in all categories (that is, for which all changes in the shares of various items were less than 10 percentage points). These included three employee-owned firms, a firm owned by a Polish investor, and two publicly traded clothing firms.

The most frequently cited change in the cost structure was a rise in the share of materials and/or energy costs (noted in 16 firms). Eleven firms from all ownership categories except NIF noted a rise in materials and energy costs. Three firms noted a rise in materials costs alone, and two firms noted a rise in energy but not in materials costs. By way of contrast, four firms (three of which were NIF or state treasury companies) noted a fall in the share of materials and/or energy costs. There did not seem to be any patterns with respect to industrial branch.

The firms in our sample seemed to have greater success in controlling labor costs, since of the thirteen firms mentioning a change in their share, six reported a drop. Here, too, we fail to observe a pattern with respect to type of ownership. Privatized firms with dispersed shareholding – that is, employee-owned and publicly-traded companies – seem to exhibit a relatively high degree of stability in their cost structures. Privatized firms with strategic investors seem to have experienced greater increases in materials and energy costs than state treasury and NIF companies. Generally, firms appeared to be more successful at limiting the share of labor costs than the share of materials and energy. This may be due to the greater ease of simply reducing the overmanning typically inherited from the socialist era as opposed to altering the production process to make it more efficient, but also to increased quality of inputs in the production process – especially through use of Western imports. Having asked respondents about changes in the structure of costs and the reasons behind those changes, we asked them what sort of cost management policy had been implemented. Seven firms provided no information on this subject. One firm admitted openly to having no cost policy, and the answers of two others indicated indirectly that they had no policy.

We have divided cost management policies into three categories: attempts to limit costs by using inputs more sparingly; investments in technology which would reduce costs, and a strategy which was intimately linked to fundamental organizational change. The first type of policy – saving by making various kinds of cuts – was found in six firms from various branches, none of which had a strategic investor. The second cost management strategy, based on investment, was applied in four firms (two with strategic investors – one foreign and one Polish). The final type of cost management strategy, based on fundamental organizational change, was demonstrated by four firms, three of them foreign-owned. In general, NIF firms seem particularly weak on cost strategy (two had none) and foreign-owned firms seem to be strongest. With the exception of one employee-owned company which has introduced cost and profit centers, privatized firms with highly dispersed shareholding have tended to focus their cost management strategies on savings in the use of inputs, rather than on deeper changes such as investment in new technology or fundamental organizational change.

Changes in the composition of suppliers

The composition of suppliers changed in 17 surveyed enterprises, while in three it remained unchanged (three firms did not provide data). In most enterprises, the problem lies not only in the change of the composition of suppliers, but also in forging new relationships between suppliers and receivers. Changes in the structure of suppliers are often caused by transformation in the sector of suppliers themselves, for example changes resulting from privatization and restructuring, closing of many firms, inability to catch up with quality requirements, obsolete structure of production by suppliers, and so on. Such changes also result from changes in wholesale trade and in turnover in some goods. The liquidation of many intermediary levels, especially in foreign trade, required from many firms to create new links with suppliers, to look for new, better sources of raw and base materials, as well as components.

In many surveyed enterprises, especially foreign-owned firms which made sizable investment in modernization of production and quality improvements, the share of imported materials and components has increased. This was often due to the fact that growing market competition required from many enterprises, especially in the food and clothing sectors, a major boost of their products' quality, which in turn necessitated finding suppliers of better quality raw materials. For many enterprises, know-how transfer or purchase of modern technologies from foreign firms meant establishment of advantageous relationships or even capital links. This referred to privatized firms with a majority stake held by foreign owners, and also to engineering industry firms covered by our survey, which changed their product strategy and became specialized in the execution of orders placed by particular customers. However, technology transfer seems to occur quite frequently as a result of normal licensing arrangements, without ownership ties.

In the analysed food-processing and engineering industries sectors, the bargaining power of suppliers declined substantially. This fact is associated by the surveyed enterprises with privatization of the economy and its opening to foreign competition. The manufacturing and financial potential of producers of both capital and consumer goods increased so markedly that in the present situation they may impose their conditions on suppliers, and the accessibility of foreign markets adds to their bargaining power.

6.4.2 Investment Processes

The investment decisions of surveyed enterprises reflect well the overall economic climate and the assessment of future demand. The completion of investment projects in a given year reflects the expectations and financial opportunities two or three years back. The necessity to invest depends mostly on the competitiveness of markets on which the enterprise operates, and on the toughness of the financial system in the economy. Our research has also tackled investment processes in enterprises, in particular the structure of expenditures on development in real and financial terms in 1990–96 and investment objectives.

Structure of expenditures on development in real and financial terms in 1990–96

In all the surveyed enterprises, the level of investment outlays has been increasing. In most firms these outlays account for 20–40 per cent of revenues. In some enterprises, investment outlays account for 5–7 per cent of total revenues, and in only one case the expenditures were insignificant and involved purchases of computer equipment, tools and protective clothing (a NIF company). Enterprises purchase production lines, machinery and technology and set up R&D departments to introduce new products or to modernize the already produced ones. Many enterprises spend considerable amounts of their financial assets on development of their distribution networks, purchases of transport equipment, new forms of marketing, promotion and product advertising.

Sizable outlays of privatized firms in the clothing and engineering industries have been spent on improving the quality of production, as well as on research and development. These outlays were the highest in firms implementing ISO 9000 standards. Large outlays are also spent on buildings. Such investments usually involve modernization and adjustment of old factories. There are also new projects being carried out in this field, including construction of new warehouses, new production departments and complete plants. Such investments are mostly undertaken by foreign strategic investors in the food-processing industry. The investment in equity or stakes of other firms is insignificant. In only two surveyed enterprises are such endeavors aimed at the establishment of new relationships with suppliers of raw materials and subcomponents. There is still very little room for joint undertakings of enterprises competing against each other, such as joint development of a product, creation of a common distribution network, development of new technologies or entering new markets.

Investment objectives and sources of investment financing
Investment objectives of surveyed enterprises are very convergent and not differentiated by either the ownership form or branch association. The analysis shows that the major objectives of investment projects undertaken by enterprises were improvement of the enterprise's market position, improvement of product quality and creating a new image of the enterprise and product. These objectives are equally important for both privatized firms and state treasury companies. The improvement of the market position is the key issue for most surveyed enterprises, due to increased competitiveness in the sectors in which they conduct their activities. Cash flow on current activities, issuing of shares, and commerciality are of key significance for investment financing. In all privatized firms with a majority stake held by foreign owners, funds provided by the strategic investor account for a sizable share of investment outlays.

6.4.3 Market Adjustments

Before starting the analyses of the market adjustment, the investigated companies should be divided into two groups. As both the markets have different profiles, a clear division into the companies operating on the investment goods markets (firms from the machine industry) and on the consumer goods markets (companies from the clothing and food sector) is necessary to appropriately estimate the intensity of the market adjustments in the investigated companies. The contrasting profile of the markets results from the different characteristics of the offered products and the final consumers, as well as the different structure of competition on the two markets. These two markets are also characterized by different key factors determining strong market position of the companies in the long run – so-called key success factors (KSF). In addition, it should be noted that in referring to types of ownership in this chapter, firms have been divided into three categories: state-owned companies (NIF and state treasury companies), foreign-owned companies and companies privatized by Polish capital.

The respondents from the companies from the machine industry, asked to list the KSF, most frequently listed advanced technologies (seven answers among nine respondents). Next in importance, the respondents listed the quality of offered products (five answers) and production costs (four answers). Only two respondents mentioned the importance of the marketing and the well-developed distribution network.

The respondents from the food and clothing industry gave opposite responses. All respondents enumerated marketing (understood as promotion activity – sales and product and trademark promotion) as one of the KSF. In the second place, they listed distribution network and quality of the offered goods (six answers among nine respondents). Only two respondents included advanced technology as the KSF in this sector. Taking into account the above observations it should be said that the companies from the food and clothing industry make the strong market position dependent mainly on the market adjustments. According to the respondents, in the companies from the machine industry, the product adjustments play a much more important role than market adaptations. Thus, we observed a larger intensity of market adjustments in the companies from the food and clothing industry than in the investment goods group.

Turnover and sales' directions

If we analyse the output in 1990s in the investigated companies in comparison with 1980s, it appears that in the most cases the production volume has decreased or remained on the same level since 1980s.

Companies from the machine industry experienced a more significant decrease of turnover than the companies from the food and clothing industries. There is only one company from the machine industry which has increased its production capacity since the 1980s. In four companies out of the nine which gave us data about the turnover in the 1980s and 1990s, manufacturing has remained on the same level. Among these companies there are two companies privatized by foreign capital, one company privatized by domestic capital and one state-owned company. The remaining four companies (three state-owned companies and one privatized by domestic capital) have decreased production in comparison with the 1980s. It is worth mentioning that the state-owned companies have decreased their output by 50–70 per cent while the company privatized by domestic capital has decreased production only by 12–15 per cent.

In the case of the companies from the food and clothing industries, we can clearly separate the group of the companies which increased their output in the 1990s in comparison with the 1980s. There are six companies in this group – four companies privatized by foreign investors and one privatized by domestic capital and one state-owned company. It should be said that this group contains the whole population of the companies privatized by foreign capital in these industries. It also observed the largest increase of output in this group in relation with the two other firms. The remaining seven companies (four privatized by domestic capital and three state-owned) have decreased the production since 1980s.

In the 1980s export was very important for the companies from the machine industry. Among ten companies which gave us data about sales directions in 1980s, half of them placed over 40 per cent of their output on the foreign markets. The percentage share of export in relation with the total production, in some cases exceeded even 75 per cent. It is worth mentioning that the companies from the machine industry exported mainly to the former CMEA countries. Export to the Western countries was marginal. Among the investigated population, in the 1980s only three companies placed more than 90 per cent of their output on the domestic market. It should also be underlined that among five companies which exported over 40 per cent of their output in the 1980s, three companies have not been privatized yet.

The companies from the machine industry were forced to look for new customers after the collapse of the markets of former CMEA countries. It resulted in increasing interest in the domestic market as well as the export reorientation to the Western markets. Therefore in the case of the companies from the machine industry in the 1990s export does not play such a significant role as it played in the 1980s. At present there are only two companies, from the investigated population, exporting more than 40 per cent of the total output – one state-owned company and one firm privatized by foreign capital. At the same time five companies place their production mainly on the domestic market – two privatized by domestic capital, and two state-owned, and one privatized by foreign investor. In contrast to the 1980s companies from machine industry export their products mainly to the Western markets. There are only two cases – a company privatized by domestic capital and a company privatized by foreign capital – where export to the former CMEA countries exceeds export to the Western countries. Additionally, there is only one company where export to the Eastern markets amounts to 20 per cent of its total output (at the same time exports of that company to the Western countries exceeds 45 per cent of its total production). However, according to the respondents, the eastern markets have increased their attractiveness for approximately two years. It is connected with the gradual increase of demand on these markets for investment goods, and larger profitability of these markets as well as the larger credibility of the Eastern contracting parties. It is worth mentioning that the companies privatized by domestic as well as foreign capital express the largest interest in the Eastern markets.

In the case of the companies from the food and clothing industry the situation seems to be different. The companies from the food and clothing industry in the 1980s were more dependent on the domestic market than the companies from the machine industry. Among the eleven companies which gave the data about the sales directions in the 1980s, five operated mainly on the domestic market (two companies did not export at all). There were only three companies exporting over 40 per cent of their total production. It is worth mentioning that all these three companies manufacture clothing products as subcontractors of Western companies. The export in the third group of companies, exporting from 10 to 40 per cent of their total output, usually did not exceed 15–20 per cent of the total production. The most important difference of sale directions between companies from the food and clothing industries and the machine industry resulted from the export orientation. Companies from the food and clothing industries in contrast to the companies from the machine industry were not so dependent on the markets of the former CMEA countries. These companies exported their products mainly to the Western countries. It was a positive heritage of the 1980s for companies from the food and clothing industries in comparison to the machine companies. In the case of companies producing investment goods, large dependence on the eastern markets in the 1980s was the main obstacle to adapting to the new economic environment at the beginning of the 1990s. According to the respondents, the export activity of the companies from the food and clothing industries in the 1980s, operating mainly on the western markets helped them, after economic transformation, to adjust their activity to the requirements of the market economy.

In the 1990s, in the case of the companies from the food and clothing industries we cannot observe such rapid shift of sales directions as in the case of companies from machine industry. This results from the much smaller earlier dependence on the eastern markets. At present, there are four companies exporting over 40 per cent of their output. Among them there are three above-mentioned clothing companies and one food company. In the case of two clothing companies the percentage of exports in relation to the total output has even increased since the 1980s. These three clothing companies still export mainly to the western markets as in the 1980s. The food company included in this group, which exported little to the west in the 1980s and nothing to the east, now exports 60 per cent of its production to the eastern markets. In the 1990s the companies from the food and clothing industries are also more interested in the domestic market than in the 1980s. Six companies among 13 companies sell over 90 per cent of their output on the domestic market. This focus on the domestic market is shared by foreign-owned firms. The attraction of the Polish market results from its size, its present and potential high rate of growth, and its high profitability. Additionally these companies were privatized mainly by international companies, which are not interested in exporting to the markets where they already operate. In the case of the food and clothing industries we can observe the gradual domination of companies privatized by foreign investors on the Polish market (especially in the case of food companies). As these companies start to squeeze out the state-owned companies and companies privatized by domestic capital from the domestic market, the latter are forced to place their products abroad or to strengthen their position on the local markets. Among the remaining nine companies, six firms started placing their surplus output on the eastern markets in the 1990s. According to the respondents, export to the eastern markets is a large opportunity for them because it is much easier to place the products there than on the more competitive domestic and foreign markets.

In contrast to the companies privatized by foreign investors, state-owned and domestically-owned private companies (with some exceptions, especially clothing companies) operate rather as local producers. Only two companies from the food industry from the remaining two groups could be consider as producers operating on the national market – one state-owned company producing vegetable oil and one company privatized by domestic capital producing food concentrates. The rest of the companies operate as local producers.

Profitability

The increased attractiveness of the Eastern markets in the last two years for companies from the machine industry mainly results from the increased profitability of these markets in comparison with the early 1990s. In the 1980s the markets of the former CMEA countries were more profitable than the domestic market. According to the respondents, in the 1980s Western markets were the most profitable but at that time the companies from the machine industry practically did not operate on them. In the early 1990s the Eastern markets become less profitable. For many companies from the machine industry export to the markets of the former CMEA countries was very often unprofitable, and many of them were forced to give up these markets. Companies had to turn their attention to the domestic, more profitable market. The strongest and the best companies from this sector started to export to the Western, most profitable markets. In the 1980s for the companies from the food and clothing industry, in contrast to the machine industry, the CMEA markets were the least profitable. At that time the domestic and western markets were much more profitable. However, respondents said that in the 1990s the domestic market was the most profitable; the western market became less profitable mainly because of the increase of production and labor costs in comparison with the 1980s.

Distribution

The types of distribution in the two investigated groups – companies from the machine industry and the food and clothing industries – are different. This results from two factors. First, the products in both sectors are aimed at different kind of final customers. The companies from the machine industry usually meet the needs of identified final individual customers. The companies from the food and clothing industries meet the demand of anonymous mass clients. Secondly, the different profiles of products require a different approach to the distribution process (in the case of the companies from the machine industry distribution of the products is connected with their assembly).

In the case of the companies from the machine industry direct sale is the most popular way of distribution. Only in two cases was the distribution system designed differently. In addition, the distribution systems in the companies privatized by domestic as well as by foreign capital should be characterized as *uniform systems*. *Mixed systems* are noted only in the case of state-owned companies. This is due to the fact that the collapse of demand after 1990 (mainly because of the breakdown of the eastern markets) more strongly affected the companies which still remain in the state hands. These companies were forced to develop secondary product lines in order to survive on the market. However, selling on new markets very often requires the establishment of the new distribution network. Without financial support and the knowledge of market conditions, these companies were forced to pass the distribution process to the final customers – the wholesalers. This process was observed with different intensity among the three companies having mixed distribution systems.

If we analyse the intensity of the distribution adjustments in the investigated companies from the machine industry, we can affirm that the most advanced adjustments are observed in the companies privatized by the foreign investors. They are more aggressive in the area of direct contacts with the final customers. The companies privatized by foreign strategic investors also spend more funds and pay more attention to the organization of distribution networks and professional training on the field of product sale, and contacts with customers.

If we consider the distribution adjustments in the remaining two groups of investigated companies, we can affirm that the adjustments in the state-owned companies are more advanced than the adjustments in the companies privatized by domestic capital. This is due to the fact that the state-owned companies have had to look for new markets to place their output more aggressively than companies privatized by domestic capital. In contrast to the state-owned companies, companies privatized by domestic capital, especially companies privatized by MEBO, usually had a good economic and financial standing in the early 1990s. These companies were not so dependent on the eastern markets in the 1980s and at present usually keep the share of the domestic market that they had in the 1980s. Consequently distribution adjustments have a very limited scope.

The distribution adjustments in the companies from the food and clothing industries are much more intensive than in the case of companies from the machine industry. This results from the fact that a well-developed and well-organized distribution system is one of the most important factors determining the company's competitive position on the market (KSF). The intensive distribution adjustments play a much more important role in the food and clothing industries than in the machine industry.

As in the case of the group of companies from the machine industry, the most advanced distribution adjustments can be observed among the companies privatized by foreign strategic investors. These companies base their distribution systems mainly on the distribution channels of their owners. We also observed that these companies separated the distribution process from the organizational structure, usually by creating trade companies responsible for distribution. This allows for decentralizing the distribution process as well as increasing its efficiency.

The distribution adjustments in the case of the companies privatized by domestic capital are less advanced than in the companies privatized by foreign investors. They distribute their products mainly through the wholesalers. At the same time they are developing their own distribution channels. The least advanced distribution adjustments are observed in the state-owned companies. The distribution process in these companies is based mainly on direct sale to the wholesalers. At the same time, the state-owned companies are developing their own distribution networks to a smaller extent than the companies privatized by domestic capital.

Sales promotion and price policy

Before starting the analysis of the intensity of the sales promotion in the investigated companies once again the different profile of the two sectors should be pointed out. Promotion adjustments – like distribution adjustments – play a much more important role, according to the respondents, in the case of the companies from food and clothing industry.

The promotion activity of the companies from the machine industry is mainly aimed at public relations activity (PR) and direct contact (direct sales) with the final clients. Among the most frequent PR activities are specialist seminars and publications in trade magazines. Among the most frequent tools of direct sales are participation in trade fairs and organization of shows and traveling displays. In the companies from the food and clothing industries the situation is different. These companies mainly focus on advertisement activity (press, TV, radio, billboards, caisson) and promotion activity (competitions, tasting). PR activity and direct sales were observed only in the companies where the sale promotion adjustments are the most advanced.

The most advanced sales promotion adjustments among the companies from the food and clothing industry can be observed as in the companies privatized by foreign capital. These companies spend the largest funds on sales promotion. They also engage in much more PR and direct sales activity than the state-owned companies and companies privatized by domestic capital. Analysing the sale promotion adjustments we can divide the examined companies from food and clothing industry into two groups. We observe a clear division, taking into account the intensity of sales promotion adjustments, between the group of companies privatized by foreign investors and the group including state-owned companies and companies privatized by domestic capital. Here, the gap between domestically-owned private companies and state-owned companies is much smaller than that between foreign-owned companies and all the others. In the machine industry we observed a similar division between privatized companies and state-owned companies. However, here the gap between foreign-owned companies (again the best performers) and domestically-owned companies is much smaller than between foreign-owned companies and state-owned companies.

With respect to the formulation of the price policy in the examined companies, we observed a clear division between privatized companies and state-owned companies. This tendency is very clear in the companies from the machine industry as well as in those from the food and clothing industries. The privatized companies formulate the price policy adopting the market price as the base price. We noticed such behavior among almost the whole population of privatized companies. There is only one exception – the company privatized by MEBO from the machine industry, having an almost monopolistic position on its market. The state-owned companies are much less advanced in the field of price policy adjustments. Among eight such companies which gave us data about the formulation of the price policy, five companies formulate the price policy adopting as the base price the production cost of the offered products.

6.5 FINANCIAL ASPECTS OF RESTRUCTURING

While analysing financial matters one should bear in mind the problems enterprises encountered in the transformation period. In the early years of this period, the recession obviously contributed to the fall in profitability and to the deterioration of financial liquidity in the enterprise sector. Systemic solutions, such as tax regulations, exchange rates and customs tariffs also had their impact on the financial standing of enterprises. Moreover, intensive restructuring may lead to a temporary deterioration of financial results, which should be taken into account while analysing efficiency ratios and financial liquidity. With this in mind, we analyse the impact of ownership status and branch association of firms on their finance, concentrating on their initial position, sources of financing, financial standing, indebtedness and problems in the field of financial management.

6.5.1 The Outset of Transformation

The situation at the starting point of the transformation was quite important. The analyses indicate differentiated initial positions at the beginning of transformation. Most enterprises were free of the troublesome 'legacy' of the past affecting their operation and financial standing. However, in nine enterprises adverse circumstances affected their situation later on.

The burden of the former system's legacy was experienced, first of all, by three groups of enterprises: all enterprises covered by the NIF program (irrespective of branch) and privatized manufacturers of capital goods. The most difficult situation was found in the NIF companies and foreign-owned electro-engineering companies. The former group's problems were due to the long-year delay in the field of ownership, economic and organization transformations, during which time they retained their status as companies owned by the state treasury. The two foreign-owned companies reported the heaviest burden of the legacy of the past and the most difficult situation at the starting point. One was a telecommunication components manufacturer producing obsolete, non-competitive products. The other had been hit by arrears in customer payments and the loss of the eastern market, which accounted for 60 per cent of sales. Less serious troubles were faced by two engineering industry enterprises privatized with the participation of Polish investors.

The analysis of the starting point position of the surveyed firms allows two groups of problems to be distinguished depending on their sources: external and internal, depending on the enterprise. The first group includes the loss of markets (the eastern market and some segments of the domestic market, for example, the falling demand of the mining industry). The problems caused by strategic errors made at the beginning of the transformation period include lack of industrial-commercial and organizational adjustments, wrong investment policy and inefficiency in settling inter-company debts. The troublesome legacy of the past resulted in the deterioration of the financial position. Negligence in the field of adjustment strategies, mounting balance-sheet losses and indebtedness resulted in the necessity of raising restructuring funds. On the other hand, thanks to export adjustments embarked on earlier, some firms in the analysed sample reported good economic and financial standing. This group included clothing industry enterprises and major exporters to the European Union countries, as well as firms operating on particularly attractive markets (in the brewery or candy branches). Strengthening positive trends in the financial indicators of these enterprises was a priority target of their privatization.

Summing up, many enterprises entered the period of transformation with a legacy adversely affecting their financial position. In some firms these factors were external, in others they were enterprise-dependent (for example, negligence in the field of adjustment strategies). The financial position of NIF companies and manufacturers of final goods in the group with foreign investors gave rise to particular concern. Hence, their new owners have been faced with considerable challenges as regards restructuring and development of these firms.

6.5.2 Financing of Activity

Despite different approaches to the role of borrowing, it should be stated that credits were not the major source of investment financing, while current activity was supported with credits, especially when it was required by the features of activity (for example, seasonal fluctuations of production). The analysis of the entire group of enterprises points to striving at self-reliance given the high interest rate on credits. This tendency was particularly strong in privatized enterprises with good economic and financial standing, although it was present in the entire group of surveyed enterprises. However, it can be seen from the analysis of surveys that changes have occurred in the field of supporting investment programs with bank credits.

Another source of financing is the liquidation of over-expanded organization and assets, for example, through sales or lease of fixed assets, and/or changes in the profile of activities. This phenomenon was recorded in eight enterprises, both state-owned and privatized. Financial operations were also of significance in some companies. They were conducted in half of the monitored enterprises, but only in six were they a major source of financing. Privatized enterprises invested their cash flow in stakes in other firms, usually enterprises operating in the same branch and/or companies dealing with marketing and distribution of these firms' products, as well as in the shares of publicly traded companies, other securities, and time deposits.

Activity financing by borrowing

Credit was not a popular source of activity financing in our enterprises. State treasury and NIF companies reported the largest needs in the field of borrowing funds for their activity. Despite their already mentioned reluctance to borrow from banks, all these groups of firms benefited from both working-capital and investment credits. Four state treasury companies avoided credits for investment activity, but lack of external financing turned out to be a barrier to development. For several years enterprises covered by the NIF program were deprived of restructuring capital due to postponements of the program implementation. Consequently, these enterprises faced a particularly hard financial barrier to development. On the one hand, boards were forced to take credits and, on the other hand, they were afraid of being dependent on banks, and of problems with repayments. Consequently, only indispensable working-capital credits were drawn, together with loans for solving financial problems. Privatized enterprises usually experienced neither the need for borrowing funds for their activity, nor the financial barrier to development, thanks to their equity capital. This referred, first of all, to firms privatized with the participation of foreign investors. The financial potential of investors allowed firms threatened with bankruptcy to survive, and speeded up the development of enterprises enjoying good financial standing. Borrowing was limited here to small working-capital credits, while investment credits were taken only occasionally. Despite its lack of popularity, in most monitored enterprises the accessibility of bank credit was evaluated positively (they could get loans if they wanted them).

Summing up, the surveyed enterprises were cautious about resorting to credits. State-owned firms were forced to take investment credits as they run into the financial barrier of development. Private companies relying on their equity usually did not take investment credit, but supported their current operation with working-capital credits. Despite the improvement of relations with banks following privatization, bank credit remained a secondary source of activity financing.

Sale and lease of assets

The restructuring of organization and assets resulted in the intensification of getting rid of assets through sale or lease. This was most important for the manufacturers of capital goods, relatively badly hit by the recession of the early years of the transformation. In state treasury companies the sale and lease of assets were a major source of revenues. Firms from this group were characterized by the extent of their over-expanded assets. Restructuring of a defensive, austere nature was accompanied by processes from the sales of assets. Among companies in this group, only one neither sold nor leased its assets. In one firm owned by an NIF, sale (and to a smaller extent also lease) of assets was also a major source of revenue (above 10 per cent of the value of sales). In the case of companies from the foreign privatization group, the sale and lease of assets meant 'paving the way' for expansive strategies. In general, unlike some state treasury and NIF companies, privatized enterprises treated revenue from the sale of assets as a short-term consequence of regular defensive activities ('paving the way' for strategic transformations). In the former groups of firms, where radical changes had not taken place, the gradual selling out of parts of assets aging both economically and materially was seen as an additional source of financing the activity throughout a period longer than in private companies, where the funds contributed by investors allow them to speed up the restructuring.

Financial operations
Financial operations were not a significant field of activity for the monitored firms. Less than half of the analysed companies were involved in major financial operations, and in only some of them were these operations regarded as a significant source of activity financing. In the group of state treasury companies and NIF only one enterprise (a state treasury company) conducted financial operations on a significant scale. More intensive activity in this field was conducted by some privatized enterprises. Examples include: equity investments by a brewing company, a well-known listed company operating in the textile branch, and an engineering industry company, and investment in time deposits and securities by the candy enterprise from the 'foreign privatization' group.

6.5.3 Financial Standing

Ability to generate profits
The analysis of gross profitability reveals an interesting and differentiated picture. The indicators for the first half of 1996 are not surprising. Privatized enterprises have better abilities to generate profits than state treasury companies and enterprises covered by the NIF program. A look at firms from the 'state' group (state treasury and NIF companies) shows similar (low) levels of profitability. On the other hand, the generally higher profitability of private companies is differentiated, as firms from the Polish privatization group record the highest profitability in the entire population, exceeding as much as three times the average indicator for the foreign privatization group. In 1995–96, the latter was the lowest in the entire sample, but has been recording a very fast growth rate since 1993.

State treasury companies are characterized by a high and increasing growth rate in 1992–94. The analysis of these companies reveals opportunities in the field of restructuring rooted in defensive adjustment strategies. State treasury companies reorganized their structures by getting rid of over-expanded assets, controlled their costs by introducing internal cost accounting and eliminated market inertia by developing marketing structures. Industrial adjustments and modernization of the productive potential were also of relevance in this context. The restructuring of state-owned enterprises stabilized at a fairly high level. This was the period of consuming the austerity effects of (largely) defensive strategies. In 1996, gross profitability declined almost threefold. State-owned enterprises deprived of external financing faced the consequences of capital barriers. A diminishing ability to generate profits is the result of a shortage of restructuring capital, as well as the exhaustion of positive effects of utilization of the existing potential.

The situation of NIF companies was different. The postponement of the program's implementation resulted in the halting of restructuring undertakings for several years. Gross profitability, low in 1992, declined below zero a year later. The implementation of the NIF program at the end of 1995 did not bring any improvement of efficiency ratios. Gross profitability dropped by 1.5 percentage points in 1995 and another 2 percentage points in the first half of 1996, when it reached the level of 5.3 per cent. If NIF and state treasury companies are taken as one group, which is justified given their long-time operation as state-owned enterprises, we shall see a gradual increase in the ability to generate profits until 1994, when gross profitability peaked, followed by a decline through the end of 1996 caused by lack of external financing.

Firms from the Polish privatization group showed, as a rule, favorable and stable profitability indicators. Interesting conclusions can be drawn from the comparison of the indicator for this group between 1994 and June 1996 and that for state treasury companies. In privatized firms profitability declined only insignificantly, while in state-owned enterprises it plummeted as much as threefold. Moreover, in the case of the Polish privatization group the decline in the average profitability ratio is caused by the diminishing ability to generate profit in only one firm (in 1995 it recorded a balance-sheet loss). There are several reasons for the high profitability of the analysed firms in this group. Six of these firms are publicly traded companies, whose finances were solid at the time of their initial public offerings. Following their privatization, these firms enjoyed financing (issues of shares, contributions made by foreign partners) as well as promotion effects connected with their status as public companies. Generally, firms from this group recorded the highest and at the same time the most stable gross profitability in the whole sample. (However, these enterprises also had the best starting point.)

A more differentiated situation was found in the group of enterprises privatized with the participation of foreign investors. On average, they recorded the lowest profitability in the first half of 1996, and by far the fastest growth rate in the whole analysed sample (the increase in the average value of the indicator for the group was almost 20 percentage points). However, the 'foreign privatization' group was not homogeneous. Two firms found themselves on the verge of bankruptcy in 1993. In both cases, profitability dropped to disastrous levels (–68.8 per cent and –79.4 per cent, respectively). Restructuring capital contributed by the foreign investor allowed them to recover from the deep collapse.

The remaining firms from this group were characterized by their stable ability to generate profits; however, apart from the above-mentioned 'convalescing' firms and one candy enterprise, their profitability declined in the first half of 1996 compared to the same period of 1995. Foreign investors interested in high rates of return in the long run were pursuing their development strategies, which incurred high costs. This phenomenon also occurred in the Polish privatization group, but on a smaller scale.

The analysis of net profitability confirms the above conclusions and findings concerning gross profitability. Better performance of 'foreign privatization' than in the case of the gross indicator results from tax incentives for firms privatized with the participation of foreign investors. In addition, the value of profitability ratios in the analysed sample was dependent on branch affiliation of a given firm. Three manufacturers of capital goods recorded negative profitability. The improved ability to generate profits by privatized enterprises is also indicated by the return on their assets. In most firms analysed, the return on assets declined in 1994 compared to the previous year. That year of favorable business trends encouraged optimistic forecasts, which were another incentive for modernization and expansion of the productive potential. The improvement of enterprises' financial results allowed for increased purchases of capital goods. With the growth rate of productive assets outpacing that of profits, the rates of return on assets were declining in that period.

The sharpest drop was recorded in the foreign privatization group where, despite an improvement, the return on assets was negative as recently as in 1994. External contributions made by investors were the main source of financing of the growing assets. After 1994, the return on assets in the group of foreign privatization had been growing steadily by the end of the period covered by our analysis. In the Polish privatization group, a drop in the return on sales caused by growing investment expenditures occurred in 1995. However, the average value of the indicator for all privatized firms has been growing (thanks to its fast increase in the foreign group). The indicators for NIF and state treasury companies were stable in the whole period of 1992–95. At the end of the analysed period, the tendencies in the field of return on assets became divergent, as the ability to generate profit is quickly declining in state treasury companies, while improving in firms covered by the NIF program.

In privatized firms, the return on assets for the entire group had been growing since 1994 and for both sub-groups since 1995, which might be an indication of this favorable trend becoming permanent. Another factor of this indicator's growth was the already mentioned sale of assets, decreasing the value of the denominator of the return on assets ratio (particularly in the case of firms from the foreign group). Considerable sales of assets were also recorded in state treasury companies, although they did not affect significantly the value of the return on assets, due to the stronger downward tendency of profitability.

The analysis of return on equity confirms the higher ability to generate profits by private companies. In this regard, enterprises from the Polish privatization group turned out to be the most stable ones, as they managed to maintain high profitability and a high return on equity throughout the whole analysed period. Favorable ratios recorded by state treasury companies deteriorated after 1995, while those of NIF companies became more favorable in 1996, which might be an indication of early symptoms of transformation. The most substantial improvement of efficiency ratios was shown by firms from the foreign privatization group due to financing from external sources and strategic adjustments made by investors. It should also be noted that the value of return on assets and equity ratios was, as in the case of profitability, branch-dependent. The most serious difficulties were experienced here by firms from the electro-engineering branch (in the foreign privatization group).

Financial liquidity

In the analysed group of companies, financial liquidity indicators were relatively favorable. Taking into account average values for the entire sample it can be argued that they were 'model' figures. Differences were found between various groups of firms and between individual enterprises. The overall liquidity ratio was more favorable in privatized firms, being 1.5 times higher than in state treasury and NIF companies. The former recorded an increase in the overall liquidity ratio in 1995, when the value of this ratio was the most favorable in the entire period. In 1995, the current ratio in the group of state treasury companies amounted to 2.0.[23] The decline in 1996 was to a small extent caused by the rise in short-term liabilities supporting current operations (in the case of lack of external financing). The main reason for the fall in this liquidity ratio was the decline in stocks of finished products and in available funds.

If we look at individual enterprises, the picture is less favorable. In 1995 one engineering industry enterprise had a liquidity ratio of 4.2. This figure indicates irrational management of enterprise's assets, leading to a rise in inventories and in unutilized cash flow. The later decline in the level of the liquidity ratio in the enterprise (to 2.6 in the middle of 1996) points to an improvement in working assets management. In the remaining enterprises, in 1995 the value of the analysed ratio did not exceed 1.5 and improved in only one case.

The current ratio reached, on average, a higher level in firms covered by the NIF program. This ratio had been growing since 1992, reaching its (irrational) maximum level of 4.0 in 1994. Then it declined to 1.8 in the middle of 1996. This rise in the current ratio must be interpreted as an unwelcome development, and its later decline indicated an improvement in assets management. The improvement recorded in 1995 was the consequence of better marketing techniques and reduced stocks of finished products. In the middle of 1996, however, the ratio fell, on average, below its welcome level. One firm still recorded a very high ratio (although it fell from 5.8 in 1994 to 3.2 in the middle of 1996), while in another firm this ratio was low (1.0), as a consequence of short-term liabilities.

Generally, privatized enterprises have the better liquidity indicators. Companies from the Polish privatization group showed the highest and most stable average liquidity ratios. Their level was particularly high in the case of publicly traded companies operating in the clothing branch, which in order to cope with competition would accumulate large stocks of finished products before the start of the season. In the Polish group, manufacturers of capital goods recorded stable levels of liquidity. One of them was characterized by excess liquidity (with the current ratio ranging from 4.2 to 5.2).

The foreign group was characterized by favorable (on average) financial liquidity. The level of the quick ratio confirms the above findings concerning better liquidity of privatized companies. The quick ratio clearly shows some slight excess liquidity of the Polish group, pointing to imperfections in managing the assets of enterprises.

6.5.4 The Structure of the Debt

Enterprises were cautious about borrowing, with short-term credits clearly dominating. Investment projects were financed mostly with own funds or contributions made by foreign investors. Despite the positive evaluation of the banking system mentioned in sub-section 6.3 and the availability of credits, enterprises were afraid of long-term indebtedness (due to high interest costs), and privatized firms clearly preferred relying on investors' contributions equity. The common application of working-capital credits, and their substantial share in the structure of liabilities, resulted from the specific features of branches.

The analysis of liabilities and receivables points to the diminishing role of inter-company debts. In all the monitored enterprises inter-company debts had no significant impact on their financial position in 1995–96. The most frequently repeated declaration of our respondents, confirmed by the analysis of their financial records, was that inter-company debts had been a problem in the early 1990s, but their significance had since dwindled.

Another problem here was the collection of overdue debts. Enterprises resorted to virtually all legal methods of debt collection. The most popular ones were contracts with debtors. When all other possibilities are exhausted, debtors are taken to court. Problems with overdue debts have led to the establishment of departments and teams in charge of debt collection. There is no apparent relationship between the ownership status or branch and the efficiency of solving this problem, which has lost importance over the course of the decade.

6.5.5 Financial Restructuring

Our analysis of financial restructuring allows us to divide the firms into three clearly distinct groups. The first of them is made up of state treasury and NIF companies. Most firms from this group concluded agreements with creditors, some with and some without debt–equity swaps. Two enterprises from this group were not taking any steps towards restructuring of their debts, which they are managing to repay without recourse to agreements with creditors.

In the Polish privatization group, the needs in the field of financial restructuring were less conspicuous. On the one hand, this was due to financing by owners, and, on the other hand, most firms from this group were publicly traded companies with good financial standing both prior to and after privatization. Among firms from the Polish privatization group only one was a party to an agreement with debtors.

In the foreign privatization group, improvement of the financial situation was secured by financing from external sources (all enterprises have been re-capitalized) and by comprehensive organizational, industrial and commercial restructuring, as well as debt reduction in firms characterized by poor financial standing.

6.6 CONCLUSIONS

In addition to the impact of initial conditions in the early transformation period on the financial situation of the entire analysed group of enterprises, ownership status is the most important factor differentiating the sample, followed by branch affiliation. Our research has confirmed the most general conclusion outlined in other studies, namely that the best financial standing or the fastest growth rate was recorded by privatized enterprises, especially foreign-owned ones. Equity capital leads to positive qualitative changes in the operation and structure of enterprises. The condition and dynamics of financial indicators constitute a composite measure for evaluating adjustment strategies. Ownership effects are apparent in the companies' profitability and liquidity measures. Financial transfers by investors and/or new issues of shares contributed to a positive change in efficiency ratios of restructured firms or financial stabilization of viable firms, especially those which have been operating for a relatively long time as privatized companies. The indicators for state treasury companies and firms from the Polish privatization group were similar through 1995, at which point these tendencies became divergent: privatized firms have stabilized, while state-owned firms have been hit by a dramatic decline caused by the capital shortage barrier. NIF companies were in decline during several years of 'privatization limbo', but showed an improvement in 1994 – a period of economic revival. However, the following years again brought some deterioration, though it may be too early for the effects of the program to crop up in the form of improved financial results. Firms from the foreign privatization group showed a fast growth rate thanks to financial contributions from foreign investors, while the fall in efficiency ratios at the end of the analysed period points to an increase in costs of adjustment to growing competition. Privatized firms also showed better debt-servicing ability.

NOTES

1. Under the first privatization program (announced in November 1990) 15 per cent of the state assets were to be privatized in 1991 and 20 per cent in each of the subsequent three years. See also '*Podstawowe kierunki...*' (1990).
2. See Ministry of Privatization (1991).
3. Moreover, in many cases an open hostility against foreign capital investment was expressed. See comparative opinion polls on the attitude toward foreign investments in Poland and Russia in summer 1992. (Blaszczyk and Dabrowski, 1994).
4. In cases in which commercial methods were used (referred to in Poland as capital, or indirect, privatization) employees had the right to acquire up to 20 per cent of their company's shares at a preferential price (50 per cent of the issue price). In cases of liquidation, or direct privatization, in which the leasing method was used, employees had the priority over other bidders. In all cases (excluding liquidation on the basis of the 1981 state enterprise law for reasons of poor financial standing), employees and management had the right to veto any privatization proposal.
5. Employees may acquire up to 15 per cent of the shares in their companies free of charge. A further 15 per cent is available free of charge to farmers and fishermen supplying a given company on a permanent basis. Former employees on retirement and disability pensions also have the right to obtain shares from this pool. The shares acquired free of charge may not be sold for two years following acquisition, and for three years in the case of managerial employees. The law also gives the government the right to extend these periods.
6. Under the new law only enterprises employing up to 500 persons the annual sales of up to ECU 6 million and own funds of up to ECU 2 million may be privatized using the direct privatization methods.
7. The shares were allocated in the following manner: 60 per cent of the total shares of each company was entrusted with the funds, 15 per cent given free of charge to the employees and the remaining 25 per cent being temporarily held by the state treasury with a view to later supporting pension funds and compensating holders of various claims on the state treasury. In accordance with the law, the 60 per cent of each company's shares distributed among the 15 funds were divided into majority and minority stakes in order to avoid excessive dispersion of shares. More specifically, 33 per cent of each company's shares was vested in one of the 15 funds, while the other 27 per cent was evenly distributed among the remaining 14. The minority stakes can be freely traded, while the majority stakes can be sold only *en bloc*.
8. Central Statistical Office (1997) p. 16.
9. As of December 1996, 66 per cent of direct privatization transactions were leasing arrangements, 21.6 per cent were direct sales, and only 6.2 per cent cases of in kind contribution to a company (see Ministerstwo Skarbu Państwa, 1996b).
10. Ministerstwo Skarbu Państwa (1996a).

11. See Central Statistical Office, *Small Statistical Yearbook*, 1994, 1995, 1996, 1997; Central Statistical Office, 'Structural changes in groups of entities in the national economy, 1991, 1992, 1994, 1995 and 1996'.
12. See Ministerstwo Skarbu Pañstwa (1996a). The State Foreign Investment Agency gathers data on the largest investments only (exceeding $US 1 million). However, such projects constitute approximately 80 per cent of total foreign investments.
13. According to official statistics, in 1989 the private sector share in GDP was only 19.2 per cent, and the share of the private non-agricultural sector 9.2 per cent. Cooperatives, then generating approximately 10 per cent of GDP, were not included in the private sector, but rather in the so-called collectivized sector. In order to facilitate comparative analysis we have included cooperatives in the private sector for the entire period; hence the 30 per cent figure. For 1995: OECD estimates. See also, Blaszczyk, Bratkowski and Dabrowski (1996).
14. Excluding non-material services, tariffs and taxes, for which the importance of GDP is systematically growing.
15. Author's own calculations based on Central Statistical Office, *Small Statistical Yearbook 1997*, pp. 352–3.
16. Most recently this opinion was voiced by Yoshiyuki Takemoto, the President of Daiva Europe Limited and Jacek Krawczyk, the President of IB Austria Securities (Warszawa) SA.
17. The annual volume of these proceeds constituted between 0.8 and 3.2 per cent of total revenues and between 0.2 and 0.9 per cent of GDP.
18. See: 'Ocena przebiegu procesów gospodarczych w 1995 r. na tle lat 1990–1994', Centralny Urzad Planowania, May 1996, and Antczak (1996).
19. See *Ekonomiczne i spoleczne efekty prywatyzacji poœredniej i bezpoœredniej. Analiza porównawcza kondycji ekonomicznej i dzialañ dostosowawczych przedsiêbiorstw ob jêtych przeksztalceniami wlasnoœciowymi w latach 1990–95* (1996), Instytut Badañ nad Gospodarka Rynkowa, Gdañsk-Warszawa, and Dabrowski et al. (1991, 1993).
20. See Carlin et al., (1995). See also Belka (1995), Pinto (1993) and Maczyñska (1997).
21. This was a tax paid by state enterprises based on the book value of their assets.
22. This was a tax paid for wage increases exceeding centrally-set norms.
23. In the literature it is assumed that the minimum value for this ratio is 2.0. See Heddenich (1988).

REFERENCES

Antczak, M. (1996), 'Income from the Privatization of State Enterprises in Poland, Hungary and the Czech Republic in 1991–1994', *Studies & Analyses* No. 80. Warsaw: CASE.

Balcerowicz, L., Blaszczyk, B. and Dabrowski, M. (1996), 'The Polish Way to the Market Economy', in Wing Thye Woo, Stephen Parker and Jeffrey D. Sachs (eds), *Economies in Transition: Comparing Asia and Eastern Europe,* Cambridge, MA and London: The MIT Press. pp. 131–60.

Belka, M., Estrin, S., Schaffer, M. and Singh, I.J. (1995), *Enterprise Adjustment in Poland; Evidence from a Survey of 200 Private, Privatized and State-Owned Firms*, London: LSE, Centre for Economic Performance, Discussion Paper 233.

Belka, M., Hausner, J., Jasiñski, L.J., Marody, M. and Zirk-Sadowski, M. (1996), *Polska transformacja w perspektywie integracji europejskiej. EU-monitoring* (The Polish Transformation in the Perspective of European Integration: An EU Report), Warsaw: Friedrich Ebert Foundation.

Blaszczyk, B. (1995), 'Various Approaches to Privatization in Poland, their Implementation and the Remaining Privatization Potential,' in W. Quaisser, R. Woodward and B. Blaszczyk (eds), *Privatization in Poland and East Germany: A Comparison*, München: Osteuropa-Institut, pp. 73–110.

Blaszczyk, B. (1996), 'Privatization in Poland', in B. Blaszczyk and R. Woodward (eds), *Privatization in Post-Communist Countries,* Warsaw: CASE, pp. 177–206.

Blaszczyk, B. (1997a), 'Privatization in Poland: Accomplishments, Delays and Things to Do', *Economic Scenarios for Poland: Conference papers*, CASE Reports No. 5, Warsaw.

Blaszczyk, B. (1997b), *Prywatyzacja w Polsce po szeœciu latach: Osilgniêcia, opóznienia I pozldane kierunki dalszych dzialañ* (Polish Privatization after Six Years: Accomplishments, Delays and Things to Do), CASE Reports No. 9, Warsaw.

Blaszczyk, B. and Dabrowski, M. (1994), 'The Privatization Process in Poland', in Y. Akyüz, D.J. Kotte, A. Köves and L. Szamuely (eds), *Privatization in the Transition Process: Recent Experiences in Eastern Europe,* United Nations Conference on Trade and Development and Kopint-Datorg Foundation for Economic Research, pp. 85–118.

Blaszczyk, B., Bratkowski, A.S. and Dabrowski, M. (1996), 'Recent Macroeconomic Trends and Policies: 1990–1995', *Eastern Europe's Tiger – Poland,* Vienna: Bank Austria.

Carlin W., Van Reenen, J. and Wolfe, T. (1995), 'Enterprise Restructuring in Early Transition: The Case Study Evidence from Central and Eastern Europe', *Economics of Transition,* **3** (4), 427–58.

Carter, L., Sader, F., and Holtedahl, P. (1996), *Foreign Direct Investment in Central and Eastern European Infrastructure,* Foreign Investment Advisory Service, Washington DC: The World Bank, September.

Centralny Urzad Planowania (Central Planning Office) (1997), *Ocena sytuacji spoleczno-gospodarczej w polowie 1997 r* (Assessment of the Social and Economic Situation in the First Half of 1997), Warsaw, July 1997.

Dabrowski, J.M. (1995), 'The Results of "Capital" Privatization in Poland', in W. Quaisser, R. Woodward and B. Blaszczyk (eds), *Privatization in Poland and East Germany: A Comparison,* München: Osteuropa-Institut, pp. 289–302.

Dabrowski, J.M., Federowicz, M. and Levitas, A. (1991), 'Polish State Enterprises and the Properties of Performance: Stabilization, Privatization, Marketization', *Politics and Society* **19**, (4).403–37.

Dabrowski, J.M., Federowicz, M. and Levitas, A. (1993), 'State Enterprises in the Process of Economic Transformation, 1992–1993: Research Findings', Gdansk: Instytut Badañ nad Gospodarka Rynkowa.

Earle, J., Frydman, R., Rapaczyñski, A. and Turkewitz, J. (1994), *Small Privatization: The Transformation of Retail Trade and Consumer Services in the Czech Republic, Hungary and Poland*, London: Central European University Press.

Glówny Urzad Statystyczny, *Prywatyzacja przedsiêbiorstw pañstwowych: Stan na koniec* (Privatization of State Enterprises as of the End of 1994, 1995, 1996), several issues, Warsaw: Central Statistical Office.

Glówny Urzad Statystyczny (1996), *Zmiany strukturalne grup podmiotów gospodarczych. Stan na koniec 1996 r* (Structural transformations within groups of businesses as of the end 1996). Warsaw: Central Statistical Office.

Grosfeld, I. and Roland, G. (1996), 'Defensive and Strategic Restructuring in Central European Enterprises', *Journal of Transforming Economies and Societies,* **3** (4).

Grosfeld, Irena and Nivet, Jean-François (1998), 'Insider Power and Wage Setting in Transition: Evidence from a Panel of Large Polish Firms, 1988-1994', paper prepared for the European Economic Association Congress, Berlin, September 2–5, 1998.

Heddenich, K. (1988), *Financial and Economic Analysis of Enterprises*, Geneva: ILO.

Jarosz, M. (ed.) (1996), *Polish Employee-Owned Companies in 1995,* Warsaw.

Kamiñski, T. (1996), 'Wplyw prywatyzacji na przeobrazenia przedsiebiorstw. Studium przypadkow' (The Influence of Privatization on Enterprise Transformation), Warsaw: CASE Reports No 1.

Koniunktura gospodarcza Polski (1997), Warsaw: Centrum Adama Smitha.

Lipowski, A. (1998), *Towards Normality: Overcoming the Heritage of Central Planning Economy in Poland in 1990-1994*, Warsaw: CASE and Centrum Adama Smitha.

Macieja, J. (1997), 'Pañstwowe jest grojyne' (State-Owned is Dangerous), *Gazeta Wyborcza*, 29 January.

Maczynska, E. and Zawadzki, M. (1997), *Zrodla finansowania rozwoju przedsiebiorstw w procesie transformacji*, in J. Mujzel (ed.), *Przedsiebiorstwa w procesie transformacji* (Enterprises in Transition), Institute of Economics, Warsaw: Polish Academy of Sciences, pp. 191–226.

Ministerstwo Przeksztalceñ Wlasnoœciowych (Ministry of Privatization) (1991), *Privatization in Poland. Program and Achievements*, 2nd edition. Warsaw.

Ministerstwo Przeksztalceñ Wlasnoœciowych (1996) *Program prywatyzacji zasobow majatku panstwowego do roku 2000* (The National Assets Privatization Program through the Year 2000), Warsaw, 25 November.

Ministerstwo Skarbu Pañstwa (Ministry of the State Treasury) (1996a), *Dynamika Przeksztalceñ Wlasnoœciowych* (Ownership Transformation Pace) No. 30, 31. Warsaw.

Ministerstwo Skarbu Pañstwa (1996b), *Raport o przeksztalceniach wlasnoœciowych w 1995 roku, w 1996 roku* (Report on Ownership Transformations in 1995, and in 1996), Warsaw.

Mujzel, J. (ed) (1997), *Przedsiêbiorstwa w procesie transformacji* (Enterprises in Transition), Institute of Economics, Warsaw: Polish Academy of Sciences.

PAIZ (The State Foreign Investment Agency) (1996), *Inwestycje zagraniczne w Polsce w 1995 r., 1996 r.* (1995 and 1996 Foreign Investments in Poland), Warsaw.

Pinto, B., Belka, M. and Krajewski, S. (1993), *Transforming State Enterprises in Poland Microeconomic Evidence on Adjustment,* World Bank Policy Research Working Paper WPS 1101.

Podstawowe kierunki prywatyzacji w 1990 r (*Basic Privatization Paths in 1990*), *Monitor Polski* No. 13/1990.

Pohl, G., Anderson, R.E., Claessens, S. and Djankov, S. (1997), *Privatization and Restructuring in Central and Eastern Europe. Evidence and Policy Options*, World Bank Technical Paper No. 368, Washington, DC, August 1997.

Rzeczpospolita, 16 April and 9 September, 1997.

Small Statistical Yearbook 1997, Warsaw: Central Statistical Office.

Statistical Yearbook, several issues, Warsaw: Central Statistical Office.

Woo, W.T., Parker, S. and Sachs, J.D. (eds) (1997), *Economies in Transition: Comparing Asia and Eastern Europe,* Cambridge, MA and London: The MIT Press.

7. Company Restructuring after Privatization in a Comparative Perspective: Lessons from Four Central and East European Countries

Iván Major

In the previous chapters we have tried to confront the facts of economic transformation in the CEE countries with the common wisdom of economic theory about property rights, privatization and the emergence of economic institutions. First we showed that the traditional approaches to East European privatization tell us little about the actual ways in which CEE countries transformed their system of state ownership into a system of private property rights. Then the country studies that are included in the book extensively discussed the ways of privatization, the new forms of corporate governance, and the successes and failures of company restructuring in the respective CEE countries after the political changes of the late 1980s and early 1990s. In this chapter we briefly sum up some of the main findings of the teams' two years research.

7.1 PRIVATIZATION: SIMILARITY IN PRINCIPLES – DIVERSITY IN METHODS AND IN PROGRESS

The four CEE countries that are represented in the book started privatization with different backgrounds and at different moments in time. Hungary and Poland had experimented with economic reforms before the systemic change, while Bulgaria and Estonia were forced to take a 'jump start'. Privatization started in Hungary and in Poland in the late 1980s, but it has only occurred since 1992 in Estonia and in Bulgaria. Nevertheless, the principles that guided the privatization process were very similar in each country, while the actual methods showed a large variety.

7.1.1 Principles and Methods of Privatization

The struggle for higher economic efficiency on the one hand, and 'to do justice' to those whose property had been expropriated either by the pre-war or by the communist regimes on the other, fostered privatization in the CEE countries. In addition, the countries' indebtedness to the West also supported the drive for privatization in the form of the sale of state-owned property to foreign investors. Moreover, the CEE governments expected sizable revenues to flow into the central budget from privatization.

There has been an ongoing debate in each CEE country as to whether privatization should be done swiftly or with care and during a longer period of time. Moreover, how can the requirements of social justice be honored, and what methods can serve this purpose the best? A multiple rather than a homogenous approach to privatization was adopted in each country. But the weight of the different methods substantially diverged country by country. An extensive free distribution of the state-owned property had dominated the Polish privatization program in its initial phase. But later, the ESOP type methods, privatization by liquidation and 'capital privatization', that is, first corporatization, then a case-by-case sale of the SOEs became dominant in Poland. In April 1993, the Act on National Investment Funds (NIF) was passed. This law formed the basis for the mass privatization program, allowing every adult Polish citizen to acquire a portion of national assets for a nominal charge. The NIF program was designed to speed up the privatization process, but its implementation did not begin until the end of 1995. In the first half of 1997, the NIF program entered a more advanced stage, with shares of the 15 funds being listed on the Warsaw Stock Exchange.

The organization and operation of the German Treuhandanstalt served as a model for the Estonian privatization. Consequently, direct sales and acquisitions by foreign investors played the most important role in that country. As was shown in the Estonian chapter, the centrally administered privatization turned out to be a very expensive venture. A large part of the revenues from privatization was deducted by the privatization agency to cover its own operating expenditures. In addition to direct sales, a voucher scheme was also applied in Estonia. Bulgaria also intended to sell its state-owned property to foreign investors. In addition, MBO, LMBO and ESOP type privatizations have been extensively used in Bulgarian privatization. A direct sale of the state-owned assets to foreign and domestic private owners set the framework of privatization in Hungary. But a complex scheme of compensation was also used that proved to be a special form of free distribution of the state-owned property.

Privatization has progressed more slowly than had been originally expected by the CEE countries. The main reason for the extensive time requirements cannot be attributed to the thoroughness of the privatization agencies. It was rather the consequence of the political clashes that surrounded each privatization deal. Still, a large part of the formerly state-owned assets was turned into private hands in Estonia, Hungary and in Poland. The process has lagged behind in Bulgaria.

Evidence from the four CEE countries shows that the companies' economic performance after privatization is not neutral to the way that these companies had been privatized. In most cases, a decentralized method of privatization proved to be more successful in terms of after-privatization performance than privatizations that had been administered by government agencies. Moreover, privatization by foreign investors resulted in better performing companies in the medium run than privatization by domestic private investors.

The expansion of the private sector went the furthest in Hungary among the four CEE countries. But Poland and Estonia closely followed Hungary. The share of the private sector approached 70 per cent as regards employment and GDP production in Hungary by late 1997. Over 60 per cent of GDP was created in the private sector, which employed over 65 per cent of the labor force in Poland in 1997. Data on the book value of national assets, which was accessible only for the end of 1995, show that the private sector had no advantage over the public sector, as the public sector's share in national assets was still 59.7 per cent in Poland. The share of the private sector was considerably smaller in Bulgaria than in the other three countries.

What can be told about the actual results of privatization in relation to the original principles and goals of the CEE governments? Although slower than had been envisioned, the economic efficiency of the privatized companies improved in all CEE countries as a consequence of privatization. But the principles of social justice have frequently been violated and the government revenues from privatization have been smaller than had been expected at the start of the process. Hungary seems to be the most successful in this regard, after the country sold a large portion of its utilities to foreign investors. However, it should be noted that a sizable share of the formerly state-owned assets vanished during privatization. A part of these assets was liquidated, but a substantial part was channeled to the loyal supporters of the ruling political parties against a nominal price. We can conclude that the most important result of the expansion of the private sector was that the former system of a monolithic state ownership and political control of the CEE economies was abolished. But the private sector still needs some time to prove its superiority over the state ownership as regards economic efficiency and international competitiveness of the companies.

7.1.2 Privatization and the Expansion of the Private Sector

The country studies showed that privatization of the state-owned property was not the only, and it was not even the most robust, form of the expansion of the private sector in the CEE countries. Start-up private businesses, green field investments of the foreign and domestic investors, the penetration of multinational companies in the CEE economies also largely contributed to the radical change of property rights in CEE. Several analysts assert that privatization has been just a minor part of the ownership changes. The above assertion may be true as regards the share of the privatized assets relative to the total privately owned assets in the CEE countries. However, it is not just the number of the privatized companies, or the value of total privatized assets that counts. The privatization of key SOEs had a triggering and it also had a multiplying effect on the ensuing private investments in the CEE countries. Privatization was an important proof of the commitment of the CEE governments to the systemic changes. It also opened up markets for additional investors. Consequently, privatization of the state-owned enterprises and the expansion of the private sector via new private businesses boosted each other. The above assertion was best illustrated by the Polish case.

The quantitative growth of the private sector in Poland was primarily due to the so-called *de novo* privatization – that is, private sector development through the establishment of brand new companies – and to a much smaller extent to the privatization of already existing state-owned enterprises. This statement can be illustrated by the following facts: as of the end of 1996, over 400 000 persons were employed in the 'privatized' sector (that is, formerly state-owned enterprises), whereas the entire private non-agricultural sector employed over 5 million persons (out of 15 million employed persons in the entire economy, of which 10 million were in the non-agricultural sector). Thus, employment in the privatized sector represented 8 per cent of private sector employment and 2.6 per cent of total employment. The entire group of enterprises which had initiated ownership transformation (whether completed or not) employed slightly less than 1.5 million persons, or about 10 per cent of the national labor force. (And 30 per cent of the employment in the private sector came from this group.) Although this figure indicates that this group of enterprises constituted an important element of the Polish economy, it does not alter the fact that the bulk of Poland's private sector (in terms of human and productive potential) is made up of *de novo* private enterprises rather than by privatized ones. It is the *de novo* private sector that was responsible for the high rate of economic growth in Poland in recent years. The sector's growth can be seen not only in the rapid expansion of the number of enterprises, but also in the rates of growth of production, sales, and investment, which are higher than those for any other sector of the economy. In short, the expansion of the *de novo* private sector has been the most dynamic phenomenon in the entire market transformation of Poland.

The high velocity of this grassroots development of the private sector would not have been possible, however, were it not for the privatization processes simultaneously underway in the economy and the shrinkage of the state enterprise sector (in addition to the favorable regulations easing market entry). First, the privatization of state enterprises and other forms of ownership transformation (for example, liquidation, bankruptcy, agreements with creditors, and reorganization of enterprises), made it possible for *de novo* private firms to acquire productive equipment at relatively low prices. Second, a large number of *de novo* private firms were created due to the withdrawal of many large state enterprises from the delivery of certain services laying outside the main sphere of their activities and the separation of the units which had provided those services from the 'mother' enterprises. This allowed many state enterprises to significantly reduce employment without causing a corresponding growth in unemployment. (We must note, however, that we do not possess sufficient data to estimate the extent to which such processes contributed to the development of the *de novo* sector.) To sum up: the current ownership structure of the Polish economy – illustrated by the statistical data contained in the Polish chapter – arose mainly through the grassroots development of the private sector, but it was aided by the privatization, demonopolization, and restructuring processes occurring in the state sector.

It can be observed that privatization was usually dominated by foreign investors in most CEE countries – for domestic private entrepreneurs lacked the necessary financial means to acquire large companies – while the activity of the domestic investors resulted in the emergence of a great number of private businesses on the first place. But a respectable number of foreign investors also started new businesses in the CEE countries. New private businesses can be preferable over privatization for one reason: the investor's commitment to do long-term business in a country is more unambiguous in the first than in the second case. But one can be sure that a great number of start-up businesses would not have been born without a massive privatization of the state-owned property, and privatization might have been much slower than it actually was without the competitive pressure of the new private businesses in the CEE countries.

7.1.3 Privatization Methods and the Economic Performance of the Privatized Companies

It is a widely shared view among analysts that the actual method of privatization does not matter in relation to the post-privatization performance of the companies (Pohl et al., 1997). What only counts is the fact whether the company was turned into private hands or not. Evidence from the four CEE countries shows that the characteristics of the individual privatization transactions do have an impact on the companies' economic performance.

First, we found a significant difference between companies that had been acquired by foreign or by domestic private investors. Labor productivity considerably improved in the former group of companies, while it even deteriorated in the latter. The financial indicators of the first group were usually better than those of the domestic private companies. Foreign companies revealed a higher level of export and investment activity than domestic private companies. Although there was not a sizable difference between the profitability indicators of the two company groups for some years, the foreign companies started performing better in this regard, too, by the mid-1990s. We should note that the above results need a careful interpretation. We could observe that foreign investors acquired many of those companies whose economic performance had been outstanding even before privatization and whose market position had been strong. Foreign investors usually outcompeted the potential domestic buyers when privatization of a company required a large amount of financial means.

The Polish team found that privatized companies were characterized by much more advanced market adjustments than state treasury and NIF companies in Poland. Moreover, among the privatized companies, the firms privatized by foreign investors – especially those in the food industry – introduced more aggressive market adjustments than companies privatized by domestic capital. It is worth mentioning that in the case of the companies privatized by foreign strategic investors, the transfer of know-how from the strategic partners in the area of adoption of aggressive market adjustments as well as the access to the cheap capital provided by the foreign owners played a very important role in faster and more comprehensive market adjustments. It is especially important to note that the Polish observed a greater extent of market adjustments in the food and clothing sectors than in the investment goods sector across all types of ownership.

Another observation of the country analysts was that government agencies were less efficient sellers of a company than its managers. Privatization took a longer time and it was not very successful when the company managers were pushed aside by the government agencies. Privatization was a learning process both for the buyer and for the managers of a company that resulted in better cooperation and ultimately in better performance if the managers could actively take part in the privatization transaction.

The experience with the ESOP type privatization is mixed. We could find some successful cases when the company was relatively small and its performance largely depended on the special skills of its employees. (Such an example was, for instance, the Hungarian chinaware factory of Hollóháza.) But in the majority of the cases, the workers of an ESOP company could not efficiently exercise the tasks of an owner and many of these companies either went bankrupt or they were sold to the managers.

The countries we analysed have not extensively used free distribution schemes in privatization so far. Consequently, we could not compare the efficiency of the sales type and the distribution type privatizations. As we could observe in the case of Estonia and Poland, selling a company to foreign investors usually resulted in more effective corporate governance and in better performance than the free distribution of the companies' assets.

7.2 CORPORATE GOVERNANCE: DOES IT MATTER?

The transformation of the SOEs into corporations started before the systemic change in Hungary and in Poland. (This process was also called 'commercialization'.) The rights and responsibilities of the owners and managers were separated and defined in a more transparent manner in the corporatised companies. Though state ownership prevailed, the jurisdiction of the state agencies was clearly set and constrained. But the new governments started to recentralize the control over the state-owned companies and they deprived the managers of the decision autonomy. Until the expansion of the private sector attained a critical and sufficient level, the state intervention into the companies' management increased rather than decreased.

An important aspect of the companies' governance is whether the dominant ownership pattern should follow the Anglo-Saxon, or the German-Japanese model. Stock exchanges and other institutions of a capital market were established in most CEE countries. This development points in the direction of the Anglo-Saxon model. On the other hand, cross ownership among banks and companies is decisive in several CEE countries, which would imply a German–Japanese type governance structure. Since many of the former SOEs have been heavily indebted to banks, and a debt for equity swap seems to be the most viable solution for the companies, commercial banks can become dominant owners of the companies. But the banks are not well equipped to exercise an efficient governance of the companies and an extensive network of asset management companies has not developed yet in CEE. Consequently, an extensive bank ownership of the companies did not emerge in CEE. The only exception is the Czech Republic, where the banks play an important role in the privatization funds which own the shares of those companies whose assets have been distributed among the people via vouchers.

A delicate problem of corporate governance emerged in many of those companies whose shares had been acquired in part by 'heavyweight' foreign investors, most of them multinationals. Another part of the companies' shares remained state-owned. Foreign investors initially acquired only a minority share of a company. But they obtained a full or dominant management control over the company. Hence, the distribution of the shares among the owners largely differed from the distribution of the management rights. This fact created a serious tension between the owners, and between the foreign owners and the company managers.

Privatization of a company in several steps seemed desirable for the CEE countries for they believed that the privatization agencies can effectively represent the 'national interests' by sitting on the board of directors. The foreign investors also welcomed this solution because they wanted to have a commitment and guarantees from the state as the seller. At the same time, foreign owners insisted that they need to obtain full management control in order to restructure the company and to change its economic behavior that will be compatible with the requirements of a competitive market. It turned out that the state lost rather than gained from the stepwise privatization of a company. It could not effectively influence the company level decisions, while it lost a great deal of privatization revenues. On the other hand, the foreign owners frequently felt themselves as being on a 'battlefield' where the representatives of the state and the managers often changed sides. Thus, where the governance structure was unbalanced and unstable it drove the foreign investors to acquire a majority share or full ownership of the company. Managerial continuity could be observed very generally in the case of Poland, and it seemed to be independent of the mode of ownership transformation. Generally, today's managers were also the managers of yesterday's state-owned enterprises under socialism.

Possibly the two most interesting observations concerning supervisory board membership are that the boards of firms owned by strategic investors tended to still include employee representatives and that there was a strong outsider presence in employee-owned firms. Thus, insider-dominated firms often appreciated the contributions that outsiders could make, and that outsider-owners often continue to find value in the employee representation which originated before they acquired their firms. The board of directors usually play a crucial role in formulating the companies' business strategy, with the supervisory board usually taking the back seat. Interestingly, there seemed to be no correlation between the type of ownership and the location of strategy-making responsibility, as all ownership types were represented both in the group of firms in which supervisory boards play a small role in strategy-making and in the group where they play a greater role. (Neither was there a correlation between branch and the location of strategy-making responsibility.) Another interesting observation was that owners – even in cases of strategic investors – seldom played a direct role. Generally speaking, the companies' management boards were firmly in charge, with supervisory boards standing off to the side for the most part. It therefore seemed that the quality of restructuring efforts was much more dependent on the vision, energy, and intelligence of the chief executive officer and his/her closest associates than on the arrangements affecting the supervisory board's makeup and activity.

We can conclude that the actual form of corporate governance may have and it does have a large impact on the companies' restructuring, competitiveness and economic performance in CEE. But an effective governance needs time to unfold, and it is also required that the property rights are stable and solid. Moreover, a well-developed market environment and a well-functioning capital market and labor market need to be in place in order to set the framework of an efficient corporate governance of the companies.

7.3 COMPANY RESTRUCTURING AND PERFORMANCE

The initial shock that had been caused by the collapse of the CMEA markets and the radical political and economic changes that occurred along with it forced the CEE companies – whether state-owned or private – to adjust to the new conditions. Consequently, an impressive adjustment process of the companies could be observed even before privatization and the expansion of the private sector. But the short-term adjustment of the SOEs did not have lasting effects. The reorientation of foreign trade occurred swiftly but the companies' international competitiveness did not stand on solid ground. An extensive restructuring and adjustment of the companies only started after privatization on a mass scale began. The country studies showed that the privatization transaction itself was not a sufficient, although it was a necessary, condition for most companies to adjust to the new market environment.

We could also observe that company restructuring took a much longer time than had been expected at the dawn of the economic transformation. And the process is not over yet. It advanced faster in Hungary and in Poland, and its first results already show in the macroeconomic indicators of these countries. But these result should be assessed with care. We found, in compliance with several other analysts, that the locomotives of economic growth are a few hundred large companies, mostly the companies that had been acquired by multinationals. Thus, economic growth is concentrated by company groups and by regions within the countries. As regards Estonia, the restructuring and adjustment process of the companies already took momentum, but it is still in its early phase. Privatization and company restructuring is lagging far behind the other CEE countries in Bulgaria.

7.3.1 Factors of Economic Performance and Competitiveness

Ownership, that is, whether a company was privately or state-owned, had some impact on the company's economic performance, but the impact was not huge in the CEE countries. And in the early years of the transformation, private companies performed even worse than SOEs as, for instance, the Hungarian case showed. An econometric analysis of the balance sheet data of the companies revealed that the dividing line between companies was not their ownership type (state or private), but the fact of whether the company was owned by foreign or by domestic owners.

Another interesting result of our analysis was that we could not find large differences among the companies' economic performance by regions. This finding contradicts the common wisdom that claims that regional location is an important variable of the companies' performance. What we could observe instead was that 'rich' regions were overpopulated, while 'poor' regions were deserted by the companies. As a consequence, huge regional differences emerged in the CEE countries. But those companies that could stay afloat in the less well-to-do regions performed as well as the companies of the popular regions.

The most significant factor of the companies' economic performance was their branch affiliation. That is, companies that belonged to a certain industry usually performed much better than companies of another industry, no matter what type of an ownership structure they had or where those companies were located. This result is very much connected to the fact that companies of different industries operated under very different market conditions. Some industries could either preserve their market positions, or they could reorient their trade more easily than others. We could also observe that companies that operated on competitive markets usually performed better than monopolized industries. We could conclude that competition, the market environment and the system of regulation of the different market segments influenced the companies' economic performance to a larger extent than ownership or regional location.

Another important factor of performance was the size of the companies. Larger companies adjusted more easily to the new market conditions than smaller ones. This can be explained by several factors. First, large companies usually have larger reserves to survive the difficult times than the smaller ones. Second, larger companies attracted more foreign investment than the small-size enterprises. Foreign investment meant more resources for investment and company restructuring and, moreover, a better access to new technologies, to advanced marketing and management know-how. In addition, foreign ownership of a company could result in better access to international markets, at least after some time. As evidence showed, foreign investors tried to 'collect' on the local markets first, before they connected the newly acquired subsidiary to their international network.

With few exceptions, labor productivity increased, the production cycle shortened, and the level of capacity utilization increased in the case of the Polish companies. These effects seem to be general and have little relation to branch or type of ownership. The situation at the starting point of the transformation was quite important. The most difficult situation was that of manufacturers of capital goods in the 'foreign privatization' group and the NIF group. Engineering industry firms from the 'Polish' group had a less troublesome legacy. Credit was not a popular source of financing. The largest borrowing needs were revealed state treasury companies and firms covered by the National Investment Funds (NIF) program, which had not acquired financing from external sources for a long time. Privatized enterprises, benefiting from external financing, were usually not interested in commercial loans (except for working-capital credits related to their current operations), despite considerable improvement of relations with banks after privatization and greater availability of credit. The processes of restructuring in the field of organization and assets resulted in the intensification of divestiture of assets. Sale or lease of assets was a tentative source of activity financing, significant in firms carrying out deep restructuring. *These activities were engaged in most frequently by manufacturers of capital goods*, relatively badly hit by the recession of the early years of the transformation. *Ownership did not seem to be as significant a factor here.*

Equity capital has been a factor in the transformation of enterprises leading to positive qualitative changes in the operation and structure of enterprises. Financial transfers by investors and/or new issues of shares contributed to a positive change in the efficiency ratios of restructured firms or financial stabilization of viable firms, especially those which had already been privatized for a longer period of time. The analyses of efficiency ratios pointed to similar figures for state treasury companies and firms from the 'Polish privatization' group. After 1995, these tendencies became divergent. Privatized firms have been subject to stabilization, whereas state treasury and NIF firms were hit by a dramatic decline caused by the capital shortage barrier. NIF companies, generally in decline while they sat in the privatization 'waiting room' (the period the Czechs refer to as 'privatization agony'), showed an improvement of efficiency ratios in 1994 – a period of economic revival. However, the following years again brought about some deterioration. In the analysts' opinion it is too early for the effects of the program to crop up in the form of improved financial results (the period of paying restructuring costs is not over yet). *Firms from the 'foreign privatization' group showed fast growth rate thanks to financial contributions from foreign investors*, while the fall in efficiency ratios at the end of the analysed period pointed to an increase in costs of adjustment to growing competition. *Privatized firms also showed better ability to service their debts.*

An analysis of the structure of debt showed an insignificant share of investment credits in the case of Bulgarian, Hungarian and Polish companies. State treasury companies and firms covered by the NIF program avoided taking expensive credits and carrying the burden of debt service in Poland. Private companies relying on equity capital did not need additional financing. The research has also shown a declining share of overdue liabilities and receivables. The growing capital barrier and – to a lesser extent – the outstanding debt were the most frequently reported problems of state treasury companies and firms covered by the NIF program in Poland.

There has been an ongoing discussion in CEE as to whether the international and the domestic competitiveness of the companies can be distinguished in a meaningful way, after the CEE markets were opened up to international competition. It is not even clear how the notion of competitiveness should be defined in a transforming economy. The traditional definitions apply for well-established companies and markets, while the size, the structure, the ownership form and probably other decisive features of the companies change in the CEE countries. We accepted the following approach: a company can be regarded as competitive if it is capable of remaining viable without accumulating a huge debt for a longer period of time. As regards international versus domestic competitiveness, the distinction is meaningful only for those companies that operate on a local market and which are not exposed to the competition of foreign companies. In all other cases, domestic competitiveness automatically equals the international competitiveness of a company, since import competition creates as tough conditions for this company as it meets on the international markets.

Competitiveness can ultimately and in the longer term be connected to the companies' profitability. We found, as was shown by other studies, that labor costs are the most decisive factors of competitiveness in the CEE countries. But other factors also had a sizable impact on the companies' profitability and thus on their competitiveness. We showed that the factors of profitability have a significantly different pattern in the case of foreign private and domestic private companies on the one hand, and state-owned enterprises on the other. The pricing of imports and exports and overhead costs were decisive factors that diminished the private companies' profitability, while banking costs and wage costs reduced the profitability of the SOEs to a large extent. Thus, the higher level competitiveness of the foreign companies can be attributed to the fact that these companies have a better access to less expensive financial means on the international financial markets. Moreover, these companies used a firm hand in economizing with employment and labor costs. As a result, labor productivity was much higher in the group of the foreign companies than in the SOEs.

7.3.2 Restructuring of Production

It has been obvious since the start of the transition that the CEE companies need extensive restructuring before they can considerably increase economic efficiency. Privatization itself is not sufficient to put the ailing SOEs on the right economic track. But restructuring is a long and painful process that would reap results only after some years. Moreover, restructuring is a complex set of measures and changes that must occur in a company. One part of the changes affect the product structure, the organization of technology and production, management and marketing of the company, while another part targets the financial state of the company. We also made the above distinction in our analysis.

There are analysts who believe that the replacement of the old managers by new ones will suffice in order to achieve a radical change in a company's economic efficiency. Evidence shows that deeper and more complex changes are needed than just to replace 'the old guys by our friends'. One of the early measures of company restructuring was the reorganization of employment in the companies. But we found that a high level of open unemployment cannot be attributed solely to the private companies. It was the result of the collapse of many SOEs, too. However, it is true that the labor productivity increase in the private companies, and especially in the foreign companies, is much faster than in the SOEs.

Another important factor of company restructuring was the increase in exports. The export activity of the foreign companies was usually higher than that of the domestic private companies or the SOEs. But we could also observe that higher export levels did not go along with higher profitability of the companies, at least for some years. This result can be explained by the fact that the private companies had to enhance and stabilize their market position first, which could imply tremendous costs. Higher profitability usually came after.

Another observation of the team was that the investment activity of the private companies started to increase only after some years. In the case of the domestic private companies this was due to the lack of sufficient financial resources. Domestic investors who had to draw loans to pay for their acquisition, used their profits to finance the debt. Many of them even went bankrupt. This was especially true in Hungary. Privatization by liquidation eased the burden on domestic investors in Poland, for they did not have to buy a whole company in order to acquire the equipment or the premises and start their new business. In the case of foreign companies, the late start of investments can be explained by the 'wait and see' attitude of the investors. Foreign investors wanted to know first if their business is stable and it can expand before they started new investments. An investment boom can already be observed in Poland since 1992 and in Hungary since 1994. The other CEE countries lag behind somewhat in this respect, too.

Finally, we showed that the change in ownership did not immediately alter the profitability of the companies, or if it did the change of ownership was frequently followed by the deterioration of the companies' profitability. What was most striking, foreign companies performed the worst in this regard for some years. The reasons behind this strange result are manifold. Some of them can be connected to the time requirement of the restructuring process. Others may be attributed to the miscalculation of foreign investors who understated the difficulties of the transformation and overstated the companies' capabilities. Another reason was the propensity of the investors to hide their profits behind costs. Such a strategy is not obvious for most foreign companies enjoyed tax privileges in the CEE countries. But those companies designed their strategies for the long run. They wanted to avoid the negative consequences of a later change in the tax rules. All the reasons outlined above show the premature state of the market economy in the CEE countries. The speed of the transformation has been fairly high in the CEE countries, still they need several years until the institutions of the market and the economic behavior of the companies and other organizations take firm roots.

7.3.3 Financial Restructuring

Centrally administered and distorted prices, ad hoc government subsidies and taxes on enterprises, an awkward statistical reporting system of the companies and centrally allocated financial means to the enterprises rendered it unfeasible to show what is how much? in an SOE in the CEE countries. Economic transformation, that incorporated the liberation of prices, in the abolition of government subsidies and in a Western type accounting and monitoring system of the companies, resulted in an effective budget constraint of the companies. State-owned enterprises carried over huge debts from the past that required a concerted action from their new owners, from the creditor banks and from the governments.

Financial restructuring of the companies included a complex set of measures a part of which were state-led, and another part market-driven. The governments made large efforts to break the chain of the inter-enterprise arrears that had been accumulated by the companies in the past, but that continued to grow after the transition began. A loan and bank consolidation program was launched in most CEE countries that eliminated a large part of the companies' debt and the unrecoverable loans of the commercial banks. In addition, new legal acts were adopted and several measures implemented in order to harden the budget constraint of the companies. It was also expected that privatization of the state-owned companies and the birth of the new private businesses will strengthen the financial discipline of all companies in the CEE countries. The country reports attested that financial restructuring takes as much time as the restructuring of production in CEE. Private companies did not perform better than SOEs as regards the indicators of financial stability, solvency and indebtedness for some years after the start of the transformation. The hardening of the budget constraint could be observed in the case of Hungary and Poland in 1993–94, but it only occurred in 1995–96 in Estonia and this goal is still to be met in Bulgaria.

A detailed analysis of the Hungarian companies' balance sheets showed that foreign private companies could improve their indicator of indebtedness first. The indebtedness of the foreign companies had declined below the indebtedness level of the SOEs by 1993. But the solvency and financial stability indicators of the foreign companies surpassed the respective indicators of the SOEs only in 1995. The financial indicators of the domestic private companies was worse at the beginning, then it was about the same as the indicators of the SOEs. Due to a radical stabilization program, the hardening of the companies' budget constraint started earlier in Poland than in Hungary. As a consequence, the Polish private companies have had better financial indicators than the SOEs since 1992. The picture is mixed in Estonia and it is gloomy in Bulgaria. We can conclude that financial restructuring of the CEE companies is a process of ups and downs and it takes a longer period of time than had been expected by most analysts.

Finally, a few comments are in order as regards the data and information that we could use during the course of the analysis. The main problems we encountered with the company level data were as follows:

1. There has not been reliable information about the ownership structure of the companies. Especially in those CEE countries where cross ownership has a significant impact, it is almost impossible to tell, whether a company is privately or state-owned.

2. The analysts had to struggle with the lack of accurate profit and loss statements and investment data of the companies. (For tax avoidance purposes investments are frequently included in costs, which makes them inaccessible statistically.) We could see, for instance, in the case of the analysis of the Hungarian companies' balance sheets that company level data are often tempered with, in order to inflate costs and deflate revenues.

3. The country analysts reported that the lack of productivity data due to lack of a reasonable measure of value added (sales is a very poor proxy as it does not reflect cost trends) rendered it extremely difficult to compare companies with different ownership structures.

4. It was a common problem for the CEE countries that many firms were unable or unwilling to provide data from the period prior to privatization or commercialization.

5. Since 1989, most statistical categories have changed – some of them a number of times – making comparisons over a series of years very difficult.

6. Many firms refused to provide information on wages, due to the fact that they have introduced a policy of confidentiality of this information in Poland and in some other CEE countries.

We can conclude that the company level data is not fully reliable in the CEE countries. But this fact is not a good reason to reject any analysis based on these data. An analysis of company restructuring that is based on data is still closer to the facts than a discourse that is deducted from assumptions and from the author's own convictions. Though we tried to pinpoint the 'hard facts' about the adjustment process of the CEE companies, we had to realize that company restructuring is a complex learning process during economic transformation. The encounter of different corporate cultures during the transition, and the dominant role of foreign investors in privatization may result in 'cultural clashes'. But this type of a cultural clash can also bring about very positive changes in the business culture of the CEE countries. Adjustment, restructuring and integration of the CEE economies into the international business community can only be successful if the 'technical adaptation' of those economies is complemented with an intensive exchange of business cultures between the West and the East.

REFERENCES

Pohl, G., Anderson, R.E., Claessens, S. and Djankov, S. (1997), *Privatization and Restructuring in Central and Eastern Europe. Evidence and Policy Options*, World Bank Technical Paper No. 368, Washington, DC, August 1997.

Index